ART AND ENGAGEMENT IN EARLY POSTWAR JAPAN

ART AND ENGAGEMENT IN EARLY POSTWAR JAPAN

JUSTIN JESTY

CORNELL UNIVERSITY PRESS
Ithaca and London

Cornell University Press gratefully acknowledges grants from the University of Washington, which aided in the publication of this book. Publication has also been aided by a grant from the Millard Meiss Publication Fund of the College Art Association.

First published 2018 by Cornell University Press

Printed in the United States of America

Library of Congress Cataloging-in-Publication Data

Names: Jesty, Justin, 1974– author.
Title: Art and engagement in early postwar Japan / Justin Jesty.
Description: Ithaca : Cornell University Press, 2018. | Includes bibliographical references and index.
Identifiers: LCCN 2018015397 (print) | LCCN 2018016468 (ebook) | ISBN 9781501715051 (epub/mobi) | ISBN 9781501715068 (pdf) | ISBN 9781501715044 | ISBN 9781501715044 (cloth ; alk. paper)
Subjects: LCSH: Art—Political aspects—Japan—History—20th century. | Art and social action—Japan—History—20th century. | Art, Japanese—20th century.
Classification: LCC N72.P6 (ebook) | LCC N72.P6 J47 2018 (print) | DDC 701/.03—dc23
LC record available at https://lccn.loc.gov/2018015397

This book is dedicated to my family.
And in memory of Michiba Chikanobu and Katsuragawa Hiroshi.

Contents

Color plates follow pages 82 and 250.

Acknowledgments

This work would never have been possible without the help of many people. It is an artifact of a network of knowledge and a willingness to explore collaboratively that I want to think is not wholly divorced from the networks that are featured in it. My deepest gratitude goes to my teachers at the University of Chicago, Michael Raine, Norma Field, and Jim Ketelaar, for their generosity, support, curiosity, and high expectations. As I have moved on, I have come to realize just how different this book would have been had it grown in other environments, and I continue to rely on their counsel and grace. Reiko Tomii's rigorous care has improved my work from the earliest stages of conceptualization to the final draft. Her independence and devotion to the field and her generosity in working with me continue to be an inspiration.

People in Japan who have shared their passion and learning have been equally pivotal. Masaki Motoi's patience, energy, and resourcefulness have made it possible to pursue questions that I would not have been able to otherwise; I have followed through on only a small subset of all the doors he has opened for me. Ikegami Yoshihiko's positive presence and tireless encouragement have demonstrated how genuine curiosity is one of the truest gifts one can give to others. Komori Yōichi, Iwasaki Minoru, and Morimura Osamu have provided both intellectual and institutional support. In relation to reportage and woodcut, I thank Ikegami Yoshihiko, Michiba Chikanobu, Toba Kōji, Tomotsune Tsutomu, and Irie Kimiyasu; Masaki Motoi, Ozaki Masato, Ishizaki Takashi, Hara Maiko, Takei Toshifumi, and Tokunaga Keita; Takemoto Katsuko, Nagasaki Yumi, and Nagasaki Yuriko; and Shirato Hitoyasu, Monden Hideo, and Shinkai Takashi. Kaneko Kazuo and Yamamoto Atsuo gave me advice and encouragement about my research on Sōbi. In relation to Kyushu-ha, KuroDalaiJee (Kuroda Raiji), Yamaguchi Yōzō, and Kawanami Chizuru have been tireless mentors; Sakaguchi Hiroshi has been an irreplaceable resource; and Gallery 58 and the Culture Section of the *Nishinippon shinbun* have been great supporters.

The people whose life and work I have been studying have been extremely gracious. In relation to reportage art I thank Katsuragawa Hiroshi, Ikeda Tatsuo, Nakamura Hiroshi, Maruyama Teruo, Yamashita Masako, Matsumoto Toshio, Segi Shin'ichi, and Hariu Ichirō for their openness and support. Katsuragawa and Ikeda have gone out of their way to help ensure my work is as accurate and complete as possible. The support of Shimazaki Kiyomi, Takamori Shun, Takako Saito, AY-O, and the inimitable Hani Susumu has been indispensable to my understanding of Sōbi, given how little the movement has been studied. Tabe Mitsuko, a former Kyushu-ha member, shared her wide-ranging knowledge and great sense of humor in many conversations and is also the person who introduced me to Senda Umeji. Taniguchi Toshio, Sakurai Takami, Kikuhata Mokuma, Ochi Osamu, Hataraki Jun, Yamauchi Jūtarō, Obana Shigeharu, and Morinaga Jun have been generous with their time, as have Osaka Kōji and Maruyama Izumi, who shared their knowledge of Kyushu poetry circles. I thank Hirayama Yasukatsu, Washimi Tetsuhiko, Maeda Tsuneo, Nakanishi Shigeru, and Kitaura Akira for sharing what they know about Bibai. Abe Seigi and Sakashita Masamichi have helped me understand Shokuba Bijutsu Kyōgikai.

Many more colleagues, friends, and mentors have helped along the way. Mōri Yoshitaka, Narita Ryūichi, Mitsuda Yuri, Nakajima Izumi, Adachi Gen, Hirasawa Go, Fukuzumi Haruo, Wesley Sasaki-Uemura, Laura Hein, Ryan Holmberg, Julia Adeney Thomas, Abé Mark Nornes, Asato Ikeda, Namiko Kunimoto, Steve Ridgely, Ann Sherif, Linda Hoaglund, Midori Yoshimoto, John Treat, Ted Mack, Davinder Bhowmik, Paul Atkins, and Ken Tadashi Oshima have all offered key guidance and support, as have Kamizono Hiroaki, Fujikawa Kōzō, Yoshimi Chinzei, Yamano Shingo, Choi Jaehyuk, Kai Shigeto, Furukawa Mika, Paek Rŭm, Iguchi Daisuke, Itō Norio, and Ōura Nobuyuki. Last and by no means least, Miyata Tetsuya has been a constant companion and source of strength.

Research and writing was made possible by a Japan Foundation dissertation research grant, a grant from the Hōsei University International Fund for foreign researchers, a Mellon grant for dissertation writing from the American Council of Learned Societies, a postgraduate assistantship from the Council on East Asian Studies at Yale University, and numerous travel and research grants from the Center for East Asian Studies and the Division of the Humanities at the University of Chicago and the Japan Program at the University of Washington. I would also like to recognize the Simpson Center for the Humanities for a Society of Scholars Research Fellowship and its director Kathleen Woodward for her vital vision and leadership. Special debts of gratitude go to the Department of Asian Languages and Literature and the University of Washington: had it not been for their extraordinary efforts to support me, I might not have remained in the field.

I thank Roger Haydon at Cornell University Press for being willing to take a risk on this project, and the anonymous readers, one of whom reached out across disciplines to share a particularly perceptive insight that contributed greatly to the manuscript.

Finally, I say thank you to Heekyoung for being everything she is and to Terin for being such a great teacher.

ART AND ENGAGEMENT IN EARLY POSTWAR JAPAN

Introduction

The *Genbaku no zu* (*Atomic Bomb Panels*) are enormous, 1.8 meters high and 7.2 meters long. There are fifteen in all. A wife and husband, Maruki Toshi and Iri, painted the panels together over a period of thirty-two years.[1] Millions of people have seen the panels since the first one appeared in 1950, as they have toured the world in the context of numerous peace movements and campaigns against nuclear arms (plates 1 and 2).[2]

One of the most striking things about them is that what fills the space on these enormous canvasses is people. There are some animals, a ship, and some floating candles, but in the early panels all that comes into and holds this space are people—over 200 in *Water* alone. There is no landscape, no reliable perspective, no consistency of scale. The figures do not walk on a stable territory, and the aerial view that made the bombing possible cannot encompass their testimony. The compositions are too rambling to be called a snapshot and they are not collage: built up from single details, the images are the cumbersome work of individually realized human forms, not an exercise in nimble juxtaposition. Though a narrative is apparent to contemporary audiences, the panels' first audiences had incomplete access to that: four years separate the initial devastation of the first panel, *Ghosts* (1950), from the beginning of *Rescue* (1954). Even with the hindsight made possible by the whole sequence, it would be difficult to claim that *Rescue* manages to undo the excesses of *Ghosts* to make them more consistent or familiar.

Although the *Atomic Bomb Panels* forego the elegance gained from regularity in time and space, they do not forsake drama. The figures are predominantly women and children. There were few adult men left in Hiroshima by the time of the bombing, but more to the point, the mother and child partake of long-standing popular metonyms for violence and shattered bonds. There are mountains of the dead, pieces of people strewn around the feet of those who stand, tendrils of skin hanging from outstretched arms. But there are also figures that have not been fully dehumanized by starvation or even injury. Many commentators have noticed how well formed they are, more nude than naked body. This is daring, even transgressive. Do we dare cross that river? Do we dare make a fiction of beauty amid tragedy? Although this was undoubtedly a risk, it may be this tension, this field of melodrama between the human and the dead, of uncertainty between success and failure, that is the source of fascination that keeps people looking at these images.[3] Would a more brutal realism or a flourish of mastery stay with us for long, would it speak to us or beckon us? Would it not run its own risk of hygiene?

The issues of speech, beckoning, and sharing are central to the production and reception of the paintings. Iri was a native of Hiroshima but was in Tokyo when the bomb was dropped. When he read of the terrible new weapon in a newspaper, he hurried home, arriving three days after the blast. Toshi followed a few days later. They did not see the scenes they painted in the first three panels with their own eyes. The sources for the scenes were the stories that survivors and eyewitnesses told, many of them Iri's relatives. Thus, the scenes the Marukis painted were based on verbal accounts, many of which were gathered in 1949 and 1950. There are other sources too. As Kozawa Setsuko's research has shown, the mother and child at the center of *Water* and the dead child at the bottom of *Fire* were modeled on photographs that had evaded the censors of the U.S. occupation and were being circulated through Communist Party networks. These panels, then, are not testimony to the artists' individual witnessing of the events but to a narration that was already part of a community: they are an amalgam of stories and carefully stewarded fugitive photographs.

The paintings are collaborative in a more immediate sense also: Iri and Toshi worked on them together, even though Toshi worked in oil painting (*yōga*) and Iri in the modern style of Japanese ink painting (*nihonga*). Oil and water, paint and ink are not easily mixed. Neither are the traditions and styles of *yōga* and *nihonga*. During the first few panels especially, the two artists were experimenting with how these divergent traditions could be brought together. In understanding the actual roles of the two artists,

Kozawa proposes a parable: Toshi, an expert in painting nudes from studio models, created corporeal figures of definite volume based on the verbal testimony of eyewitnesses, while Iri, who arrived much closer to the actual blast, washed the veil of memory over them in the watery grey of ink.[4]

The wobbly, irregular human forms emerge too close to each other and then too far apart. That the tension between death and survival, between anger and humanism, between mourning and melodrama should come in such unbalanced compositions and such a hodgepodge of styles and images is testament to the human scale of this memorial. No one approach dominates, no experience rises above others. No single line establishes a rule of consistency or finality over what in the community of memory is such a multifarious and unruly event.

Beyond the community that supported the imagery that appears in the paintings, there is the extended community that enabled the visibility of these images as paintings. Images have long suffered suspicion and persecution in the argument that vision is an unavoidably alienating sense that both represents and enables the inhumanity and violence of modernity.[5] Images undoubtedly do have their own power, which is often experienced as being direct or immediate.[6] But they are also exceedingly unwieldy and fragile. They require tremendous effort and resources to produce, display, and preserve. As a corrective to the idea that images have agency or power in and of themselves, we must remember how much capital, infrastructure, and work is necessary to make and keep a given image visible. What were the communities of support that were called into being in order to carry the *Atomic Bomb Panels* around the world so that they might in turn bear their own form of witness?

The first five panels were made during the U.S. occupation. Public mention of the atomic bomb was forbidden under occupation policy. If the first exhibitions had been discovered by the police or the military police, the panels could have been confiscated. The occupation censorship authority banned a picture book about the bombing the Marukis produced in 1950 titled *Pikadon* (*Flash-Boom*) and the police regularly confiscated pirated copies of it from shops. Until the landmark August 6, 1952, edition of *Asahi gurafu*, which, with the end of occupation, was finally able to "break" the seven-year-old news, many Japanese people had little idea of what had happened in Hiroshima and Nagasaki and few had seen any pictures.

The *Atomic Bomb Panels* could intervene, but it was not a matter of images spreading of their own accord. In 1950 and 1951, the Marukis themselves carried the panels from place to place on a countrywide exhibition tour. With nothing but the national railroad and their own feet to move the huge canvases, the Marukis held exhibitions in fifty-one locations. Of course they had help, most notably from the Japanese Communist Party (JCP) and the Nihon Heiwa Iinkai (Japan Peace Committee). These organizations helped the Marukis make contact with people in the places they visited who could help them set up the exhibit. The exhibits were held in department stores, country inns, schools, universities, and temples. Local groups such as students, teachers' union members, and people in the peace movement helped to organize publicity and integrate the program with the local community of the concerned. Each exhibit would stay in one place for three or four days, and each day one of the Marukis, usually Toshi, would make a presentation. Toshi's presentations were in the form of a dramatic performance. She told stories based on the panels, sometimes half-sung in an improvised vocal style reminiscent of traditional popular oral narratives, shifting frequently from one character's voice to another's. She often spoke laments from the perspective of the dead. These performances created a space for extreme emotional involvement and participation. Contemporary reports claim that 649,000 people saw these exhibitions.[7]

Near the end of 1951, two young activists agreed to take over the exhibition tour. In 1952 and 1953, Nonoshita Tōru and Yoshida Yoshie brought the paintings to 794,200 people in ninety-six locations. Although they could not mimic Toshi's verbal performances, they held four or five teach-ins per day when the panels were on display. They discovered that survivors of the bombings lived all over Japan, and when one was in the audience, he or she would sometimes take over the explanation. Visitors were given the chance to express their reactions. Yoshida later described how some crushed their pencil tips into the paper as they tried to write out their emotions. In at least one case, these reactions were collected and hand printed as a booklet.[8]

The *Atomic Bomb Panels*, therefore, are not simply images, and they are certainly not images that captured or legislated reality. Rather, they are one part of an expanding network, part of a community and a communication that was only possible to the extent that people sustained it, kept contributing to it, and kept the images visible. Just as the panels themselves were born of the unevenness of human community, memory, and capacity, their exhibition was a forum for multiple ways of identifying and reacting to the paintings. Performance studies scholar Shannon Jackson has argued that art's institutionality—something I might broaden to its social existence—is best thought of as a durational, performative process rather than a static structure: "less a sculpture than a drama."[9] We can bring that idea to bear here: what we see and what we look to as art always rests on the activities of people and collectivities. The work of the artists in this study brings this to light. Their work was realized in pen, paint, film, and performance, and this is what survives as art. But their work was also a gesture within a movement, a gesture that they themselves had to carry through to the audiences they hoped it would reach. Their work includes not only their visual artistry but also the actions they took to create the conditions that would make their work visible and relevant. Only when we take these together can we understand the testimony embodied in their work.

Goals

This book is a cultural history of the relationship between art and politics in a particular time and place: Japan from 1945 to 1960. The investigation has two main goals. One is to reframe the history of that moment and its relevance to the present day, something that has specific relationship to Japan but also addresses understandings of the Cold War more broadly by revisiting possibilities obscured by subsequent consolidations of political and cultural life. The other is to demonstrate a method of examining the relationship between art and politics that approaches art as a mode of intervention, but insists artistic intervention move beyond the idea that the artwork or artist unilaterally authors political significance, to trace how creations and expressive acts may (or may not) actually engage the terms of shared meaning and value.

In both of these efforts, my project is aided by—indeed, relies upon—the formation of art and culture in the early postwar. It was a time of tremendous transformation globally. For Japan, the end of the Fifteen Year War (1931–1945) left people destitute and dislocated, stranded as refugees around Asia and in Japan. But by the end of the subsequent fifteen years, Japan was fast allies with its former enemy and occupier, dreams of mass prosperity were coming within reach, and hardly a shadow of empire remained in public memory. That transformation was anything but neat and even, and its results were far from foregone. Its elements were contested, the sites of prolonged political struggles across the 1950s. Within those struggles, particularly at the popular level, culture played a central role. Practices of self-expression and self-representation flourished. Hundreds of small-scale associations formed around writing, performance, singing, visual art, and film and music appreciation, and became stages for organizing creative and expressive work into a mode of semi-public subjectivity that fed into and formed out of social movements both large and small. Preserved today mostly in the pages of hand-printed (*gariban*) pamphlets and journals, eked from busy workdays and material adversity, this cultural engagement was undertaken with evident seriousness of intent: it was not something done with an excess of time or money but as work that was apparently necessary to its present. There is thus ample evidence within the field of culture of deep popular engagement with the urgent questions that faced Japan, along with the idea that culture itself would be a tool of its refashioning.

Histories of postwar Japan have often overlooked both the crisis and engagement of the early postwar, instead taking the social stability, political quiescence, and economic expansion of the period 1960–1990 to be definitive. Modernization theorists hailed Japan's postwar transformation into a prosperous, capitalist, democratic nation as evidence that it had redeemed itself from the error of fascism. A later generation of critical "transwar" historians worked to undermine that view by arguing that the roots of the postwar order were to be traced to wartime mobilization and rationalization, not postwar liberalization.[10] One thing these narratives have in common is that neither of them has much use for the hybridity and outright conflict of the early postwar and neither gives weight to the reality of roads not taken. This book revisits the early postwar for its difference from what came immediately after it, but also for its apparent kinship to the present, when once again visions of the future are openly contested and the foundations of stability less evident.

The study also endeavors to rethink the relationship between art and politics. Theorization of the politics of modernist and avant-garde art has been dominated for some time by ideas such as intervention, disruption, and critique, which tend to ascribe the political significance of an artwork to the incisiveness of its indictment of mainstream systems of value and meaning and its disruption of those systems through provocation or displays of antagonism or parody. The art forms that appear in this study occasionally partake of this logic, but it alone cannot account for their politics. Put simply, along with disruption (and its more ambitious cousins, destruction and revolution), the artists herein were in a situation whose instability demanded some degree of creation. While their work is not short on critiques of fascism, capitalism, and the Cold War, these were paired with efforts to build something different in the present. Hence our theories of art and its politics must be able to account for constructive and creative work which is carried through at the level of practical action as well as theory and artistic practice. Writers such as Grant Kester, Shannon Jackson, and Doris Sommer have recently begun to call for a recognition of the aesthetic and political value of duration, commitment, interdependence, solidarity, and sustained dialogue between artists and non-artists.[11] This study will show how art, and culture more broadly, became both a field and a tool for imagining and enacting delineable social change, not simply marking the need for it.

The two goals are closely interlinked. The task of pursuing them follows a similar logic. The history of Japan 1960–1990 has understandably focused on the dominant trends of economic development, depoliticization of public life, and the astonishing standardization of everyday culture. Similar trends are to be found in France, the U. K., and the United States. Keenly sensitive to these trends, political artists began to address them in their work as early as the late 1950s. The political aesthetic of estrangement, disruption, critique, and parody emerged from that work, as artists and theorists faced increasingly hidden and pervasive forces of social organization, and in the absence of organized radical alternatives. In film studies, this aesthetic has been codified as political modernism. In art history, Guy Debord may be the best-known theorist in the Euro-American context, while William Marotti demonstrates Akasegawa Genpei's importance to the Japanese context.[12] Beyond these examples, most scholarship on the politics of the avant-garde of the long 1960s relies on some version of an aesthetics of disruption and critique, which assumes a well-defined and clearly dominant mainstream culture, against which a small, critical minority of artists position their works to political effect. This aesthetic is highly invested in the artwork and the artist as privileged bearers of political significance, yet in many cases it envisions little actual change. As Rebeccca Solnit observes, "Sometimes radicals settle for excoriating the wall for being so large, so solid, so blank, . . . rather than seeing a door."[13]

While it is true that I find this political aesthetic fundamentally limiting, my project is primarily historical. I seek to historicize 1960s interventionism by setting out an alternative. While risking great oversimplification, we can characterize the contrast with reference to Yuriko Furuhata's recent study of the image politics of Japan's avant-garde filmmakers of the 1960s. She shows how "cinema—itself an apparatus of the spectacle—became a testing ground for the reflexive critique of media spectacle" precisely as new media formations (particularly in relation to television) were coming to dominate the intersection of culture and politics.[14] The political aesthetics traced here, however, developed in a different context. The reach of visual media was not nearly so broad as it was in the 1960s, while the question of what the mainstream was to be was itself in dispute, as multiple hegemonic articulations of meaning and value clashed. In the cultural field, production was less capitalized, less centralized, and more permeable than it would become in the 1960s. This made divisions between producer and consumer, high and low, avant-garde and vernacular less easy to draw and maintain. Most important, however, the instability in the cultural field was invested with value. The idea of a "testing ground," something legitimated by separation from other milieu of culture, was rejected (in practice as well as rhetoric), while—to coin a term for the sake of comparison—the aesthetics at play are characterized more by flexivity than reflexivity: the idea that both art and action were unavoidably part of a transforming reality.

The aesthetic and political convictions of the movements investigated in this book vary considerably, but one common thread connecting them is the importance each accorded to what I call democratic culture. In the ideas and activities to be chronicled, we will repeatedly see creative expression taken to be a fundamental aspect of participation. Further, ideas and creative practices were paired with concrete efforts at extending the franchise of creativity and expression by building the space and capacity for anyone to articulate an idea and position. Thus, in addition to the ideal of creativity, we see an investment in practices and organizations by which the fruits of *any*one's authorship might find some degree of publicity. Democratic culture is not a term that was used at the time in the way I am proposing, and the mode of its appearance is uneven. But the advantage of using the concept is that it allows us to see the constitutive commonalities among a variety of cultural movements of the early postwar, in which self-expression, self-representation, and the structured sharing of those expressions became key modes of political subjectivity and action. As a working definition, I use the term to denote an organization of values and competencies that aims to make possible the participation of the widest number of people as public authors of their own ideas, and aims to build the material and institutional forms by which those ideas could be heard and weighed most widely. This is a study of how cultural producers conceived of and worked in and around that ideal in the early postwar.

It is also a study of how these efforts were informed by the experience and assessment of war and fascism. Questions of responsibility emerged out of concrete and deeply personal experiences of war, defeat, loss, and survival. Artists implicitly and explicitly contrasted the peace and democracy that energized so much postwar debate and political organization with their darker shadows, war and fascism. For the groups in this study, who tend toward the liberal and radical left, the figures of war and fascism were doubled: the Cold War was reanimating the monstrosities of the war that had just finished. The push by successive conservative governments of the 1950s to "correct the excesses" of the early, liberal occupation reforms was indistinguishable from a resurrection of fascism. The Korean War, the remilitarization of Japan by U.S. forces, and the beginnings of Japan's own rearmament, revived the socioeconomic structures of the war as well as people's memories of it. Early postwar adversity was thus riddled with urgency. And yet—though the word optimism can be misleading in this context—animated by a belief that the future could be shaped by intervention in the present.

Although the patterns of the early postwar's democratic culture faded with the consolidation and homogenization of culture in the 1960s, certain aspects of it can provide resources for understanding the present-day pluralization of political aesthetics, as seen in a renewed interest in community arts, amateur production, and experiments that seek a place for art in fostering civic engagement. Both the early postwar and the present are characterized by having witnessed a massive decentralization of cultural authority and a deprofessionalization of production. Both are characterized by an awareness of empowerment and progressive change existing as possibilities, but as possibilities imperiled by the consolidation of new patterns of military expansion and conflict, as well as political repression. Both seem to be characterized by an opening of conceptions of what art is and who should be doing it, while understandings of the politics involved concentrate as much on creating contexts for changing the terms of culture as on protesting its perceived immobility. Both seem to demand new models for understanding the relationship between art and politics.

Cases and Method

The three movements in this study each center on the visual arts, but they share an essential characteristic common to many varieties of cultural group in the early postwar. In each movement, we find people devoted both to their artwork and to the task of finding new terms for art and culture's social existence. Artists experimented with ad hoc, nonhierarchical, and noncoercive ways of relating to one another and explored a range of media and exhibition formats to find new ways of relating to a public. This kind of experimentation is familiar territory for avant-garde movements throughout the twentieth century, but as will be described in part 1, artists were not the only ones looking for new ways to participate in building a new culture in the early postwar. They were joined by large numbers of amateur producers who gathered in workplaces and neighborhoods or through a common interest or experience to share in a creative and expressive activity. Poetry writing, theater, dance, singing, painting, and film and music appreciation, were some of the more common activities of these circles, as they were often called. Circles were informal forums where people met outside their usual social roles. Many held performances or exhibitions or produced their own hand-printed publications. Although each circle was small—usually little more than a handful of people who got together a few times a week to exchange their work and talk—circles were where the franchise of authorship was expanding. People who joined them used their own hands and voices to take hold of the cultural means of production and to alter, if only incrementally, the terms of the culture they were to share. They included artists, filmmakers, and intellectuals on the one hand, and workers, teachers, housewives, and a whole range of people on the other, each involved in experiments in finding new terms of organization and new modes of creative and expressive agency. It is at the junctures between these two trajectories, between the widespread impulse toward creative externalization on the one hand, and the more familiar realm of creative expression, that is, art, on the other, that I situate the movements I now introduce.

The subject of part 2 is the reportage artists. These artists formed a loose movement whose work is part of what made the 1950s a golden age of documentary. The movement was born around 1950, when the conservative shift in U.S. occupation policy was reaching a crisis point. The late 1940s had already seen U.S. policy move away from its early commitment to democratization and demilitarization toward rebuilding a strong, capitalist Japan as a bulwark against communism in the East. But in 1949–1950, with the beginning of a purge of suspected communists and the Korean War the backsliding became a rout, and the reportage artists saw society returning to the military-industrial authoritarianism so familiar from just a few years before. Although the word "democracy" now fell easily from the lips of those who had recently been urging wholesale sacrifice for Japan's wartime empire, the reportage artists did not see a break with the fascist past. They saw instead a sinister repetition of the structures of war and oppression, and their work was undertaken to reveal it.

The practice of reportage involved traveling to places such as U.S. military bases and factory districts, where the violence of militarism and military-driven capitalism condensed. But for the reportage painters, the problem Japan faced was one whose source was also on the inside. As artist Katsuragawa Hiroshi saw it, their mission was to "dredge up that cause that in so many forms has raised us over the past twenty years, has driven us toward a hateful war, has so decisively eaten away our youth. We have to get inside this and express it."[15] The source lay deeply buried, not only in social structures but also within individual psyches, and the reportage artists used surrealist techniques of deformation and montage to get at the depths of that interpenetration. Their works tend to be crowded, heavy with contorted and overripe bodies, crowds, shanty towns, constructions sites, and bases. Though heavy, the embodiment is unstable, pulled apart and squeezed together in grotesque reconfigurations. All-over, montage compositions likewise refuse to settle down, teetering, jangling toward an uncertain future that the artist seems able to capture only a distended instant of. While many people sought to disavow responsibility for fascism, to cut off any personal role in it beyond that of victim, the reportage artists insisted on digging up uncomfortable histories and finding them doubled in the present. Peeling back the skin of Japan's supposedly postwar society revealed that everything still teemed with rot underneath, setting the terms for the political failures of the present as they saw it. Reportage works insisted on sewing the subject back into history and opening out its vulnerability in the process, challenging people to face the deeper causes of war and corruption, both inside and out, that could not be exorcized otherwise.

Their devastating artistic critique of postwar society was paired with concrete—and surprisingly optimistic—efforts to realize something that would operate on different terms. This played out on a number of levels. At one level, the artists undertook experiments to alter the place and role of their artwork. As with the other movements in this study, they were concerned with the issue of how and under what terms their work could become visible. They organized their own exhibitions and published small, hand-printed works of criticism so they would not be beholden to the hierarchy of the more prestigious exhibition societies that had existed since before the war. At another level, the artists attempted to realize new terms of social relationship in their relations with others. They supported each other through a fluctuating network of short-lived groups of fellow travelers. These groups self-consciously avoided hierarchy and role specialization that would disenfranchise people from certain kinds of production. Although we might be tempted to accord these little weight, it was through such ad hoc groups that the artists received much of their considerable cultural education, and it is thanks to them that their work has survived at all. They also crossed boundaries to work with amateur artists and poets who had formed their own circles. This type of contact was a defining element of reportage practice, since research could only be done through a network of relations that constituted an (admittedly fleeting) alternative to a more stratified and concentrated organization of cultural production. In these ways, reportage consisted of both artistic and social practices, although, as will be seen, in a highly conflicted and unstable combination.

Part 3 examines a more loosely organized grouping: the Society for Creative Aesthetic Education, the work of the documentary filmmaker Hani Susumu and, tangentially, artists of the Asocio de Artistos Demokrato and

Fluxus. What draws these actors together is a modernist belief in the possibility of personal and social liberation through the unfettered exercise of creativity. The Sōzō Biiku Kyōkai (Society for Creative Aesthetic Education), Sōbi for short, was one of a number of nongovernmental education movements (*minkan kyōiku undō*) that flourished in the decentralized environment of early postwar education. Sōbi advocated a radically child-centered education that afforded each child the time and space to explore the world for themselves and work through challenges by exercising their innate creativity. Sōbi members believed that the full actualization of individual human energies would loosen and eventually destroy the bonds of the repression that they saw surviving through the war and into the present. The cycle of modern authoritarianism by which adults stamped "good" behavior into children to satisfy the parochial demands of rationality, was enabled by the devaluation of human beings' innate aesthetic sense. The child, if allowed to discover their own process of growth through creative exploration, could achieve an aesthetic accord with the world around them, one ultimately governed by fleeting intuitions of fit and balance. Schools, and society more broadly, needed to encourage this process of growth, in all its messiness and unpredictability. Teachers paid close attention to each artwork a student produced, but what they would produce *next* was of even more concern. The necessity of that work-to-come would appear in retrospect, while in the moment of anticipation it was an intensified awareness of as yet unformed possibilities. How could the teacher orient themselves and their students to welcome change, how could society come to welcome it, how could it be represented?

While Sōbi advocated a non-repressive approach in the classroom and school, the teachers in the organization also attempted to realize a certain art in their working lives. The movement was constituted at its base by schoolteachers interested in the pedagogy who formed local study groups to learn about it. As learners, they undertook their own process of exploration in a self-conscious pursuit of knowledge and tried, through openness and good will, to create an atmosphere where personal expression and creativity would be encouraged and shared. The aesthetic became a model for a spontaneously emerging order. It was to be the model for all education.

Hani Susumu and his family were peripherally involved with Sōbi, but the primary connection to be traced is in the way his early work explores the problems that the unpredictability and excessiveness of human creativity present for filmic representation. While film, particularly documentary film, might be taken to lock reality into an image that is frozen at the moment of shooting, Hani hoped to achieve the opposite: to create films that brought the inherent liveliness of reality to life by helping the audience appreciate the tension and unpredictability of each moment as it unfolded into its own future. If the Sōbi teacher attempted to adopt a certain humility before the complexity of each child's development, Hani saw film as a medium that let the viewer assume a similar relation to the world. And much like the Sōbi teacher who stepped down from the front of the class to stand "on the side of the child," Hani's film practice brought the camera down to a position among the children he was filming, a move that would have a lasting impact on the practice of social documentary in the 1960s and 1970s.[16]

Part 4 examines a regional group of avant-garde artists, Kyushu-ha. While the first two parts find their protagonists among the relative elite, part 4 takes the opposite position. Kyushu-ha was a group of talented artists, but none had formal education in the arts and all had full-time jobs. They worked on their art in the time they could find outside their work as train conductors, teachers, copyeditors, store clerks, and printers. While it is difficult to avoid the impression that the reportage artists were going down to work with workers' circles, Kyushu-ha is a case where the energy was bubbling up from below. And far from nature sketches and still lifes one might expect from aspirants on the outskirts of the cultural hierarchy, Kyushu-ha's work was an eruption of hard-edged social comment that was realized in viscerally suggestive materials such as tar, rope, wood, and metal scraps. There are continuities between Kyushu-ha's exploration of embodiment and that of the reportage artists. Although Kyushu-ha's exploration carries through in material associations more than in figuration, they shared a belief that the work of art could reveal primal interpenetrations among people and things. Kyushu-ha is usually understood as one of the flag-bearers of Anti-Art, which began around 1958, and developed parallel to proto-pop assemblage in the United States and *nouveau réalisme* in France. But as is the case with some assemblage artists in California who also worked in the late 1950s, it is difficult to judge whether Kyushu-ha was acceptably iconoclastic or whether they were closer to outsider savants whose poor taste, erratic energy, and atavistic anti-modernism make even the label "Anti-Art" too bounded and coy.

Kyushu-ha developed toward the end of the 1950s, and its experience embodies the tension between the ideals and practices of democratic culture that were so characteristic of the early postwar and the increasingly professionalized and centralized field of contemporary art. At the beginning, Kyushu-ha had all the features of a circle: it was open to all comers, it avoided infrastructure and hierarchy among members, and was committed to altering how art became visible. Outside Tokyo, the regional art world was dominated by large exhibition societies with exclusive memberships.

These societies acted as the cultural gatekeepers in areas where there were no dedicated art museums or galleries. Kyushu-ha undermined this cartel by building an alternative: they organized their own exhibitions in which any artist could exhibit. They also organized semiannual trips to Tokyo. Their works and some of the antics surrounding them attracted the attention of Tokyo-based critics, and for a time Kyushu-ha enjoyed a degree of recognition as a vanguard group. The pull of Tokyo, however, created unresolvable pressures. The Tokyo art scene was tied increasingly to contemporary developments in New York and Europe, and critics did not suffer laggards gladly. While there were a few artists in Kyushu-ha who had the ambition and talent to succeed in that fast-moving world, its open-door policy hampered its fortunes, as did its project of remaking the regional art scene. These contradictory demands split Kyushu-ha and the group dissipated in the first half of the 1960s (though it resurfaced in altered form during the political turbulence of the late 1960s). If the commitment to democratic culture meant increasing access to authorship, Kyushu-ha was remarkably successful in doing that for the dozen or so members who passed through it. But this commitment was in tension with the emerging system of contemporary art, which was based on individual careerism and a demanding distinction between authorized and unauthorized producers.

Each of these movements made their art political. They shared a basic understanding that art emerged from and answered to reality in a special way. Reality itself was radically fluid—emergent in growth and creation for the progressive educators of Sōbi, metamorphosis and revolution (*kakumei; henkaku*) for the reportage artists—and was conceived as encompassing subject and object in inherently unstable fields. Art, in its modernist and avant-garde modes, was uniquely able to attend to such change and make it sharable as a social artifact, its value lying in its profound and multiform sensitivity to the tumultuous transformations so in evidence at the time. In this way, change implied radical freedom and unbounded possibility. But the artists I describe in this book did not conceive of liberation in terms of rarefication or purification, and they did not see it as something to be achieved by attaining distance. It could only be approached through engagement with the churn of reality, and we will see how the human body, the collective body, and a multitude of everyday objects figure prominently, even heavily, as the most important sites of art's work. Art provoked and marked involvements that moved across divisions between the internal and the external, interweaving individual and world, yet insisting that that had no given form. It was not an escape route but a way of opening oneself into a reality intensified by the realization that it was undetermined, and of all the greater gravity because of it.

We might also say that these groups made their politics artful. In doing so, however, we must take care not to exoticize the creative work of people with few resources. Whatever picture we get of the artfulness of their political activities is retrospective, something people at the time would have been unlikely to recognize. But there is room to be sensitive to—even admire—the creativity and resourcefulness of their interventions. Most were not blessed with comfort, and the transformations they lived through showed little mercy. Both in spite of and because of this, they realized new possibilities in many responsive and crafty ways, finding crooked paths through success and failure that defy reasonable prediction. To introduce some examples, when the Marukis brought the *Atomic Bomb Panels* to Hakodate in December 1951, Inoue Yoritoyo, one of Japan's most prominent cellists, happened to be in the city at the same time and gave a free, impromptu recital at the exhibition for about 300 people. He observed that performing music for the sake of peace was the truest form of performance.[17] In the same year, author Abe Kōbō, who had just received the Akutagawa Prize, Japan's most prestigious literary award, made the unusual career move of relocating to a small apartment in working-class south Tokyo where, as a Communist Party activist, he taught a group of worker-poets how to write poetry and assemble self-printed magazines, using the same techniques he and his circle of avant-garde colleagues had used to produce their own experimental publications. Some years later, a major publisher put out a book of writings by inmates in a juvenile detention center as a mass circulation publication.[18] The collection became the basis for a film starring a cast of young men who had juvenile records but no acting experience. Director Hani Susumu let these young men "write" many of the scenes through improvisation on set. The film, *Furyō shōnen* (Bad boys), was voted best film of 1961 by the leading film magazine *Kinema junpo*, outdoing films by cinema giants such as Kurosawa Akira and Ōshima Nagisa. Members of Kyushu-ha lay in wait on the day that people would be bringing their works to submit to the prestigious Fukuoka Prefectural Exhibition in order to convince as many of them as possible to ditch it in favor of their own low-budget Kyushu Independent Exhibition, held in the assembly hall of a local newspaper company.[19] (The exhibition also gave Kyushu-ha the chance to exhibit their collaboratively assembled pile of junk, which had had the dubious distinction of being rejected by the open-submission Yomiuri Independent Exhibition a few months before.) In these examples and many others we find people collectively refusing to recognize stability in place or identity. Artists thrived in coal mines, workers were artists and authors, teachers became learners and vice versa. Liberation was not a free-floating or unaccountable state but something that happened through the discovery of possibility in response-ability: a creative taking in and setting out with whatever was at hand, which enabled audiences and collaborators not fully conceived at the start to appear and proliferate in the process of the works becoming public.

Yet even as we may find interest in the unusual trajectories that pop up here and there over the course of this narrative, we should not lose sight of the effort, almost always collaborative and repetitive, that was required to make the work actual and sharable. In one of his early considerations of culture, which also dates from the late 1950s, Raymond Williams insisted on two aspects to the term. "We use the word culture in . . . two senses: to mean a whole way of life—the common meanings; [and] to mean the arts and learning—the special processes of discovery and creative effort. Some writers reserve the word for one or other of these senses; I insist on both, and on the significance of their conjunction."[20] In their practices, the movements in this study also insisted on both of these understandings and on the significance of their conjunction. The work of conjoining the two modes of culture in the early postwar—the one the proleptic attempt to realize the not-yet-real, the other to build vessels adequate to sharing value and meaning—was not smooth, but part of an ongoing and always partial work.

In attempting to follow this process, I avoid reducing one mode of culture to the other, by claiming, for instance, that the avant-garde led social change through sheer force of vision or that the artworks were embedded in a system of meaning like any other aspect of culture. Doing so both raises and lowers the bar for intervention: it demands concrete accounts of relations between thought, vision, speech, and action, but thereby forces us to confront the persistent gap between visions and actual, enduring achievements. Conjoining the two meanings of culture in practice always involves contradiction. We cannot help but notice that the reportage artists' attack on the autonomous subject and their simultaneous organizational and educational efforts undermine each other, or that Sōbi's attempt to lead liberation and Hani's attempt to represent indeterminateness are fundamentally contradictory, or that Kyushu-ha was in a state of inconsistent denial about its contradictory need for Tokyo as both a scorned foil and a necessary ally. Attempts to represent or achieve ideals always entail such contradictions. The potentialities suggested by word and art are never instantiated purely in reality. If we do not accept the separation between word and deed, art and reality, we are forced to devalue one or the other: to long for utopias that promise resolution through perfect realization or be driven to a cynicism that takes the continuing gap between words and reality as evidence that words mean nothing.[21] Attempts to conjoin them will be far from consistent, we might say far from pretty. But it is in the attempt at conjunction and its unpredictable results that my greatest interest lies.

Understanding art's relationship to social change in this way requires us to traverse different idioms and modes of culture. No single artwork is sufficient in and of itself to creating social change. Rather, when read as gestures that unfold in the context of wider movements, we can see each work as part of an arc, or a heterogeneous forest of arcs that, taken together, establish the possibility of collective change as being present. For example, when Katsuragawa Hiroshi went with Abe Kōbō to teach woodcut to workers in south Tokyo, both his actions and his art at that time and place can be understood not only in the context of his other attempts to work across class lines but also as one instance of a broader interest in woodcut as a teaching and learning tool in the early postwar. Katsuragawa's work is but one small fleck in that larger movement, though an irreducibly important one.[22] The collection of juvenile delinquents' writings that was the source for *Furyō shōnen* (Bad boys) is one of dozens of such books, where the work of marginalized people created in a local circle was subsequently published for a mass audience. Writers, editors, activists, and consumers moved cultural products all over the cultural field as they participated in movements that neither capital nor the state had much interest in supporting. The Kyushu Independent exhibitions of 1958 and 1959 were comparatively small, but in the context of the art scene in Fukuoka, which had no venues for exhibition outside those provided by the prefectural exhibition and the large art societies, even such a small venue was an important opening. Further, the Kyushu Independents occurred in the context of at least a dozen similar independent exhibitions that sprang up in early postwar Japan. The open exhibition is a simple format, but one that is radically pluralistic: not just emblematic of, but actually instantiating equality of access to a public, albeit in a short-lived, episodic form. This kind of consideration is the core of my account of the political: each artwork and each act is a small moment that can be understood within the wider context of the many movements of the early postwar years. When written as history such reading is contextual, with the caveat that the context is not pre-constituted background but was itself being made and remade in each of the actions I recount and in many more that took place outside the bounds of what can be included here. It is in the accumulation and extension of such accounts that we can begin to appreciate political significance as something that does not explode in sudden clashes but emerges in resonances among many single steps.

Part One

Arts of Engagement and the Democratic Culture of the Early Postwar

Chapter 1

Participatory Culture and Democratic Culture

The battles over culture after 1945 were battles for the heart and soul of Japan. Government officials responded to defeat by proclaiming the goal of rebuilding Japan as a nation of culture (*bunka kokka*), a campaign that Carol Gluck notes was intended to displace politics with culture, particularly in relation to the imperial institution.[1] On the other side of the political spectrum, the Japanese Communist Party strove for a cultural revolution (*bunka kakumei*) that, while hostile to the emperor, trumpeted its own version of a "healthy" national history and heritage. Despised by both was the entrepreneurial and irreverent bootleg (*kasutori*) culture that thrived in strip shows and pulp magazines.[2] Intersecting with these battles was a groundswell of popular desire to self-educate and have culture enrich daily life. Surveying the top ten bestselling books in Japan each year from 1946 to 1949, John Dower concludes that they "collectively conveyed an impression of cosmopolitan breadth and serious purpose never again to be matched, as ordinary citizens proved responsive to writings that addressed abiding issues of human nature and social responsibility."[3] Kitagawa Kenzō has shown that titles in the Prange Collection, which includes nearly every journal and newspaper published in Japan in the period 1945 to 1949, affirm this passion for high culture. Within the category of entertainment and culture magazines, literary magazines make up the largest number of titles (879), followed by *haiku* (673 titles), then *tanka* (497 titles). By contrast, there are only 133 sports titles.[4]

Culture was deliberately and intensely politicized, and particularly noteworthy is how active the investment was at the grassroots. Dower concludes his analysis with a consideration of *Kike Wadatsumi no koe* (Listen to the Voices of the Sea) (1949), a collection of diary writings by young soldiers who died at war. It was a runaway bestseller, but the sales figures are only part of the story. The book spawned numerous reading groups where participants reexamined their own experiences of the war, some of which produced their own self-published writing, again to be shared with others.[5] There are many examples of this kind of active readership in which readers formed groups to discuss issues raised in major publications.[6] Active listenerships and viewerships also flourished, in the form of music and film appreciation societies.[7] Along with these active receivers of culture were groups of producers: amateur poets, nonfiction writers, historians, painters, woodcut makers, and performers in theater, dance, and chorus groups. Some film appreciation societies even got involved in film production.[8]

These groups were generally called circles. Thousands existed nationwide, their membership possibly reaching into the millions.[9] Their sheer number and variety makes generalization difficult, but we can group them roughly according to how they were affiliated and what kinds of activity they undertook. Workplaces undoubtedly had the highest concentration.[10] A given company might have dozens of culture circles, which were popular among young, single workers who had time in the evening and on weekends to participate in regular meetings. Workplace circles were generally sponsored by the company or the union, although some were independent of both.[11] Large workplaces often had multiple circles in a particular genre with competing identities. Circles that formed outside the workplace are more various. They sometimes grew out of, or into, grassroots social movements. They could be affiliated with local governance initiatives such as the New Life Movement. They could be linked with Japanese Communist Party (JCP) organizing. They could be unaffiliated, such as groups that used a *kōminkan* (community center) or a member's home to hold their meetings. Finally, the activities of many circles had little to do with specific social campaigns: many, if not most, were "just for fun."[12]

What circles might mean is at least equally complex. Participation does not have a political valence in and of itself, nor is it in a privileged relationship with left, right, or center on the political spectrum. Andrew Gordon writes that workplace recreation appeared early in the twentieth century when owners of textile mills recruited rural women by promising "to educate and cultivate them in place of their parents."[13] He also points out that company-sponsored recreation activities existed throughout the war. However, Kurahara Korehito, a leader of the proletarian literature and arts movement, introduced the term "circle" (*sākuru*) to Japan from the Soviet Union in 1931.[14] Kurahara hoped to use culture circles as staging points for political dissemination and mobilization—an aspiration that was soon to be crushed by the state. The strategy was revived as part of the JCP's cultural strategy in the early postwar years.

The competing investments in circles in the 1950s grew more complex with the mid-decade importation of mass society theory (*taishū shakai-ron*) to Japan.[15] Mass society theory laid out a critique of modernity that contrasted with what at the time was a widely accepted understanding of Japan's descent into fascism: Maruyama Masao's theory that fascism was a symptom of Japan's incomplete modernity, its failure to fully liberate individual energies from feudalistic superstition and prejudice. Mass society theory raised serious questions about the modernity Maruyama championed, focusing on its negative effects such as the isolation of the individual and the consequent opportunities for increasingly sophisticated forms of bureaucratic administration. Within this critique, the small group, or *shōshūdan*, was promoted as a social form that could intervene between the nation and the individual and be a theater where alienation would be ameliorated and overbearing state apparatuses kept at bay. As Mizutamari Mayumi explains, the discourse of *shōshūdan* "created great hope in the circle movements of the late 1950s by indicating an alternative to established political institutions." It showed how the small group had an important role to play in overcoming the perceived top-down character of communist mobilization on the one hand and the top-down bureaucratization of the postwar state on the other. In sum, people took circles seriously in the 1950s. Although intellectuals, union organizers, company managers, and political and civic activists promoted them toward different ends, one common thread among their ideas was that through circles, individuals would become more self-consciously and actively involved in a collective process and that that engagement would improve both the individual and the process as a whole.

Circles have received renewed attention recently. Reflecting the diversity in circles at the time, recent studies have been careful to emphasize that the circle movement as a whole did not entail a particular politics: some circles were politically active, some were not, and those that were politically active worked toward different ends and used a variety of tactics and organizational styles. The tendency in scholarship after 1960 was to dismiss circles as JCP staging points. That is clearly an incomplete picture. Michiba Chikanobu has argued against that tendency, writing that we should "imagine people's desire for expression and its concrete realization as being sustained by liberation under the postwar constitution, the expansion of opportunities for free subjective self-expression, and a hope for progress that foreshadows recovery and high growth," not the JCP's narrow idea that Japan was being "colonized" and "militarized."[16] Speaking to a more general question, Narita Ryūichi has proposed a classificatory division between leisure (*goraku*) circles, which came together primarily to share the joy of reading, talking, and socializing, and circles that had some relationship to a social movement or public concern.[17] While the division between these two categories is not precise or stable, it is important to keep in mind that while many circles did form out of or feed into grassroots political movements, such circles represent only a subset of participatory culture as a whole. Many circles had no identifiable political goals at all.

It is in response to this issue that I propose the term democratic culture as a way to draw together the politically or publicly oriented subset of participatory culture. This term allows us to delineate the dispersed, diverse, and politically active associational experiments of the early postwar period as related phenomena.[18] Four basic characteristics warrant the term democratic culture. These can be further subdivided into two categories that correspond with two ways of using the term "culture." According to one usage, culture designates a collection of works published or performed in recognized genres, such as poetry, theater, (auto)biography, and music. This understanding of culture deliberately refines and invests certain forms of activity with significance: the "new observations and meanings," the "creative," the "finest individual meanings," to return to the words of Raymond Williams.[19] As it relates to this meaning of culture, the democratic aspect of democratic culture is apparent in two ways. The first is in the value and effort placed on overcoming barriers of class and education to find contexts for association and creative endeavor: a movement toward greater accessibility and cultural enfranchisement that involved both elites and non-elites. The second is in the attention given to taking control of the means of cultural production so that publicity, publication, and the development of networks of reception would remain in the hands of people concerned with the message.

The term "culture" can also designate more commonplace patterns that permeate all behavior, meaning, value, and expectation, what Williams termed the "ordinary processes of human societies and human minds."[20] In the ongoing, self-conscious attention to protocols of participation and representation within participatory cultural groups, particularly their care in trying to make all voices audible, we can see attempts to enact patterns of behavior that often explicitly contrasted with the repressive elitism of fascism. Finally, in the way that these small groups connected issues of local concern and self-development with the big questions of Japanese public life in the early postwar—particularly peace and democracy but also the rights of the individual, gender roles, and public health—they can be thought of as the grassroots of larger movements that pushed for change in large-scale patterns in Japanese society.

These four characteristics constitute my definition of democratic culture as it can be seen as a subset of the more general efflorescence of participatory culture in the early postwar. The first characteristic of the early postwar's democratic culture is the emphasis on interaction between elites and non-elites, the attention to finding value and meaning in creative border crossing, and the idea that cultural production should be open to anybody. After 1945, many intellectuals attempted to overcome their failures during the Fifteen Year War, and many of them conceived that as a project of building a more direct relationship with the great mass of Japanese people. On the other hand, at the same time that elites were attempting to build a new common culture, there was great popular interest in culture developing at the grassroots. These two trajectories often met in circles. Some examples of the most direct experiments in intellectual leadership are the free schools of the late 1940s that were organized by intellectuals who had moved to the countryside to escape aerial bombardment during the war. Leslie Pincus analyzes one such example, the Hiroshima Culture Movement of 1945–1947, led by Nakai Masakazu.[21] Nakai had been on Kyoto University's prestigious philosophy faculty before being stripped of his position during the war for thought crimes. In 1945, he began a project of teaching European Enlightenment philosophy to local farmers in Hiroshima prefecture. One of his goals was to undo patterns of thought and life that had led to people's unquestioning participation in militarism. The problem as he saw it was that "peasants have found themselves trapped in a formation where they are continuously confronted with crises that threaten to destroy whatever cultural foundation they have managed, at great cost, to build," leaving them no space for culture or reflective thought. Nakai hoped to help people develop a "salon of the soul" (*tamashii no hiroma*) as a space for such reflection and questioning.[22] Nakai's movement developed into a traveling summer university in 1947, with lecturers including prominent left-leaning intellectuals such as Hani Gorō, Hirano Yoshitarō, Taketani Mitsuo, and Shinmura Tōru.

Although the creative activity of these groups was often initiated and led by intellectuals, it cannot be written off as the effect of elites mobilizing the unsuspecting into pliant "democratic" citizens. To continue with the example of free schools, the students in those schools took things from their experience that exceeded, or were simply different from, the investment of teachers (and are available to us thanks to the small publications that were the original vehicles of the students' public expression). Amano Masako relates how the co-ed student body at the Kyoto Jinbun Gakuen (Kyoto Institute for the Humanities) became a forum for the first blossoming of postwar feminism.[23] In part 2 of this study we will see how reportage artists interacted with a group of worker-poets in South Tokyo. The artists undeniably brought technical knowledge and cultural access to the amateur producers while gaining valuable material for their own artwork. But neither that artwork nor the activities of the circle in question (which continued for ten years after their visits) can be defined by the interaction. This aspect of democratic culture was something that existed uneasily, episodically, and imperfectly across class and amateur-professional divisions. I suggest that what brought together groups that might otherwise have been distant was the idea that whatever the common culture might turn out to be in form or content, it would and should involve the expressive involvement and creative work of many.

The second characteristic of democratic culture is the deep investment in material aspects of communication. Producer groups staged their own performances and published their own hand-printed journals; they were engaged in semi-public production. This entailed not only producing the content of their work but maintaining new public contexts that they controlled. The condition of culture's visibility and audibility itself was a central issue, and circles attempted to lay hold of the means of their cultural production. Participants in many movements believed that it was the practice of written expression that would create a space where self-consciousness and self-examination might develop. But it was the practice of printing and distribution that made this part of a publicly shared process. While these independently maintained material supports for culture remained small in scale, there was considerable permeability in the cultural field. As already seen in the case of *Listen to the Voices of the Sea*, collections of amateur writing regularly became bestsellers and films. In this sense, the small local contexts for independent cultural production were not subcultures: "independent" was not constituted in antagonism to "mainstream." Rather, producers and audiences at all scales seem to have recognized the value of a culture constituted by many channels leading back and forth from local to international.

The work of publication also made it possible for networks of circles to develop communities of interest that were not tied to locale. Historian Sasaki-Uemura introduces the Yamanami no Kai (Mountain Range Society), a network of circles whose members gathered to share experiences of the war. Though the network originated as an alumni group, it grew and became geographically dispersed, and members' self-printed publications became the primary way of staying in touch.[24] For all the groups in this study, the conditions of a work's visibility were a primary concern: self-publication, self-organized exhibitions, traveling exhibitions, and public speaking were the mundane but indispensable practices that sustained visibility among members and an identity visible to a wider public. Many of the tiny journals that were the intellectual lifeblood of these groups were printed using a mimeograph technique (*gariban*) in which each master sheet was etched by hand into a waxy template and each page was printed by pressing ink through the template, one sheet at a time. They are testimonies wrung from scarcity, evidence of the tremendous effort people invested in fashioning expression into something that could be shared, but at the same time, testament to the energizing potential of freedom even amidst adversity.

In addition to these characteristics that relate to the concern with broadening cultural enfranchisement, there are two further elements of democratic culture that are more conventionally associated with democracy. First, there is a self-conscious examination of the forms of association that governed a group, in particular an occasionally obsessive attention to ensuring equal voice in discussions and decisions. Democracy in this aspect means direct democracy, something that emerged from the process of ongoing collective activity. Articulations of this varied: from the ongoing churn of group dissolution and reformation in the case of the reportage artists, to the unstructured scrum of Kyushu-ha, to Sōbi's attempt to model an organizational culture where disagreement and discussion could form an identity (even as that made it difficult to maintain any particular identity). Circles typically had little to no institutional self-interest, existing only insofar as they continued to work for the participants, often shifting, dissolving, and reforming in the process. This was enabled to some extent by the small scale of circles: they existed most basically as regular face-to-face meetings and commanded few resources or power. But such things also became values. What might be considered the *locus classicus* of circle study is a volume produced by the Shisō no Kagaku Kenkyūkai (Institute of the Science of Thought), *Kyōdō kenkyū: shūdan* (Collaborative research: The collective).[25] The study profiles sixty-three circles and includes a number of theoretical essays that argue that the defining characteristic—and primary virtue—of these small groups was their fluid nature, emerging wholly from the evolving needs, interests, and interactions of their members. The general model, therefore, was voluntarist, and a group's identity was coextensive with the activity of its members. It is worth noting that this model is not necessarily successful at protecting minority views, and the case of Kyushu-ha will show how the need for constant participation could be as exhausting as it was exhilarating.

Finally, many cultural associations were connected to social and political movements. Ōsawa Shinichirō highlights areas where this commonly happened: education, aftercare and convalescence, agricultural reform, improvement to daily life skills, democratization of the workplace, regional social reform, and opposition to war.[26] Circles were thus a part of political processes writ large, although the manner and scale of that connection varied and could change unpredictably over the lifetime of a circle. Involvement in politics seems to have been less an identity and more something that happened as the situation came up. Sasaki-Uemura's work portrays the impromptu nature of political engagement with particular clarity. In one case, a group that came to be called the Kusa no Mi (Seeds of Grass), formed out of a writing daily life (*seikatsu tsuzurikata*) practice. In 1951, the *Asahi shinbun* began a column that featured writing from female readers that proved to be immensely popular. Women around Tokyo who contributed to the column began to form study and discussion groups, and soon such groups were forming in other regions. The groups started their own journal in 1955, which freed them from newspaper editors. Discussion and writing led to research: members investigated the effect on families of aging and other health and economic issues. They used their research "to make policy recommendations to city officials, the Health Ministry, Diet members, and the national pension agency."[27] Their interest in education initially involved them in campaigns to oppose the conservative education reforms of the mid- and late 1950s, which then led them to oppose a revised police law in 1958, and finally to oppose the revised Anpo Treaty (The Treaty of Mutual Cooperation and Security between the United States and Japan) in 1960. This seemingly organic relationship among discussion, research, expression, and political involvement is the most important aspect of the linkage between cultural activity and public participation that characterizes the early postwar's democratic culture. Examining the manner of this linkage forms the core of much of my analysis of reportage, Sōbi, and Kyushu-ha.

Before moving on I must address the term "democratic" itself. Invoking democracy is undoubtedly contentious and there is a polemical reason for doing so, in addition to the four substantive reasons just outlined. Few terms have been more claimed, contested, and scorned than democracy as it relates to post-1945 Japan. The United States used it to legitimate military occupation, the JCP made it the centerpiece of its revolutionary project, and the

Minshutō, the most explicitly reactionary of the postwar political parties, adopted it as their name. Such vagaries fed and continue to feed suspicion regarding its usage. Of specific relevance to this discussion is the way that a rejection of postwar democracy (*sengo minshushugi*) came to be codified in the late 1950s, when a younger generation of critics and activists used it to stake out their rebellion against their elders in the form of an excoriating critique of what they saw as the soft-headed half-steps and compromises that formed an arc of consistent failure, starting with the failure to resist war and fascism and repeated by the same people in the postwar in their failure to connect with the masses or defend a true democracy. The caricature of democracy as a wilted fig leaf used to cover over repeated political inadequacy stems from this polemic and feeds into the critique of enlightenment and modernization that lies at the foundation of post-1960 critical cultural politics in Japan.

One of the most influential figures in developing this discourse is Yoshimoto Takaaki (b. 1924). The crux of his success in destroying the legitimacy of left-wing intellectual leaders was his exposure of the continuity between their wartime and postwar behavior. His public attack began with a 1955 essay that showed just how little the postwar work of prominent communist poets had changed from the work they'd written over a decade earlier in support of the war: entire metaphors were reused in the name of democracy that had first appeared in the name of war.[28] Joined quickly by many more voices, Yoshimoto's attacks widened over the next five years, reviling those on the organized left for their hypocrisy, lack of self-reflection, servile devotion to power and orthodoxy (he referred to opponents relentlessly as "turncoat fascists" [*tenkō fashisuto*]), and an inability to take stock of the chasm between their ideas and social reality, in particular their irrelevance to the Japanese masses. Out of this firestorm the *apres-guerre* generation emerged victorious, having struck down their elders with notable vengeance.[29]

The capstone to Yoshimoto's campaign was an essay he wrote in the wake of the 1960 Anpo protests titled "Gisei no shūen" (The end of fictions), which captured the zeitgeist on the radical left, particularly the members of the activist student organization Zengakuren.[30] One of the many fallouts from the 1960 Anpo protests (fought against renewing the Treaty of Mutual Cooperation and Security between the United States and Japan—the kingpin of the Cold War alliance between the two nations) was to cement the split between the radical and organized left. This happened definitively when the Communist and Socialist Parties joined the general public criticism of Zengakuren's actions on June 15, when Zengakuren members had forced their way into the Diet compound through armies of police, resulting in many injuries and one death.[31] The parties' abandonment of the principles of the protest and their failure to defend the students' right to petition the Diet was the end of the fiction that they stood for any commitment to democracy. Yoshimoto also criticized what he called the "citizen/democracy theorists" (*shimin/minshushugi shisōka*), meaning the liberal and progressive thinkers associated with the Shisō no Kagaku Kenkyūkai such as Tsurumi Shunsuke, Maruyama Masao, and Takeuchi Yoshimi. He argued that their continuing inability to take a truly defiant stand against the state was due to internalized trauma rooted in the repression they had suffered during the war and that this also prevented them from confronting the selfishness and cunning of the common people they so hoped to redeem. Writing at the conclusion of his essay that "the 15-year fiction of the postwar" had ended with the Anpo protests of 1960, it is clear that the fictions in question are enlightenment and democracy, be they of a progressive or revolutionary kind.

Yoshimoto's influence grew during the 1960s, and he became a figurehead for the student movements of the late 1960s. His critique of postwar democracy, the organized left, and Maruyama Masao were taken as hallmarks of a more radical, often anti-modern position that, broadly speaking, shares substantial commonalities and intellectual field-positioning with thinkers such as Michel Foucault, Roland Barthes, and Jacques Derrida. While in the present context that commonality is to be seen in Yoshimoto's sensitivity to the hypocrisies that haunted Enlightenment projects, Scott Richard Mehl has shown how his anti-expressionist poetics are also similar to those of his French contemporaries.[32] The intellectual shift, of which Yoshimoto's project is emblematic, is a major reason why the grassroots democratic experiments of the early postwar have tended to be overlooked. The experiments themselves were dismissed as misguided and failed but, more pervasively, the polemical position—characterized by a belief in the inextirpable continuity between prewar and postwar, an insurmountable distance between intellectuals and everyone else, and the moral equivalence of progressivism, fascism, and communism—make it difficult to take the core ideals of democracy seriously at all.

My use of the term "democratic" is therefore intended to draw attention to the historical contingency of its denigration and to signal an unwillingness to cede the idea to its abusers. For starters, no one in this study appears in need of apologists. No one would have invoked democracy as a transparent term, or as a description of their present situation. The Asocio de Artistos Demokrato, which I discuss in chapter 10, represents a rare case where a group *did* lay claim to the word. But their 1953 manifesto is tellingly aware of the complications associated with it. "The word 'democracy (*demokurashii*)' passes among us like a papal indulgence. Everybody knows how this convenient word, in dressing up any injustice, can put a person's conscience to sleep, turn lies into truth, and conceal all non-democratic (*himinshuteki*) intentions from proper criticism. . . . We must take this word made filthy with bad intentions and throw it back one more time into the faces of our enemies."[33] Those living at the time—even those who went so far as to invoke democracy as a value—seem in little need of latter-day wisdom. I reclaim the term in a similar spirit, not as something actual but as a possibility, embattled to be sure but calling for even greater attention for that reason. I do not conceive of democratic culture as a state that was achieved, but as a limit or horizon that emerges as a shared sense of possibility from a forest of uncoordinated actions that has become ever clearer in the context of recent scholarship on the early postwar.[34]

Though I will come back to diachronic questions in more detail in the epilogue, it is worth mentioning in this context some possible genealogies between early postwar democratic culture and what went before it. It bears a strong resemblance to what Sho Konishi has described as anarchist democracy, which flourished as consciousness and practice in the early twentieth century and emphasized mutual aid, equality, multiplicity, a symbiotic connection with the natural world, and the idea that the thoughts and actions of "the people" (*heimin*) in their everyday lives could best guide collective progress, without reference to the state.[35] The relationships that can be theorized and built in such cooperatist anarchist organization are responsive to the special capacities of each person and to the world and human needs within it. They coalesce where needs or interests bring people together, according to a logic based not on credentials (least of all those backed by the state) but oriented toward problem solving—finding answers to new needs with resources to be found through experiment, exploration, and study. Anarchist democracy relies on an ad hoc, eclectic, associative logic that allows each individual theoretically unlimited capacities and enables all manner of unauthorized connections to be made, among fields of knowledge as well as people. Although this history had been largely effaced, Konishi reveals how anarchists' collective work effected lasting cultural change without resorting to violence, and altered common understandings and values related to literature, art, education, agriculture, science, and language. Culture was both the field and the tool of transformation, and not just transformation but *progress*.

I am not the first to call attention to the similarity between the anarchist democracy that Konishi describes and the democratic culture of the early postwar. Konishi himself suggests it, and his argument is one that contributes to (and reframes) a school of thought and action that argues the seeds of civil society and democratic ways of life in modern Japan are to be found in the daily practices and thinking of the common people.[36] The popular tradition of mutual aid (*sōgo fujo*), which goes back at least to the Tokugawa period (1600–1868), is often referenced in this school of thought. Although Konishi may have been the first to connect Japan's mutual aid tradition to modern anarchism (he shows how deeply the tradition affected Kropotkin's thinking on mutual aid, for instance), he is not the first to take an interest in mutual aid itself.[37] The above-mentioned *locus classicus* of circle study, *Kyōdō kenkyū: shūdan*, also points to the intellectual and practical traditions of mutual aid as a historical forebearer to the spontaneous organizing and networking patterns of the early postwar circle movements.[38] Entertaining such a connection places the democratic culture of the early postwar in a lineage of civil society–like traditions that predate the modern state and survived in an unevenly submerged form long after its founding.

CHAPTER 2

Art and Engagement

The previous chapter presents the work of the networked small groups of cultural producers as attempts to make culture anew in the here and now by means of ad hoc association and self-determined cultural production. But it does so from a perspective that is retrospective and general. This chapter begins at the opposite end, from questions arising from the perceived gap between idea and effect and from the related question of what role art and the aesthetic were to play in bridging that gap.

After all, why would art and culture seem so necessary at this time? "A time," as historian Oguma Eiji writes, "when the social order was not settled, when phrases like 'the world can be changed' had reality,"[1] yet also a time traversed by brutal tides, from the remilitarization and reactionism of the early Cold War to the trauma, hunger, and uncertainty of the day to day. Why would creativity appear, as if so naturally, as a response to adversity? The framework for the answer that I fill out in this chapter is that unformedness called forth efforts to form collective meaning: adversity was also an irresistible field of potential. The work of forming was affirmative and attractive even when it entailed sacrifice. (And often it was just plain fun.) But at the same time, the re-forming, in its materiality and sociality, proceeded with the very tools and materials of adversity and was oriented toward its most urgently felt sphere—that of daily life—lest its radical potentials—its dreams—fail to take root in reality in a way that might bear fruit in the present and future.

In elaborating on this idea, I also lay out an argument about intervention. Examining the patterns of early postwar intervention provides an opportunity to consider them in contrast to more recent paradigms, from which they differ on key points. Specifically, it is an opportunity to find value in terms such as commitment, organization, goal-directedness, and incremental change that were for a long time out of fashion in the politics of avant-garde art in the capitalist west. Such an examination is also an opportunity to relativize and critique the tendency to find the greatest aesthetic value in spontaneity, disruption, and immediacy. Emphasis on the latter qualities constitutes what I call a volcanic model of the avant-garde: value is taken to emerge through a sudden disruptive energy that punctures the formal, ethical, or epistemological assumptions of the audience (and by extension, those of mainstream culture). As an organizational/institutional ideology, such moments stand for an absolute break, a sort of anti-institution, always a step beyond a collectivity's tendency to settle meaning and cause it to ossify. The spectacle of eruption and the curious ejecta that harden as they fall to earth stand in as memorials of radical independence and unscripted possibility, albeit ones that, in contradictory fashion, must be framed and kept public by the highly codified worlds of museum, critic, historian, and parts of the art market in order to maintain their visibility and establish broader cultural relevance.

The art and culture movements of the early postwar were different. They presumed that there should be no privileged access to the process of grasping and sharing something emergent: *anyone* could do that. But if everyone were to do it, new organizations would be needed so that anyone's aesthetic work could become visible. This was necessarily a work that moved less concisely than the volcanic avant-garde. To continue the geological metaphor, we might call it a metamorphic avant-garde in that art attained value not by claiming a monopoly on disruptive insight but by expanding the possibilities of public expression and by precipitating qualitative change through the effect of sheer density, thereby shifting, incrementally, the lay of the cultural landscape.

The case of Senda Umeji (1920–1997) illustrates these points. At age 20, Senda had the short-lived good fortune to be taken in as a student by the established painter Nakagawa Kazumasa. When he was drafted a few months later, his hopes of becoming an artist vanished and, returning from China four years later, he found his family home destroyed by the air raids along with all of his artwork to date. Like many in those lean years right after the war, Senda set out for coal country. The liberation of Korean and Chinese forced labor had left a shortage, and coal was a priority for the national economy.

The mines had food, and that drew people of all classes and backgrounds to them to eat, sleep, and work together. Most of the migrants returned home as the economy began to restratify a few years later. But Senda stayed, married, and had two daughters while working in pit #1 of Nihon Tankō's Takamatsu mine in northern Kyushu. It was his health and his father's health that brought him back to Toyama in 1958 to take up the reins of the family roof-tiling business.[2]

After arriving in Kyushu, he began painting again as soon as he could afford supplies. His work caught the eye of Ueno Eishin (1923–1987), a Kyoto University dropout, who headed the management committee at the workers' dormitory Senda had moved into. In that capacity, Ueno put out a hand-printed journal featuring the poetry and writing of dorm residents, and he invited Senda to contribute something. This was Senda's opportunity to try woodcut. Over the next decade, Ueno and Senda produced many hand-printed arts magazines that were made for and included the work of fellow miners. They produced five "picture stories" (*ebanashi*), which were simple tales, almost parables, that Ueno wrote and Senda illustrated on each page with a woodcut. Senda also published an illustrated collection of miners' work songs on his own, though Ueno probably helped him with interviews as he compiled it. These publications involved dozens of original woodcuts, virtually all of which Senda hand-printed at his home with the help of his wife, Aiko, and two comrades from the Nihon Kikanshi Kyōkai (Japan Newsletter Association). They made roughly 30,000 prints for the five picture stories alone, using handheld barens as their only tool.

A great paradox of Senda is that it was *only* during his time in the mines that he thrived as an artist. After he returned to Toyama, his artistic production dropped off markedly. Why should that have been? One would think that being the head of the family business, living in his ancestral home, his children off at school, he would have been able to pursue his art with much greater freedom. But for Senda this was not the case. It was working a swing shift, living in a cramped worker's row house with his young family, sharing the company of people not usually known for their aesthetic sensibility that seems to have sustained Senda's work.

This probably wasn't so rare. Kido Noboru, one of the more active members of the small collective of worker-artists called the Keihin E no Kai (Keihin Picture Society), worked thirteen hours a day between his "job" as a day laborer in Tokyo and the supplemental piecework he took in to support his family of four. And yet, unable to bear the emptiness of a life encircled by work and sleep, he took up woodcut with some of his friends, stealing time to carve during work breaks, discovering in the process "a hidden blossom" within himself.[3] At the same time, Kido was acting editor of another group's self-published, hand-printed poetry magazine, *Ibuki* (Breath; Life), that featured writing by workers in and around the Shibaura factory district on Tokyo Bay.

These examples attest to the attractive, affirmative energy of shared creation as something that bends not just the spaces for art and reception but the conventions that presume to organize the time of work into equivalent units. Though seemingly paradoxical, many if not most of the countless nearly anonymous creators who contributed to democratic culture were writing, talking, singing, and printing on stolen time or, to adapt Kido's idea, time that bloomed. Their work was not assigned to them by activist unions or the Communist Party (though its dissemination was enabled by them). Its proliferation hints at the thrill of producing something with and for a particular group of people, something that is both one's own and has clear meaning beyond oneself, bearing connection to others and the wider world. It was not leisure or distance but quite the opposite—potential connection—that drove such production. Here is the first sense in which the term engagement applies. An engagement is a promise, a commitment, but one that is not coerced. It is founded on mutuality and is inherently proleptic: only future behavior will settle how well an engagement, as a mutually recognized enunciation of a shared future, is actually realized. As an ongoing condition, engagement therefore entails an ongoing assumption that the engaged parties will respond to each other: even if each and every missive and action is not reciprocated, there is enough give and take to affirm the viability—the real virtuality—of shared but unsettled futures. In this respect, engagement is simultaneously subjective and objective: it sustains an idea that one's expressions and ideas might have some place in the present and future and that they might be reflected back in the work of others and in society broadly.

A second paradox of creators like Senda and Kido is that despite their tumultuous and demanding lives, their artworks exhibit great poise. They are quiet and spacious and curious. Make no mistake: they are political and unabashedly so. But the legibility of their politics may cause us to miss, first, the somewhat mundane fact that they were meant to be enjoyed. Ueno's style in the picture stories reads like a well-worn folktale and Senda's prints appear equally warm and familiar. Ueno imagined in his afterword to the 1954 hand-printed edition that after a day of hard work and a meager meal, "the one stretch of enjoyable time remaining" was when "parents and children lie down together around the oil lamp to chat amongst themselves and laugh while reading children's books and manga to each other."[4] The picture stories were designed for such a reception, and according to Ueno and Senda, people at the Takamatsu mine were enthusiastic about them.[5]

But also, second, we should not overlook the way these liminal productions open politics into a mode of sensitivity to daily life as a microcosmos. The narrator of the first of the picture stories, "Senpuri Senji Laughed" (Senpuri Senji ga waratta), tells us that the sour expression of the title character is what earned him his nickname of *senpuri*, a bitter herb he always seems to have just tasted. He never laughs and hardly speaks, and his newborn child takes after him. At work in the pits on the day in question, the shift boss begins making demands to tidy up because the company president is coming to tour the worksite. The workers respond with a call to down tools and vote whether to take the action or not. It comes down to the final vote and all eyes turn to Senji. When he speaks up in favor of the work stoppage it is an occasion for his comrades to celebrate him, but the story continues. He goes back home to his wife and, while playing with his child, begins to smile and laugh, to which the child responds with his own laughter. The story ends as Senji dances around the room laughing. The title refers to this moment of opening up, of shared enjoyment. Although the action of speaking up in the mine is what changed the objective situation, the reverberations of that expand into humor, a playful kind of back and forth with the world.

The first four of Ueno and Senda's picture stories all center on humble miners or housewives who find a public voice. The stories frame these expressions as having consequence, but go further to show a correspondence between the public restoration of justice and the familial/neighborly opening out of an emotionally enriched communicative space. The resolution is not in the public or the private realm but in their implicit connection: in the way the most intimately felt legitimacy becomes public and vice versa. Thus, while they do not gloss over the struggle for life and while the roughness of Senda's woodcuts communicates something of the stark environment of the mine town (as well as the poor materials of their production), these are redeemed when the forces of the larger world and those of feelings among family and friends move into alignment to open up new qualities, depths, and possibilities that emerge from the discovery of interdependence. The pivot that achieves this is always the same: the voice of the formerly silenced.

In "Oya to ko no yoru" (A night for parents and children), Komine's family goes hungry because the company is paying wages in worthless scrip. Her children will have to stop going to school. She goes to the company offices one morning to get the paperwork to withdraw her children from school. There, the boss tosses 500 yen at her to ease her situation but extracts a promise from her in return: to spy on the union for the company. With the money she buys food, but the thought of betraying her family eats away at her (fig. 2.1). She is tormented by guilt through dinner, which her children notice. They push her to explain and she confesses. The information is relayed to the union, which

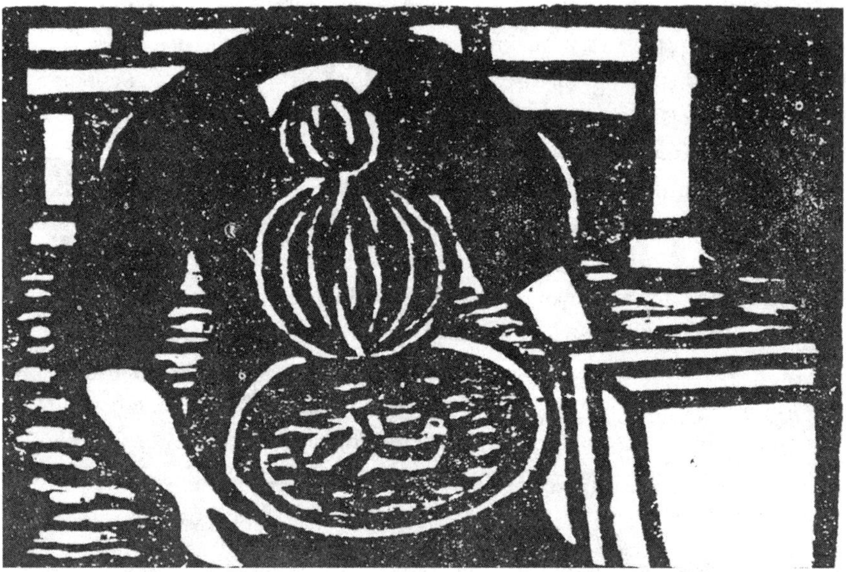

Figure 2.1 Senda Umeji, from "Oya to ko no yoru" (A night for parents and children), 1954. Woodblock print on paper. 19.9 cm x 25.2 cm. Tagawa City Art Museum.

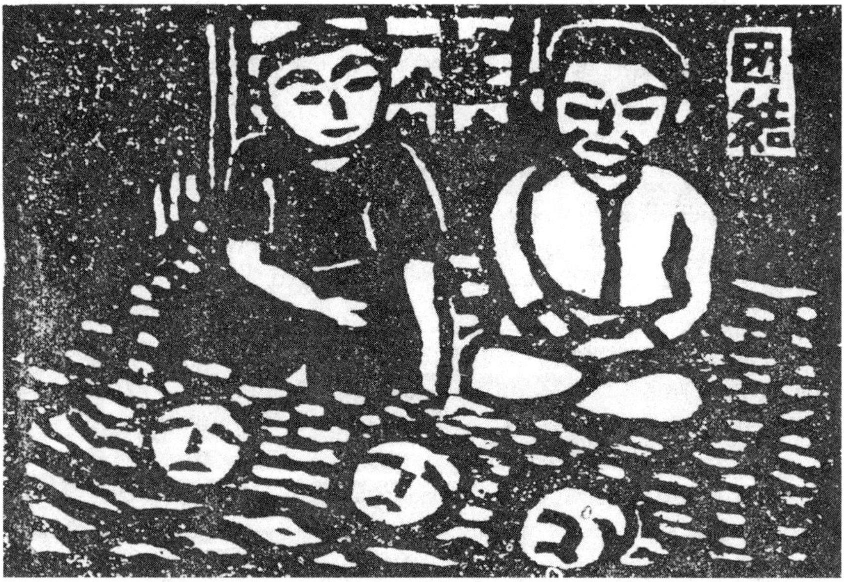

Figure 2.2 Senda Umeji, from "Oya to ko no yoru" (A night for parents and children), 1954. Woodblock print on paper. 19.9 cm x 25.2 cm. Tagawa City Art Museum.

confronts the boss and extracts back pay for all the workers—something the narrative dispenses with in summary. The final resolution is the restoration of harmony and dignity that comes with communication in the family (and the union): Komine and her husband sit near their three sleeping children, "exchanging a smile brimming with happiness, the most beautiful smile parents of this world can exchange." We can see that the structure of two images, one before and one after Komine's confession, are similar (fig. 2.2). But in the final image, the "reflection" is created between the faces of the parents and children.

Senda's cover for the inaugural issue of *Sākuru mura* (Circle village) implies a similar reflection (fig. 2.3). The miner looks at the viewer and in the positioning

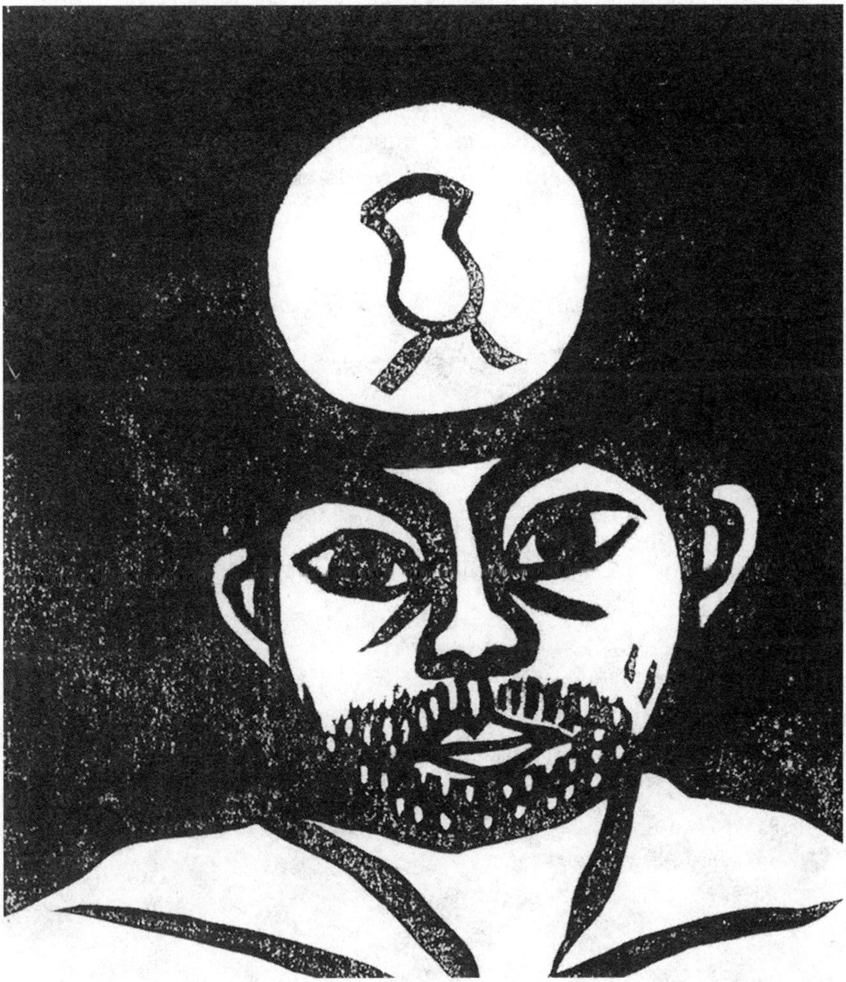

FIGURE 2.3 Senda Umeji, cover of *Sākuru mura* (Circle village), 1958. Woodblock print on paper. 34 cm x 25.7 cm. Tagawa City Art Museum.

of his body seems to be spatially accommodating us. Senda has written that he imagined the viewer also wearing a headlamp, which explains why the miner's face jumps out with such clarity and candor. It is completely available to us, as we might be to it. The realization of mutual implication is not exactly shocking, but it is arresting. These works have a clear political setting and valence, but they also expand the political into the very small. Senda realizes varying states of reverie in the mundane, the best of his works opening out a sensitivity to the potential in the world even in the most familiar encounters, showing the environment of the mine opening up as if on a hinge to the swirl of the stars, the movement of the earth (fig. 2.4). The defamiliarization is enlivening, not threatening. Everyday life is shown to be infiltrated by possibility, as small-scale alignments at home, in the union, in chance meetings, settle things into a slightly different but wholly better place than where they started. This is cosmic in the sense that it describes an immanent belonging, an interrelationship that elevates as it relates. And the aesthetic is the mode by which we can enjoy and share that vision of unforeclosed interrelation and the absolute equality in belonging that derives from it. This open interrelation is the second sense

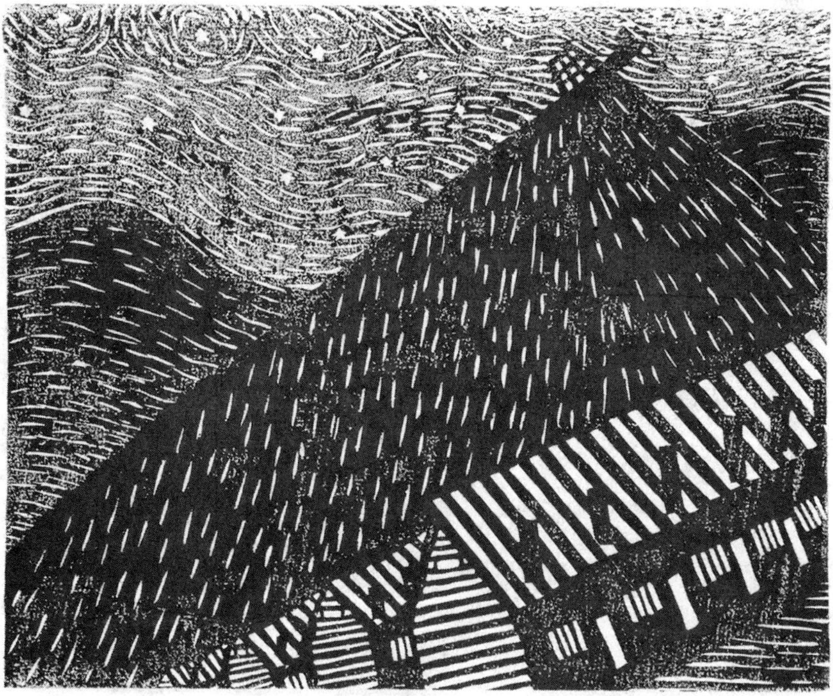

FIGURE 2.4 Senda Umeji, *Hoshizora no shita no botayama* (*Slag Heap under a Starry Sky*), 1956. Woodblock print on paper. 39.5 cm x 45 cm. Tagawa City Art Museum.

of the word engagement, denoting an assumption of unavoidable relatedness but one that is as yet undetermined. The miner on the cover of *Sākuru mura* is momentarily connected to us: we are not strangers, yet there is no indication of how this moment of passing each other in the dark will turn out.

The power of these works, however, would be nil had they never been seen. They might not even have been made without the substantive possibility of responses to the miner's quiet address to the viewer. Those possibilities were built and rebuilt by organizational work coordinated among many actors in shifting capacities. There were, certainly, historical factors that enabled this work: near-universal literacy, a large and diverse mining work force, strong unions, the concentrated living environment of the mine. But these factors do not address the question of what motivated the labor of responsiveness and curiosity that instantiated the networks in question. Ueno's introduction to the second edition of the picture stories (1955) is often cited as giving insight into why he devoted so much of his life to the Chikuhō coal fields. Years before, he had injured his leg deep in the mines and was carried out by another miner, a stranger, who sacrificed a day's pay to crawl up steep, narrow passages with Ueno on his back. Ueno positions himself as recipient of a gift that can never be fully returned: the gift of life that that miner and many after him gave without a second thought. For Ueno, the picture stories were a gift in return. Though he lived out the rest of his life in Chikuhō, he didn't claim to be a miner or a native, only that his work was sustained in relationship to miners. Senda is also difficult to place. Artist, miner, artisan's son? None of these identities is sufficient. Judging by his works, his tie to the mines was less freighted than Ueno's. Instead of returning gratitude for salvation, he strikes an affectionate appreciation, not for his coworkers but for people their grandparents' age—something his coworkers might well have been able to share. His selection of work songs combines happiness and grief, tragic deaths with underground trysts, the taste of a one-cent cigarette, though one you can hardly afford anymore (fig. 2.5). While the emotions of the songs Senda collected are ambivalent, the style of his woodcuts is more consistently affirmative. He renders the incidents and feelings in the songs with near-uniform fullness, balance, and strong rhythm. They are evidently distant enough to be admired as forms of life past (fig. 2.6).

The artists' relationships to the mines is only one part of the picture, however. Their work was part of a movement that enabled multitudes to participate in creating culture by building spaces and circuits of recognition where their voices could be heard. One mode of such building was ethnography and investigative reporting. Examples include Senda's collection of

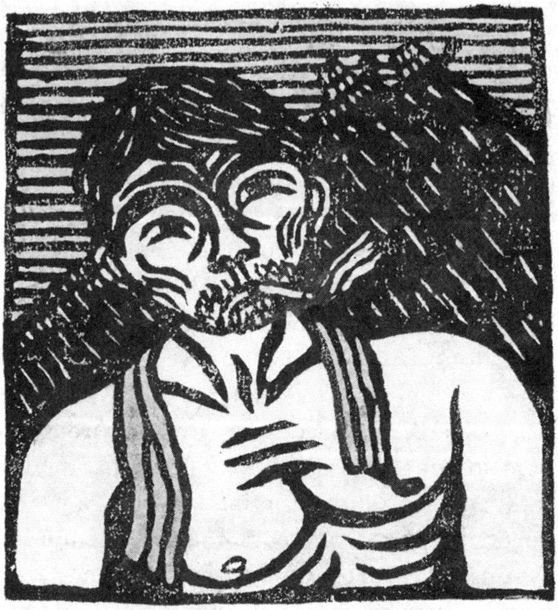

FIGURE 2.5 Senda Umeji, from *Tankō shigoto uta bangakan* (Illustrated collection of mine work songs), 1956. Woodblock print on paper. 18.7 cm x 22.1 cm. Tagawa City Art Museum. "Rice goes up, wages go down, can barely smoke a one-cent Bat." (Bat is a cigarette brand.)

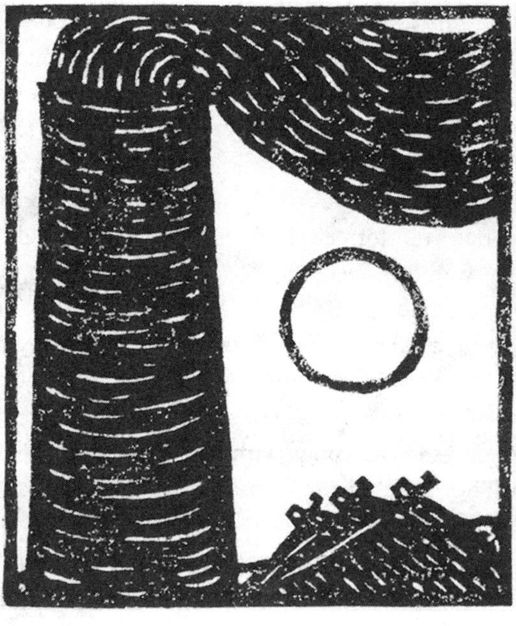

FIGURE 2.6 Senda Umeji, *Tankō shigoto uta bangakan* (Illustrated collection of mine work songs), 1956. Woodblock print on paper. 14.7 cm x 13.5 cm. Tagawa City Art Museum. "If you'll be my girl, I'll blow my feelings from that smokestack."

work songs, Morisaki Kazue's published oral histories of female mine workers, and Ueno Eishin's book-length documentations of the havoc wrought in the lives of miners at the small mines, stories that rarely reached the headlines as the coal industry was slowly dismantled. Another mode was providing venues for people to write their own works, usually fiction, poetry, and reportage. The majority of works that appeared in the hand-printed periodicals at the mines were produced by people who subsequently did not become full-time authors or artists. Some of these worker-artists published only once. Most did a few times. Some became leaders or respected artists, even if not household names. Examples of the latter include Kunikami Nobuo, who collaborated with Ueno Eishin and went on to produce his own hand-printed periodical *Tankō nagaya* (Mine tenement); the poets Ishigaki Rin or Ejima Kan; and of course Senda and Kido. We must avoid saying these figures arose "out of nowhere": more properly they arose out of the material and spiritual context of a democratic culture.

The small groups of collaborators that sustained so many people's cultural production cohered primarily through shared passion, interests, and concerns. The groups were usually connected to each other and to similar groups around the country. In some cases, local groups were affiliated with a large-scale publication, in which case the network of groups was maintained by the publishing company with the goal of developing its audience. In other cases, groups were affiliated through a labor union or political party, which supported them because they could build solidarity and were useful in political and social campaigns. Some groups developed and maintained their own networks, with little reliance on preexisting organizational infrastructure. These networks were rarely exclusive though, and many groups participated in all three types. All the groups in this study engaged in and/or built a number of overlapping networks in a somewhat eclectic manner. This situation created a uniquely shaped audience: one that had extreme specificity in a work's most local reception and extreme unpredictability in its eventual visibility to a wider audience.

The Keihin E no Kai, for example, self-published two collections of their woodcut prints. Some of them subsequently appeared in a textbook for the woodcut education movement led by Ueno Makoto.[6] They also submitted works to large exhibitions, each with slightly different audiences: the Japan Independent Exhibition, which the JCP-affiliated Nihon Bijutsu Kai (Japan Art Society) held each year; the annual exhibition of the Shokuba Bijutsu Kyōgikai (Council of Workplace Art), a network of union-sponsored art circles; and the third Nippon Exhibition, which was run by the avant-garde reportage artists discussed in part 2. Ueno and Senda's picture stories were reprinted with moveable type in 1955 and sold nationwide. The same year, selections from the first five stories were reprinted in the Japan Coal Miners' Union newspaper *Tanrō shinbun*; in the JCP daily, *Akahata*; and in a magazine that featured large amounts of circle-based writing, *Bungaku no tomo* (Literature companion).[7] They were also included as volume 7 of an experimental series of artfully produced books on social problems, the Testimonies of Japan Reportage Series, which featured the work of some of the avant-garde artists I discuss in part 2.[8]

In the process of traversing these different contexts, the picture stories were claimed for different purposes. This was evident already in the first 1955 reprint. Manabe Kureo, a prominent activist and writer, claimed in his afterword that the stories succeeded in making literature "something for all people (*kokumin zentai*)," and that they were faithful works of reportage that described the "contradictions" of miners' lives in concrete terms. Manabe thus framed the stories as models of what was then the mainstream JCP line. Ueno pulled in the opposite direction with his extremely personal introduction, described above. He also explained the optimism so evident in the picture stories by introducing a microhistory: they had been written at a moment when he and other activists at Nittan Takamatsu were just starting to sense the first stirring of new movements after the devastation of the 1953 "rationalization" campaigns, which had been used to root out activist union members. He called them "fables" (*meruhen*) for a time of new hope.[9] Their inclusion in the more experimental Testimonies of Japan Reportage Series, meanwhile, put them alongside writers and artists who were increasingly blurring the boundary between fiction and nonfiction, reality and fantasy, in their work of reportage. The same works thus afforded mulitple connections and readings. Activist unions and the JCP sustained information and distribution networks that were important for the circulation of Ueno and Senda's work and for the work of some of the reportage artists. But as both examples also demonstrate, those networks ended up supporting truly eclectic cultural production and could be activated in a nonsystematic manner by entrepreneurial actors. The trajectories of the various instantiations of Ueno and Senda's picture stories show that they were made possible by the initiatives of just a handful of people, usually writers or editors, when we trace the actual connections.

These movements and associations were built and maintained primarily through the efforts of the artists and writers themselves. Their networks often piggybacked on those of union or JCP organizations and they lent their social capital to a variety of social movements as the need arose. While sustaining their own micropractices of gathering, writing and discussing, cutting templates (*gari*) for printing, and distributing and exhibiting their work, these groups had a generally outgoing orientation, an unwillingness to settle for what was given at any one moment. Wherever we choose to enter and begin to trace the networks of interconnections, we quickly find constellations of association opening out: the examples above focus only on the connections that appear when we trace the journey of the picture stories in the first two years after they were first published as a hand-printed volume.

We can see similar patterns in the three groups I examine in the remainder of this study: all of them put a great deal of energy into building new organizations and networks that would keep their work visible while also using existing organizations' infrastructures in an ad-hoc manner. In each case, teaching, small publications, traveling exhibitions, regular gatherings, and public speaking were the most important techniques of organizing. By themselves, each of these activities was potentially mundane, but their accumulated patterns opened new possibilities. In the language the reportage artists used, the avant-garde project had to be both a political and an artistic avant-garde, although, as we will discover, this was a fraught combination that involved tremendous effort and only patchy success. In the language of Sōbi, creativity in both children and adults was made possible by a "creative atmosphere," something that had its most important stage in the classroom but that also required openness and flexibility from school administration and family. Creativity might blossom most vibrantly in open (i.e., uninhibited) spaces, but concerted effort on the part of the teacher was needed to protect creative atmospheres from outside pressures to close them down. In hoping to bring as many on board as possible for its forays into Tokyo, Kyushu-ha was as much an amateur circle as a contemporary art group. And the case of Kyushu-ha in particular helps us see that the specialization and professionalization of the cultural field that caused the group to founder was at base a process of splitting the repetitive, reproductive work of creating context from the properly creative work of art.

In order to bring these observations to bear upon contemporary discussions of art and politics, I focus on Jacques Rancière, a thinker whose early work, *Proletarian Nights*, has been an inspiration for this project from the beginning. His work sheds light on the capacities ascribed to the art and culture of the early postwar in a number of ways. Recently Rancière has interpreted Emerson and Whitman as some of the earliest examples of modernist poetics because they identify the spiritual potential of small things and everyday activities—the farmer contemplating his oats; the lunatic carried off to the asylum; the plumb bob, trowel, and scaffold; the steam saw; the handpress; the awl and the cobbler's kneestrap; billiard sticks; milliners' ribbons; and of course, leaves of grass—yet admit no separate world of the spiritual beyond the interminable linkage of things into the chain of beings.[10] Analogously, political change emerges potentially anywhere, always coming from outside current distributions of expectation to extend the chain of beings into new instantiations of previously unrecognized equality. Unprejudiced sensitivity to the equality of such beings rejects the concept of margin and center for an equivalence of non-identity. Making sensible the pregnant possibility in and among every person and object is a question of aesthetics, which makes the aesthetic a faculty that is uniquely able to open the field where radical democracy might flourish.

Rancière's ideas, however, are at best able to apprehend only half of what I mean to call attention to. The limitation of his work stems from the way valuation of the new and unexpected forces an equivalent hostility toward organization, and blocks recognition of the important admixture of repetitive and predictable work that is necessary to make the new possible and subsequently shareable. While he uses the term "distribution of the sensible" to describe the social order that politics and art alter, his model is not one of silence becoming sound but of speech once heard as noise being recognized as discourse. Such moments, however, turn out to require considerable cultural expertise on the part of the speaker. His examples of politics almost always assume shared language, if not the gift of effective polemics; he often visits the courtroom as a site where voices once heard as noise are heard as political speech.[11] But how is the knowledge and skill necessary to being heard in such places to be built?

Rancière's most sustained consideration of literacy and learning is *The Ignorant Schoolmaster*, which follows the story of Joseph Jacotot, a university lecturer who discovers by chance that there is a way to teach students without sharing a common language. While the book is not framed as an account of literacy and should not be judged as such, it is nonetheless revealing in its structured absences. Particularly striking is how thoroughly Rancière represses any mention of reproductive work. Jacotot's pedagogy requires an enormous amount of memorization. At a number of points in *Schoolmaster*, Rancière invokes the student memorizing the first three words of the prose epic *Les aventures de Télémaque*: "Calypso," "Calypso could," "Calypso could not." Then, without any indication of what happens in between, the students have succeeded and are composing soaring extemporaneous compositions: they are either learning their first three words or are (magically) fully empowered speakers in a new language.

If Rancière is unconcerned with how the work of building literacy can be a potential barrier to politics as he conceives them, he also avoids examining the material conditions of visibility and audibility. Although Rancière speaks in terms of a collective political subject, nothing in his work can account for collectivity as a lived process, and the anecdotes he typically deploys emphasize symbolically invested individual acts much more than collective work. Why, for instance, does Jacotot have students at all, and why do they engage in such labors under his aegis? Although he is in a newly humble position of ignorance, he apparently remains well connected, such that the vista extending outward from his standing makes his classroom possible as a stage for the future. We might imagine the pushy librarian as a counterexample to the ignorant schoolmaster. Although the pushy librarian would be well positioned, intellectually and materially, to implement a similar pedagogy, she or he would face considerable social and institutional barriers to behaving as a leader of students and would also provide a far less gallant hero for historical narrative.[12] In his inability to recognize the institutional supports, the mundane actions and transactions that create the opportunities for more spectacular moments of disruption, Rancière is typical of a political aesthetic that fails to acknowledge the interdependence of autonomy and support and disavows the maintenance work that support entails.[13]

Rancière is far from the only figure to theorize the relation between art and politics in this way. Ernesto Laclau and Chantel Mouffe develop the concept of antagonism in *Hegemony and Socialist Strategy* as arising from the "impossibility of [society] fully constituting itself."[14] They deliberately place antagonism beyond objective social relations and resistance to them, staking out the ground of politics as something categorically separate from the social. Such theories, however, obscure the phenomena I wish to emphasize. They are based on a radical separation of politics from any actual social situation and invest heavily in devaluing organization, solidarity, and repetitive labor. Moments of insight are necessarily fugitive, and the work of building better relations and the structures necessary for sustained visibility is not only secondary but entirely misguided. Michel de Certeau perfects the fetishization of the fleeting, elevating it into a sublime mode of experience while explicitly rejecting a route to revolution or even systematic disruption. In his opposition of tactics to strategy, he builds an account of the significance of tactics against a (drastically overstated) theorization of technocratic administration in which the only possible mode of autonomy emerges within the instability of enunciatory moments.[15]

Rather than investigating the relationship between politics and the social order—that is, the *way* that politics emerges and in turn alters a social order—many of these thinkers, and post-*Schoolmaster* Rancière in particular, appear to be more concerned with policing the border between politics and society in order to ensure that politics (and aesthetics) remain a pure space of possibility that is never tarnished by actuality. Breaking with this tradition, I start with the idea that rebuilding the contours of a culture or a society does not happen only through an event or disruption or disagreement. Although disruption may be necessary, creating access to that moment of disruption, that unbidden moment of public authorship, requires organizational work to prepare and to communicate the significance thereof. The continued appeal to the power of the event, or to the power of the artwork in and of itself, provides no way to value this process and, worse, enforces the continued invisibility of the work that is necessary to make certain events and objects visible and relevant. The logic of the event, insofar as it celebrates something self-generating and self-propagating, repeats the myth of self-sufficient creativity, effectively banishing the work of repetition and renewal to conceptual darkness. Further, the attack on institutions that is often a corollary of this logic, is in this aspect an attempt to sever the umbilical connection between types of work designated as creative and those designated as reproductive: a devaluation aimed to remove the stain of dependency from view.

The three movements in this study provide an occasion for investigating how their participants developed new *and* stable conceptual spaces and patterns of transmission so that they could share their experiences and share the possibility of authorship with others. Critical battles entailed practical commitments. Ideas and words were crucial, but they were not enough by themselves. Writing and discussing might have been practices of opening out a range of responses to the present, but organization of some sort was needed to extend experience and make it available to a time and a place beyond the first embodied moment of its birth. *Shared* experience, an experience or idea living and moving beyond the individual, is the basis for a political presence that can sustain through time and between spaces.

While my need to think outside the paradigms of the volcanic avant-garde has arisen in relation to the project of understanding the early postwar period in Japan, the move has contemporary resonance. Grant Kester has criticized inherited assumptions about autonomy, critique, and the aesthetics of rupture for the way that they recode political transformation "into a form of ontic disruption directed at any coherent system of belief, agency, or identity" and how they reduce the artist or intellectual to "[supervising] the process through the composition of axiomatic texts (writing, poetry, film, objects, events, etc.) that seek to destabilize the viewer or reader through essentially individual hermeneutic engagement."[16] The patterns of democratic culture laid out here clearly entail more diverse modes of engagement. Doris Sommer's work shows how practices in a variety of unlikely contexts demonstrate art's power to make room for possibilities within seemingly intractable "spirals of power and passion."[17] In this, art's freedom is not a claim of separation from the world nor does art serve as reified placeholder of endless potential; art renews itself in its work of actually finding the world anew. As Sommer points out in her reading of Schiller, the freedom he identified was double-edged: it gave birth to uncertainty in the indeterminateness of the present state while simultaneously implying that every individual was equally an artist in their capacity to transform it.[18] Schiller burdened the aesthetic with no small thing when he conceived of its importance in light of man's unique power "[to transform] the work of blind compulsion into a work of free choice, and [to elevate] physical necessity into moral necessity."[19]

While the groups in this study never referenced Schiller in this capacity, someone whose work they were very much aware of—Jean Paul Sartre—captured a similarly double-edged freedom in his pronouncement that "man is condemned to be free."[20] As participants in a moment of tremendous historical transformation, artists could hardly claim a monopoly on disruption. Art was a way of engaging with something already in motion beyond them. Growth was a force beyond the control of the Sōbi educator. It could only be received in a certain way: stunted at great peril to the child and the world, encouraged with nothing more than the *hope* that the child could assume its alien power as creativity. The reportage aesthetic of avant-garde realism strove to apprehend historical crises that similarly operated beyond individual control. One prominent theorist exemplified avant-garde vision with reference to William Tell, a man condemned by a tyrannical foreign lord to save himself by shooting an apple from his son's head. The moment when all the old forms of vision finally fell away was a moment of absolute contingency, but one that was focused through a crisis of absolute inescapability. This is freedom, but freedom that comes only by letting go the illusion of individual control.

As such comparisons also demonstrate, however, there is considerable difference between the art forms and theoretical emphases of the early postwar years and those of the present day. One difference is that the specter of failure took a more vivid and specific form in the early postwar period. The tremendous suffering of the war and occupation made the stakes high in Japan: collective failure portended a return to fascism and war in Asia, two things that seemed quite possible in the uncertainty of the 1950s. Some of the failures that were most commonly invoked in considerations of fascism in Japan were intellectuals' separation from the masses, their inability to make their critical insight matter in the runup to war in the 1930s, and the masses' structural inability to make use of knowledge even if they encountered it. It was, that is to say, a problem of disengagement, of separation. The specter of disengagement took many interrelated forms. Intellectuals' alienation from the masses is one form, something many cite as motivating the experiments in crossing boundaries and building contexts for a more inclusive culture. Alienation of high culture from low culture is another, and we can see many corresponding attempts to take "low" culture seriously and to make "high" culture accessible. Yet another figure of disengagement arose between the individual and the world, and even within the individual subject. This was a split between ideas on the one hand and embodied behavior on the other. The term "engagement" can also be understood to apply to the interlinked projects of overcoming these perceived splits in the cultural and social fabric. And it was at the final site—the split between ideas and actions—that art and the aesthetic were often invoked in the early postwar.

Although there is a considerable range among the groups in this study, a general observation to be made is that each in their own way held the idea that art and the aesthetic worked through some area or way of meaning that was closer to people's embodied being than other forms of knowledge. Critic Hariu Ichirō, who was close to the reportage artists, argued that the artists' task was to "build a new relation between thought and body, politics and literature,"[21] a formulation that coded thought and politics as abstract and the body and literature as concrete. The problem was often expressed in terms of how the inside (the world of embodied consciousness) and the outside (the social, historical world) could be brought into meaningful correspondence. The assumption was that the two *were* inextricably working through one another but that ideas and representations had yet to find a way to make that interpenetration visible and available to intervention. For Sōbi, human being was part of a natural pattern of growth. The "suffering of twenty million" Japanese children that leader Kubo Sadajirō identified in 1949 was a suffering born of repression: forced alienation from the process of natural growth. Teachers in the movement and the artists who found common cause searched for a form of representation and organization that would get out of the way of growth and find ways to instigate full participation in growth as a present process. Attunement to the aesthetic was the key to connecting inexorable but easily stunted biological patterns to practices of organization and representation. Although Kyushu-ha was more mixed, the artists Sakurai Takami, Tabe Mitsuko, and Kikuhata Mokuma each explored the interpenetration of the social and the embodied individual. While Sakurai nursed a romantic vision of the self undivided from the natural world and mourned the traumatic rupture of individuation, Tabe and Kikuhata each developed a more complex vision of the interdependence of self/society and the natural world. All three imagined the tension and friction generated by the clash of forces as playing out across the terrain of the human body and its everyday milieus.

The different mechanisms will be interrogated more deeply in each chapter, but the commonality lies in the way that art and the aesthetic were taken as special for their ability to describe and make manifest the potentially abstract political and historical questions of the early postwar with a specificity and suppleness that could actually get at individual experience. Art was thus a potential link between the deeply personal and the larger problems of human relation and historical change.[22] Hariu Ichirō, for instance, credited reportage art (as opposed to filmic documentation) with being uniquely capable of capturing the full-body significance of a site or event because of the intervention of the artist's embodied experience in the process of production. Similarly, Sōbi's discourse on child art hinged on the idea that art bore an indexical correspondence to the embodied consciousness of the artist. The aesthetic was a special form of knowledge that worked at the threshold between mind and body, between ideas and actual habits of seeing and acting. In this way, it held some promise of making mind matter, this time around.

Raymond Williams's early work calls attention to the underacknowledged fact that people are constantly recreating their social world. "Everything we see and do, the whole structure of our relationships and institutions, depends, finally, on an effort of learning, description and communication. We create our human world as we have thought of art being created."[23] We may detect a similar insight running through many of the culture movements of the early postwar period. But few at that time mustered the explicit optimism that runs through Williams's *Long Revolution*. Though art and the aesthetic had special potential, and though artistry could be reconceived as everyone's affair, few were optimistic that it could achieve relevance easily.

Awareness of the mutual implication of subject and history came not only from an excitement about the potential of liberation but also from having witnessed the dire effects of such mutual implication under fascism. Because of its ability to communicate beyond reason and consciousness to the twilit areas of meaning that were *still* pulling the country towards violence, art became a vital tool for change. The depth attributed to the participatory process of culture was thus at the same time an appreciation of the stubbornness of its roots and the immensity of the task ahead.

Part Two

Avant-Garde Documentary

Reportage Art of the 1950s

CHAPTER 3

The Tales of *The Tale of Akebono Village*

Yamashita Kikuji's *Akebono mura monogatari* (*The Tale of Akebono Village*) (1953) is a landmark of reportage painting (plate 3). It is the single most reproduced of all reportage works and often stands in for the movement as a whole. It can be approached as a microcosm of reportage.

The reportage movement began around 1950, as the Cold War heated up in East Asia. The People's Republic of China was founded in 1949, the Korean War began in 1950, and from the perspective of the United States, Japan was becoming an ever more important bulwark against communism in East Asia. American bases in Japan were busy. Japanese industry benefited from a boom in U.S. military procurement contracts for the Korean War, which set it on a path for growth after the considerable uncertainty of the late 1940s. Only a few years after the end of World War II, war and two-tier capitalism were returning, and back with them was oppression. Suspected communists were summarily fired from both public and private sector jobs in a series of red purges from 1949 to 1952, while communist activists were arrested and prosecuted for crimes under suspicious pretenses in a number of incidents. One symbol of the intense polarization of the period was the May Day protest of 1952, which erupted into violence just three days after the official end of the U.S. occupation, leaving two dead and hundreds injured after clashes with the police. This was the perilous world the reportage painters hoped to make visible and change.

Yamashita Kikuji (1919–1986) painted *The Tale of Akebono Village* in 1953. The painting is based on events that occurred in a village deep in the mountains of Yamanashi prefecture, about half a day's train ride west of Tokyo. Akebono Village was extremely poor; the primary economic activity was wood gathering. The land reform carried out under U.S. occupation had not affected mountain holdings, so the social structure of Akebono Village had remained little changed from before the war. To begin to understand the tale of Akebono Village that Yamashita was trying to tell, we can follow curator Ozaki Masato's approach and contrast it with the incident of Akebono Village.[1] The incident occurred when a group of protesting villagers ransacked a local landowner's house, injuring some of the family members. It was reported in the local papers as an outbreak of thuggery (*bōkan*), but the report contained no explanation of the reason for the protest. Yamashita's work aimed to restore the story the newspapers had omitted.

The tale as Yamashita painted it contains no reference to the incident at the landlord's house at all, concentrating instead on the before and after. The strife in the village began when a landlord destroyed a tenant's fields in order to construct a new access road to his property. The person in the middle of the painting, head bowed, is the woman whose fields were destroyed as she protests against the landlord. The reported ransacking of the landlord's house was the third protest related to the construction of the new road. A few days after that incident, the corpse of Ishimaru Kaname, a Communist Party activist who had been working in the village, turned up in the river. Ishimaru's body lies at the bottom of the painting, the face disfigured in the way it had been found, apparently by a sharp implement. But the painting provides a deeper past as well. The woman on the right-hand side of the painting had hanged herself in 1931 after losing all of her savings in a bank collapse that was connected to the same landlord's family.[2] By including her suicide, Yamashita suggests a story not only of the precariousness of life in poor villages, but of repression repeating across generations. The deep continuity between the pre-war, the war, and the postwar is the underlying refrain of the tale as Yamashita tells it.

To this we should add the tale of the painting's creation. The incidents in Akebono Village were not reported in the national press and did not become a cause célèbre of the 1950s. How did Yamashita discover the story? Answering that question provides an entry into the networks that the reportage movement depended on and created through research and direct political engagement. The key link between Yamashita and Akebono Village lies with a group of worker-poets who lived in the south Tokyo neighborhood of Shimomaruko. Close to the Tama River and Tokyo Bay, south Tokyo was home to many factories and working-class neighborhoods, and the Shimomaruko poetry circle was one of the most prolific of the many hundreds of poetry circles of the period.[3] Over the decade of the 1950s, the circle published dozens of journals and poetry collections, including a rousing special issue about the May Day protests mentioned above. This group provided the social context that made Yamashita's painting possible. Such is true of many reportage works: information and access spread through networks that crossed class barriers and existed well outside any established social systems for art.

In 1951, the Shimomaruko circle began to be visited by three young communist activists: novelist Abe Kōbō, painter and future filmmaker Teshigahara Hiroshi, and Katsuragawa Hiroshi, an artist discussed below. Abe moved into the neighborhood to teach classes on literature, while Katsuragawa taught woodcut and mimeograph publishing. Katsuragawa also happened to be close friends with Yamashita Kikuji. It was through Katsuragawa that Yamashita met a member of the Shimomaruko circle named Maruyama Teruo, who had been born into a Buddhist temple near Akebono Village. Maruyama had been working as an activist in the village but was lucky enough to have left for Tokyo before the incident.[4] The people who were killed and arrested were Maruyama's comrades, and it had originally been his idea to get the story out about what had happened.[5] Maruyama's idea had been to make a *kamishibai* based on the events. *Kamishibai* is a popular form of storytelling that uses a set of picture cards that a storyteller narrates. Before television, *kamishibai* was a popular form of entertainment for children, and in the early postwar years it was used in education and political organizing as a low-cost version of a slide show. Maruyama would write the text and Yamashita would create the artwork. "The Tale of Akebono Village" thus began as a collaborative project, conceived as a tool for enlightenment and agitation.

Maruyama and Yamashita traveled together. They stayed at Maruyama's family temple for about one month while they interviewed villagers and activists and Yamashita made sketches. After Yamashita returned to Tokyo, he set to work on the *kamishibai* (some of his preliminary sketches survive). It never came to fruition, however. As Maruyama explains it, he had been getting signals from the Communist Party that they wanted to forget the entire Akebono incident, probably in an effort to distance themselves from the ill-conceived armed struggle campaign of 1952. The tour Maruyama had been planning would have been impossible without the party's assistance, so he let it drop and made no further attempt to contact Yamashita about it.[6] At some point, Yamashita stitched together two jute bags to create a large canvas and began to work on *The Tale of Akebono Village* as a single painting.

With the benefit of the above historical explanation we can understand the events Yamashita juxtaposed. But without it, it would be difficult for viewers then or now to understand the tale in any detail. Yamashita originally conceived the tale as a narrative in the form of *kamishibai*, but the painting is necessarily different. The question of how to render ongoing social realities in the form of a single work is a challenge for any form of socially concerned realism. The reportage artists answered the challenge through use of montage and deformation. The human body as well as space and time were bent and rearticulated to expose the inescapable bodily significance of political events. The technique sewed together the world-historical and the private, the inside and the outside, injecting the individual and the everyday with the pain and pressure of an inescapable historicity while infesting the political with all manner of unsightly animal appetites and weakness. This was the mode of representing both the urgency and ubiquity of politics and the precariousness of the present at all scales.

The chosen site often condensed that precariousness: the U.S. base, the factory, the village, opened out to larger social forces while focusing them into a dense impact on a specific place. Visually crowded all-over compositions that squeeze out neutral space are common. Heteronomous forces burst from the ground to infiltrate and imperil the figure. In *The Tale of Akebono Village*, the deep mountains are a massive though ill-defined wall across the background: an expression of entrapped consciousness as much as geography. The agents of village reproduction—the policeman, the schoolgirl, the farmer—are painted as dogs, in a uniform earthy brown. Lithe and indecorous, they slip greedily into any potential gain, their biological tenacity sustaining the village if not the individual. The composition cuts off or partially obscures the human figures and fastens together incongruous scales and perspectives in a rough and ready way that lends it an unfinished dynamism: the spaces do not resolve, there is no single center, and something is still afoot, although the four main figures are the victims rather than the agents of what is happening. It is a history painting that suggests a dark future as much as a dark past.

The human figures bear the marks of larger forces. Yamashita was fascinated by metamorphosis and the grotesque throughout the 1950s.[7] Although those motifs are not dominant in *The Tale of Akebono Village*, the detail of the mucus, bulging eyes, and tongue of the hanged woman, for instance, change the tone significantly. Her image is not redeemed in death, and her corpse is shown to be subject to material movements that know no more pity than the dogs. Such "gratuitous" details are symptomatic of the avant-garde realist technique of using the flesh to dramatize the workings of the political, often in the mode of abjection. Another work by Yamashita, *Shokuminchi kōjō* (*Colonial Factory*), is an excellent example: a tangle of hand-like limbs overflows the bars of what is presumably a munitions factory supplying U.S. forces (fig. 3.1). They are clearly a figure of dehumanization, whose power comes in the attenuated glimmer of consciousness still apparent in their fragile effort to congregate. The body becomes a place where consciousness and alien forces cross. It is torn and distorted but still connected to itself. Sinews that were invisible so long as they performed their appointed function are left painfully exposed and strained. Injury, mutation, monstrous proportions, and metamorphosis hold open an uncomfortable moment of change in the figure of bodily dislocation. Theorists of avant-garde realism sometimes used the metaphor of the scalpel: documentary was to cut through and peel back reality's surface. In order to expose the world being torn apart, the artist needed to cut deeply lest the transformation fail to fully manifest. The intervention might take the form of going deep into the mountains to investigate an uprising or of dredging up grotesque imagery, but in these and other ways, the task was to hold the present open in the form of a wounded landscape and body. While signs of pain and disempowerment, the wounds were also the site of untold possibilities.

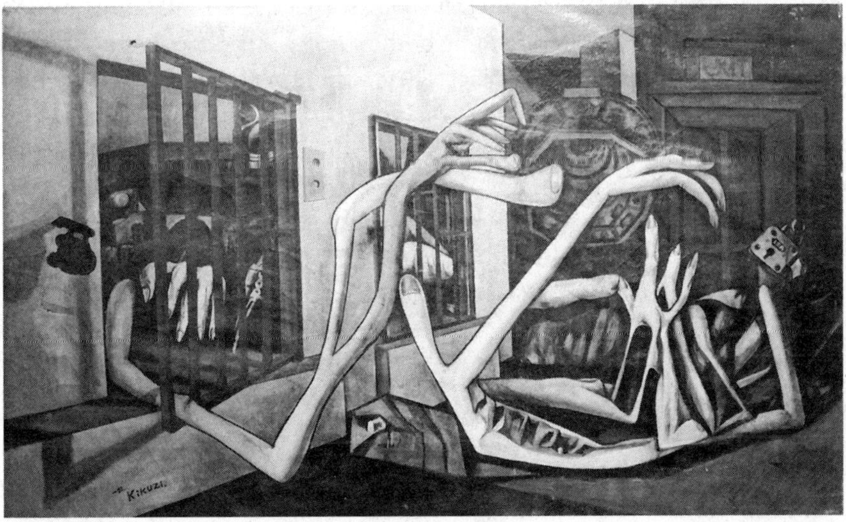

FIGURE 3.1 Yamashita Kikuji, *Shokuminchi kōjō (Colonial Factory)*, 1951. Oil on canvas. 72.5 cm x 116.5 cm. Courtesy of Gallery Nippon / National Museum of Modern Art, Tokyo.

The question of where the source of oppression and authoritarianism was to be found was one of great importance in the early postwar years. Why and how had Japan plunged so easily down the path to war? Why was it all happening again in 1953? Individual experience fleshed these questions out in disturbing ways. Yamashita himself had been a foot soldier in China in the late 1930s and never recovered from the horror and remorse he felt at having taken part in brutal killings.[8] He was one of a small minority who consistently made their feelings of responsibility public after the war. For the rest of his productive life he investigated the military and the emperor system and the ways they preyed on human fear. Many others who had participated in the war were inclined to keep their complicity private or to deny that their responsibility was personal. But for Yamashita and the other reportage artists, it was precisely in this twilit space of daily, embodied vulnerability that the key to the persistence of systematic violence seemed to lie. If the political failures of the war and Cold War were ever to be overcome, it was at this level, at the depths of human habit and feeling, that change had to happen. Reportage artists had to expose the interpenetration of the personal and the historical because they took it to be the very medium of change.

This put reportage artists in an uneasy position. On the one hand, they took part in numerous movements that addressed workers' and tenants' rights, protested the presence of U. S. military bases in Japan, and attempted to share the tools of artistry and authorship widely. Artists felt it was their primary task to immerse themselves in the most traumatic events of the present, to go to the places where history seemed to be unfolding, and to bring back and pass along something of the shock of that encounter as something that was still open and in peril. They worked in popular forms and with nonprofessional artists, usually as teachers. This practice of encounter and exchange both relied on and formed the unusual creative communities of the early 1950s, such as the one that supported *The Tale of Akebono Village*. How their artwork could reach an audience was also a question that preoccupied them. They experimented with *kamishibai*, ink drawings and illustrations, political cartooning, and woodcut and organized their own exhibitions where their works could be shown. Yamashita's painting was displayed at the independently organized Nippon-ten in 1953. All of these activities required effort over and above the process of painting or drawing and demonstrate hope that change was possible and that their work meant something.

On the other hand, their faith in humanity was so deeply shaken by the experience of the war and the postwar, their vision of the interpenetration of individual and society was so dark, that it threatened to crack any faith in the possibility of redemption. Their artistic vision left little room for the ideal of an autonomous modern subject: no matter how enlightened, there would always be something untrustworthy, dependent, and exposed at the core of any actual subject. Many in an older generation of artists—the "naturalist realists" as I will refer to them below—believed the cause of fascism was a lack of enlightenment. But the reportage artists were beginning to question whether there wasn't a problem with the entire project. Instead of looking for a way to build something that was missing, their artwork was more concerned with investigating the mechanisms of repeated failure at the foundation: failure of a politics of enlightenment, not its incompleteness, was coming to seem like the most basic reality.

In looking for a way to understand the tension between their artistic approach and their political engagement, I am reminded of something John Berger wrote around the same time, 1954, about Goya, one of history's great reportage artists.

> The despair of an artist is often misunderstood. It is never total. It excepts his own work. In his own work . . . there is the hope of reprieve. If there were not he could never summon up the abnormal energy and concentration needed to create it. And an artist's work constitutes his relationship with his fellow men. Thus for the spectator the despair expressed by a work can be deceiving. The spectator should always allow his comprehension of that despair to be qualified by *his* relationship with his fellow men: just as the artist does implicitly by the very act of creation.[9]

The anguish of many works encountered in the coming pages strikes me in the same way: it is best approached with appreciation of the participation of all of the people, including the artist, whose work to make the works visible can only be considered a sign of considerable caring, even optimism. While their works insisted on keeping the present open no matter how painful it might be, that implied a genuine question, a yet-to-be-seen that in turn demanded action.

As time went on, the tension within the reportage artists' position generated splits. The Japanese economy began to recover in the mid-1950s. As mass media grew, even politically hot issues found many channels to the public and the actions of individual artists, like Yamashita's visit to Akebono Village, became less significant. Kruschev's criticism of Stalin and the Soviet suppression of the Hungarian revolution in 1956 split the artistic and intellectual left around the world. This loss of faith was compounded in Japan by the JCP's misadventures in the early 1950s. In the latter half of the 1950s, many young radicals, students, artists, and writers abandoned their sympathy for the party. Although reportage was always a loose group of fellow travelers, it began to disintegrate during this period as artists began to follow different trajectories. The final section of chapter 6 takes up one such trajectory, that of Nakamura Hiroshi, whose work demonstrates both the persistence and the transformation of the reportage aesthetic in the 1960s.

To end this chapter, however, we can briefly examine the trajectory of Yamashita Kikuji. Although the reportage movement dissipated in the late 1950s and early 1960s, Yamashita continued to explore the interpenetration of the personal and the political in a disturbingly dark, surrealistic style. In the mid-1960s, he began to incorporate references to the emperor and The Fifteen Year War (1931–1945) in his paintings. In the 1970s, these developed into a series of collages in which he joined images of the emperor with images of the victims of the war. His investigation was partially rooted in his own experience but was also conceptually sophisticated. He saw discrimination as the fundamental social structure and structure of feeling that made the simultaneously extreme and casual violence of war possible. Discrimination was the theme of a series of forty-one collage works about the Sayama Incident, in which an illiterate man, Ishikawa Kazuo, who was a member of Japan's traditionally discriminated-against minority (*burakumin*), was convicted of kidnapping and murder after a dubious police investigation.[10] In these works, Yamashita combines a range of imagery denoting the war, state authority, suffering, and oppression in collages that include written statements of facts that undermined the prosecutor's case against Ishikawa. Thus, the end of the reportage movement in the late 1950s and early 1960s did not stop Yamashita from continuing his investigations of war as something hidden within the consciousness and the social structures of postwar Japan or from continuing to be involved in specific social causes. Many such individual stories of engaged artwork emerge from the reportage movement.

CHAPTER 4

The Social Work of Documentary and Reportage Art as Movement

This chapter approaches the question of art's relation to social movements from two perspectives: first a broad-stroke sketch of the efflorescence of documentary practices in the early postwar with reference to the reportage artists' work within the larger field, and second, an investigation of the reportage artists that examines their organizational practices and how they viewed their relationship with other practitioners of their time.[1]

Documentary and realism have rarely been at the center of histories of postwar art, literature, or film in Japan, a pattern that goes hand in hand with the tendency to overlook the tumultuous cultural politics of the 1950s. In a negative sense, the neglect is structured by paradigms of expectation about the politics that are proper for both art and Japan after 1945. Insofar as conceptualism, performance, and parody have been established as the critical art forms most appropriate to cultural standardization under Cold War capitalism, realism, documentary, and earnestness have been outsiders to both political and aesthetic tastes.[2] In a positive sense, the twinned neglect of documentary and the political struggles of the 1950s hints at a substantial connection between the two. Documentary was not only intertwined with political and social movements but was itself a social movement, involving both interventions into public discourse resulting from research, critique, and advocacy, while calling into being a different social and cultural map, one established in the shifting collaborations among socioeconomically and culturally diverse associations that were and are a necessary part of documentary practice. There is therefore historical overlap and logical consistency between documentary as a mode of artistic engagement and the movements toward democratic culture discussed in chapter 1. Both operated through a pattern of making the otherwise invisible visible and legitimate. Both inhered in the work of creating material structures through which the words of new participants and creators could be heard. Both demand that we open the concept of media from intensive concentration on particular material forms (paint, film, etc.) to include the positions and logistics that enable participation.

Documentary is by its nature a form of displacement: its basic rhetoric claims that existing distributions of information need to be upset and its production is possible only through social displacements. But there are many approaches to documentary, and the reportage artists were one group among many. Because their artistic and political stakes developed in discussion and dispute with others, we must understand what and who they responded to in order to understand their position within the larger field. This section approaches documentary as a field riven by disagreements over politics, tactics, and modes of representation yet, for all the disagreement, sustained by the proximity and provisional conjunction of different actors and approaches. Narratives that cast an avant-garde group as their protagonist sometimes lapse into assuming the group's own critical positions, resulting in unexamined dismissals of large territories of human endeavor. This chapter develops a more complex picture. While the reportage artists had deep differences with other practitioners and political actors, the cultural landscape of the 1950s was such that those other practitioners "talked back" and engaged in debate over representation and action. Amateurs and professionals encountered each other in ways that allowed for differences to exist while maintaining general solidarity in the context of a particular goal or issue. Below I consider three issues that seeded such solidarity: coal mines, the Matsukawa Incident, and the Sunagawa Struggle. In the context of such issues we can see the connection between small-scale, local writing practices and politics writ large, as well as the juxtaposition and collaboration of diverse actors responding to their world in ways that were importantly different yet linked in practice.

Coal Mines

In postwar Japan, larger workplaces supported many cultural groups that often competed with one another, forming around different affiliations, with the union, the company, or independent of both. Coal mines were some of the most culturally active workplaces. This is partly because of their size and their relative wealth compared to other industries. They also had highly integrated work and living spaces that were often cut off from the world outside. Finally, the education level of workers in early postwar mines was extremely mixed. In the late 1940s, when unemployment ballooned elsewhere, mines were a magnet for people searching for work and food. Returnees from the colonies, demobilized soldiers, people displaced by the bombings, people of all classes and backgrounds, made their way to the mines. Ueno Eishin, a major figure in reportage writing who himself followed work from mine to mine around Kyushu, remembers that it was this rich cross-fertilization that sustained the literature and culture movements of the early postwar years.[3]

Coal mines were one of a number of "social problems" in the 1950s. Notwithstanding modernization, mining remained dangerous and dirty, something that is especially emphasized in photographs from the time. Mining could express modern industrialization and exploitation through more primitively recognizable figures of labor, such as children picking through slag or men emerging from pits glistening with black sweat. The combination of strong unions, a volatile energy market, and battles over rationalization produced epic struggles between management and labor throughout the 1950s, which made mines a major site for understanding and representing labor issues. Mines appear in every media imaginable from *manga* to *haiku*, from film to *nihonga*.

But mines and miners did more than provide material for images of labor and exploitation. Miners themselves were active cultural producers. A case that illustrates this begins with Domon Ken's photobook, *Chikuhō no kodomotachi* (The children of Chikuhō) (1960), which he photographed during a two-week visit to the mines of Chikuhō (a region in northern Kyushu). As with many works of documentary featuring children, the collection celebrates the energy and innocence of the children of Chikuhō but also uses them as powerful figures of precariousness and deprivation. Domon's approach was a hit. The photobook quickly sold 100,000 copies and was adapted into a movie the same year.

But not everyone working in the mines appreciated the approach. Ueno Eishin and Senda Umeji also worked in Chikuhō (see chapter 2), as did members of the Nittan Takamatsu Photography Circle. Shōda Akira, a miner and a member of the photography circle, criticized Domon for the way he ended his collection with a few photos of the ongoing strike at the Mitsui-Miike mine, as if to imply that such large-scale labor organizing was the way to save the precarious innocence depicted on the previous pages. That stance, Shōda argued, ignored the economic disparity between unions at large mines like Mitsui-Miike, and the artisanal systems at small and mid-sized mines, which were the ones bearing the brunt of rationalization in the industry. He also criticized Domon for failing to represent labor inside the mines, asserting that in the end, "children were the most appropriate way for him to express what he was able to appreciate given the limits [to his understanding]."[4] Children, in other words, were a faithful representation of Domon's own ignorance. Some of the photographs Shōda took, along with fellow circle members Yamazaki Fujio and Yamaguchi Isao, documented conditions at small and mid-sized mines and were published as part of two book-length reportage works written by Ueno Eishin that told the story of the deteriorating working and living conditions of artisanal miners and their attempts to defend their livelihoods.[5] These photographs became the starting point for a multi-volume set of amateur photography of and by miners that has now reached ten volumes.[6] Although the work of the Nittan Takamatsu Photography Circle never approached the stature and influence of Domon Ken's work, the network of mine-based culture producers at Nittan Takamatsu made it possible for Shōda to publish his critique of Domon, and the publication of Ueno's book by Iwanami demonstrates how major publishers interacted with and supported local cultural production and locally produced knowledge.

In another case of multiple viewpoints emerging from distributed documentary practices, Ikeda Tatsuo, one of the reportage artists discussed below, visited the mines of northern Kyushu three times in the 1950s, producing a number of ink and painted works. One of these, *Botayama* (*Slag Heap*) (1954), depicts a slag heap as a monster made of human bones (fig. 4.1). Ikeda's allegory imagines the pile of castoffs from the mining process as a pile of bones that he refigures into a malevolent force bent on consuming more human life. When Ikeda and his collaborators in the Seisakusha Kondankai (Producer Workshop) were holding an exhibition of their works in the industrial city of Kokura, about an hour from the Nittan Takamatsu mines, Senda Umeji came to see it and told Ikeda that he would never depict a slag heap in that manner. For Senda, the slag heap was "something that grew taller with each day that it sucked in the blood and sweat of the miners," but because of that, it evoked not terror but reverence, "something like a crucifix."[7] This affection for the life of the miners comes through in many of Senda's works, particularly his *Tankō shigoto uta bangakan* (Illustrated collection of mine work songs). The interest in ethnographic interviewing, in collecting local folk tales, and in the unpublicized experiences of women, artisanal miners, and miners who traveled to South America and beyond typifies the documentary practice of Ueno, Senda, Morisaki Kazue, and others who worked in the Chikuhō area.

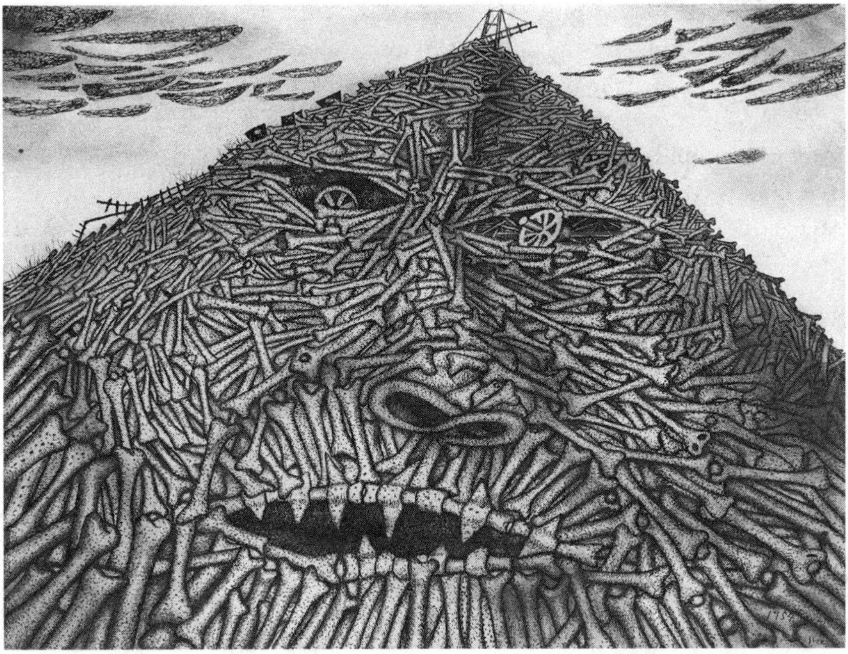

FIGURE 4.1 Ikeda Tatsuo, *Botayama* (*Slag Heap*), 1954. Ink, water color, and conté crayon on paper. 29.2 cm x 37.6 cm. Courtesy of Ikeda Tatsuo / Hiroshima City Museum of Contemporary Art.

These cases demonstrate not that one or the other of the perspectives is more legitimate or that a divergence of views is itself unique. What *is* unique in this period is the tremendous scale of cultural production in and around mines and other workplaces, composing a mosaic within which these two instances constitute a handful of tiles. But more importantly, and what may also account for some of the scale of the cultural production that survives, is the permeability of relations among diverse authors and artists. Though it is not surprising that Chikuhō miners would have been critical of Domon Ken's presentation of the children of Chikuhō, what is remarkable is that their critiques were written, printed, and published and that, beyond that, we have their own photographic work, undertaken in part to correct the failings they detected in Domon. Although it is not surprising that residents of a mine community would have different associations with a slag heap than an artist seeking material for a more general statement about extractive industry, what is remarkable is that there was direct exchange over the issue and that both viewpoints had their artistic expression, as did many more beyond this rather stereotypical binary. The exhibition where Ikeda and Senda met was organized by a group of young artists with the express intention of reaching new audiences by holding exhibitions in areas, such as Kokura, that avant-garde art usually did not reach. As with many of the examples above and below, the organizational work needed to realize such unusual exhibitions or to publish amateur photos or to publish workers' essays and poems was undertaken in each case by a handful of people who were acting with no institutional demands to drive them, yet connecting with similarly small-scale actors around particular issues.

The Matsukawa Incident

One of the motivations for such widespread interest in documentary in the 1950s was distrust of established media. To be sure, on the far left, the JCP dismissed the established broadsheets as *burushin*, "bourgeois newspapers." But as Toba Kōji has argued, there was a more general public skepticism of media rooted in a foundational postwar narrative that claimed that the majority of Japanese citizens had fallen victim to a cadre of militarists who had used the media to deceive them by fabricating stories of continuing victory during the final years of the war.[8] Skepticism of the media was thus a major element in the early postwar environment, fed by the availability of a number of competing informational spheres that did not tell the same story. One area where the battle over information and public narrative comes out most clearly is in cases of suspicious police behavior and criminal prosecutions, the so-called frame-up incidents (*detchiage jiken*), of which there are at least eight.[9]

The Matsukawa Incident was by far the most prominent of these. It occurred in 1949 near the town of Matsukawa in Fukushima Prefecture when a national railroad train overturned, killing three of the operators. Police and prosecutors quickly charged a group of twenty, many of whom were active members of the radical National Railway Workers' Union, with having sabotaged the track. The first trial, which reached a swift verdict in 1950, found all twenty guilty and sentenced five to death. News of the trial circulated quickly through union, JCP, and JSP (Japan Socialist Party) channels. But it was cultural production—poetry, long fiction, songs, films, and art—that brought the issue to the attention of a wider public. As Toba Kōji has shown, the tremendous variety of creative activity surrounding the Matsukawa Incident may be the best single demonstration of the richness of the media mix that developed around critical political issues.[10]

Poetry was the first to proliferate. A number of the accused had begun to write poetry in prison, and many on the outside used poetry to voice their support. Within a few years at least six poetry collections appeared featuring work by the imprisoned and by members of hundreds of poetry circles around Japan. One notable achievement among this early poetry production is a three-part epic poem composed as a collaboration among three circles of worker-poets in Tokyo (the Chiyoda Poets Collective, the Shimomaruko Culture Collective, and the Bunkyō Poets Collective).[11] By 1954, the practice of writing poetry about Matsukawa had become so widespread that the editors of *Matsukawa shishū* (Collection of Matsukawa poetry) received 3,000 submissions in response to their call for poems.[12]

The interpenetration of different kinds of cultural production is sometimes demonstrated in a single volume. *Shinjitsu wa kabe o tōshite* (Truth passes through walls) featured a section of diary entries of the prisoners, a section of poetry by both amateur and established poets, and a final section of essays by leading critics.[13] In another example, Satō Hajime, one of the accused, wrote a fictionalized account of his experience while he was convalescing with tuberculosis. While at a sanatorium, he joined a poetry circle (circles at sanatoria were so numerous that they drove their own subgenre of literary production) and worked on his manuscript in the company of other amateur writers, including the soon-to-be-published Yamada Utako.[14] Satō's *Hikoku* (Accused) became a bestseller.[15] While the Matsukawa Incident provides a window into the ways amateur and professional production were integrated into the context of a political movement, we can also detect an investment in empiricism: the idea that the process of establishing truth was something that should be undertaken by many actors. This was similar to what can be seen in, for example, the practice of the Kokuminteki Rekishigaku Undō (People's History Movement) and the Kusa no Mi (Seeds of Grass).[16]

The Matsukawa Incident also inspired documentary and fiction films and a number of reportage artworks. Yamashita Kikuji completed a three-piece series that was exhibited at both the Art Exhibit for Peace and the Nippon-ten in 1959. One of the prisoners, Sugiura Saburō, produced a picture titled *Kanbōzu: benki o dai ni mado kara nozoku* (*Depiction of the Cell: Looking from the Window, Using the Toilet as a Stool*) with the help of the established realist painter Okamoto Tōki. The work was included as part of a charity exhibition in 1956 to raise money for the cause, together with calligraphic signature boards (*shikishi*) that eminent supporters such as Shiga Naoya and Uno Kōji donated.[17] The Matsukawa Incident became a focal point for a multimedia cultural movement that called into being and relied upon interactions between amateurs and professionals, a commitment to a permeable cultural field, and an attempt to intervene in an ongoing legal and political battle that involved the status of the new postwar legal system and the question of who was entitled to speak in the name of truth. All of these attempts to find public voice in relation to the fate of the twenty accused happened before a final verdict had been reached and were therefore not only expressions, but interventions into the function of the legal system that went well beyond the everyday milieu of most of the participants. All twenty of the accused were finally cleared of charges in 1963, a result many see as having been secured by the movement that supported them.

The Sunagawa Struggle

U.S. bases in Japan were another site that stimulated the formation of cultural-political movements through the practice of documentary art. The Tachikawa air base in western Tokyo attracted the greatest amount of attention in the 1950s. Because of its location less than an hour from downtown Tokyo, it was easily accessible to activists, students, artists, and cultural figures who were concerned with the issue of the U.S. military presence more generally. While the U.S. occupation of Japan had officially ended in 1952, a condition of its end was that Japan remain locked within a chain of American military bases that spanned the Aleutians, South Korea, Okinawa, the Philippines, Guam, and, later, Vietnam. When Japan resumed sovereignty in April 1952, 260,000 U.S. servicemen remained in the country, stationed at 2,824 separate facilities.[18] The Tachikawa air base featured in reportage throughout the 1950s, but with the beginning of the Sunagawa Struggle in 1955, it became the site of a battle waged across the fields of Sunagawa and across the political and cultural landscape of Japan.

The struggle was triggered by the U.S. military's plan to extend the runways at the base so the new jet aircraft coming into service could land. Japanese national authorities had agreed to the plan, which necessitated taking two parcels of land (#4 and #5) from the neighboring farming village of Sunagawa. Local residents immediately organized against the confiscation and were joined by student groups, union members, and cultural leaders from Tokyo who supported them in a series of battles that focused on Japanese authorities' attempts to survey the land in preparation for construction. The battle against the second of these attempted land surveys, in October 1956, drew the most support, including hundreds of students, workers, three busloads of prominent intellectuals from Tokyo,[19] and features centrally in Kamei Fumio's film *Ryūketsu no kiroku Sunagawa* (Record of blood: Sunagawa).

U.S. bases embodied highly legible interconnections between local situations and global- and national-scale issues. The first issue was militarization. Peace was a tremendously popular ideal in the early postwar period. Although the word was used regularly as political currency, it had powerful resonance beyond political divisions. The bases in Japan and Okinawa served as staging points during the Korean War and remain active to this day. While peace and neutrality were popular as international ideals during the 1950s, in Japan the idea of peace also tapped a more self-centered hope that the horrors of war would not again descend upon Japan's increasingly prosperous daily life. If a wider war erupted, the U.S. bases in Japan could make it a target. A second issue was sovereignty. While the general public did not share the anti-Americanism of many on the radical left, bases crystallized the issue of sovereignty in ways that had obvious broad appeal. In the case of Sunagawa, farmers were being threatened with eviction by Japanese police acting as proxies for a foreign military. Few if any could defend the legitimacy of the state in such action. Even the national newspapers took the side of the Sunagawa residents—that is, until a group of students and unionists broke into the base compound during the third confrontation with surveyors and were arrested. As a side note, the district judge who was the first to hear the case against the trespassing protestors cleared them of any wrongdoing on the basis that the U.S. base itself was in violation of the Japanese constitution. Although that decision was overturned, it demonstrates the contention around issues of peace and sovereignty that bases could bring to the fore.

The Sunagawa Struggle became a focal point around which multiple movements and actors coalesced, giving rise to a multivocal and multimedia sphere of cultural activity. Partly due to the nature of the struggle itself, visual media—film, photography, and art—feature more prominently than they do in the case of Matsukawa. All kinds of artists went to Sunagawa: older generations of naturalist realists, younger generations of avant-garde realists, and future members of the Neo-Dada movement who were still art students at the time. The 1956 and 1957 Nihon Independent exhibitions included particularly large numbers of artworks based on the Sunagawa Struggle. A selection of works from the 1956 exhibition was subsequently exhibited at a Sunagawa junior high school as the Sunagawa Bijutsu-ten Bijutsuka ga Toraeta Tatakai no Kiroku (Sunagawa Art Exhibit: The Struggle as Documented by Artists). After the junior high school exhibit, the artworks circulated to union halls, factories, and a cafeteria on the south side of the Tachikawa train station.[20]

Although I return to Sunagawa in subsequent chapters, Takei Toshifumi's work highlights the work of two artists, Shinkai Kakuo and Mita Genjirō, whose work complements that of the avant-garde realists that are the main focus of my research. Shinkai (1904–1968) was one of an older generation of realists. He was active before the war and in the postwar and he represents that generation's commitment to naturalist realism, humanist values, and the JCP-affiliated democratic arts movement. Shinkai's main work with the people of Sunagawa is a series of thirty-seven watercolor portraits which he had planned to integrate into a large oil work that was never completed. Portraiture was a major element of naturalist realist practice in the postwar years. Many of the works feature crowds that are highly individualized, composed of portraits of actual people. Portraiture was invested with ethical significance: it was best done, according to Shinkai's colleague, Uchida Iwao, when one had a close rapport with the sitter.[21] True to this humanist ethic, Shinkai wrote that he saw the "recovery of humanity" as the most important task of the realist method.[22] The practice meant that Shinkai had to return to Tachikawa many times, and not just for the most intense confrontations with the police.[23] A commemorative photograph shows him accompanying a group of Sunagawa residents to the Tokyo Metropolitan Museum to see the 1956 Nihon Independent, evidence that he saw the people he painted as an important part of the artwork even after their sitting for the portrait had finished.[24] Although little has been written about the relationships that might have developed through the practice of portraiture, it is noteworthy that Shinkai was the only artist mentioned in a book of reminiscences published on the fiftieth anniversary of the beginning of the Sunagawa Struggle.[25]

Mita Genjirō demonstrates a slightly different articulation of the work of art and the work of politics; he painted oil paintings on canvas for display at venues such as the Nihon Independent while also producing woodcut prints, often using the same composition for both. Mita's work illustrates an awareness of the power of different media for different venues while also implicitly claiming that both media were relevant to political struggle. Woodcut was common in reportage, and perhaps more than in any other visual art we can see the clear influence of China in it. Japanese artists deliberately adopted both the graphically simplified expressionism and the claims of political and popular legitimacy from Lu Xun and the Chinese woodcut movement. Mita, who had been fired from his position as a schoolteacher in the red purge of 1950, brought his interest in education to woodcut, advocating woodcut as a form that was inexpensive and relatively easy to learn. After joining the Atarashii E no Kai (Society for New Pictures) in 1955—which will be discussed further in chapter 8—he advocated for the practice of visual reportage as a way to develop socially conscious ways of looking at one's daily surroundings.[26]

Shinkai and Mita are just two of the many artists to work the Sunagawa Struggle into their artwork and to work their artwork into the Sunagawa Struggle. Many other artists were involved, as were photographers, filmmakers, academics, poets, writers, and songwriters. One should not assume, however, that these cultural producers were a homogenous group. Documentary practice entailed certain common elements: interactions between professionals and amateurs, efforts to expand cultural enfranchisement so that the voices of those otherwise silenced could be heard, involvement in specific social movements, and mixing of mediums. But beyond this there was considerable disagreement about what the value of documentary was and what specific aesthetic and social forms were best suited to it. We can begin to understand these differences by concentrating on the reportage artists as a distinct subgroup within the broader practice of documentary.

Reportage Art as Movement

Reportage art began to coalesce as a coherent movement around 1950. What makes reportage coherent is the movement's artistic practices and theoretical stakes. Those will be the subject of the next chapter. Here I seek to understand the way their historical stakes manifested in their relationships with other groups of artist-activists in the 1950s. As we will see, the historical and theoretical stakes answer to each other, so the picture that begins to develop here will continue to develop in the next chapter.

The reportage artists were far from the only ones interested in organizational experiment. There were many attempts in the field of art to face up to the legacy of the fascist past by building more democratic structures in the present. Indeed, the response to the question of war responsibility in the art world in the late 1940s is notable for the way that it conceived of wartime failure not in personal terms, but as rooted in deficiencies in the way modern art (*bijutsu*) had been established as an institution. Artists and critics paired critical assessment of wartime failures with concrete ideas for reorganizing art's social existence to prevent such failures in the future.[27]

The network of small, loosely affiliated avant-garde groups that fed the reportage movement can be seen as one aspect of those attempts at reorganization. Instead of describing each group in this network—a number of studies have already done that—I focus on features common to them: their self-conscious approach to organization, their intermedia practice, and their works of publishing and exhibiting.[28] That will provide a way to understand the thought they put into organization and identity formation, as well as the effort they invested in securing their own means of visibility. One thing that becomes apparent is the emphasis these avant-garde groups put on openness and permissiveness regarding artistic form, something that distinguishes them from the polemics of the realism debate in the 1940s, which had tended to entrench rigid links between art forms and their supposed political relevance. The groups I discuss put more emphasis on position and orientation while allowing that many media and artistic forms could achieve political relevance.

The avant-garde collectives of the early postwar were fluid. Memberships were constantly changing, as were the missions of different groups. Although certain activities were common to most, each group was also a unique experiment in association. Organizational styles could be carefully egalitarian and collaborative, as in the case of NON, which painstakingly diagrammed schedules to orchestrate the production of collaborative paintings. Or they could be less formal but more hierarchical, as with the Yoru no Kai (Night Society), where a handful of established artists and writers held court. Missions could range from the extremely specific, such as the efforts of the Jinmin Geijutsu Shūdan (People's Art Collective) to get Abe Kōbō to Poland to represent Japan in the Sekai Seinen Gakusei Heiwa Yūkō Sai (World Youth and Student Festival of Peace and Friendship), to the vastly open, as in the case of Seibiren (Nihon Seinen Bijutsuka Renmei; Japan Young Artists League). Seibiren emerged as a network that brought together artists and small groups of artists scattered around the country. Although it focused on young artists, it went to great lengths to avoid a prescriptive identity beyond that. In one telling exchange, Takeuchi Kingo contributed to the first issue of the group's small journal with a call to take a defining stance on what kind of art would be appropriate for this new generation of artists. His essay, "Against Tableau," was a call to abandon the two-dimensional picture plane as an outdated convention that was not up to the task of representing present-day reality.[29] This idea was criticized in the following issue for being too dogmatic; Ōno Saiji argued that no style or medium could be ruled out.[30] This exchange is an example of many similar exchanges that took place in these small groups, which were searching for modes of organization where identity would be openly negotiated and would not be limited by genre, style, or enduring hierarchies.

The groups consistently brought together cultural producers who worked in different media, and many attempted to produce multimedia works. Poets, writers, and aspiring filmmakers were prominent alongside visual artists. In the case of the Seiki no Kai (Century Group), a large group of young avant-gardists that formed in the late 1940s, some of the many seminar topics included surrealism, Picasso, Sartre, the critique of modernism, Weber, and Marx.[31] In addition to shared study, many groups engaged in multimedia production. In 1950, the Seiki no Kai, which by then had become much smaller and more tightly knit, produced a series of booklets called the *Seikigun* (Century collection).[32] These featured translations, original poetry and fiction, and art criticism. Each was lavishly illustrated by members of the group. In the process of producing them, Abe Kōbō, Katsuragawa Hiroshi, Teshigahara Hiroshi, Segi Shin'ichi, and others tried their hands at different tasks: drawing, writing, and actually producing the books. Although ten years later these four would be known as a writer, an artist, a filmmaker, and a critic, respectively, the production of the *Seikigun* refused such professionalized divisions.

The *Seikigun* is just one example of the kinds of printed works these small groups produced. In the context of reportage art, these included agitation pamphlets, posters, and *kamishibai*; newsletters and journals; and work designed for mass media such as newspapers and books. Each of these will be introduced in greater detail in chapter 6. Here I will make three general observations. First, while self-published journals and newsletters are a feature of many self-organizing cultural groups, the journals these young artists produced are particularly important records of discussions of organization and group identity. Such discussions could be mundane. The journal Seibiren produced served partially as a publicity board, publishing the names of new members as they joined and introducing members' work in reviews as a way to knit together geographically dispersed artists. The discussion of identity also remained a feature of the journal: all but the last issue raised the question of what Seibiren should be, eliciting continuing participation from members.

Second, the artists usually produced the publications, at a considerable cost. Katsuragawa recalls that paper was so scarce around 1950 that he had to lug rolls of it across Tokyo from the black market to put together the *Seikigun*. Many journals were *gariban*, meaning the text was etched into a waxy template that could be used only a few hundred times before it wore out. Artists often handled printing, binding, and distribution themselves.[33] While artists used these self-created spaces to find autonomy and wrote about them in terms of attaining their freedom from older generations and dominant organizations, the investment of time and energy necessary to sustain that freedom was considerable. As material objects, these small journals demonstrate how the groups perceived sustained collective work to be the enabler of both artistic and political significance.

A third and final feature worth noting is that reportage artists demonstrated an enduring interest in manga, caricature, and print art, something that remains central to avant-garde and underground culture of the 1960s.

Exhibition was another public format that these small groups experimented with in a characteristically self-conscious fashion. Although reportage as an artistic and social practice had been brewing since before 1950, it definitively came on the scene with the first Nippon-ten in 1953.[34] While the exhibit was not all reportage works, it is rightly remembered as the main public vehicle for the work of reportage artists. It was also important organizationally. It brought together the two main groups of reportage artists: the Zen'ei Bijutsu Kai (Avant-Garde Art Society), a group of slightly older artists that had been attempting to link activist politics with experimental art since the late 1940s, and Seibiren, a group founded in 1953 as a network of younger artists around Japan. Seibiren brought together Katsuragawa Hiroshi, Ikeda Tatsuo, and Nakamura Hiroshi and at its height reached 160 members. It was thus a much more ambitious organizational project than the small groups that the artists had been experimenting with up until then. An exhibition held the previous year, the Heiwa-ten (Heiwa no Tame no Bijutsu-ten; Art Exhibition for Peace), provided some of the social capital for the first Nippon-ten. It was organized by essentially the same group of artists as those who organized the Nippon-ten and was designed to overcome divisions in the art world in order to foreground how art could address the contemporary theme of peace. Participants came from most of the large exhibition societies, they came from both parts of the recently split JCP, they included older artists and newcomers, and *nihonga* and *yōga*.[35] Although participants in the Heiwa-ten did not come together for much longer than the duration of the exhibition, it modeled a style of exhibition where the contents would not be arranged according to formal similarity or because the artist was a member of a particular group. It was a grouping of artists who shared a particular goal and its organization was ad hoc and voluntarist.[36]

The Nippon-ten continued in a similar spirit. The idea behind it reconfirms the themes already apparent: an orientation toward present-day reality, the importance of positionality, openness towards artistic forms, and self-consciousness about issues of organization and representation. One of the founders, Katsuragawa Hiroshi, proposed some ideas for the exhibition in the first issue of Seibiren's journal, *Konnichi no bijutsu* (Art of today).

> We must build ourselves up to the point where the intentions, actions, and expression of our group, our "group artist," become equal to the task of dredging up that old energy that is the deep source of war, and changing it into a new energy. So what can we do toward this? We must dredge up that cause that in so many forms has brought us up over the

past twenty years, has driven us toward a hateful war, has so decisively eaten away our youth, we have to get inside this and express it, and this will be a moment of change. This bodily mass "Nippon" contains a terrible ancientness [*furusa*] but at the same time is what forms the categories of all our thoughts and determines the nature of our expressions. . . . [To capture this] we need to have an exhibition based around a "theme without a theme," for example, "Exhibition of Japan's Conscience," or "The Theme without Theme Nippon."[37]

His idea, "The Theme without Theme Nippon," turns on the double meaning of the word theme, meaning both a unifying concern or idea and the visible content of a painting. One of the most common criticisms of naturalist realism was that the politics of its art was judged by the subject matter of a painting: scenes of strikes, protests, work, and domestic life were taken as guarantors of both realism and political righteousness. *Tēma shugi* (themeism; content-centrism) was a pejorative word used to critique the superficiality of naturalist realists' reliance on content. The idea of an exhibit with a theme but without a theme captures the sense in which having social concern was important (for Katsuragawa, nothing less than coming to terms with the cause of fascism deep in Nippon's bodily mass) but that it was equally important to affirm that there was no one way to represent that theme. As was true with the Heiwa-ten, the Nippon-ten was an artist-organized affair. At the first exhibition in 1953 there were around 170 pieces, mostly paintings and drawings, most done by members of Seibiren. Two works that have since become part of the canon of art history debuted there, Yamashita Kikuji's *The Tale of Akebono Village*, and Kawara On's *Yokushitsu shiriizu* (*Bathroom Series*).

Seibiren and the Nippon-ten are interesting for the way they reiterate certain characteristics of what art historian Reiko Tomii has called the "*dantai*" form of collectivism, which dominated the formation of modern art (*kindai bijutsu*) before 1945.[38] The *dantai* were large exhibition societies that developed to provide a stable context for exhibition (including developing an audience for modern art) and for artists' careers (by developing hierarchies of taste and skill that would legitimate individual achievement). Tomii has shown that *dantai* fulfilled many of the public institutional needs of art in Japan during the first half of the twentieth century—needs that in the western context were filled by museums, critics, and the art market. While the political crisis of the 1950s motivated the reportage artists to strike out on their own, the forms they turned to as they developed their organizations implicitly aspired to the broad public presence of the *dantai*.

The Nippon-ten was held at the Tokyo Metropolitan Art Museum in Ueno, a site whose primary function was to be an exhibition space the *dantai* used on a rotating basis for their annual exhibitions. The scale also resembles a *dantai* exhibition: generally the Nippon-ten exhibited around 200 works, divided into separate rooms, as a *dantai* exhibit would be. While avant-garde artists continued to develop new forms of publicity and collectivity to support their work in the 1960s, they did so on a much smaller scale than the *dantai* and the groups discussed here. And, as Tomii observes, they were not as invested in developing stable institutional structures.[39] Tomii calls this later pattern of collectivity the *shūdan*; it outsourced the institutional work of maintaining exhibition space to a small network of galleries and museums, which, by the 1960s, had begun to support contemporary Japanese art more actively. The young avant-gardists of the 1950s had fewer of those options.

The Seisakusha Kondankai (Producer Workshop), which Ikeda Tatsuo and film critic Kasu Sanpei started in 1955 as Seibiren was starting to dissolve, was likewise a large and varied group of young artists, critics, and filmmakers. They organized themselves into sections, including the photography section (*shashinbu*), the painting section (*kaigabu*), and the film section (*eigabu*) which, incidentally, included Hani Susumu, Satō Tadao, and Yamagiwa Eizō, who started the important film journal *Eiga hihyō* (Film criticism) in 1957.[40] Such size and organizational complexity largely disappeared with the more informal *shūdan* organizations in the 1960s. The painting section, which Ikeda led, organized a traveling exhibit for their work, one of which allowed Ikeda and Senda Umeji to discuss the symbolism of the slag heap as introduced above. Traveling exhibits were a familiar part of art's institutionalization pre-1945; the Nitten Exhibition and the large *dantai* shows generally toured the country after opening in Tokyo. The goal of the traveling exhibits of the Seisakusha Kondankai partook of this form, though with the aim of bringing their work to more out-of-the-way places than the large exhibition societies ever would: Kokura, Ōita, Toyama, among others.[41]

In sum, the *dantai* was an ambitious organizational form. It entailed an attempt to sustain a public for artists' work when there were few other institutions that could do so. The reportage artists attempted to sustain this type of organization through their own labor with little to no funding. While the large art societies had membership fees and were at the center of the domestic art market, Seibiren and the Nippon-ten had no comparable resources. Likewise, the artists did not have the cultural capital that went along with such institutions. Whereas artists in the Nika Kai could expect a respectful audience even in regional cities, when Ikeda took his avant-garde works to rural or industrial areas with his colleagues in the Seisakusha Kondankai, they faced quite direct questions from their audience. What did their works *mean*? Why were they so dark? The young avant-gardists faced audiences in ways that those protected by the institutional aura of established art never would. Thus, they present a remarkable combination: extremely ambitious horizons for establishing public relevance and a support system that consisted primarily of the energy of the artists themselves. The combination is emblematic of the way the reportage artists' stance was not anti-institutional or anti-art despite their "dark" works, and demonstrates the stakes they imagined in building a different social place for art, but one that did not cede the field of broad public relevance.

The Reportage Generation

While the reportage artists' interest in establishing the terms of their works' visibility and political relevance was shared to greater or lesser degree by many cultural organizations in the early postwar, they also marked their distance from parallel movements in the art world, as discussed here, and on the left, as discussed immediately below. The reportage artists often used the idea of generation to define the gap between their work and the work of others. Most of the reportage artists were born in the 1920s and early 1930s. Ikeda Tatsuo, who was born in 1928, illustrates some of the experiences that were common to this generation. At age fifteen, Ikeda had been drafted into the *tokkōtai*, the corps of pilots trained to fly planes laden with explosives into U.S. ships. After he completed his training, Ikeda was stationed at a forward operating base—probably no more than a few days from being sent to his death—on the day Japan surrendered. By coincidence, that day was also his seventeenth birthday. Even though his life had been spared, he remembered that rebirth as more trauma than joy. "Young people had grown up being fed the lesson that sacrifice for the country and becoming a god enshrined at Yasukuni [i.e., dying in the war] was the road to eternal righteousness. We were all hurtling down that road with no time to think. When the road suddenly cut off, it led to great sorrow and confusion." Almost a year after the war ended, he wrote in his diary, "And what's time, what's the universe, what's space, what's life, aren't they all but nothingness?"[42]

These words illustrate the completeness of the ideological collapse that the end of the war brought for people of Ikeda's generation. They reached school age in the mid-1930s and had lost out on much of their education due to total mobilization in the final stages of the war. They knew little outside imperial ideology and had no inkling that many of their parents and teachers harbored doubts about the empire. Mixed with the trauma of such a sudden end to their world was survivors' guilt stemming from the fact that so many of those who had been sent to their deaths in the final days of the war had been their peers. Although they had been old enough to die in the war, Ikeda's generation was too young to face the questions of collaboration or responsibility that their elders did. From their vantage point, the question of responsibility was stark, and they were not inclined to be forgiving of their elders. The sudden about-face in 1945 in which people who had so recently been sending them off to become gods now began to extol democracy made them angrily skeptical of both imperial ideology and democracy.

Although in the previous section I argued that the Japanese art world changed in response to assessments of wartime failures, the reportage artists would not have agreed with that argument. All of the *dantai*, which had been active until the government forcibly folded them together in the early 1940s, began to reappear after their wartime hiatus. Even though their members reflected on the immediate past and professed a commitment to democracy after the war, they did not fundamentally alter their hierarchical structures. Even less palatable organizations resurfaced alongside them: in 1946, the Nitten Exhibition, the embodiment of state control over the arts, reopened after just one year of hiatus, drawing criticism from all over the art world.[43] Universities also remained largely unchanged after the war. Ikeda Tatsuo recalls a moment of truth shortly after he arrived at Tama Art University in Tokyo in 1948, when he saw a painting by one of his professors, Ihara Usaburō, featured in a magazine: it was a portrait of the imperial crown prince on a ski holiday.[44] Ikeda soon dropped out. The reportage artists' investment in the idea of generation thus developed against a backdrop of specifically discredited authority.

It also developed against a backdrop that called into question the artist's role in a society that seemed to be heading back down the path toward war and fascism. The concept of generation was productive: it energized the youth networks and experiments in boundary-crossing collectivity that the reportage artists created and moved through. As Katsuragawa summarized in 1960, five years after Seibiren had dissolved,

> The Heiwa-ten in 1952, and following this, the reportage movement initiated by artists of the younger generation, had already laid the ground for the coalescence of this generation of artists into a group. In addition, even among the general majority of young artists who did not participate in the [reportage] movement, the political and social crisis of the Korean War, together with the reemergence of the old

guard . . . with its old value system and authority . . . [populated by] an older generation who devoted themselves to painting war pictures during the war, but in the postwar made another easy switch of allegiance to modernism, these things all sowed suspicion toward the shameful older generation.[45]

The threat of war, a return to oppressive values, and the untrustworthy behavior of those in authority loomed large and came together in the idea of a rift that divided generations. The response of reportage artists to this insight included attempts to participate directly in the political and social crisis they saw unfolding. These practices aligned them with the cultural left, particularly the JCP, but that relationship was also riven by the different experiences of generation.

The Question of the JCP

In their belief that their artwork could and should intervene in the history of their present and that the institutions of art in Japan needed to be reformed to become more democratic, the reportage artists were largely in step with the Japanese Communist Party. Many of them were members of the party. But their relationship with the JCP over the course of the 1950s was complex and ended in bitter rejection. Examining this process can shed light on the general disillusionment with the Communist Party that affected the cultural politics of many countries at this time, including Japan. By the end of the process, the JCP had lost whatever political and cultural credibility it might have had as a vanguard party. Virtually all cultural figures—party members and fellow travelers alike—had severed ties with or had been expelled from the party by the early 1960s. One result of that process was to make the JCP a target of persistent vilification on the cultural left in subsequent years: the birth of an independent student movement and the origin story of 1960s radicalism more generally are inextricably intertwined with rejection of the JCP. While there are clear reasons for this rejection, a reevaluation is necessary, especially since the standard narrative has no way to account for the popularity of the JCP among young radicals up until 1955.

Immediately after the war, the JCP enjoyed significant legitimacy. It provided a well-developed historical account of what had led to the Fifteen Year War and a robust alternative narrative to the one that had just been shattered. Its platform of peaceful revolution and accommodation of the U.S. occupation made it widely palatable. As the occupation progressed, however, its appeal became narrower. In politics, this emerged in the context of the occupation's reverse course, which sought to marginalize and then persecute left-wing political organizations which in turn drove those organizations into more radical positions. In the field of culture, that narrowing was most apparent in the critique of modernism in the arts, which began in 1947 and gathered strength through the late 1940s.

The year 1950 was a turning point. Early that year, the Cominform (Communist Information Bureau) in Moscow criticized the JCP's peaceful revolution strategy, which accommodated the U.S. occupation and worked within the structure of parliamentary democracy. The JCP split over how to react. The group that advocated acknowledging the criticism and denouncing the occupation became known as the international faction (*kokusaiha*). This was the smaller of the two groups but it contained much of the JCP cultural establishment, centered on the editorial board of the literary journal *Shin Nihon bungaku* (New Japanese literature). Among these were many former members of the proletarian literature and arts movement of the early 1930s. The group that advocated ignoring the criticism as inappropriate to Japan's situation was the mainstream faction (*shuryūha*); it was in the majority and controlled most of the party apparatus. Within weeks of the initial criticism, China's Communist Party echoed the Cominform critique, which caused the mainstream faction to change its position. Thus, both factions of the JCP ended up advocating a break with the peaceful revolution strategy. But the split had already occurred and the two factions remained split until 1955.[46] The chaos in the JCP leadership intensified in 1951, when the party adopted a strategy of armed struggle against the Japanese government and the U.S. occupation. This radicalization made the party illegal and forced many leaders to flee to China or go underground in Japan. The absurdity of the armed-struggle strategy would be a major focus of criticism of the party when it finally renounced the strategy in 1955.

Recent research has called attention to two aspects of JCP policy during the period of the split that have been relatively neglected. The first was a shift toward supporting worker and farmer culture at the grass roots, which played out through the party's relationship with grassroots circle movements.[47] An important defining characteristic of the mainstream faction was its outgoing involvement in these circles. The editorial policy of the mainstream faction's literary journal, *Jinmin bungaku* (People's literature), heavily emphasized interaction between intellectuals and artists from all walks of life. It also published large amounts of material submitted by working-class writers. The people tasked with establishing the connections to local and worker culture included Katsuragawa and Abe in their work as cultural activists (*bunka kōsakusha*), which I discuss in chapter 6.

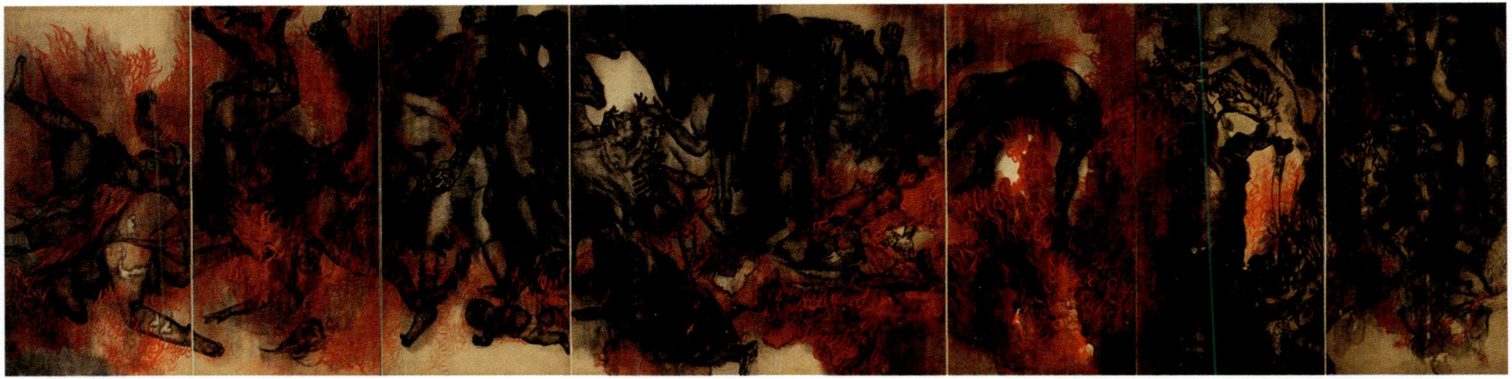

1. Maruki Iri and Toshi, *Genbaku no zu dai ni bu: hi* (*Atomic Bomb Panels 2: Fire*), 1950.
Japanese ink on paper. 1.8 m x 7.2 m. Maruki Gallery for the Hiroshima Panels.

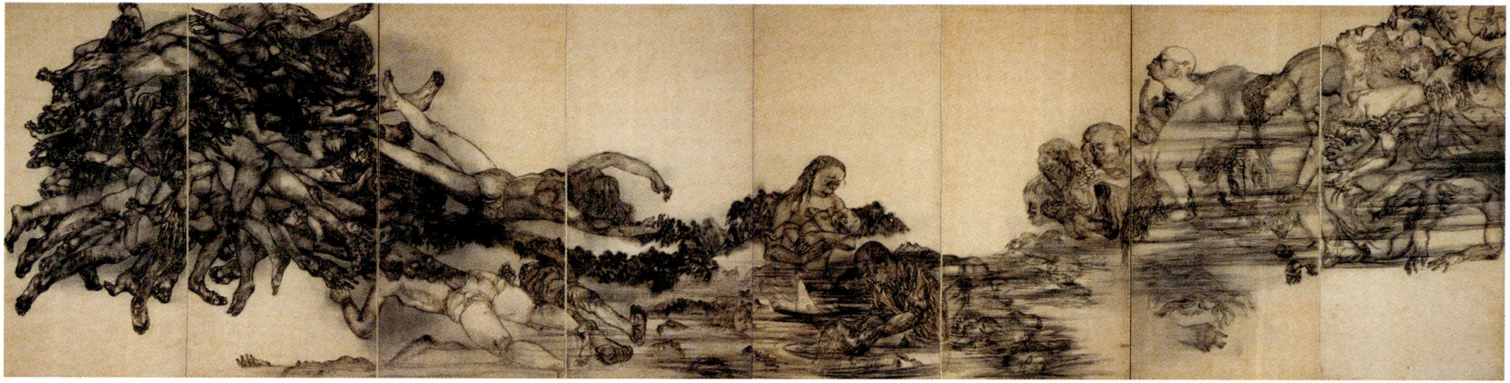

2. Maruki Iri and Toshi, *Genbaku no zu dai san bu: mizu* (*Atomic Bomb Panels 3: Water*), 1950. Japanese ink on paper. 1.8 m x 7.2 m. Maruki Gallery for the Hiroshima Panels.

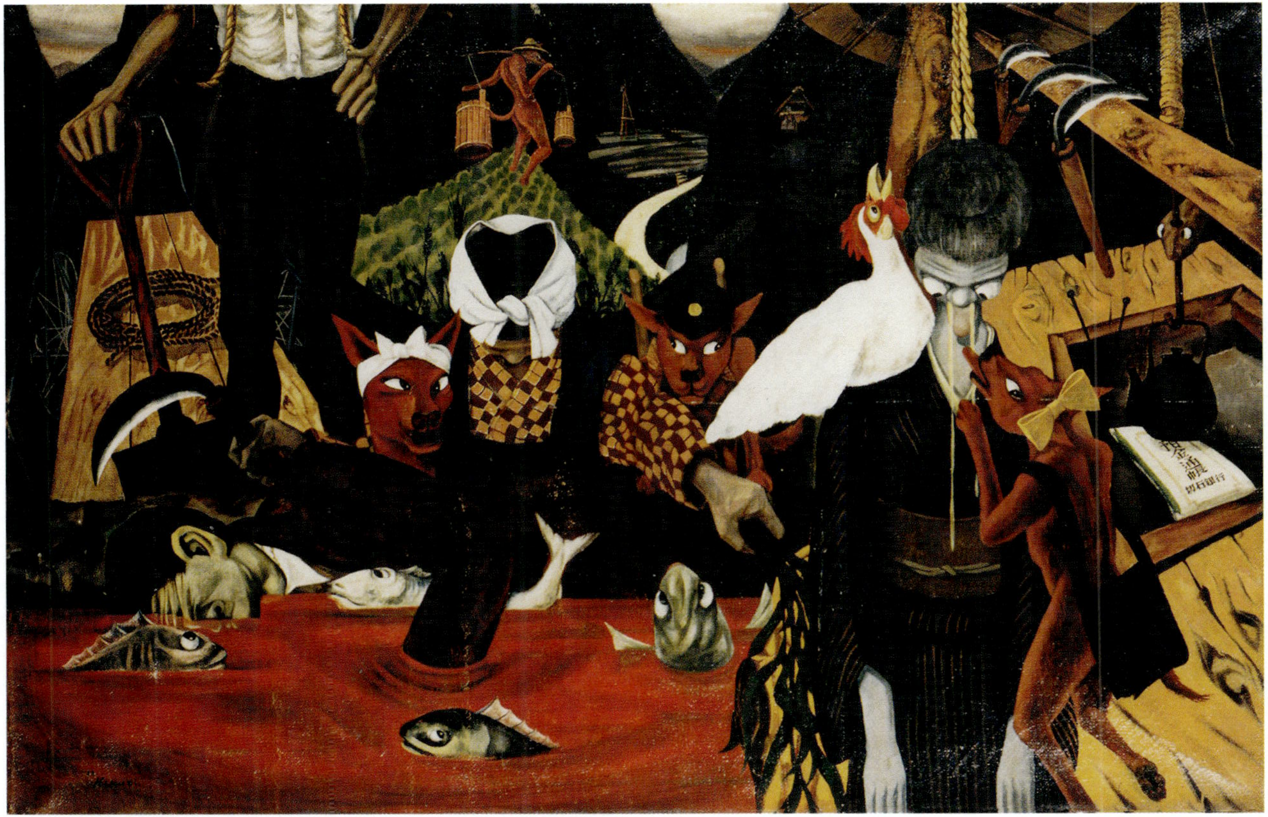

3. Yamashita Kikuji, *Akebono mura monogatari* (*The Tale of Akebono Village*), 1953. Oil on jute. 137 cm x 214 cm. Courtesy of Gallery Nippon / National Museum of Modern Art, Tokyo.

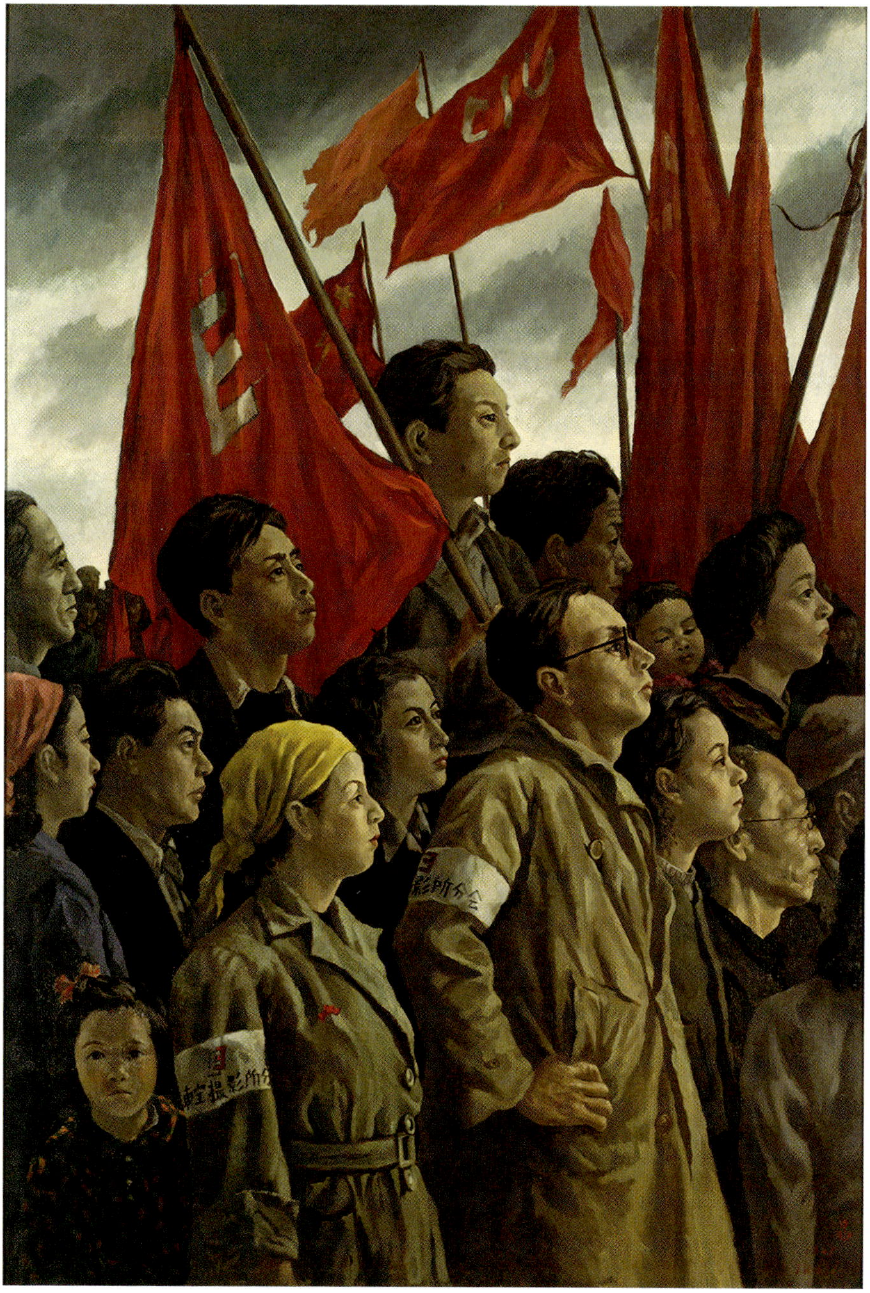

4. Uchida Iwao (aka Gan), *Akahata: utagoe yo okore (bunka o mamoru hitobito)* (*Red Flag: Raise Your Singing Voices [People Protecting Their Culture]*), 1948. Oil on canvas. 195 cm x 130 cm. National Museum of Modern Art, Tokyo.

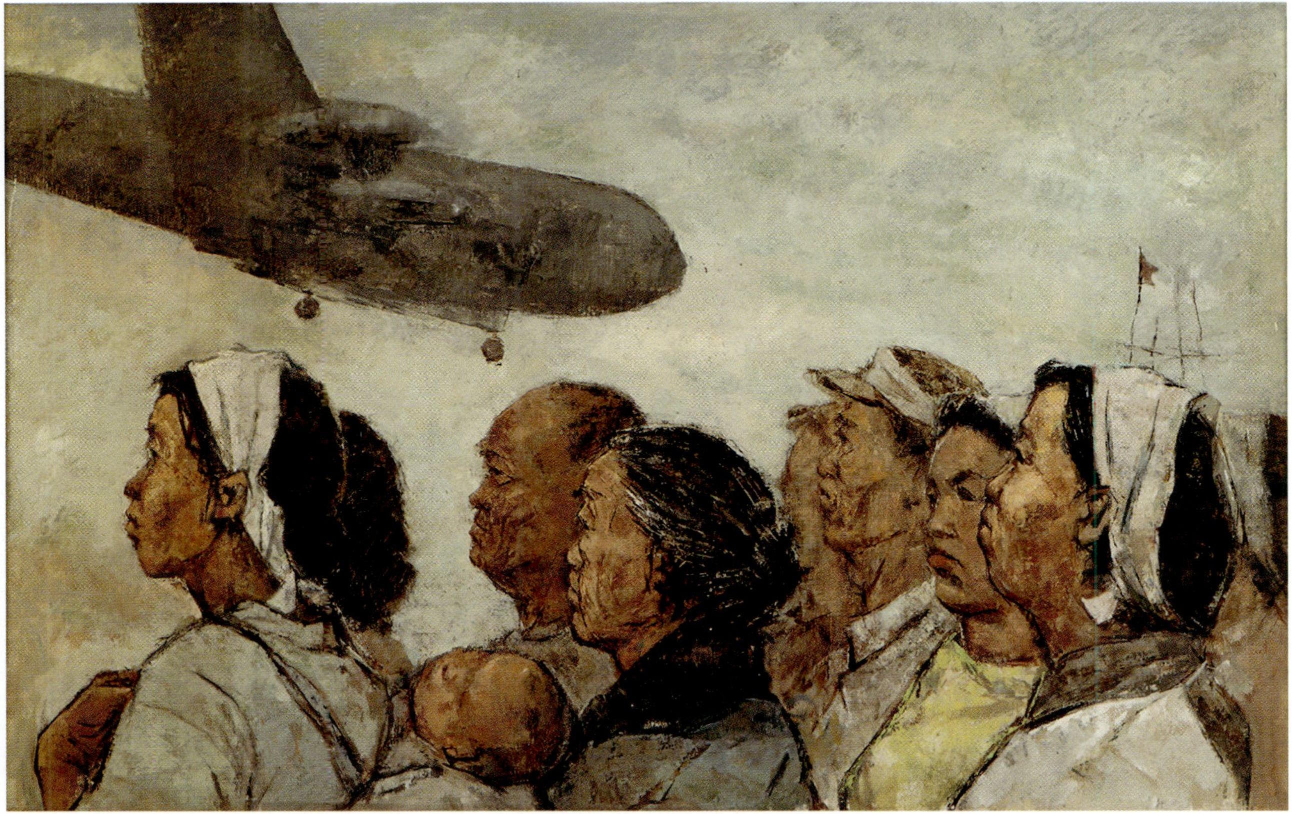

5. Mita Genjirō, *Sunagawa no hitobito* (*People of Sunagawa*), 1957. Oil on canvas. 71.6 cm x 116 cm. Courtesy of Mita Takashi / Itabashi Art Museum.

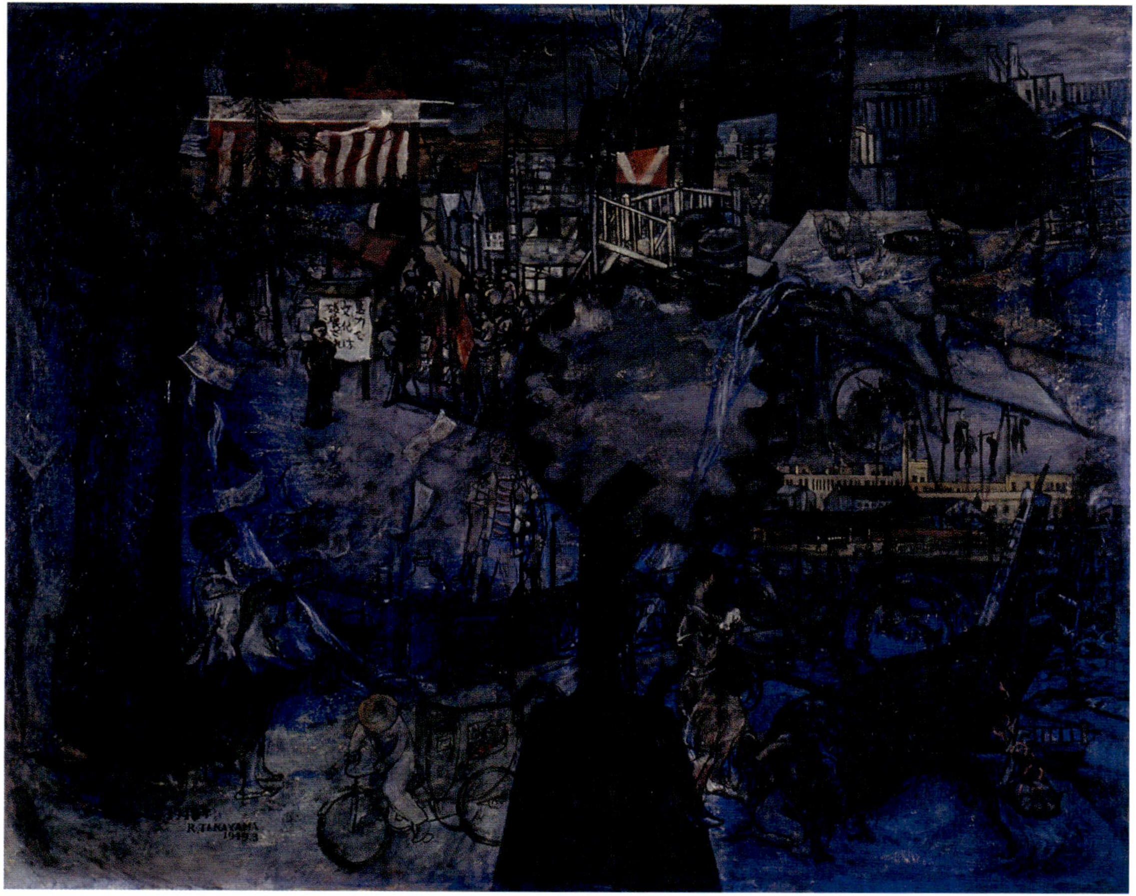

6. Takayama Ryōsaku, *1948 A.D.*, 1949. Oil on canvas. 112.5 cm x 145 cm. Courtesy of Saitō Masako / Itabashi Art Museum.

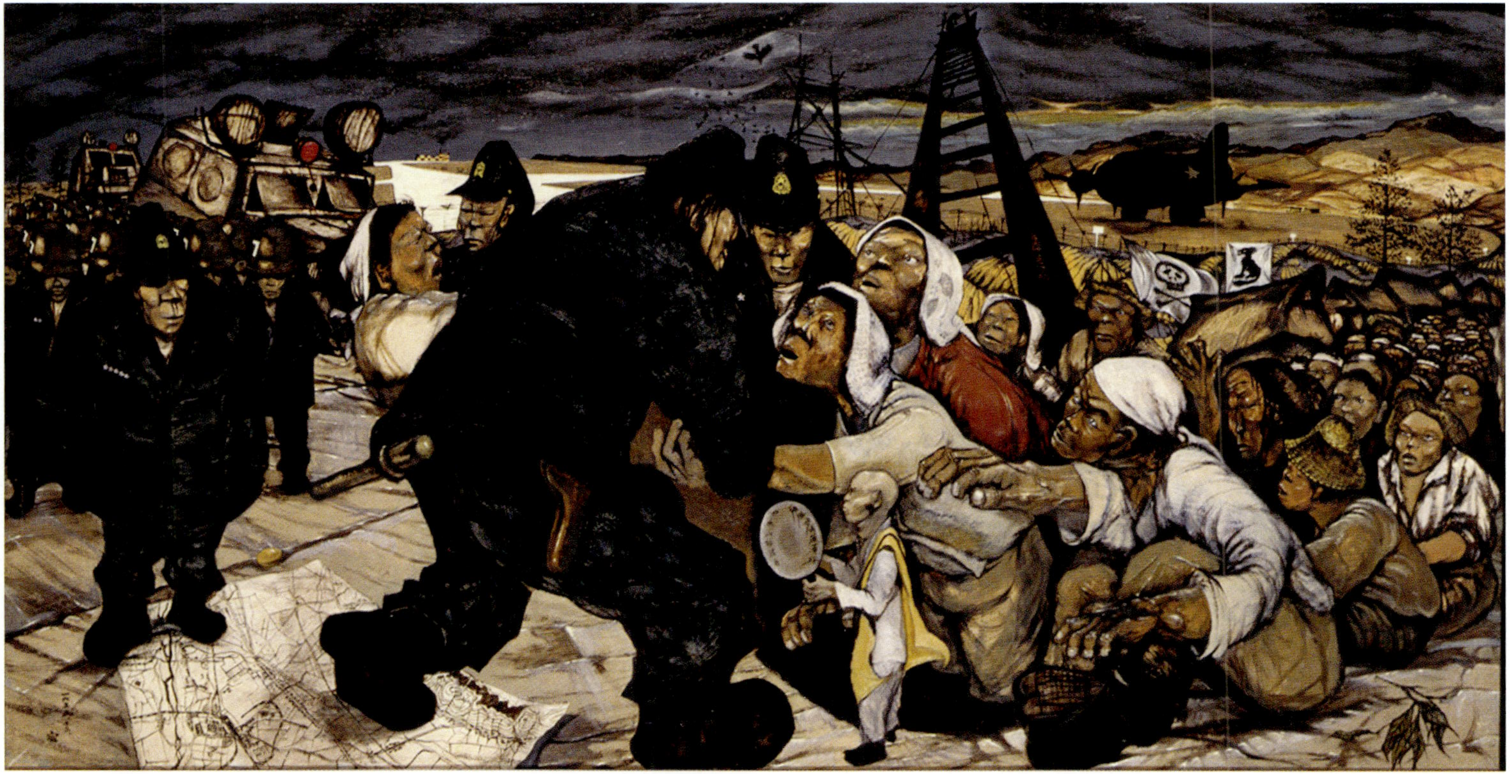

7. Nakamura Hiroshi, *Sunagawa go-ban* (*Sunagawa No. 5*), 1955. Oil on board. 92 cm x 183 cm. Courtesy of Nakamura Hiroshi / Museum of Contemporary Art, Tokyo.

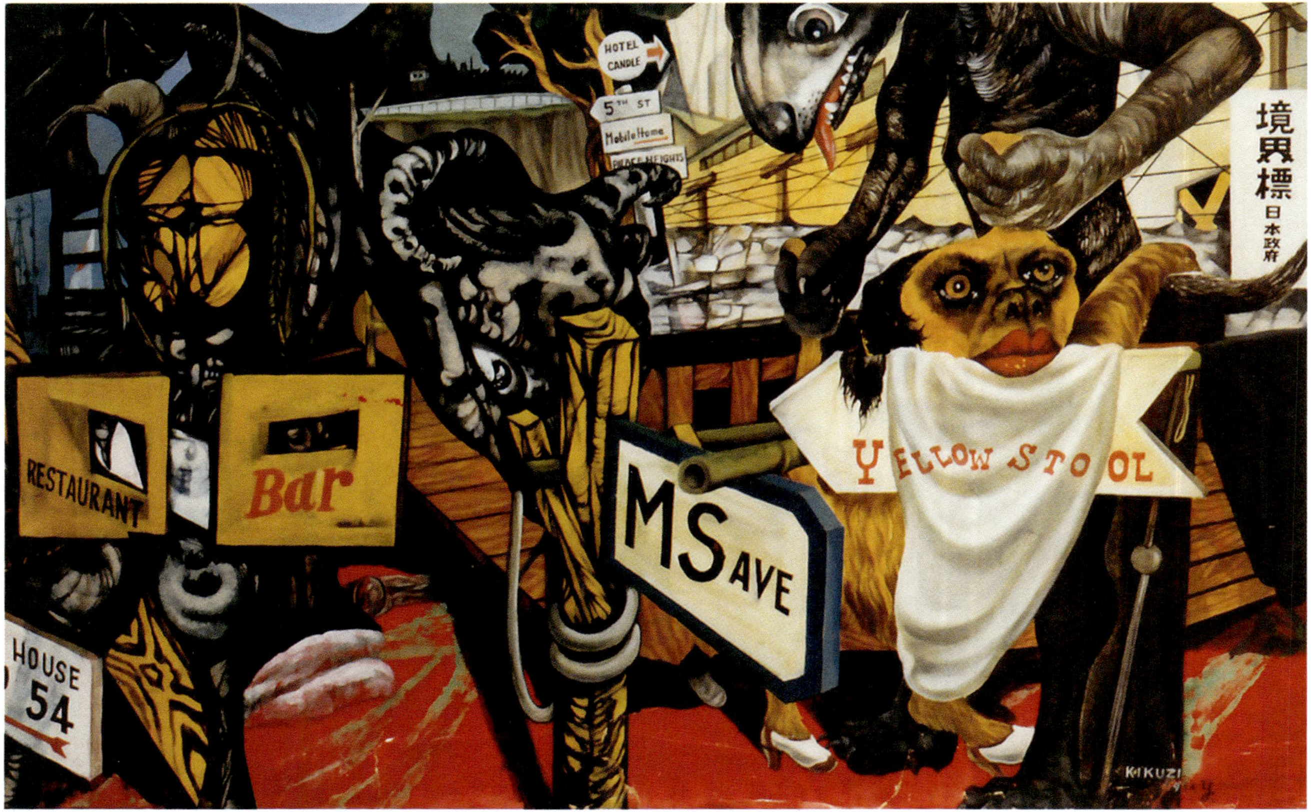

8. Yamashita Kikuji, *Shin Nippon monogatari* (*The Tale of New Japan*), 1954. Oil on canvas. 72 cm x 116 cm. Courtesy of Gallery Nippon.

Another reason the split is important is that it ushered in an era of official agnosticism regarding artistic form. The party abandoned the critique of modernism, using its policy statements to assert a separation between questions of politics and questions of artistic technique.[48] The focus shifted to action: the party did not pass judgment on artistic form so long as artists were engaged in political struggle. In an article often cited as a defining statement on JCP artistic policy from the period, Nanjō Tōru praised the Heiwa-ten and Seibiren for working to link art to pressing political needs: peace, anti-imperialism (meaning anti-Americanism), and nationalism.[49] As Segi Shin'ichi later aptly noted, Nanjō's praise was for the politics of the artists and made no mention of the artworks at all.[50] The journal *Jinmin bungaku* (*People's literature*) also regularly featured political reportage, including a piece on the Tachikawa base by Ikeda Tatsuo's group Enāji (Energy), discussed at greater length in chapter 6. Thomas Schnellbacher has argued that the JCP split set the stage for this shift in cultural policy, when the group most active in attacking surrealism and other forms of modernism (i.e., the international faction) lost control over cultural policy, providing "an opportunity for 'modernists' like Abe Kōbō to gain a foothold."[51] While the reportage artists do not appear to have had specific allegiance to the mainstream or international faction, the leveling of leadership the split caused provided them with an opening. Looking at the main publication of the JCP-affiliated Nihon Bijutsu Kai (Japan Art Society), *Bijutsu undō* (Art movement), one can see the editorial board swung wildly during this period. At first it was dominated by older-generation naturalist realists, then the reportage artists, then back again, and then back once more. This demonstrates that the young reportage artists stood on a more equal footing: it is hard to imagine them becoming the editors of this publication—which a few years earlier had fired the first shot in the critique of modernism—without the split. But the footing itself was much less stable: the new opportunities for the reportage artists were born out of chaos, not systemization.

Perhaps even more important was the party's emphasis on action over identity. Instead of totalities of substance, Schnellbacher writes, "the movements between 1950 and 1955, based on Stalinist and Maoist doctrines, tended towards totalities of action. . . . The change broke the deadlock between two kinds of identity [modernism and realism] that had characterized the first five postwar years of the literature movement."[52] As we will see, the reportage artists also emphasized action and rejected the idea that certain forms of art were automatically more political than others. One can argue therefore that in 1950–1955, the JCP provided them with a structure for what they wanted to do anyway; that is, to be actively involved in ways that their elders had failed to be during the war and were failing to be at present. It provided an apparatus and social context for artists to pursue their artwork in ways that were explicitly and concretely trying to intervene in the cycle of war and oppression.

Another turning point came at the Sixth Party Congress in 1955, when the feuding factions reunited and renounced the policy of armed struggle. The sudden about-face sent shock waves through left-wing and progressive culture. Over the next few years many of those who had lived through the period of the split argued over how to diagnose its failures. Some criticized the misadventures in their entirety. Nagai Kiyoshi, painter and spokesperson for naturalist realism during the realism debate of the 1940s, is one such figure. In a piece he wrote in 1957, he noted how the populism of the grassroots strategy had tipped into anti-intellectualism and reduced artists to making handbills and placards, with even the least attention to artistry being denounced as art-for-art's sake.[53] He also said that membership in the Japan Art Society suffered because local chapters began to ignore the center. The journal *Bijutsu undō* illustrates this disinvestment. By 1953, it had transformed from a broadsheet set in moveable type with a number of inset images to a clumsily mimeographed (*gariban*) pamphlet. Whatever financing had existed had apparently dried up. We can imagine that as an established artist and critic in the late 1940s, Nagai saw a great deal being lost in the chaos of the split. He welcomed the call for self-criticism after 1955 but asserted that some needed to undergo it more than others: not everyone was equally responsible for the mistakes.

But for the reportage artists and those of their generation, the fallout from the change of course in 1955 was more complicated and intense. Someone like Nagai, who easily identified with the pre-1950 party, could welcome the change of course as a return to normal. But to the young students and artists who had been involved in grassroots activism, the change was a betrayal: many had been jailed for their activities and the about-face seemed to prove that their sacrifice had been for nothing. With the change in strategy, Japan lost its only revolutionary party and doubts began to surface about the party's commitment to revolution even during the "armed struggle" period. As official policy, armed struggle had lasted from 1951 to 1955, but the actual armed struggle had lasted for only about six months: the so-called Molotov cocktail campaign (*kaenbin tōsō*) in 1952. Had the old guard of party leaders really believed that armed struggle could work? If they had, why hadn't there been more actual armed struggle? Had armed struggle been a case of the leadership saying one thing but believing another? Had they let the young sacrifice themselves for a position they never thought feasible? Critics among the younger generation began to draw parallels to the failures of leadership and the sacrifice of the young during the war. *Tenkō*—the process of ideological conversion that the police had forced many activists in the proletarian movement of the early 1930s to undergo—became a rhetorical weapon of choice. The young critics of the JCP highlighted the older generation's *tenkō* into fascism in the 1930s, followed by *tenkō* to democracy in 1945, followed by *tenkō* to armed struggle in 1951 and then *tenkō* to peaceful coexistence in 1955. The pattern demonstrated an absent or fundamentally corrupt political subjectivity, most evident in those who claimed to lead.

For younger generation critics, it was not *tenkō* itself that was most problematic but the failure to properly recognize the damage it caused. Yoshimoto Takaaki, whose work is often taken to stand for this younger generation as a whole, wrote in the introduction to *Bungakusha no sensō sekinin* (The war responsibility of writers), which he co-authored with Takei Teruo in 1956, that if one is to "write about the failure of literature and poetry during the war" one would have to approach it "specifically as a problem of the inner self. . . . Yet, as expected, none of my opponents do this. They happily forget their experience of the war, and blithely ignore that this is a problem of the inner self." He continued, invoking the sacrifice of youth both during and after the war: "They pay no heed to how we have spent this past 10 years [1945–1955], fighting both in reality and within ourselves to come to terms with our experience of the war. . . . I for one cannot forget that there is blood that runs beneath this peace, and that the voiceless voices of the dead cry out, only to fall silent again."[54] Matsumoto Toshio joined Yoshimoto's assault on the JCP leadership in the name of betrayed ideals and squandered innocence in the field of documentary film, as did Nakamura Hiroshi, Mōri Yuri, and Katsuragawa Hiroshi in the field of visual art.

The charge they led was also undertaken in the name of artistic expression. Failure to examine the problem of *tenkō* as a problem of inner consciousness had implications for artistic form. Naturalist realism came to be linked explicitly to willful blindness, an unwillingness to face up to personal involvement and responsibility. Yoshimoto examined elder poets' wartime poems alongside their postwar poems, showing that their style and imagery had not changed at all and that only the ideological keywords had flipped.[55] In the world of documentary filmmaking, Matsumoto Toshio connected the unproblematized realism of postwar left-wing expository documentary to wartime documentary and prewar proletarian film.[56] In the realm of art, Katsuragawa Hiroshi may have been the first to explicitly link postwar naturalist realism with war painting. In an essay published in 1954 that actually predates Yoshimoto's first attack on the older generation of poets, Katsuragawa upbraided naturalist realists for failing to come to terms with the flaws in their belief that reality could be apprehended through disinterested visual observation. He argued that insofar as realism was tasked with representing dialectic transformation, faithful description of things as they were would never be adequate because the idea of faithful description assumed a stable, mutually respectful distance between subject and object. Artists who continued to put faith in that approach failed to realize that there was no neutral "non-aggression zone" (*fukashin ryōiki*), no position that left the observer or the observed safely uninvolved. Foreshadowing Yoshimoto's tactics, he criticized a recent painting of a group of workers by Koiso Ryōhei (1903–1988), asserting that the only difference between it and Koiso's war paintings was the subject matter, not the way of thinking, which still stopped at the "meaningless, superficial" boundary of the human. A more aggressive, transgressive stance toward the human, Katsuragawa argued, was necessary to avoid the failures of war painting. Although the disparagement of naturalist realism has become naturalized in Cold War capitalist countries, that disparagement was culturally constructed. This moment in the mid-1950s is when that construction begins.[57]

An invaluable document for understanding the reportage artists' reading of this history is a collection of essays by Bito Yutaka, Katsuragawa Hiroshi, Nakamura Hiroshi, and Mōri Yuri that was published in the independent journal *Keishō* in 1960.[58] Nakamura's essay took on the period 1955–1960, after the JCP reversed course at the Sixth Party Congress.[59] According to Nakamura, "[The turnaround] displayed nothing more nor less than the desire to find a nice safe shelter from the dangers of the Molotov cocktails. Realism's comeback is exactly this: safety, in terms of both politics and art."[60] He examined a number of exhibitions, the Nippon-ten, the Heiwa-ten, and the Nihon Bijutsu Kai Independent, to show how flaccid their missions had become. In addition to a political dumbing down of exhibitions, the JCP began a positive revaluation of the large art societies like the Nika Kai. That the JCP would now find the art societies attractive signified a decisive renunciation of the whole concept of avant-garde art, historical necessity, and artistic subjectivity to Nakamura and the other young partisans.

Along with their frustration that the spaces for serious exhibition had been lost, the reportage artists were disappointed with the level of critical debate. Critical questions in *Akahata* now turned on whether kitchens or strikes were the appropriate subject matter for left-wing painters. The shift drove Nakamura to write his first critical essay in 1957. "When you compare the weakness and falsity of the so-called postwar socialist realist painters with the dissolution of the prewar proletarian arts movement, when the artists committed *tenkō* to become war painters, you can't help but notice how many points of similarity there are. The general cause of this was the failure of artists to take on the laws and contradictions of society *as something that was within them*."[61] This drive to locate the problem of *tenkō* as something existing on the inside is definitive of the cultural critique of this moment. We will see that it resonates with and amplifies the theorization of avant-garde realism that began developing in the early 1950s. After 1955, the theory of avant-garde realism generalized into a critique of failed subjectivity among the older generation and the organized left as a whole.

As can be deduced from Nakamura's essay and the issue of *Keishō* that it was part of, the reportage artists did not object to political radicalism and direct action. They objected, rather, to the JCP's sudden conservative shift away from it. They also objected to the tendency in the late 1950s to call the entire period of the split and armed struggle a mistake in left-wing adventurism, to sweep it under the rug and let bygones be bygones. Indeed, the older generation's lack of responsibility and failure to engage in critical self-examination were the main grounds for the reportage artists' indictment of the JCP. Katsuragawa Hiroshi wrote the section of the *Keishō* issue that dealt with the period 1950–1955. A major focus of the essay is his response to those such as Hariu Ichirō who dismissed the art of that period as formulaic and content centered and who argued that the artists who produced such works were misguided victims of the party.[62] Katsuragawa countered this dismissal of that body of work with an account of how the reportage artists' involvement in cultural activism (*bunka kōsaku*) had been an expression of their own desire to engage in the politics of the time, and how their approach to their artwork was anything but formulaic. He argued that their trips to various sites presented them with problems that were sociological, anthropological, and artistic—problems of how to create a work that captured the reality of people enmeshed in a particular sociohistorical moment. While he rejected the attempt by Nanjō Tōru (and the party) to claim their activity as a new kind of "people's art,"[63] he vindicated the activity itself in his own terms: what drove their work was "a desire to revolutionize art based on a thorough rejection of the methods of naturalism and nineteenth-century realism that clung to impressionistic perceptions and, simultaneously, to compose a material real-ness [*genjitsusei*, glossed as *riariti*] of the outside world through an active, praxis-based subjective eye."[64] Thus the reportage artists who refused to renounce their work were the stalwarts, the outliers, the embarrassments to the reformed party. As their writing attests, they aimed to redeem the politics, the art, and the engaged aesthetics of the armed struggle period, the JCP and its craven doddering be damned.

CHAPTER 5

Avant-Garde Realism

Artistic form and practice are the most consistent defining features of reportage art (*ruporutāju kaiga*).[1] In this chapter, I trace the theories and practices that would come to define the reportage style, a style I call avant-garde realism. Realism was a key concern for artists, writers, and critics of the early postwar worldwide. The "battle for realism," as James Hyman has described it, shaped Britain's art world in a field of competing positions on "internationalism and nationalism; liberalism and Communism; overt politicization and artistic autonomy; individual genius and collective action," all of which organized themselves around competing ideas about realism.[2] In Japan also, realism was a central value and source of legitimacy and a term through which many other ideals found shape. The realism debate (*riarizumu ronsō*), which began in earnest in 1946, shows how important realism was to artists and critics.[3] For all of the contention and disagreement over what constituted the best form and practice of realism, all of the partisans shared a similar view that the opposite of realism was not another artistic form, but a failure to attempt relevance. While the reportage artists shared this basic investment in realism, beyond it there was considerable disagreement between them and other realists over understandings of reality itself and the individual's place within it.

I begin the account of avant-garde realism's development in the late 1940s by attending to two distinct (though by the early 1950s highly intermixed) groups: the Zen'ei Bijutsu Kai (Avant-Garde Art Society), whose members were in their 20s at the end of the war and had been active as artists before 1945, and a younger cohort whose members were mostly in their teens at the end of the war and became active around 1950. As early as the late 1940s, some members of the Zen'ei Bijutsu Kai were developing artistic forms that foreshadowed avant-garde realism. The Zen'ei Bijutsu Kai had formed when the Bijutsu Bunka Kyōkai (Art Culture Association), a larger group of surrealists that had formed in 1939, split. Citing the wartime resistance of Picasso and Matisse in their founding manifesto, the Zen'ei Bijutsu Kai declared that it would work toward human liberation and avoid both the "narrow ideas bestowed by the proletarian art [movement] of the past" and "the frivolous and decadent tendency to make a show of eccentricity."[4] Whereas the rhetoric of the realism debate of the late 1940s tended to solidify a split that linked political engagement with naturalist realist forms on the one hand and experimentalism with artistic liberation on the other, the Zen'ei Bijutsu Kai's manifesto signaled that its members wanted to break this impasse by bringing political engagement and artistic experimentalism together.

The group included Yamashita Kikuji, Bito Yutaka, Ide Norio, Takayama Ryōsaku, and Ōtsuka Mutsumi, all of whom were important to reportage in the 1950s. Many members of the group were also members of the larger, JCP-affiliated Nihon Bijutsu Kai (Japan Art Society), but they diverged from the JCP cultural establishment on the question of artistic form. In the late 1940s, that establishment consisted mostly of people who had been active in the proletarian arts movements of the early 1930s. They tended to promote a form of realism that depicted scenes of everyday life and struggle in a style that looks much like nineteenth-century realism in its subject matter and its emphasis on verisimilitude. Further emboldened by the critique of modernism (*kindaishugi hihan*), some in that establishment declared that techniques such as deformation ran counter to the task of realist art, which was to represent historical (i.e., socialist) truth. The most dogmatic of these critics rejected the entire modernist canon from Cezanne on. The Zen'ei Bijutsu Kai found itself the target of criticism and, for its part, responded to criticism in its self-published journal.

We can see how the difference between avant-garde realism and naturalist realism played out in art by looking at some paintings about struggles. Uchida Iwao (aka Gan, 1900–1953), painted *Akahata: utagoe yo okore (bunka o mamoru hitobito) (Red Flag: Raise Your Singing Voices [People Protecting Their Culture])* in 1948, during the massive third strike at the Tōhō film studio (plate 4).[5] The work is typical of naturalist realism in its attention to the individuality of the strikers and the absence of any attempt to depict an enemy.

Instead of confrontation we are presented with a collection of portraits whose faces are the main vehicles of emotional appeal, expressed in the mode of stoic outrage. Portraiture and landscape dominate the oeuvre of this cohort of artists to such an extent that we may wonder whether their education in conventional studio practice limited their ability to portray dynamic events. Almost ten years later, in *Sunagawa no hitobito* (*People of Sunagawa*), a work about the Sunagawa Struggle, Mita Genjirō used similar strategies, although he included a U.S. plane in outline form and his brushwork is more impressionistic (plate 5).[6] In both works, the composition is simple and static, the color palette is muted, and the figuration is somewhat rough. The figures and the settings are anything but heroic; they portray instead a quotidian view of struggle that emphasizes the formal and moral wholeness of its protagonists.

The paintings of the same struggles by Takayama Ryōsaku (1917–1982) and Nakamura Hiroshi are different. Takayama's work, *1948 A.D.* (1949) integrates the Tōhō strike into a vision of the year 1948 and may be the first work to demonstrate the elements of avant-garde realism that would become prominent in the years to come (plate 6).[7] Nakamura's work, *Sunagawa go-ban* (*Sunagawa No. 5*) (1955) depicts a clash between police and protestors in Sunagawa (plate 7). Both use multiple references to particular sites and incidents, while the human figures are more symbolic than individual. Affective charge is prioritized over consistency in scale or style, to the point that some figures border on caricature. There are no clear heroes. Quite different from the moral clarity accorded the figures in Uchida and Mita's works, the farmers in Nakamura's work appear desperate, as if impelled by a primitive force emerging from the earth. Both works employ montage. In Takayama's, the composition brings together about a dozen major elements that share no common ground or sky. Nakamura's work combines elements that are all taken from the site but in a way that corresponds to no actual point in Sunagawa's geography or to traditional rules of perspective. Nakamura experimented with four-point perspective to make the composition's center jump out at the viewer. The artists, therefore, marshall the subject matter to create maximum emotional, even kinesthetic impact, not through any single figure but through the force that can be generated by recombining them. The style of the works is also highly eclectic. Takayama's swirling blue atmosphere imitates Matsumoto Shunsuke's cityscapes but replaces Matsumoto's lyricism with a shadowy current of anger and violence. According to Nakamura, *Sunagawa No. 5* combined figuration inspired by Rivera, dramatic perspective modeled on Rapin's *Barge Haulers on the Volga* (1873), and an attempt to create an overall impression like the genre paintings of Bruegel the elder.[8] These do not come together neatly. However, the rough and ready cacophony of the compositions is itself a source of their energy.

At about the same time that Takayama Ryōsaku was painting *1948 A.D.*, Hanada Kiyoteru and Okamoto Tarō were starting to develop a theorization of avant-garde art that shared the Zen'ei Bijutsu Kai's desire to link the artistic avant-garde to political involvement. Hanada and Okamoto were important sustainers of a rich intellectual milieu in the late 1940s and early 1950s that was characterized by a heady mix of existentialism, Marxism, and surrealism. Their theories were built and elaborated in the context of informal study groups and salons. Some of the more important groups were the Yoru no Kai (Night Society), which included Hanada Kiyoteru, Abe Kōbō, and Okamoto Tarō; the Avangyarudo Geijutsu Kenkyūkai (Avant-Garde Art Research Society), which included Okamoto, the young Ikeda Tatsuo, and future members of Jikken Kōbō (Experimental Workshop); and Seiki no Kai, a large group of primarily young writers and artists that included Abe, Katsuragawa Hiroshi, and future filmmaker Teshigahara Hiroshi. These and other groups sustained an intellectual ferment that was integral to cultural life in Tokyo and vital to developments in poetry, philosophy, fiction, theater, filmmaking, music, and the visual arts. They provided an informal infrastructure for multimedia experiment and profound, albeit eclectic, learning about avant-garde movements from the previous century. Two of the artists I write about in the next chapter, Katsuragawa Hiroshi and Ikeda Tatsuo, came to Tokyo from far-flung provinces with the dream of entering art university in the late 1940s. Despite the sacrifices they'd made to do that, they both dropped out within the first year, alienated by the education in studio practice. The education they received instead took place within the context of these informal societies, and they and the others in their cohort became highly literary and theoretically sophisticated as a result. Their multimedial experimentation, their intellectual curiosity, and their penchant for theoretical writing is characteristic of the reportage artists and the practitioners of avant-garde realism more generally.

The theory of avant-garde realism began to take shape in the thinking of Hanada, Okamoto, and Abe Kōbō in the late 1940s and continued to develop through the 1950s. Of this group, Hanada Kiyoteru was by far the most important. The writing of Hanada, a famously nonsystematic thinker, is a cobweb of double meanings, abrupt reversals, jumps of perspective, a dizzying range of intertexts, and dark humor. This set of rhetorical traits and pedagogical strategies interestingly corresponds to those of reportage. Hanada and Okamoto distinguished their ideas from the naturalist realists of the JCP establishment by moving the question of realism away from consciousness and representation toward embodiment and being. A roundtable discussion that took place in 1948 is the first instance of the emergence of the avant-garde paradigm of realism and well illustrates two of its most important features.[9] In the discussion, Hanada, Okamoto, and others debated painter, theorist, and prominent defender of naturalist realism Nagai Kiyoshi. Nagai presented what by that point in the realism debate was a familiar idea: that realist art must empower people by helping them understand their historical situation. Art failed when it turned away from faithful portrayal of the historical world, a failure Nagai and others in his camp saw as embodied historically in the figure of Cezanne, whom they pilloried for his perceived political dilettantism and his theory of realization, by which painting achieved its own order of reality. The apparent experimentalism and destructiveness of avant-garde art grew from this misrecognition of realism's mission, which for Nagai was rooted in a neo-Kantian constructivism that ultimately took place only within the mind of the artist.

In response, Okamoto argued that the avant-garde was not a form of cognition at all but a movement of being (*jitsuzontekina mono*). It was prior to any knowledge of it, and therefore the structures of Kantianism (thing-in-itself v. phenomenon) and the specter of idealism that went with them were irrelevant. The avant-garde, as the embodiment of ceaseless material change, was not and could not be abstract. Hanada emphasized the avant-garde's rootedness in actuality: he proposed that its dynamic flux emerged between the opposing poles of the rational and the empirical (as opposed to Okamoto's more conventional opposition of rational and irrational). Nascent in this debate were two fundamental disagreements, the first over the concept of reality. While other participants in the realism debate understood reality to mean historical, culturally mediated reality, the avant-garde realists conceived of it as partly acultural, as biological or material. In positioning the empirical as the polar opposite of the rational, Hanada implied that reality itself was a destabilizing and nonhuman(ist) entity. The second disagreement was over the work of art. For the avant-garde realists, the issue was one of embodiment and action, not knowledge and representation. The artist was in the paradoxical position of embodying and attempting to channel what was essentially undetermined—a potential for unlimited change and instability—and it was this that led to the ceaseless destruction and experiment of the historical avant-gardes.

The avant-garde's claim to realism rested on the ontological priority it gave to change. The inherited forms of the western modern tradition had reached their limits: naturalism, abstraction, and surrealism were each unable to accommodate the dynamism of the inner and outer worlds' interdependence.[10] Surrealism remained trapped in the subject's unconscious while discounting its interaction with the rest of the universe. Naturalism failed in a similar way, by assuming that the looking and transcribing subject was independent from the outer world. The task of realism was to portray reality as a process that traversed the boundary between inner and outer. What stood in the way was established forms of seeing and thinking. Objecting to the general assumption that the avant-garde position was in opposition to realism, Hanada claimed it as "an advanced form of realism."[11] It was in their mutual rejection of established form that realism and the avant-garde came to be inseparably linked for Hanada and the avant-garde realists.

Process and change is central to one of Hanada's most discussed essays, "Ringo ni tsuite no ichi kōsatsu" (An examination of apples).[12] As the title indicates, the essay is about apples, and how modern artists had tried to represent them. Hanada argued that Dali, in his depiction of instinct; Cezanne, in his depiction of rationality; and the naturalists, in their depiction of surface characteristics had all failed to apprehend the apple. What they depicted instead was a thought and value system in the skin of an apple. To break the structure of these failures, Hanada proposed the thought experiment of William Tell. Forced by a tyrannical lord to shoot an apple off his son's head as a punishment for defiance, William Tell stands in a relationship of absolute necessity to the apple. Hanada wrote that artists "should try imagining for a moment, standing a hundred paces off, with the bow string taught, bathed in the dazzling light of the sun, and aiming resolutely at the bright red apple on top of their child's head. It is only in this situation that the apple in itself is revealed."[13] William Tell's situation dramatizes a paradox: that it is at the moment of being most trapped, of being most inescapably committed to a particular here and now that the absolute indeterminacy of things becomes real. The apple is not contingent upon belief or will; it is absolutely indeterminate until it becomes part of the past. It is at that moment that the individual becomes most tightly bound to it. Commitment, therefore, staking one's life, is the way to grasp the fundamental indeterminacy of the world and the pivotal (if unpredictable) role of one's actions within it. Commitment is the path to discovering the terrible (but possibly redemptive) entanglement of oneself with the world.

The idea has existential overtones. The way the alien nature of others' existence feeds existential instability is reminiscent of Roquentin's encounter with a tree in *Nausea*, while the temporal, proleptic aspect brings to mind the arrow left in midair at the end of Camus' *The Rebel*. Likewise, Hanada's arrow offers no account of the state of the world at the end of its arc: realism is at best an orientation, not a final state. Although Hanada and others almost always described releasing the arrow as a moment of crisis—one that "leaves no recourse but regeneration through a desperate resistance"—we should remember that the moment of crisis is open ended.[14] Although dire, William Tell's world is responsive (irresistibly so). One can find a similar emphasis on commitment as the starting point for realism in Abe Kōbo's writing. Abe rejected the attempts of surrealists and older naturalist realists to position themselves as bystanders to reality. In an essay linking "new realism" to the practice of reportage, he countered that "the eye of praxis is not an eye that gazes but one that seeks to move."[15]

The emphasis on action resonated with the radicalization of JCP policy in the early 1950s. Maoist ideas of indigenous revolution fed the imaginations of young radicals both inside and outside the JCP as they turned increasingly to direct action. The theoretical emphasis on process and embodiment was the counterpart to such action. The reportage artists' practice of going to a site to experience oppression and the struggle against it motivated and expressed these ideas in equal measure. As Hanada conceived it, commitment to the present promised to unite the political and artistic avant-garde. The moment the arrow flies—irretrievably, to an unknown end—is the moment of radical possibility, in both art and politics.

While Hanada focused on the movement of the avant-garde into the future, the practice of painting (or writing, or filmmaking) entails a different temporality, and his theories have little to say about the nature of that mediation. Hariu Ichirō's work provides a more explicit theory of that mediation, centered on the body. In an essay titled simply "Kirokusei" (The question of documentary), Hariu explained why the practice of painting had such an important contribution to make to reportage. "Newsreels (*nyūsu eiga*) often expose unusually dramatic contradictions from within the stuff of reality itself, beyond the intention of the cameraman. . . . But compared to that, all of the images in a painting are expressed with the tint and tone of the artist's emotions and thought. Therefore, to a much greater degree than is the case in the cameraman's pursuit of reality, a complete grasp of reality on the part of the painter must necessarily be coupled with a revolution of the self."[16] For Hariu, the artist's work entailed the artist's own inner state, so if the artist was successful in painting a realistic painting, it would involve more than just the artist's struggle to understand the "miserable and crushed" structures of the outer world. The painting would also become an index of the artist having internalized those structures while at the same time externalizing the structures of his inner world. More than film, painting as a practice was necessarily a melding of inner and outer realities and Hariu argued that paintings were successful to the extent that they embodied that interpenetration.

Reportage did not depict physical landscapes and human figures per se, but the appearance of these in particular times and places, as they were shaped by human emotion, interest, and value. According to Hariu, in order to understand how the emotions of, say, fishermen fighting an artillery testing range in their fishing grounds intertwined to weave the space and time of the theater of struggle, one had to go to the place and experience the struggle. Going to a place, "sharing the experience of people's lifestyle and psyche, their joys and suffering," was integral to making any eventual painting part of "a living reality, a process of always unfolding as dynamic change."[17] If they were to align their own inner being to the same historical arc as the subject they hoped to relay, artists would have to grind down their own subjectivity and put themselves in the position of fighting for life and livelihood. "If [the artist] has thoroughly demolished his everyday self in that reality, when he begins to paint the subject on a canvas, the form and color will not spring only from resemblance to the subject matter, nor will they be aimed only for visual effect, but rather become none other than the trace [*shirushi*] of the artist's deep human emotion."[18] When that happened, the painting itself would become a "thing" (*mono*).[19] Thus, the whole practice of reportage—the bodily, mental, and emotional involvement of the painter in interaction with the people and places she or he hoped to depict—was the guarantor of documentary relevance.

These ideas attest to the importance of direct experience and embodiment to avant-garde realism. The physical hardship of war and occupation and the need to redeem survival through action, all come to bear upon the embodied subject. The critical field surrounding reportage art overflows with corporeal metaphors. In his essay "Ruporutāju no igi" (The meaning of reportage), Abe Kōbō conceived of reportage as wielding a scalpel to peel back the skin of everyday common sense to discover new things in the "darkness" (*ankoku*) underneath.[20] Looking at works of reportage from that time, we can see how particular locales such as the factory, the military base, or the site of protest appear in a visual form that attempts to represent the interpenetration of those locales with people. The tortured human body remains a dominant theme in reportage, as it was generally in figurative painting at this time. But I argue that instead of simply being expressions of suffering or being implicitly connected to the project of (re)building a modern subjectivity after the war, other ideas are at work in reportage art and avant-garde realism.

Abe Kōbō put material (*busshitsu*) at the center of his theory of what he called "new realism." Like Hanada, Abe insisted that reality was essentially the process of contact between material and consciousness. Material and consciousness, however, did not map onto the division between inside and outside: both were within and without the embodied subject. For Abe, consciousness was already decentered because it was social, meaning that one's words weren't really one's own, that individuals were always thinking with other people's thoughts. But material was even more powerfully decentering: a dark, destabilizing, libidinal energy that expressed itself through "movements of the flesh" that were beyond good and evil and the abstractions of science or historical understanding.[21] The elemental force of material worked constantly to destabilize human values and meanings and, Abe argued, could be felt as a parasite (*kiseichū*) within consciousness, a seed of unassimilated life.[22] While naturalist realists criticized the avant-garde realists' exploration of the dark forces that constantly pushed themselves up into consciousness as being decadent, Abe insisted that whether one liked it or not, this was the most fundamental reality. New realism began with the task of "apprehending the laws of [reality's] fluctuation and struggle."[23] Rather than an exploration of how the modern subject could be rebuilt, the theories of avant-garde realism laid the groundwork for a rejection of the modern subject's possibility, one whose antihumanist and antimodernist implications became more explicit over the decade of the 1950s.

The theory of avant-garde realism provides insight into why deformation, metamorphosis, the grotesque, and montage are so important to the visual vocabulary of the reportage artists. Metamorphosis is perhaps the most literal realization of the body as a material process; it marks the progress by which obscure forces remold an individual. Ikeda Tatsuo's *Bakemono no keifu shiriizu* (*Monster Genealogy Series*), imagines social ills in the form of mutant organisms, usually without eyes, that (re)produce their noxious effects in the unthinking mode of a biological imperative. In many avant-garde realist works, human hands grow to enormous prominence, overtaking the rest of the human form (fig. 3.1). The prominence of hands, which are so deeply involved in an individual's sensing and shaping of the world seems not only to be an allegory of dehumanization but a figure of consciousness turned inside out upon the world, intelligence that is not afforded refuge behind the eyes. The overcrowded, all-over montage compositions likewise attest to the lack of head space, the lack of distance between self and other, the press of the material world. While reportage artists inherited the surrealist respect for the unconscious and for techniques of defamiliarization, their canvasses are markedly different from the Dali-inspired mainstream of surrealism in Japan. The clear horizon and desert-like expanses scattered with unlikely exotica are replaced in reportage by compositions that are spatially shallower and have lost the horizon to a maelstrom of brightly colored, enlarged bodies, familiar from everyday life but uncannily exposed and uncomfortably packed in lurid *dépaysement*.

Although we can see similar compositional strategies in the work of André Fougeron, for instance, I would argue that the intensity of the psychological and social critique in the reportage oeuvre is unique to Japan. A comparison of *Atlantic Civilization* (1953) and Yamashita Kikuji's *Shin Nippon monogatari* (*The Tale of New Japan*) (1954) can be instructive (plate 8). While both use montage, Yamashita's is denser and the various sectors of the composition are more difficult to disaggregate. In *Atlantic Civilization*, each figure is presented more or less independently from the rest of the painting and we can easily imagine removing them to reveal a grassy hill and ocean, which provide a firm ground to the painting. The use of imagery is almost entirely iconic. Although the work aims to communicate the confusion of American-led decadence, the method remains rational and highly legible. While *Tale of a New Japan* includes similar anti-American icons, there are many elements that are less legible but more menacing, such as the mass of muscle and bone on the left and the inexplicably red ground. The glassy-eyed copulating dogs are symbols of sexualized power relations, disturbing both for how graphically they are depicted and for their complete disinterest in having been caught in the act. They are depicted as animals—beings from which we expect no decorum—rather than as animal*ized*. They thus hang in an undecidable state in which they are both undeniably allegorical and intransigently, impassively, repulsively material and alien. *The Tale of New Japan* provokes outrage, to be sure, but it offers no countervailing safe perspective; every position is like a crimp on a continuous surface of inhuman transformation that enfolds all.

A shift was taking place in the early 1950s that was only just beginning to be articulated in art and words. When artist Katsuragawa Hiroshi saw a "terrible ancientness" lurking within the "bodily mass 'Nippon,'" he and his fellow reportage artists were doing something that many others were doing: trying to assess the interlinked failures of the present and the recent past.[24] But their conception of that problem and the implicit solution had diverged from those of older generations and inherited realisms. For Nagai Kiyoshi and other practitioners of naturalist realism, the implicit cause of fascism was a lack of modern humanism. In line with the dominant Kōza-ha interpretation of Japanese history, these realists saw the Meiji as an incomplete bourgeois revolution: feudalism had remained intertwined within Japanese society despite technical modernization. Japan's artists, it followed, had yet to achieve the objectivity of vision that realists in nineteenth-century Europe had achieved. We might say that in striving for objectivity, realists of the older generation were trying to distance themselves from the bodily mass "Nippon" as fast as they could. Their canvasses display an aspiration to rationality, justice, and human dignity: people stand at the center as manifest moral anchors. Within the theorization of avant-garde realism, however, the task was not to keep trying to build something that was missing but to "find the cause" (to return to Katsuragawa's words) of the repeated failure at the foundation of that building. For the reportage artists, the problem was not something that could be overcome simply by trying harder this time around. Failure of a politics of enlightenment, not its incompleteness, was coming into view as the most basic reality.

CHAPTER 6

Katsuragawa Hiroshi, Ikeda Tatsuo, and Nakamura Hiroshi

Katsuragawa Hiroshi was born in 1924 and grew up on the northern island of Hokkaido. Of the three artists examined in this chapter, he was the only one who seemed destined for a career in fine arts from an early age. He submitted his first work to the Hokkaido-ten (Hokkaido Exhibition), a regional juried exhibition, when he was still thirteen and submitted another four or five works over the next few years.[1] This work does not survive and his subsequent work, which includes oil paintings, drawings, and collage, is not as prolific as this precocious beginning might suggest. Drafted in the final year of the war, Katsuragawa was spared the front lines, but only because army training had broken his physical and mental health.[2] After a period of recovery, he finally came to Tokyo and entered Tama Art University in 1948, selling his books to get together enough money, four years older than his nearest classmate.

Ikeda Tatsuo was one of Katsuragawa's classmates at university. Through Ikeda, Katsuragawa began to have contact with the Yoru no Kai and, through that, the members of the Seiki no Kai. As Thomas Schnellbacher notes, the Seiki no Kai illustrates how young artists were trying to set the groundwork for an organizational structure that went beyond patronage and personality.[3] The group established three basic principles: first, that it should include "comrades" over thirty despite its focus on youth; second, that the administrative positions should be assigned based on ability and not on "name value"; and finally, that the character of the group should not be determined by the personalities of its functionaries. The Seiki no Kai was important because it gave the young members their first experience in independent publishing. In addition to a newsletter, they published a series of small books called the *Seikigun* (Century collection) that featured translations and original poetry and fiction that members Abe, Katsuragawa, Teshigahara Hiroshi, Segi Shin'ichi, and others wrote and illustrated.

This was the context in which Katsuragawa and the other members began to read and discuss existentialism, communism, and avant-garde realism. The group was deeply connected with Hanada Kiyoteru through Abe Kōbō, who was already well recognized as a brilliant critic and author despite his youth. The group became increasingly political, especially after the Korean War began in June 1950. Following Abe's lead, Katsuragawa joined the JCP in the spring or summer of 1951. As part of their cultural strategy, the JCP sent Katsuragawa, Abe, Teshigahara, and other young artists, writers, and activists to industrial areas and farming villages to educate, organize, assist, and mobilize the people living there. This activity was called *bunka kōsaku*, which can be translated as cultural activism. The group's first assignment was to work with a group of worker-poets in Shimomaruko, a community on the industrial south side of Tokyo. The poetry circle predated the arrival of JCP activists and was already quite radical.[4] Shimomaruko was home to the factories of Mitsubishi and Hokushin Denki, both of which were manufacturing military supplies for the Korean War. Katsuragawa, Abe, and Teshigahara worked closely with the circle for over six months, meeting with them a number of times each week. Abe rented a room and lived in the area during that period. Putting his experience from the Seiki no Kai to use, Katsuragawa made the woodcuts for the covers of the circle's first two poetry collections and helped assemble the publications. Abe taught classes on poetry writing and literary theory. This project involved everyone in the processes of writing, artwork, publishing, and teaching. Although the collaboration continued for only a few months, it was a context where people met who didn't usually meet, both sides reaching across divisions of class and expertise to work on a project together.

How did Katsuragawa's artwork function as part of a collaborative project and political movement? His cover for the group's second poetry collection is informative (fig. 6.1). It depicts an industrial neighborhood of jaunty houses, people overflowing into the street, smokestacks smoking, the sun shining. Katsuragawa succeeds in creating tremendous energy with visual rhythm, a feature that marks many of his drawings and woodcuts. The surfaces jostle each other almost playfully and the people outside add life to the formal dynamism. A comparison can be made to *Kōzui no machi* (*Flooded City*), an oil painting from 1950 that Katsuragawa produced before his involvement in *bunka kōsaku* (fig. 6.2). The painting shares the same composition as the cover for the poetry collection: a vertical axis runs down the middle and

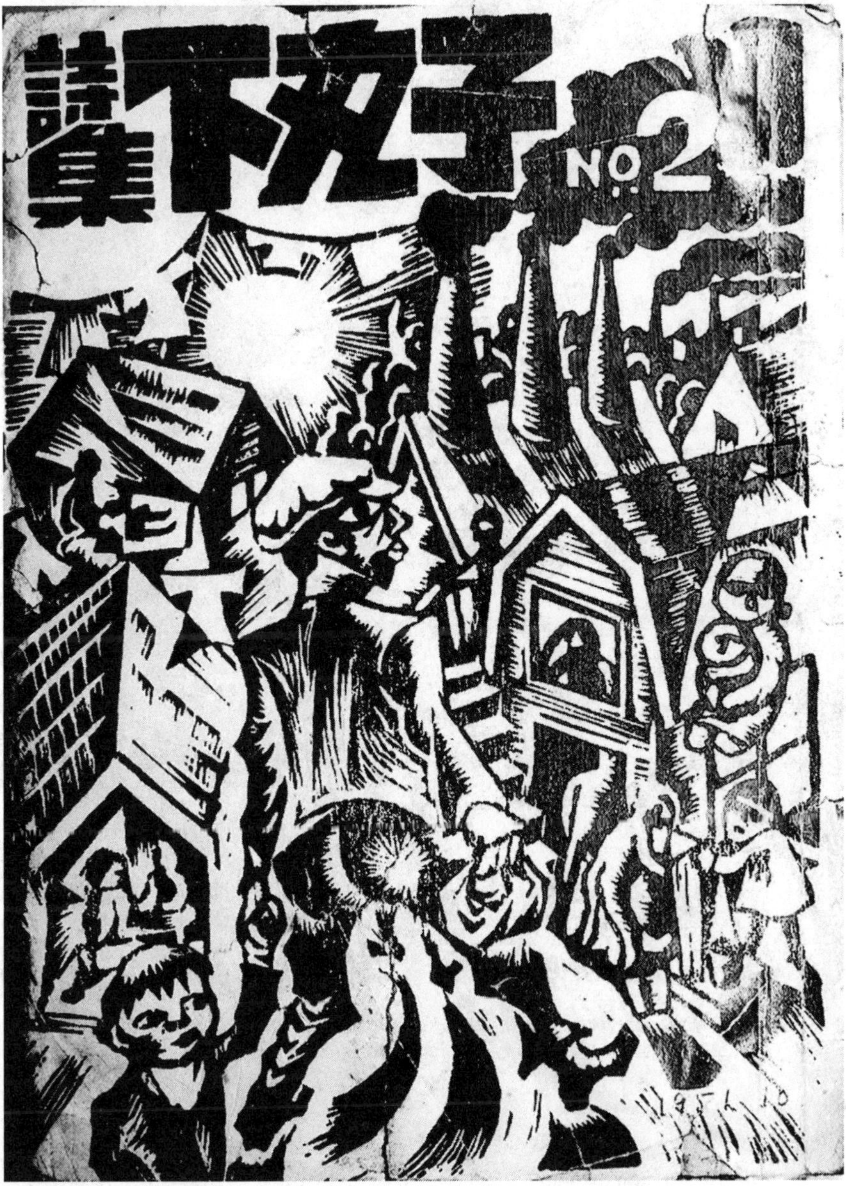

FIGURE 6.1 Katsuragawa Hiroshi, cover of *Shishū Shimomaruko* 2 (Shimomaruko poetry collection 2), 1951. Woodblock print on paper.

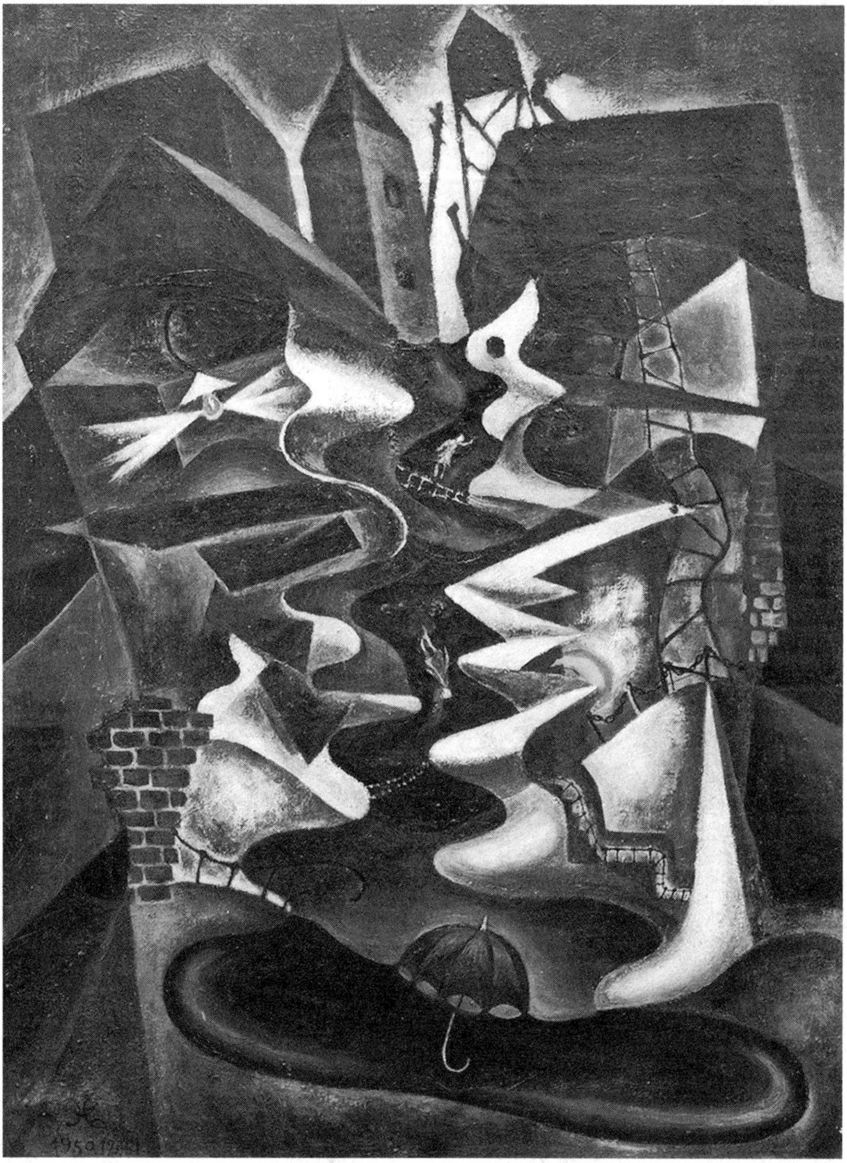

FIGURE 6.2 Katsuragawa Hiroshi, *Kōzui no machi* (*Flooded City*), 1950. Oil on canvas. 77.3 cm x 56.7 cm. Courtesy of Katsuragawa Jun / Katsuragawa Akane / Museum of Modern Art, Tokyo.

elements of a cityscape rear up on either side. The center is a twisting road that two waifs float down toward a forlorn umbrella. The buildings at the top lean backward forbiddingly and offer no sign of life. On the cover of the poetry collection, however, the road leads into a bustling community.

A man walking to or from work with some energy in his step occupies the central axis. This change over one year from lonely souls washed away in an alienated landscape to a dynamic community energy is evidence of what the structure of cultural work provided for Katsuragawa. Whereas many of the young people of his generation felt the urge to do *something,* the JCP grassroots strength provided a way for young artists to connect with other classes and become involved with them in a process of social engagement through shared expression and mutual recognition.

The cover of the poetry collection invites us in. This particular collection runs to sixty-eight pages and includes twenty-six poems by twenty-four people. The group published many more similar collections during the 1950s.[5] Providing a synopsis is challenging, but I have chosen to excerpt a poem that is itself a work of reportage, evidence that reportage was not only a movement where cultural elites took it upon themselves to interact with people outside their station but a practice that was available to people of all classes. In the poem "Rinjikō" (Temporary worker), by Inoue Yotarō, the narrator is a temporary worker who goes to the Mitsubishi munitions factory for a day.[6] The "you" in the poem refers to the full-time workers that he is separate from as a temporary worker. The selections I quote represent about one-eighth of the poem.

> Today for just one day I worked as a temp at Mitsubishi Heavy Industry
> and clipped the slave badge to my chest.
> It was the first time in my life
> but when I passed the guard men armed so sternly
> my chest swelled. . . .
> . . .
>
> In your waiting room
> the walls, the desks
> were all painted yellow in foreign paint
> but your sweat sunk in as you sat there
> staining your clothes black.
> The haughty yellow walls and desks
> were miserable that morning
> in the room filled with the stench
> of your sweat. . . .
> . . .
>
> I sat next to one of your old friends
> a man sparkling with silver stubble
> leaned over and whispered that

they didn't need geezers
like him now.
Chased from your workplace
I felt that whisper
grow into a terrible storm
shrieking of the future. . . .
. . .

When I passed the guards
to return the slave badge, I was searched
to the bone, but still my chest swelled full
of all that I would sing
about my day with you.

The poem goes through a number of vignettes, two of which I've quoted, and at the end of each, the narrator, his chest swelling, must calm himself before he bursts into a song of rage. But in his final line he pledges to sing of the things he couldn't inside the walls of the munitions plant, to carry the old man's whisper, the stench of the sweat, beyond the yellow walls the United States had boxed them into. The Shimomaruko collections contain many voices of work, daily life, outrage, protest, and hope. Together, and further accompanied by the words and images of Katsuragawa, Abe, and Teshigahara, they form a chorus that is trying to realize a world of values over and beyond the walls of the factories fueling war that surrounded them. Although Katsuragawa, Abe, and Teshigahara left the circle after a little more than six months, the Shimomaruko group continued to produce poetry, fiction, and a substantial volume of critical work through the end of the 1950s.

After Shimomaruko, Katsuragawa's next assignment took him to Ogōchi, a town in the remote mountains of western Tokyo that was the site of a hydroelectric dam project. A group of young students and artists were sent there in the summer of 1952, originally with the idea of mobilizing residents who were going to be displaced by the dam. They carried a mimeograph press, waxed templates, ink, and paper deep into the mountains and worked in a lean-to to make woodcuts and drawings for newsletters. When the group arrived, however, very few of the original inhabitants remained. Their subsequent attempt to mobilize the construction workers failed and ended with the police chasing the group out of their camp. The work Katsuragawa and his companions did in Ogōchi was not intended for exhibition. It was meant to function within the (largely fantasized) context of a community that would recognize itself in the representations being produced.

One of the newsletters the group produced was a small booklet that depicted the story of a strike unfolding (fig. 6.3). Each of the images had a

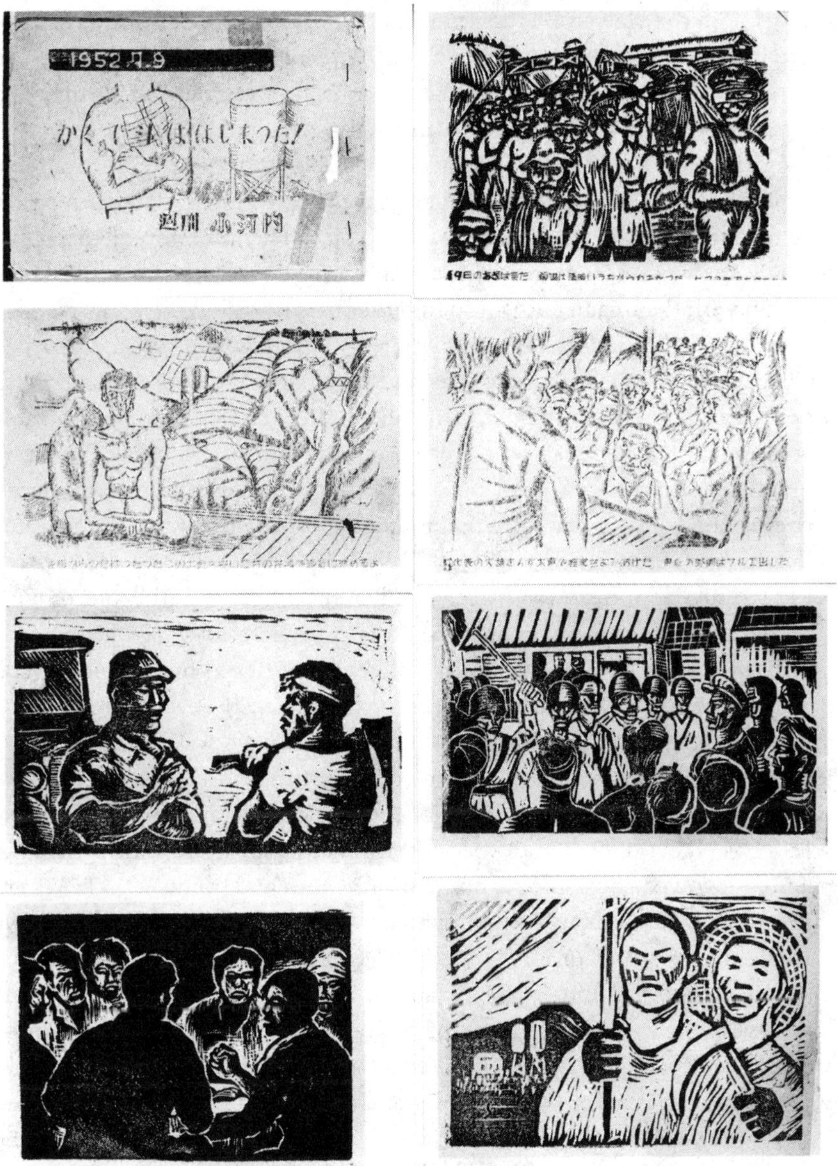

FIGURE 6.3 Katsuragawa Hiroshi et al., illustrations for *Shūkan Ogōchi* (*Weekly Ogōchi*), 1952. Woodblock print and mimeograph on paper (8 stapled sheets). 13.5 cm x 18.7 cm. Courtesy of Katsuragawa Jun / Katsuragawa Akane / Itabashi Art Museum.

small caption underneath that narrated the story or portrayed the voice of one of the characters. With two exceptions, the people in the pictures are facing each other, leaving the viewer outside the circle. Tang Xiaobing has noted that the subjects in Chinese revolutionary woodcuts rarely make eye contact with the viewer. It is assumed that "the voice comes through as even more proactive and more visceral than that constituted by eye contact [so that] the deepest conviction . . . is that the conventional poetic of seeing must be translated and transformed into an empowering politics of speaking and voicing."[7] In this booklet also, the lack of inclusion of the viewer through eye contact reveals an assumption or hope that the conversations in the pictures extended to the audience through shared voice. The intention of the artists was that the workers would do more than simply establish an emotional relationship with the image but would find themselves within the conversations depicted in the narrative. The visual representation, which invoked the river valley, the mess hall, and the bridge, and then connected these locales both visually and verbally to other narrative arcs, linked the fiction to recognizable places and people. The pictures thus have some indexical function, pointing the audience toward places in their actual lives. Unlike Chinese woodcuts, however, the political structure that might have made that narrative possible in reality was sorely lacking.

There are a number of striking differences between the pieces Katsuragawa produced for exhibition and the ones he made for Ogōchi: they clearly have different audiences and different logistics in mind. Both *Ogōchi mura* (*Ogōchi Village*) and *Tachinoku hitobito* (*The Evicted*) were painted in 1952 and exhibited in 1953 in Tokyo (plate 9, fig. 6.4). Tokyo was less than a day's journey from Ogōchi but the two works seem to register the significance of the distance between the two locations. Katsuragawa produced these works based on sketches and woodcuts he had made on site. The process of painting involved combining a number of venues and events. *Ogōchi Village,* for instance, includes both a man with an eyepatch, an image Katsuragawa included in his woodcut in the *Weekly Ogōchi* pamphlet, and a man with a chest injury, a figure Bitō Yutaka had used for the cover. But there are some obvious differences in the mode of address. The people in the exhibited works have stopped talking to each other and now face the viewer directly. Individuals are placed front and center and their living spaces are diminished in the background. This difference is particularly striking in the case of the woman and child, who are dwarfed by their house in Katsuragawa's onsite sketch (fig. 6.5). The narrative has also disappeared, and unless the viewer knew the local history in detail, they would have no way of knowing why *The Evicted* are being evicted or why *Ogōchi Village* is behind barbed wire.[8]

A more pervasive difference, however, is how still the exhibited works appear. The inhabitants of *Ogōchi Village* stand as if dumbstruck, and the mother and child do not seem to be doing anything in particular, whereas in the sketch the mother tends a fire while her child demands attention. It

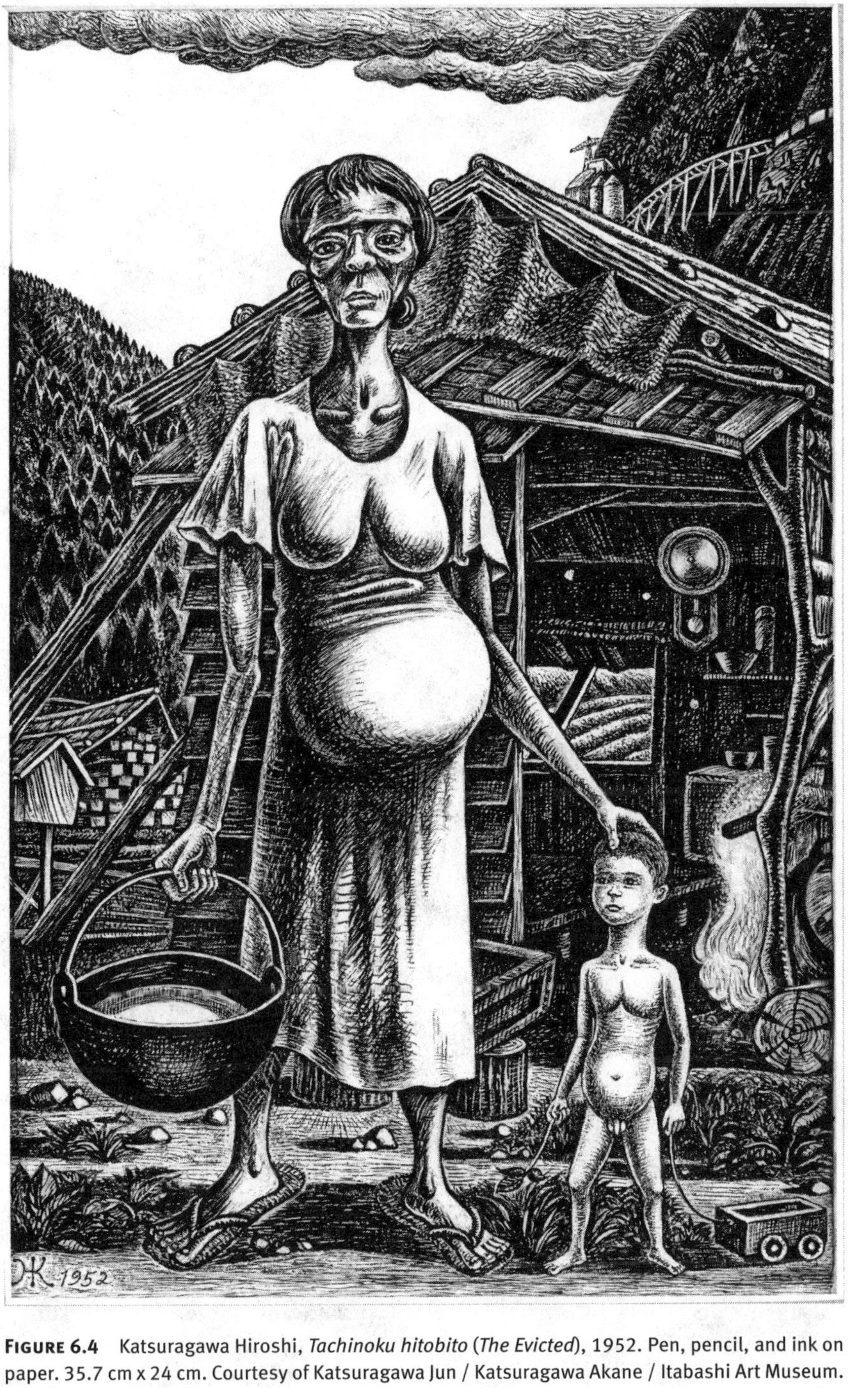

FIGURE 6.4 Katsuragawa Hiroshi, *Tachinoku hitobito* (*The Evicted*), 1952. Pen, pencil, and ink on paper. 35.7 cm x 24 cm. Courtesy of Katsuragawa Jun / Katsuragawa Akane / Itabashi Art Museum.

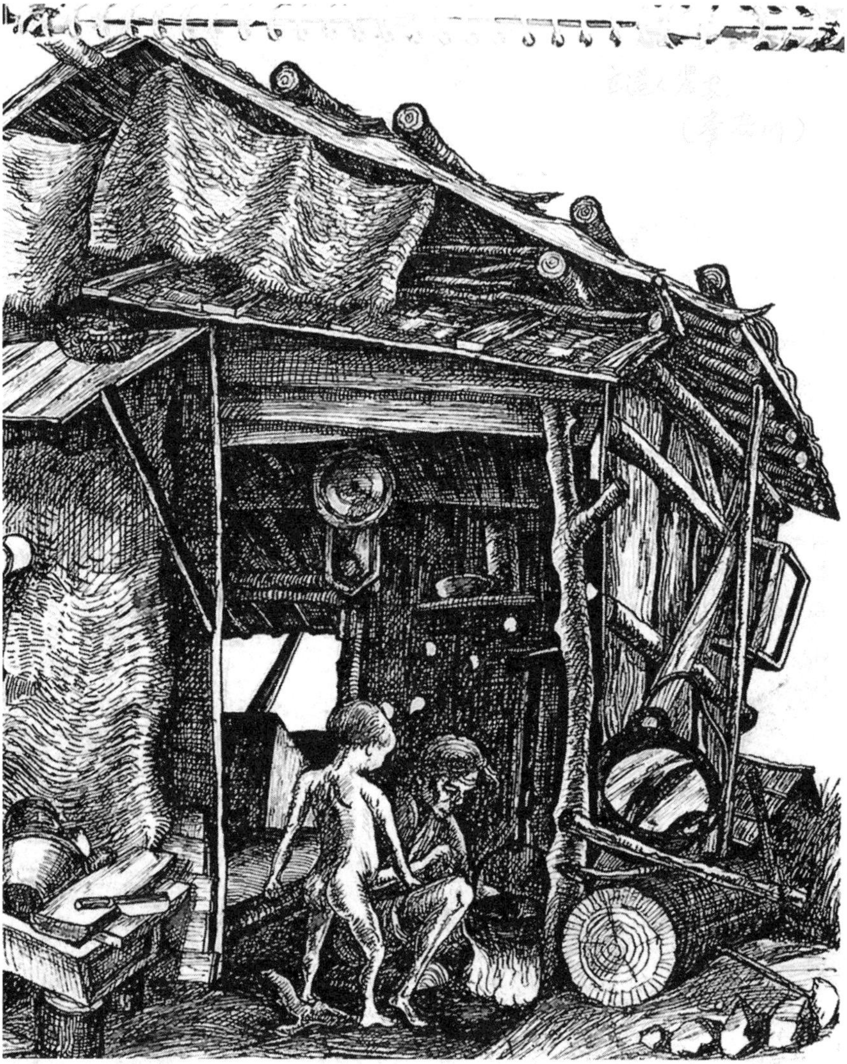

FIGURE 6.5 Katsuragawa Hiroshi, sketch done near Ogōchi Village, 1952. Pencil on paper. Courtesy of Katsuragawa Jun / Katsuragawa Akane.

is as if *all* of the tension and concern the artist hopes to mark and capture is carried in the bodies themselves, whereas in the onsite productions it was shared across the narrative and lived environment. Though the viewer has been put decisively into a relationship with the characters in the painted versions, it seems that the price of that has been to remove those subjects from their context and to render them motionless. This translation suggests to me some of the different interests and expectations running through the works, and I read the pose of eternal waiting as a testament to the limits of exhibition. The eyes looking directly out of the paintings impel the viewer into a relationship of caring, or of interest, or of being implicated. The meeting of gazes might establish a momentary communication or sympathy, but without the surrounding narrative, it is unclear what the viewer could be expected to do with that feeling of connection. The figures risk becoming objects, instead of occasioning new openings in the self or world of the viewer. While the exhibited paintings embody an accumulation of actions that included going to and coming back from the site, laden with equipment and a sense of mission, the actual coordinates of that journey are effaced in the pieces that were produced for exhibition in a gallery, and the artist seems unable to convey a dynamic connection to the site depicted in them.

Katsuragawa's experience introduces us to some of the attempts to find a place for art in creating new networks that would be alternatives to the repetition of war and exploitation. Through *bunka kōsaku,* Katsuragawa participated in a brief though significant exchange with worker-poets and artists in industrial Tokyo. That exchange continued to affect both him, as he continued industrial reportage over the next few years, and the worker circle, which continued to produce collections of poetry and criticism through the 1950s. The Ogōchi project shows, however, that the standard technologies and institutions of art, paintings or sculptures produced for an exhibition, provided a difficult environment for works that aimed to rally audiences to political involvement. And this is true even when they were organized independently of established art institutions. It is with this problematic in mind that I turn to the work of Ikeda Tatsuo.

Ikeda Tatsuo and Media Experiments

Ikeda, who was born on August 15, 1928, was seventeen years old on the day the war ended. Unlike Katsuragawa, his first dream was not to become an artist but to be a teacher. The occupation unfortunately closed this road to him: as a member of the *tokkōtai*, his rank in the military was too high for him to hold any public post immediately after the war. After becoming involved in a small theater group and local culture circles in his home province of Saga on the island of Kyushu, he began to develop an interest in art. He painted his first self-portrait in 1947 and entered Tama Art University in 1948. He dropped out of university just as quickly, after his encounter with the Yoru no Kai in late 1948.

In addition to his self-study and his activities within the network of small groups that were springing up around 1950, Ikeda held a variety of part-time jobs to make ends meet. He worked in a radio repair shop, sold flavored ice from a wooden box slung over his shoulder, painted the graphics for pachinko machines, and painted portraits for American GIs on their way to Korea based on snapshots they carried with them. He had his first experience with the power of mass reproduction while he was working at a commercial design company. One of his designs was used on a margarine container that then appeared in stores around him.[9] A more significant instance of mass reproduction was in 1953, when his work *Amimoto* (*Net Boss*), appeared in print in the Yomiuri newspaper. When Ikeda had gone to the exhibition and saw his small pen drawing hung high up in one corner of a large gallery, he wrote in his diary, "Just like I thought, would've been better off not submitting it."[10] But Abe Kōbō singled it out in a review of the Yomiuri Independent Exhibition as being noteworthy, and the newspaper carried a reproduction alongside the review (fig. 6.6).[11] Abe wrote that the picture had "discovered the face of Japan."[12] These experiences catalyzed Ikeda's interest in the possibilities of mass print media as a platform for reportage.

The *Shimomaruko Poetry Collection* and other collections like it might be thought of as mini-media (*minikomi*). They were read by a relatively small

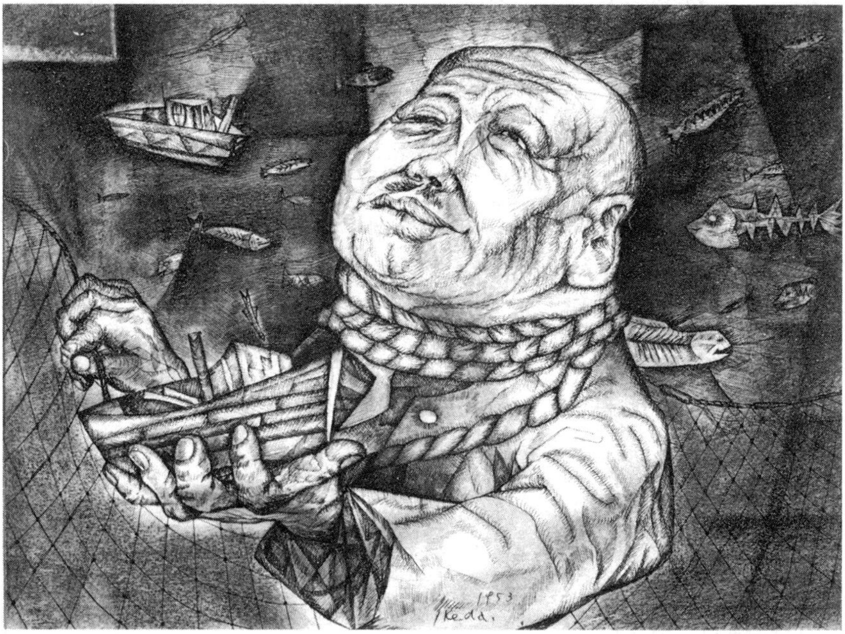

FIGURE 6.6 Ikeda Tatsuo, *Amimoto—Uchinada shiriizu* (*Net Boss: Uchinada Series*), 1953. Pen, ink, and conté crayon on paper. 24.7 cm x 32.2 cm. Courtesy of Ikeda Tatsuo / Museum of Contemporary Art, Tokyo.

group of people, including members of the circle, people in other circles around Tokyo, and various writers and editors of higher circulation publications who sought out poetry from circles. Ikeda, in contrast, was fascinated by the potential of mass media, particularly newspapers, books, and *manga*. During the period from the early 1950s to the early 1960s, Ikeda constantly came back to the question of art's relation to politics, asking the simple and vexing question of how the single artist could change the world. In 1952, he had a chance to see an exhibition of the *Atomic Bomb Panels* when they were on one of their tours. He wrote in his diary, "I could feel the anger and sorrow that drove them to create these paintings, in other words I could feel their humanism. But the problem was with the *paintings*. Are paintings really enough? How can a picture succeed in resisting reality's slide towards war?"[13] These are fundamental questions. Although I argued in the introduction that the *Atomic Bomb Panels* were a whole movement in addition to being paintings, they were in that respect something of an exception. If Abe had not singled out Ikeda's *Net Boss* for the Yomiuri, how visible would that work have been? Against the reproductive powers of the mass media, what chance did a single painting have?

What precipitated an answer for Ikeda was a trip to the Tachikawa air base to prepare a piece for *Jinmin bungaku* (The people's literature), the literary and culture journal of the mainstream faction of the JCP.[14] After this first experience with published reportage, he began to focus much more of his energy on pen drawings.[15] These pieces, therefore, were formative. The Sunagawa Struggle began in earnest in 1955, when the plan to expand the runway came to light. At the time Ikeda went there in the spring of 1953, he was not reporting on the clashes or the sit-ins that Shinkai Kakuo, Mita Genjirō, or Nakamura Hiroshi would later address. Rather, he and his companions—Yamano Takuzō and Fukuda Tsuneta, who were fellow members of the group Enāji, and the poet Sudō Shin'ichi—were investigating how the presence of the base affected life in the town.

The piece depicts how the base created a war zone within Japan—planes take off in the night and head "west, west, west" (toward Korea) or line up on the runway as they await rearmament. It pits residents of the town against each other, threatening farms but providing employment. It corrupts young women, encouraging them to cover their "yellow Japanese faces" with "poison strawberry" rouge. Finally, it pollutes the air and the water: the smell of gasoline greets the narrator as he steps off the train, and the water pulled from wells is so polluted it catches fire. It plays on some of the most familiar tropes used to stir nationalist sentiment: the landscape, the female body, and the future of children. But it does make some effort to point out the complications of colonialism: some people are making a profit by selling gasoline from the wells, the laborers at the base are making a living, and the women of the cabarets and bars are mentioned together with shoeshines, rickshaw pullers, and students forced to be pimps.

The three pictures Ikeda drew all feature children. The first is a little girl peering through barbed wire (fig. 6.7a). Her left eye has been replaced with a U.S. Air Force insignia, her right eye with the silhouette of a plane. The second drawing is of two children playing in the road. The composition is focalized through the gaze of the little girl, who looks up at a serviceman and a (presumably) Japanese woman (fig. 6.7b). The third one seems to be drawn from the perspective of a child looking through the legs of a couple at the multiplying forms of servicemen and Japanese women (fig. 6.7c). Ikeda's three drawings are obsessed by childhood and vision. The simple explanation of course is that children are perennial foci of anxiety as they are both impressionable and a community's future.[16] But the composition implies that the viewer too might be childlike and that education and vision are closely linked.

The second picture presents this mechanism most clearly. While the little girl stares up toward the couple, the frame of the picture limits our own view to the couple's waist. Their posture comes back to us only as a shadow, among the other shadows that blanket the children's world. We can't see the tops of the buildings in the background and are thus trapped in this place, where the girl's gaze and the shadow of the couple keep pulling us around in a circle, a dynamic that might one day pull the girl up and into the "light" where the couple stands. It's interesting to note the boy so fascinated with his toy plane. Will he fly one day? The tension, both visual and symbolic, is generated by the pull of vision. Sight and light not only show, but also impel the viewer, arousing interest in, curiosity about, attention to things already happening in Tachikawa, just beyond the frame of the picture. Even if we choose not to look, the sights will multiply, replicating themselves in our children's eyes. Although the community of voice discussed in relation to Katsuragawa's work is one way for sympathy to propagate, Ikeda's work portrays the physical effects of vision, its involvement in people's bodies and the worlds they make. Images have mass and gravity: they begin to act on bodies before the person is aware of it, and in this sense the person is constantly growing up and out through vision. This is one of the assumptions of visual reportage and is a key to Ikeda's interest in mass media.

Ikeda worked on a few pen and pencil series through the 1950s that had titles such as *Kinjūki shiriizu* (*Beast Chronicle Series*) and *Bakemono no keifu shiriizu* (*Monster Genealogy Series*). The *Monster Genealogy Series* is essentially a series of portraits: each has one humanoid figure that illustrates some aspect of the

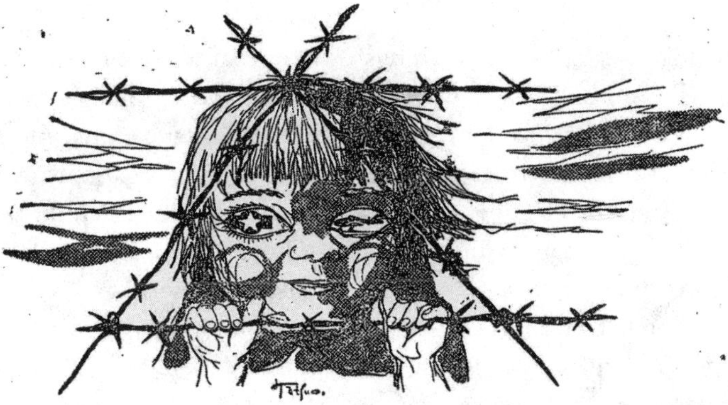

(A)

類行機を
められてい
れ出して立
の下を流れ

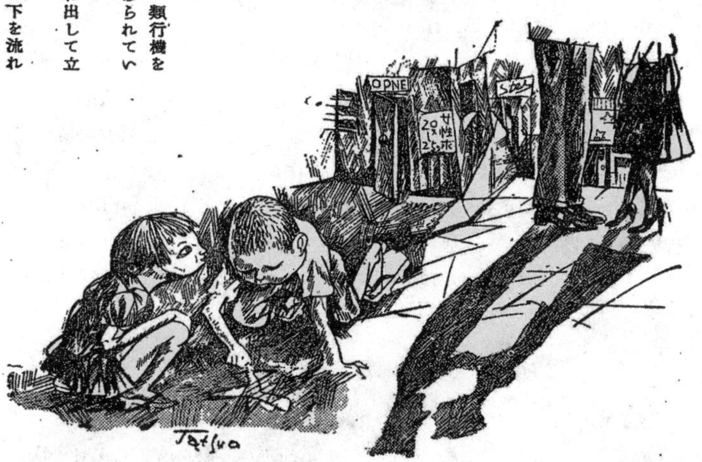

(B)

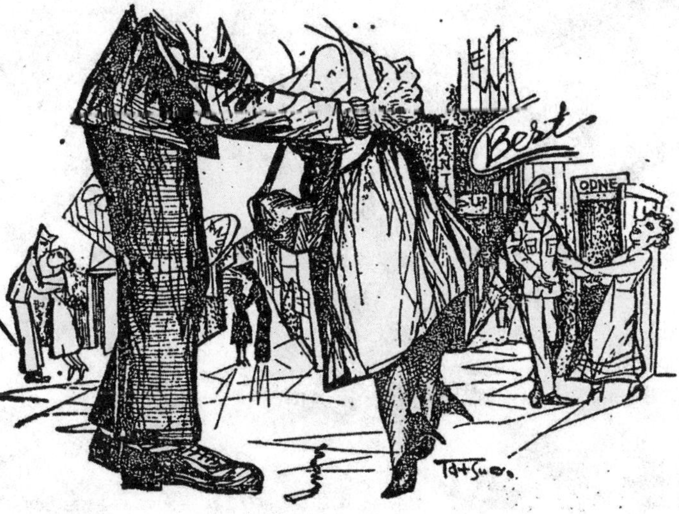

(C)

FIGURES 6.7A, 6.7B, AND 6.7C Ikeda Tatsuo, drawings from "Kichi Tachikawa" (Tachikawa base), collaborative reportage in *Jinmin bungaku* (The people's literature) (July 1953): 46–50.

present. Like *Net Boss*, the drawings rely on caricature to carry their critical message. Although the satire is considerably more ominous than in most newspaper cartoons, these portraits aim for the same jab of insight that political cartoons do. Ikeda's pen work also made these drawings easily transferable to various kinds of printing. The image of netted fish, which Ikeda adapted to a number of contexts, illustrates this. The first appearance of the image is in the ink drawing *10,000 Count* (1954). The title refers to a Geiger counter reading (fig. 6.8) and it was first displayed in a solo show of Ikeda's work at the Takemiya Gallery in 1954. The subject is the *Lucky Dragon* Incident, in which a U.S. hydrogen bomb test showered a fishing vessel (the *Lucky Dragon*) with radioactive fallout, killing one of the fishermen and causing panic about the safety of the food supply. After exhibition, Ikeda's drawing appeared in 1954 on the cover of the first volume of the Testimonies of Japan Reportage Series, on the topic of nuclear power (fig. 6.9).[17] The image pops up again in 1957 in the pages of *Akahata*, the JCP daily broadsheet. There it is part of a serialized story by the prominent reportage author Sugiura Minpei: "Chōkai giin ichinensei" (Freshman on the town council) (fig. 6.10).[18] The replication of the image, from exhibited pen drawing to book cover to newspaper cartoon, shows how versatile and powerful the pen drawing format was for Ikeda.

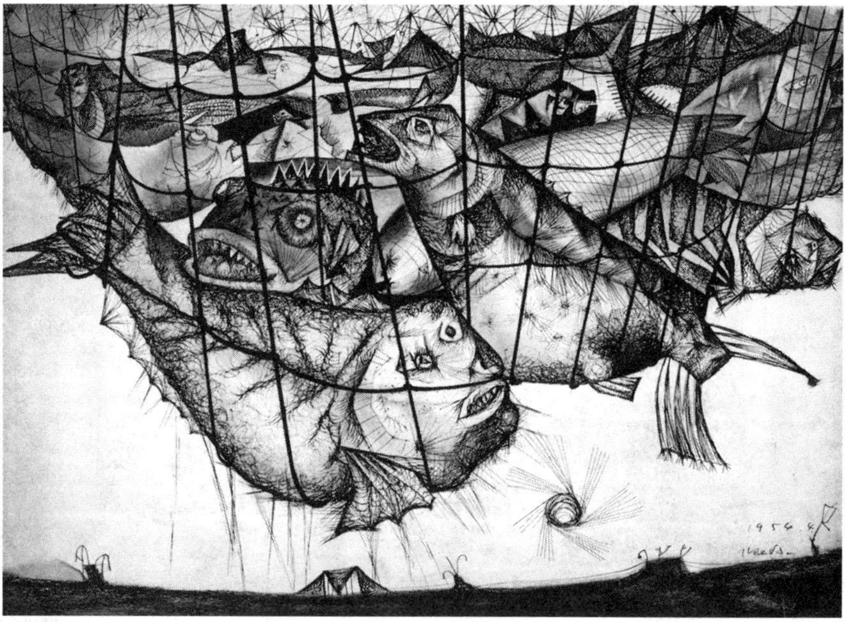

FIGURE 6.8 Ikeda Tatsuo, *10,000 kaunto* (*10,000 Count*), 1954. Pen, ink, and conté crayon on paper. 27.8 cm x 37.3 cm. Courtesy of Ikeda Tatsuo / Museum of Contemporary Art, Tokyo.

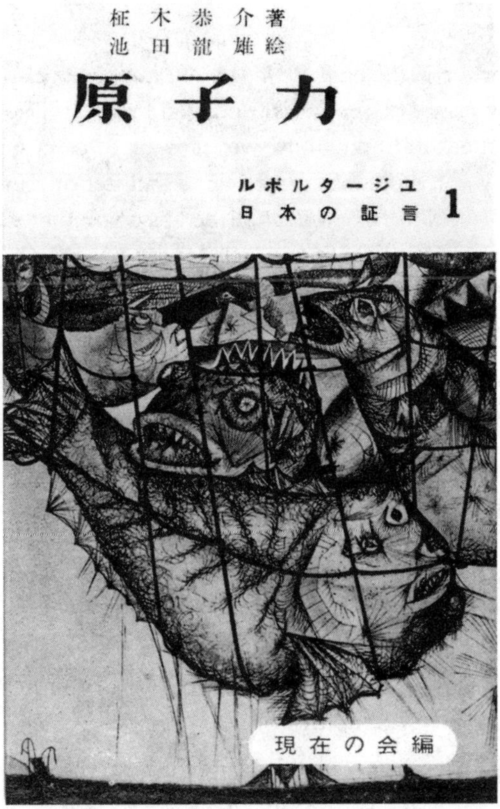

FIGURE 6.9 Ikeda Tatsuo, cover of *Nihon no shōgen: genshiryoku* (Testimonies of Japan: Nuclear power) (Tokyo: Hakurin Shobō, 1955).

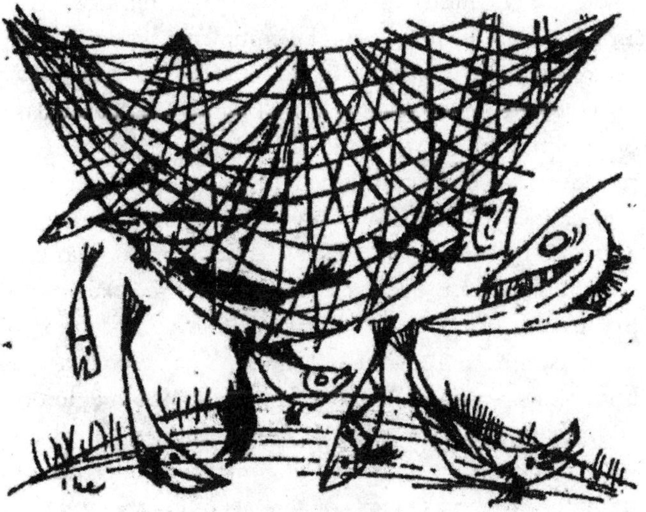

FIGURE 6.10 Ikeda Tatsuo, illustration for "Chōkai giin ichi-nen sei" (Freshman on the town council) by Sugiura Minpei, episode 78, serialized in *Akahata* (1957).

But the cover for *Testimonies of Japan: Nuclear power* also came at a turning point in the nature of the mass produced image in Japan. In addition to being an experiment in finding new ways for art to carry a compelling message, reportage was a mode of correcting the failures of journalism. By 1955, however, when *Nuclear power* was published as a volume of the Testimonies of Japan Reportage Series, there was little for reportage to add to the topic. In 1954, there had been a veritable boom in publications on the topic in the wake of the *Lucky Dragon* Incident—around thirty books had been published.[19] Paper was no longer scarce, and soon a new format, the weekly magazine (*shūkanshi*) emerged and began to dominate popular visual and print culture. Close on its heels was TV. The tide of visual and written information that was building in 1955 eroded one of the primary functions of reportage. It is from within this flood of visual mediation that I consider the work of Nakamura Hiroshi.

Nakamura Hiroshi: Enter the Machine

Nakamura, who was born in 1932, is the youngest of these three artists. His work provides a salient example of one way the reportage aesthetic and ethic changed and developed in the late 1950s and 1960s. He did not begin painting until 1953, and although *Sunagawa No. 5* (1955) has become one of the best-known pieces of reportage painting, his approach to reportage changed not long afterward. In 1951, he came to Tokyo from Shizuoka to study art at Nihon University. Nihon University was not an art school, which meant that Nakamura did not encounter the same academism in postwar art education that Katsuragawa and Ikeda had, and he completed his course of study.[20]

Universities were some of the most politically radicalized sites in Japan. In the early 1950s, members of the Zen'ei Bijutsu Kai, such as Katsuragawa, toured Tokyo campuses speaking about their experiences with *bunka kōsaku*. Nakamura came into contact with the reportage movement at one of these meetings. He joined the first meeting of Seibiren in 1953 and joined the Zen'ei Bijutsu Kai two years later.[21] In keeping with the movement's practice of combining artistic production and activism, Nakamura began to work with a painting circle at the National Railways facility in Shinagawa, a major hub in southern Tokyo. He visited the circle once a week to teach basic painting skills. Unlike Katsuragawa's experience in Shimomaruko, the union-based circle he worked with was not expressly political and remained mostly focused on painting.[22] What Nakamura got in return was access to people's working lives and to parts of the facility that were not open to the public. These experiences formed the basis for his first reportage canvases, one of which is *Kokutetsu Shinagawa* (*JNR* [Japanese National Railways] *Shinagawa*) (1955) (plate 10).

Although spare, this painting demonstrates great skill for such a young artist and a sense for dramatic composition that characterizes most of Nakamura's subsequent work. The draftsmanship around the edges of the picture is smudged, while the middle portion of the train has more detail and more clarity of line. This is also the spot where the worker is looking, mimicking the focal point of an eye's visual field. If we take foreground to mean the part of the painting with greatest visual immediacy, then the foreground here is created by the worker and the middle portion of the train, while the rest fades into background. Cinematic framing cuts the worker at the waist and the pole he is carrying at the top, and the torsion of the body indicates he is walking. Together these create a dramatic snapshot of motion: the moment of a glance that establishes an axis of visual articulation. Although the subject of the painting is a train and a rail worker, the motif is something about the operation of vision.

Nakamura's interest in vision continued to develop, as did his self-consciousness about the canvas as a tool of mediation: a "machine," as he would later call it. In 1979, a quarter-century after *JNR Shinagawa*, Nakamura painted *Shasōhen TYPE 7 (Kyabin)* (*Window Scenery Type 7 [Cabin]*) (fig. 6.11). Much has changed in the composition, but some points of commonality remain: as in *JNR Shinagawa*, the viewer of the painting encounters the back of someone's head looking at something inside the painting. The doubling of the viewer's act of looking is subtle in *JNR Shinagawa*, but in *Window Scenery Type 7 (Cabin)* it is heavily emphasized. The window frame doubles the picture frame and the viewer joins the receding line of floating schoolgirls, looking for something inside the rectangle. Nakamura uses a reticulated composition to create an inversion of perspective: the distant "outside" of outer space, which all our gazes are oriented toward, become the depths of the canvas's "inside." This self-consciousness about vision and the institution of the canvas is a trajectory Nakamura was already embarking on in the second half of the 1950s.

His turn in the late 1950s is emblematic of a number of changes under way at that time. Generally speaking, artwork began to move away from reportage as it had been practiced in the first half of the 1950s. A quick glance at the later work of the artists I have discussed shows that socially concerned figurative painting and drawing continued but was tied less and less to the practice of visiting a specific site. Namiko Kunimoto has argued that Nakamura's 1957 work *Shasatsu* (*Gunned Down*) marks his turn away from the site (*genba*) as a ground for meaning.[23] The shift away from the site

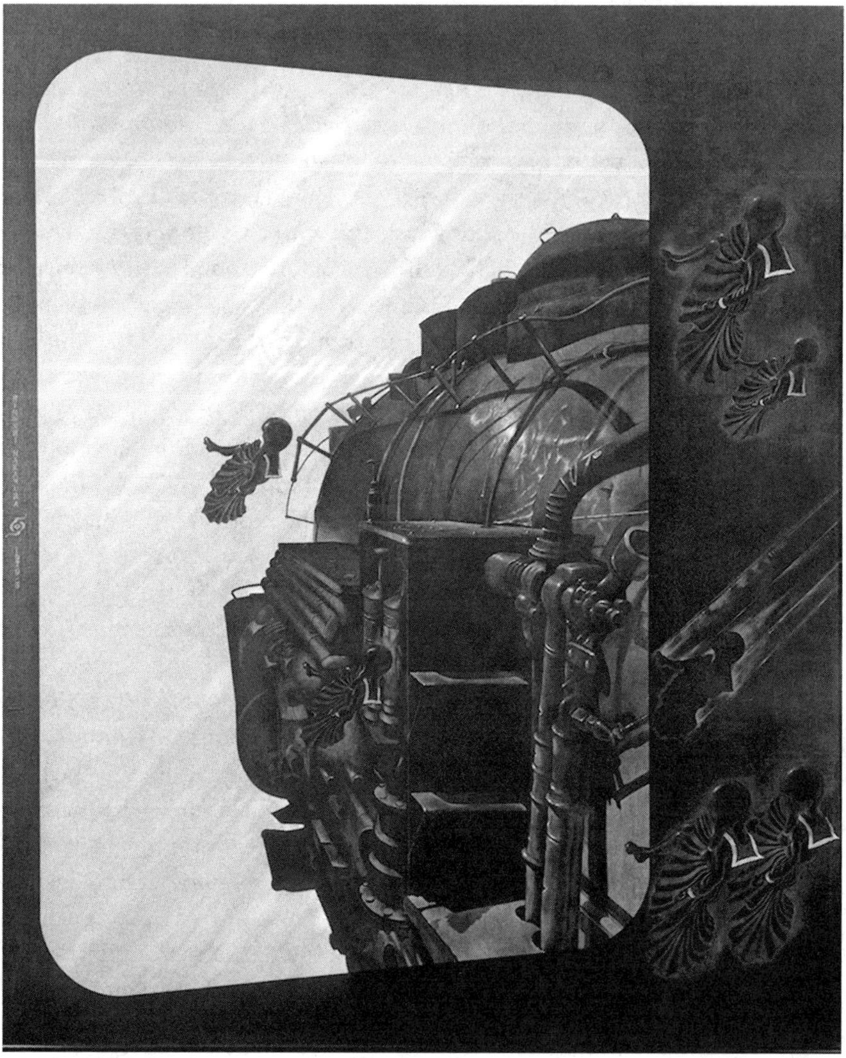

Figure 6.11 Nakamura Hiroshi, *Shasōhen TYPE 7 (Kyabin)* (*Window Scenery Type 7 [Cabin]*), 1979. Oil on canvas. 162 cm x 130 cm. Courtesy of Nakamura Hiroshi / Hamamatsu Municipal Museum of Art.

and the practice of going to it entailed a major change in the conceptualization of realist and documentary practice. Research was central to reportage. First, the transgression of boundaries of geography, class, and expertise was something that enabled learning and exchange between artists and amateurs. As visits to sites decreased, this mode of creating networks and associations faltered. In theory as well, joining the struggle was thought of as the basis for reciprocal transformation of self and world. As Hariu and Hanada theorized, artists had to put themselves fully within the scene in order to break the obfuscating structures springing up both inside and outside. In Hariu's words, this practice enabled the artist to "thoroughly demolish his everyday self."[24] Movement, therefore, was part of the project of defamiliarization.

But a number of forces drove the avant-garde realists away from this conceptualization of documentary. First was a shift that was taking place in the way documentary was conceived in relation to popular culture and the everyday. Recent studies of documentary in Japan highlight a split that appeared in the latter half of the 1950s as artists and theorists moved away from the idea of documentary serving to establish connection, toward greater insistence that it serve as a tool of estrangement from everyday values.[25] This split was already nascent in the theorization of avant-garde realism: in Katsuragawa's idea that the territory of the human should not be protected as a "non-aggression zone" and Abe Kōbō's vision of cutting into the surface of everyday reality as with a scalpel. Writing slightly later, in 1957, Sasaki Ki'ichi escalated this rhetoric, arguing that the documentary spirit needed to be "barbaric" and "destructive."[26] A number of sources propelled this change in how avant-garde realists theorized their art. First, as argued in chapter 4, the downfall of the JCP as a legitimate voice on questions of culture vindicated and amplified the ideas of the avant-garde realists: aggressive, pitiless pursuit of the dark forces at work on the inside as much as the outside was painful and disturbing but increasingly necessary in order to escape the failure of subjectivity that was so evident in the older generation of realist. Second was the continuing rude health of popular self-writing practices. Such movements experienced their peak in the mid-1950s, and by that time many of the intellectuals and artists who had at first engaged with such movements were becoming more critical of them. An undertheorized (though accessible) ideology of writing things "as they are" (*aru no mama*) had come to pervade this type of writing. Margaret S. Key has shown how Abe Kōbō, for instance, was increasingly concerned that the practice of recording daily life reinforced the idea that truth was basically manifest. In response, he reconceived his documentary practice to problematize the correspondence between representation and reality.[27]

Last was the increased prosperity and apparent stability of daily life. The explosion of visual media in the late 1950s, which tended to reinforce a vision of peace and plenitude, changed the site of struggle. Ishii Shigeo—an artist whose work captures a sense of generalized unease—wrote in 1957 that he believed the victimizer and the victim, the dominator and the dominated might not be as separate and easy to recognize as recent realist painting tended to portray them (as in figures of police or the downtrodden). The task for contemporary artists was not to "direct our eyes only to localized incidents . . . but to discover and give form to the uncanny [*hinichijōteki*] world that lurks within the everyday world."[28] Ishii's words signal a spatial distribution and visualization of political struggle that took on the main features of avant-garde realism but discarded the idea that certain sites were privileged condensations of politics. The sinister forces that pulled the individual and society inexorably toward war were to be discovered not in clashes between easily identifiable groups but within the context of everyday life, where they worked in ways and through agents that were more obscure and pervasive. William Marotti has shown how the Neo-Dada artists and Akasegawa Genpei grappled with this challenge in the 1960s.[29]

Nakamura's work responded to this challenge while remaining in many ways true to the aesthetics of avant-garde realism. In the late 1950s, when Nakamura rejected the call to engage in self-criticism for work carried out during the JCP split, he used the battle cry, "the tableau does not perform self-criticism."[30] This was in part a fiery rejection of the JCP's demands. Through it, Nakamura developed a particular concept of "tableau' (*taburō*) that continued to evolve along with his paintings. For Nakamura, the tableau stood for a space that "rejects any direct political efficacy in art" and was free from any need for political self-criticism. It was also primarily concerned with "beginning to problematize its own surface." Rather than seeing the canvas as a conduit, Nakamura saw the canvas itself as the focal point that received ontological priority. "The tableau has become the avant-garde."[31]

The elevation of art and the assertion of its independence from political movements is a common feature of the discourse of the post-1955 break with the JCP. But this did not entail a rejection of politics. Nakamura's work up to the present can be viewed as a form of reportage. His paintings remain topical: they address the 1960 Anpo protests, lampoon the 1964 Olympics, and most recently use the iconic star from the American flag and the crescent moon of Islam in paintings and photomontage. But more fundamentally, Nakamura turned his critical eye upon vision itself. Instead of trying to inhabit vision as a committed participant (like William Tell) or to legitimate vision through proper placement and orientation, Nakamura became concerned with vision as the very thing that needed to be made visible. Although vision was still primitively powerful, it was increasingly colonized by consumerism and mass media. Nakamura's painting in the 1960s took particular interest in tourism, a practice that robbed travel of difference. In tourism, visibility signaled availability, a process that made the site less compelling as a place of destabilizing transformation. *Enkan ressha A—bōenkyō ressha* (*Circular Train A: Telescope Train*) (1968) alludes to the solipsism of tourism (plate 11). A train carriage filled with female students on a school trip bends around on itself, implying travel is nothing but a mechanism of repetition that keeps the subject at the center no matter how far he or she may move. The site for contestation thus became vision itself, as it operated within and was operated upon by mass mediated visual culture.

Nakamura was aware of painting's potential complicity in mass media's colonization of vision. In the late 1960s and 1970s he developed the idea of the "tableau machine" (*taburō kikai*), a concept that foregrounds the way the painted surface manufactures visual interest and instigates a process of attraction that pulls the viewer to it. We can see in a photograph how the work *Jogakusei ni kan suru geijutsu to kokka no shomondai* (*Problems of Art and Nation as They Relate to Schoolgirls*) (1967) multiplies the act of looking (plate 12). We see a reproduction of a photograph of a mannequin dressed as a schoolgirl, who is looking through binoculars at a painted lens over a painting of Mt. Fuji. The arrangement makes it impossible to think of the canvas as an expanse simply made available before us: the reticulation establishes the viewer as being the last iteration of a multi-layered biomechnical mechanism of looking and focusing. The viewer is part of the machine, not master of it, just like the schoolgirl/mannequin. It is no accident that the image being viewed is Mount Fuji, a loaded symbol of nation and empire that is also ubiquitous on stationary and bathhouse walls. Tableau machines are extensions of capitalism, nation, and war. But the basic fuel of the machine is eroticism. The snow that the lens enlarges on Fuji's peak is molded to suggest a creamy, gooey fluid, and the round tip of a military plane is just poking into the magnified area above it. Most surfaces in Nakamura's works from the 1960s appear sexualized: in addition to the focused sexualization of the figure of the schoolgirl, his works flaunt a pervasive but unfocused erotic charge in their lush coloration, taut shiny surfaces, and suggestive curls and ridges.

Nakamura's vision of vision as something that pulls people into the thrall of the nation and the operations of commercial culture might seem to be the ultimate repudiation of the idea that art could serve as a conduit for some understanding of or emotional transfer between two entities that are assumed to be far apart and in need of bringing together. Looking, for Nakamura, always makes the subject vulnerable to machines of mediation fueled by erotic forces which, within the operation of commercial enterprise such as tourism become oriented toward self-satisfaction. Although the self-satisfying loop of vision may be antithetical to the practice of reportage, Nakamura's belief in vision's power to transfix is not at odds with the theory of avant-garde realism. Just as William Tell stands transfixed by the apple, the schoolgirl in *Problems of Art and Nation* stands transfixed before the image of the image of the image of the image of Mount Fuji. The difference is not about vision's role in establishing the mutual implication of the historical moment and the body. Embodiment remains central. What has changed is what is being looked at and, more broadly, the *dispositif* of viewing. Instead of focusing an inescapable moment of transformation toward an unknown future as the apple did for William Tell, Mt. Fuji pulls vision into a system that integrates desires into a larger complex of social machinery that promises no change. Vision, even in the form of travel, now flatters the ever-central subject instead of destabilizing it. It works to extend the biomechanical machines whose system offers no hope of transformation. Nakamura was in the position of having to illustrate this process of entrapment, but to do so visually, by implicating the viewers themselves in the extension of the tableau machine.

Survivals

Reportage was never a monolithic movement, and the three artists examined in this chapter exemplify three different paths. For Katsuragawa, reportage was one part of an activist project that included mobilization, education, and collaborative production across class lines. Katsuragawa's art work was in dialogue with this social work. However, there was an intractable gap between his "on location" works and the ones he prepared for exhibitions. Although the dream of the *bunka kōsaku* project was to share knowledge and empower diverse actors, the institution of art was not able to realize that dream for its audience. In the end, the reportage artists had limited success in making their art of or for the people they tried to work with. Katsuragawa's rate of production fell in the late 1950s and remained low thereafter.

Although Ikeda was also an activist, he gradually moved away from long-term engagements with local people. He placed more hope in the potential of pen and pencil drawings and their reproducibility. Alternative publishing was a crucial element of reportage for writers and for artists. Working with elements of surrealist deformation and caricature, Ikeda produced series of single legible images to crystallize a complex of problematic social relations. But the end of censorship and the growth in popular print media over the 1950s undermined hopes that even that strategy could be effective. Following the failure of the Anpo demonstrations in 1960 and the continuing rise of mass culture, Ikeda became disenchanted with politics. He has remained a productive illustrator and painter, but his art did not continue to aim toward specific activism.

Finally, Nakamura's path as an artist began in the maelstrom of the mid-1950s. Soon after he began painting reportage works, the JCP renounced armed struggle and reunited, although Nakamura and other artists took that as a demonstration of the JCP's intellectual and moral weakness. By 1960—when Yoshimoto Takaaki wrote his essay declaring the "end of fictions"—the party no longer had any credibility as a cultural or political vanguard. Young radicals struck out on their own during this period, but in doing so many rejected not only the JCP but also any suggestion that art could or should be linked to an organized political movement or a mass movement. As artists ceased to go to sites of struggle, they had less contact across class and geography. As their aesthetic became more confrontational, they moved away from popular documentary practices and stopped working with amateur artists. Collaborations such as the *Shimomaruko Poetry Collection* became much more difficult.

These are the reasons why many mark an end to reportage in the late 1950s: the stubbornness of the institution of art, the rise of mass image and print culture, and the implosion of the JCP as a legitimate cultural force. But I would like to end with some suggestions about ways avant-garde realism and the project of reportage resonates with some of the art and film of the 1960s. These comments are speculative, suggesting possibilities to be investigated further. One continuity is in political prints and pen and pencil drawings. Grotesque caricature was a mainstay of political artistry, from reportage art to Akasegawa Genpei's work in the late 1960s. In Nakamura's work, a more specific observation can be made, that repetition—both graphic and thematic—takes on a particular tenor and set of associations. Around 1960, graphic repetition emerges as a major feature of his painting practice. The line of urinals that feature in many subsequent works appear in a painting for the first time in *Kaidan nite* (*On the Steps*) (1959/1960) (plate 13). The painting demonstrates how repetition establishes structure and serves the basic mechanics of figuration—in the black and white alternation that forms the columns and stairs in the background, for instance. Subsequently, the urinal, the man with glasses, viscous fluids, and of course the schoolgirl would join the train as figures that proliferate conspicuously across multiple works. It was also around 1960 that Nakamura began to make prints, often for publication covers and event posters. This practice kept him connected with underground and radical political cultures through the 1960s. The prints repeat elements of his paintings and the high contrast of the painting technique lent itself to the print form, as seen in the cover to a small book that assessed the fateful storming of the Diet on June 15, 1960 (fig. 6.12).[32]

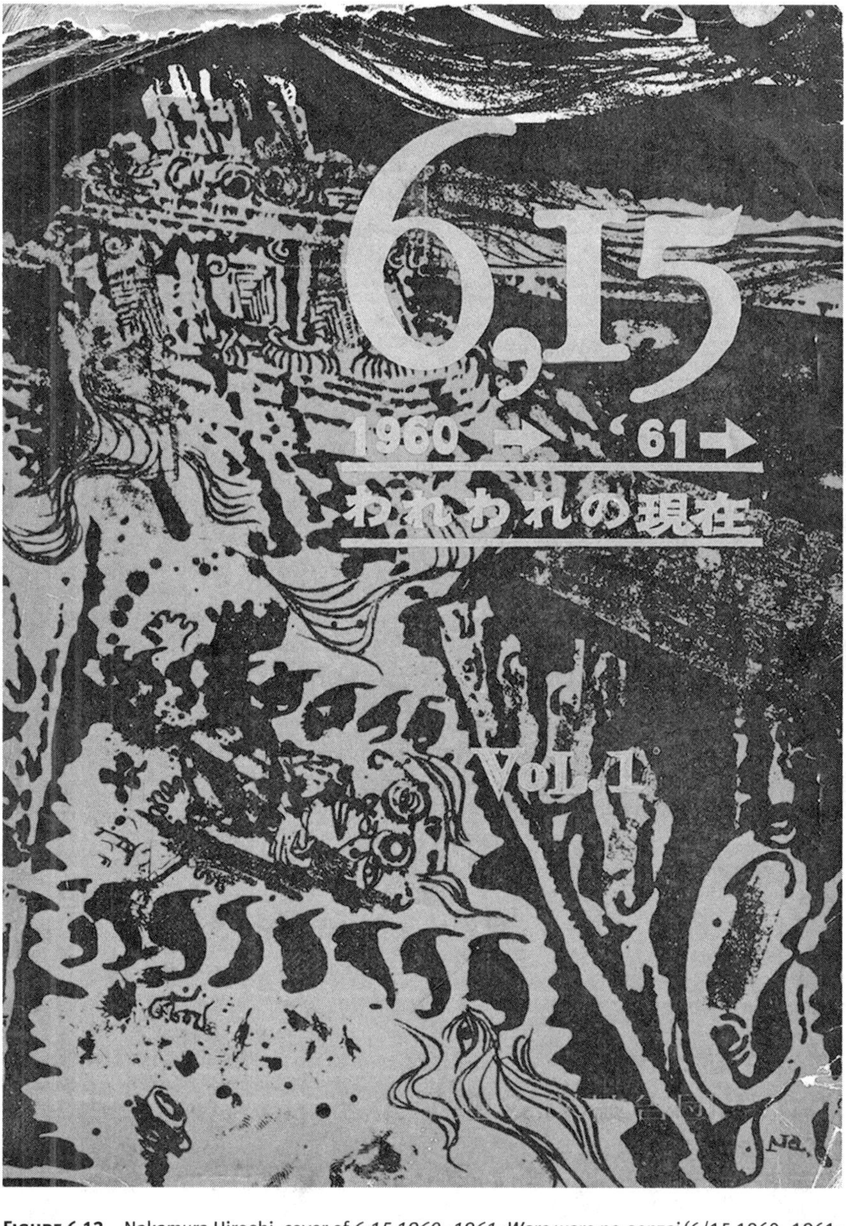

FIGURE 6.12 Nakamura Hiroshi, cover of *6,15 1960–1961: Ware ware no genzai* (6/15 1960–1961: Our present) (Tokyo: Zengakuren Anpo Hikokudan, 1961).

Thematically, Nakamura links repetition to history, particularly to empire and militarism. The idea that debased repetition lay just beneath the surface of increasingly prosperous postwar society was a central tenet of avant-garde realism. It is found as early as Yamashita's *The Tale of Akebono Village* in 1953 and appears explicitly in the work of Nakamura (and many others) in the 1960s. The parallels that artists and critics drew between the war and the World Expo in 1970 were therefore variations on a trope that had already been evolving for two decades. In addition to the thematic continuity between the 1950s and 1960s, it is interesting that graphic repetition also tends to take on a gothic aspect in the work of Yokoo Tadanori and Awazu Kiyoshi, for instance. In Nakamura's work, as in theirs, repetition is sinister. The schoolgirls who appear in his works are vacant and increasingly disfigured, the clouds and plant life are threatening. Repetition implies the malicious heteronomy of a doppelganger or parasite. The focalization is not from the perspective of a master of puppets or a carefree automaton savant but from that of the degraded subject: the doubled "original" that has been left behind or hollowed out as the now defective, lesser copy.

A related theme is the linked symbolism of sexuality and domination. This is important to Nakamura's work, as it was for many (generally male) creators of the 1960s. Sexual transgression, often in the form of violence, was a major part of 1960s underground culture. Steven Clark has suggested that "the conspicuous amount of attention paid to the relationship between sex and violence in the late 1960s might best be understood as an attempt to expose the erotics of war as a first step to desconstructing that relationship." But he then goes on to argue that "sadistic narratives failed in the greater project of decoupling sex from violence and, in fact, may have served to further concretize and naturalize that association."[33]

Although Nakamura is adept at creating moments where viewers might realize their own role in replicating the mechanism of looking, the eroticization in his works, particularly of schoolgirls, runs the risk of repeating the mechanism rather than making it visible. His works still play upon attraction and repulsion and are interested in showing how vision pulls the subject out of themselves and attaches them to the outside world—a mechanism that Hariu Ichiro among others claimed underwrote the value of reportage practice and gave paintings power in the world as "things." But in the theory of avant-garde realism, the transfer between inside and outside was unpredictable. It was shocking and painful, it was a moment of change, quite unlike the gratification promised by the solicitations of consumer culture. In the practice of reportage, moving to the location of struggle and throwing oneself into it was key to the practice of (self-)transformation. Against the background of realisms that had failed to motivate the inside and modernisms that had withdrawn from the outside, this theory and the activism it was tied to emphasized embodied location and movement as a way to bring the inside into contact with the outside in new ways. But as the social movement fell away the structures of violence that were taken to be lurking on the inside began to lose any worldly attachment beyond their channeling into the bio-mechanical machinery of the national consumer economy. With this, war came to be on the inside, and the only way to address it was by purge or parody, which became endless repetitions of their own.

Part Three

Opening Open Doors

Sōbi and Hani Susumu

CHAPTER 7

Touching Down at the Sōbi Seminar

As they disembarked from their trains, Sōbi members who had arrived for the group's summer seminar in the mountain resort region of Nagano knew immediately that they were in the right place. A corps of volunteer fellow members had been waiting at the station since morning, holding welcome banners and wearing matching red porter's caps to symbolize their "willingness to help" (*sābisu ishiki*). Brimming with enthusiasm—occasionally bursting into song—they greeted each new arrival with a handshake and insisted on helping them with their bags. Hot spring resort towns were used to accommodating large groups, but there was something special about Sōbi.[1] Perhaps it was the members' smiles and bright eyes, their outgoing talkativeness, or their habit of shaking hands instead of bowing, but something about the Sōbi seminar seemed to alter the atmosphere of its venue. The spectacle attracted puzzled newspaper coverage, one *Asahi* report declaring that it was as if "a small independent country of unknown origin had sprung up." Sōbi members were equally apt to emphasize the group's deviation from the norm. As one member enthused, it was like "an Independent Nation, just touched down from the planet Mars."[2]

The annual summer seminar was a meeting of teachers, almost all of whom worked in Japan's public schools, most in rural areas. They came to the seminar to pursue their interest in the philosophy and pedagogy that the Sōzō Biiku Kyōkai (Society for Creative Aesthetic Education, Sōbi for short) had been championing since the early 1950s.[3] The pedagogy rested on a deep faith in the natural virtue of the individual and in the idea that each child was central to their own education. They were part of a tradition that ran from romantics such as Rousseau through early twentieth-century progressive modernists such as Dewey, to the figures most proximate to Sōbi: Franz Cižek, Homer Lane, A. S. Neill, and Herbert Read. Within these traditions, self-determination and self-actualization were the keys to personal and social emancipation. But such things could only emerge out of an individual's creative engagement with the world. Growth was ultimately "a part of the cosmic process,"[4] and the aesthetic (as opposed to the rational) was what allowed insight into that virtuous correspondence, in the form of fleeting intuitions of balance, fit, and rhythm. For many in Sōbi, aesthetic education was not just one subject among others, it was the model for *all* learning, a pedagogy that would free children to develop according to their own immanent creativity, even when that implied messiness, disobedience, and danger. At its extremity, Sōbi advocated complete noncoercion, which would resolve the distinction between work and play, natural growth and creativity, and promised to ameliorate the rationalist repressions that lay at the root of so many modern social ills, particularly violence and war.

We therefore begin with a certain exoticism and eccentricity, acknowledged—even flaunted—at the time, but possibly magnified as we look back through the lens of established historical assumptions. Not without reason the decade or so after 1945 calls forth images of suffering and trauma against which Sōbi's relentless optimism and progressivism seem unlikely: an exotic island among the dark tides of debilitating loss and embittered political struggle. But Sōbi was not exactly minor and was not as isolated as that metaphor suggests. It was one of the largest of many postwar nongovernmental education movements and certainly the largest in the field of art education, reaching a peak membership of 2,360 in 1956. Sōbi also became something of a cultural phenomenon in the mid-1950s as the subject of Kaikō Takeshi's semi-fictional *Hadaka no ōsama* (The emperor's new clothes), which won the Akutagawa Prize in 1957, and Hani Susumu's documentary film *E o kaku kodomotachi* (Children who draw), which I discuss in detail in chapter 10. Finally, Sōbi can be seen as one of a number of late-flowering progressive modernisms. Ming Tiampo has shown how Yoshihara Jiro's unconditional faith in internationalism and individual originality animated early Gutai. InSEA (the International Society for Education through Art), formed by UNESCO in the early 1950s under the guidance of Herbert Read, espoused the hope that "the right of man 'freely to participate in the cultural life of the community . . .' and to create beauty for himself in reciprocal relationship with his environment, would become a living reality."[5] Though this hope was framed with a startling optimism, such convictions and the movements to establish them as a social reality were equally born of the lessons of fascism and war.

Sōbi's clearest enemy was the authoritarianism of prewar and wartime pedagogy, which leaders of the movement saw surviving in the postwar. More broadly, the authoritarianism and violence demonstrated in the 1930s and 1940s were but the most concrete examples of a more fundamental problem in modern, adult, civilized society. Built on division, repression, and an overdevelopment of reason, modern society had lost its balance. Schools played their role in enforcing the imbalance, as they beat and intimidated the natural creativity of children into efficiency. An early and much-cited essay by Kubo Sadajirō, Sōbi's founder and leader, ended with the claim—particularly provocative in 1949—that the source of the "unhappiness of twenty million" Japanese children was not material deprivation but psychological repression.[6] Delinquency, neurosis, and war were the inevitable results of the cycle of repression that was needed to maintain modern social order, and that cycle, Kubo asserted, was alive and well in the postwar.

Sōbi's mission was to break the invisible bars of that prison. And although one might say that investing in children as figures for liberated existence was a displaced rejection of modern capitalist society, Sōbi actually applied and to an extent realized their ideas by establishing and defending a space for responsive teaching and for noncoerced human relationships more generally. The Sōbi teacher stepped down from the head of the class to stand "on the side of the child," in the phrase made famous by A. S. Neill.[7] Their work did not stop with the classroom, but committed them to a decentralized administrative environment where pedagogical experiment was possible; the administrator had to make room for developments emerging from the bottom up. Sōbi's intellectual commitments involved practice: its members experimented with new modes for actual human relationship, first and foremost in the classroom and school, but also as a movement that would embody the same respect for engagement and creativity that they espoused for the classroom.[8]

The annual summer seminars provide a good example of the ethics that Sōbi's ideas entailed. The topics of lectures and study groups were various. Many addressed classroom practice: how to *teach* with such a child-centered pedagogy. Punishment and direct instruction were discouraged, but then how could the teacher motivate students? Other groups studied how to evaluate artwork. As an index of a child's creative growth, artwork provided vital information, but analyzing it was devilishly case specific. Yet others tackled the question of why children abandoned art at puberty and how Sōbi ideals could challenge or at least survive social differentiation. At the 1956 seminar, the keynote speaker highlighted the importance of dialog between teacher and student. The teacher could no longer impart instructions deemed necessary in the outside world. The children were already *in* the outside world, and it was already real time. In real time, small encouragements, openness, humor, and improvisation were the things the teacher could use to generate a "creative atmosphere" in class. The teacher, therefore, had to be something of an artist themselves. "The teacher is one who, as a creator themselves, finds those moments of communion with their students' hearts that flare like fireworks between them."[9]

The Sōbi seminar gives us some hints as to what this "creative atmosphere" was like. From the moment the red-capped volunteers met the new arrivals at the station, the participants lived in a social environment of their own creation, full of energy, play, and mutual support. The "seminarians" (*seminaryan*), as they sometimes called each other, shared their sleeping quarters, and after the day's lectures and activities, conversations went deep into the night. "There were always some companions to be found in the cafeteria . . . chatting until late at night, as from a cocktail, the pulse of friendship flowed out in beautiful electric waves."[10] Humor also abounded. Groups from different prefectures introduced themselves as the "Aichi romantic group," the "Fukui mambo mania," and the "Hyōgo loony buffoons" (*ikarebonchi*) in the newsletter that circulated at the gathering.[11] No one was required to go to any of the events: teachers played hooky, even slept in class. In this atmosphere, learning and work took on new qualities. One member of the volunteer corps recalled, "Work itself had joy and value. So there was no reason to cut out and steal breaks. . . . Very similar to how a child's artwork is a child's life, and not a form of leisure or flight from reality."[12] These observations echo those made by Herbert Read about the work of a craftsman: absorbed body and soul in his creation, there is no such thing as leisure, "only rest and freedom."[13] As something shared, the "creative atmosphere" was not expressing a desired future but enacting a way of relating in the present, one that would continually call itself into being as long as people participated.

Though the effects of Sōbi's efforts are difficult to see in the present day, their experiments in reforming how classrooms and schools were organized flourished in the decentralized administrative environment that existed prior to the education reforms of the late 1950s. Sōbi was a grassroots movement, comprised at its base by local study groups of teachers who gathered to discuss their teaching and ideas. But when the reforms of the late 1950s set the stage for a recentralization of the school system under the Ministry of Education, the space to apply their ideas in the classroom began to narrow, as did the horizon of what was possible. For that very reason it is important for Sōbi to find a place in postwar history as an example of what was possible: an anti-conservative, noncommunist, grassroots movement fired by modernist idealism.

Sōbi's ideas were not entirely unique to Sōbi. Children's art has long been a point of interest for modern artists, and art education was a productive endeavor for many artists in the early postwar years. Gutai is one such case: the group's early activities drew from and contributed to a similarly expressive and emancipative education movement in the Kansai area centered on the journal *Kirin* (Giraffe).[14] The artists closest to Sōbi were those of the Asocio de Artistos Demokrato (Association of Democratic Artists), as well as Ay-O and Takako Saitō, who would later join Fluxus. I do not have the space to treat these artists' organizational and artistic work as fully as it deserves. But I discuss them briefly in closing because their work indicates how a shared principle of uncoerced futures might be found in daily life, both in our relations with others and with art.

The artist whose work I consider most closely is filmmaker Hani Susumu. Hani had a long relationship with Sōbi, although he was never a member or a teacher. He spent his own student years at Jiyū Gakuen (Freedom Academy), a progressive school founded by his grandmother Hani Motoko. He was thus part of a lineage of Japanese progressivism that managed to survive through the war. Many of his early films, both fiction and documentary, take an interest in children, and one of them, *E o kaku kodomotachi* (Children who draw, 1956), was filmed in a working Sōbi classroom. But the connections go deeper than this. If, in the classroom, Sōbi teachers put themselves on the side of the child, letting their own active growth become the driving force of education, Hani's film practice sought to let the unedited documentary image become the structuring force of his films. Both child-centered education and film are profoundly concerned with how to understand change in real time: if the child shows us change unfolding in a uniquely embodied, specific entity, so does film. And just as Sōbi pedagogy put great emphasis on respecting the sanctity of each child, on insisting above all else, that children be granted *their own future*, Hani's films also insist that the reality documented on film be granted its own future, as something unfolding for itself in its own time. Both sought to steward the new as it came into the world and to protect the sanctity of its unpredictability.

It is in this shared commitment to the principle that each person's individual experience is sacrosanct and that social organization and representation must find a way to delineate and protect a space for the full playing out of that experience in time that I see the connection between Hani's films and the Sōbi movement. The common thread running through their work is the attempt to represent and realize in society the principle that each person has a legitimate experience of the present and a future of their own.

Chapter 8

Sōbi as Organization and Movement

The Sōzō Biiku Kyōkai was founded on March 2, 1952, and continues to the present day. Sōbi's own timelines, however, always put the beginning of the movement in 1936. These two beginnings provide rough markers to two phases of Sōbi. In the first phase, a small, elite group of artists and intellectuals pursued an interest in children's art through public exhibitions and study groups. In the second phase, which began around 1950, Sōbi became a mass movement. Following the organization's official founding in 1952, membership jumped to 1,584 in 1954 and reached a peak of 2,360 two years after that.[1]

Kitagawa Tamiji's (1894–1989) return to Japan from Mexico in 1936 is the event that marks the beginning of Sōbi's timelines. Kitagawa is best known in Japan as a painter, but he was also a long-practicing teacher. The youngest son in a landowning family, Kitagawa dropped out of college prep school and left Japan in 1914. He did not return for twenty-one years. He spent most of his time in Mexico, where he worked for a decade as an art teacher in the *escuelas de pintura al aire libre*, or open-air schools of painting, a system of experimental schools that were part of Mexico's revolutionary education reforms.[2] The mission of these schools was to make art accessible to children from traditionally disadvantaged populations such as farmers, workers, and indigenous peoples and to revalue Mexico's "native" art, which had become newly nationally significant.[3] Broad strokes and forms, free and expressive use of color, indifference to rules of perspective, and respect for inborn creativity were elements of the pedagogy of these schools that had deep resonance with Sōbi as it developed in the postwar. Kitagawa stayed out of the educational arena after his return to Japan in 1936, but he reemerged after the war as a leader of one of the first experiments in student-centered education: the Nagoya City Zoo School, which was held in the summers on the grounds of the zoo from 1949 to 1951. The Zoo School was Kitagawa's attempt to replicate his experiences in Mexico. He was thus an important early member of Sōbi, but it is fair to say that in putting him at the beginning of their timelines Sōbi was laying claim to him as a figurehead. Kitagawa himself became critical of the group by the late 1950s for reasons to be detailed in the next chapter.

Sōbi's true founder and leader was Kubo Sadajirō (1909–1996). Like Kitagawa, Kubo was born the second son in a wealthy landowning family. Although he studied education at the graduate school of Tokyo Imperial University, he never taught in a classroom. His interest in children's art seems to have come about almost by chance.[4] Once he became involved in collecting child art and holding exhibitions, however, he dedicated much of the rest his life to the cause of art education. Kubo organized his first publicly judged exhibition of child art in honor of his father's 80th birthday in 1938. Over the next four years, he organized seven more exhibits. Judges for these exhibits included artists such as Kitagawa Tamiji and Ei Kyū, and progressive elites such as Hani Gorō, a respected Marxist historian, and Hani Setsuko, a progressive educator, who were also Hani Susumu's parents.

The foundation for Kubo's project was laid during a nine-month tour of the United States and Europe in 1938 and 1939. Kubo took with him a collection of 3,000 works of Japanese child art and traveled east from California, giving lectures, meeting educators, and assembling a collection of art to bring back to Japan. During his trip, Kubo met the British reformer R. R. Tomlinson, and visited A. S. Neill at his famous Summerhill School. He also learned of the renowned Austrian educator Franz Cižek.[5] Kubo was not himself a teacher, an artist, or an original theorist in the field of education. His real achievements were as an art collector, a networker, and an advocate. After he returned from his trip abroad, Kubo organized exhibitions of the art he had collected and began a collaborative project of studying and translating the works of the people he had met. The war interrupted these activities during the years 1943–1946, but after the war, Kubo and his group continued their work with even greater energy, visiting schools, giving lectures, holding exhibitions, translating, publishing, and generally promoting the ideal of child-centered aesthetic education. By the time Sōbi formed in 1952, there was a substantial body of artworks and translated theory to serve as the basis for Sōbi's second phase as a broad social movement.

It is no accident that Sōbi's membership and public visibility peaked in the mid-1950s. During the U.S. occupation, the highly centralized wartime education system was replaced by a decentralized one. The 1947 Fundamental Law of Education laid the legal basis for this change, stipulating that education was to be "directly responsible to the whole people."[6] The administrative framework was set out in the 1948 Board of Education Law, which gave locally elected boards power over curriculum, textbook selection, and teacher evaluation, an arrangement that allowed for local pedagogical innovation and experiment.

Numerous nongovernmental (*minkan kyōiku*) groups made up of teachers interested in designing new curricula and improving their teaching sprang into this space for experiment. Ōtsuki Takeshi counts fifty-four *minkan kyōiku* groups for the period 1945 to 1981, although the actual number could easily have been twice that.[7] Twenty of these groups formed during the 1950s, most of which were characterized by a shared conviction that "the education of Japanese children could not be left up to power or its administrative organs."[8] Their hostility toward the central government was fueled in part by a sense of atonement for the role teachers had played in mobilizing children during the war. However, while most were sympathetic to the left-wing Japan Teacher's Union, the *minkan kyōiku* groups were not officially connected with the union. These groups were thus independent of the two main power blocks in the 1950s educational environment.

At its base, Sōbi was a nationwide network of locally organized study groups. These were formed by teachers in a geographical area who were interested in the Sōbi approach. Sōbi had a remarkably strong following in Japan's rural and semi-rural prefectures, such as Gifu, Fukui, and Saitama.[9] Study groups, known as seminars (*semi*), met a few times a month for members to discuss examples of their students' artwork and evaluate their own teaching.[10] Discussion of artwork was particularly important: learning how to see a child through their art was central to Sōbi's teaching practice. These study groups were small, almost always under ten people, and they were wholly voluntary. They existed only to the extent that teachers participated in them and their activity was unregulated by the regional and national levels of the organization. Any group could call itself Sōbi if it wanted to, and there was never a case of the larger organization charging a person or group with having inappropriate ideas.

Sōbi's organizational footprint was light; the regional and national levels of administration were extremely thin. Sōbi had a standing committee (*jōnin iinkai*), a head office (*honbu*), and slightly over a dozen branches (*shibu*), although the number of branches changes through the years. The standing committee was in charge of articulating the general direction and mission of the organization. The first standing committee was made up of Kubo's colleagues who had been active in the first phase of Sōbi. As the original members moved on, they were replaced by others who were active in the organization. The head office and the regional offices were mainly responsible for organizing events and publications. None of the administrative entities had dedicated housing. "Offices" were located in the homes of office holders. All office holders were full-time teachers and there was no professional administrative staff.

Like the study groups, the relation among these various levels of the organization was characterized by volunteerism, meaning that anyone could participate so long as they could devote the time to it. Branches could establish themselves whenever and wherever there were enough people: a branch could form when there were fifteen or more people, although this threshold was never specified in writing. There seems to have been little horizontal connection among study groups outside the auspices of the branches. But it might be more appropriate to see the branches themselves as the expression of horizontal connections: they were not pre-given, but coalesced whenever there were enough study groups in an area to populate them. The head office was theoretically open to anyone, but there were practical barriers to participation. People who wanted to participate had to be physically present to do so, and as the head office moved from one office holder's house to another, it tended to stay close to Tokyo. Sōbi has never been headed by a woman.

The fact that Sōbi was volunteerist does not mean it was technically democratic. A particular branch might select a head who would run the office and attend the annual meetings of branch heads, but this kind of decision was made on the fly, not necessarily by means of a formal voting process. The standing committee proposed new committee members each year at the national seminar, and everyone at the seminar voted on them. There was never a case of someone being voted down or of someone who volunteered to serve on the committee being turned away. Volunteering did depend on the level of access and visibility a person had within the organization, but it seems that there was not a lot of competition for administrative positions. The work demanded time and offered little power. No office had disciplinary power over other offices, and the budget of each office was separate, so there was no financial leverage among them.

Thus, Sōbi members were free to conduct their teaching, reading, writing, and study groups in whatever way they saw fit. Although it is difficult to prove that all voices were heard in this informal organization, there is much evidence that Sōbi's institutional and intellectual practices respected debate and responsive exchange. Sōbi's art exhibitions always had public judging so that people could hear the reasoning behind the judges' choices. At the annual seminars, the attendees were divided into two teams and members took turns publicly praising and defending the artwork from their team in front of the whole seminar. A welcoming attitude toward criticism is another notable feature of the group. The annual seminars always had an elective session called "Sōbi Critique," where participants debated criticisms and complaints. In 1952, Sōbi published a small pamphlet that collected common criticisms of the creative approach to art education but the pamphlet did not provide any answers to the critiques; it left that up to the readers.[11]

What made Sōbi a coherent endeavor was not organizational rigor but shared ideas and practices. Sōbi was an intellectual community of active learners and practical experimenters; events and publications were the main vehicles by which individual groups and members shared the goals and intellectual stakes of the movement and connected to others within it. Events included national and regional seminars, lectures, and children's art exhibitions. For a member in Fukui prefecture, for example, the calendar of events for 1956 would have included the following, in addition to the regular local study group's meetings:

January 4–6: West Japan seminar, Hiroshima (217 attendees).
March 4: Meeting of the infant art study group, Fukui (40 attendees).
April 29: Fukui regional branch general meeting, Fukui. Activities included an exhibition of children's art, discussion of the national seminar, and a slide show of children's artwork from Yamagata.
July 1–8: Third annual Sōbi children's art exhibition, with public judging, Fukui.
August 5–10: Fifth national Sōbi seminar, Nagano (1,441 attendees).[12]

The summer seminar is discussed in chapter 7. Children's art exhibitions were at least equally important for Sōbi. They provided an opportunity to educate audiences about the Sōbi approach, especially through the explanations the judges gave. They also provided a context where local art teachers could be professionally recognized. If a student received an award in a regional, national, or international show, it would give the student's teacher professional credibility in their local school, which could help in cases where teachers were unpopular with administrators.[13]

Members of Sōbi were prolific writers and translators. Through their collective work, a large body of theory in both art education and progressive education became available in Japanese. The *Sōbi nenkan* (Chronology of Sōbi), published in 1978, lists approximately 280 full-length books in its "Sōzō Biiku bunken mokuroku" (Bibliography of Sōbi books). These were not all written by Sōbi members, but they constitute a coherent body of theoretical and practical knowledge that provided a reference for members and an entryway to those who were curious. The 1978 list is the grandest version of this kind of bibliography, but even in the late 1940s and early 1950s, when Sōbi publications were hand printed (*gariban*), they usually included a list of suggested further reading. By 1954, Kubo and his colleagues had translated the works of most of the European forebearers of the Sōbi philosophy into Japanese. Also by 1954, the two early leaders of Sōbi, Kubo Sadajirō and Kitagawa Tamiji, had published their own books.[14] Sōbi published a series of eight pamphlets in the period 1952 to 1957, each of which dealt with a specific topic at some length, in addition to a monthly newsletter titled *Sōzō biiku* (Creative aesthetic education).[15]

An account of Sōbi as an organization would not be complete without an appraisal of the role of Kubo Sadajirō, its most powerful advocate. Kubo used his position and personal wealth to support the arts throughout his life. He made contributions to the development of art education and print art and to the dissemination of western art and theory in Japan. He was an energetic leader and organizer, a prolific writer and translator, and a renowned Esperantist. A dyed-in-the-wool enlightenment intellectual, he saw new ideas from Europe and the United States as keys to reforming Japanese society and he worked to bring world recognition to Japanese artists. His considerable connections gave him access to ideas and the clout to publicize them. Kubo had a forceful personality, but he does not seem to have been a charismatic leader. He himself never claimed leadership of Sōbi and no one seems to have confused their passion for Sōbi with a passion for Kubo. Nor was he a particularly original educational thinker.[16] The value of his intellectual work lay more in collecting and promoting the theories of others, creating a field of educational, aesthetic, and psychological knowledge that members of Sōbi were free to explore and apply for themselves.

Kubo also provided Sōbi members with opportunities to meet young artists by inviting artists he knew to participate in the summer seminars. Another of Kubo's projects, known variously as the Yoi E o Yasuku Uru Kai (Association for Selling Good Pictures Cheaply) and the Shō-korekutā Undō (Small Collector Movement), further blended art and education by bringing together up-and-coming artists and novice art collectors. It was headed by a committee that consisted of Kubo, Ei Kyū, Fukushima Tatsuo, and Ōno Motoaki, who selected artists to submit works that could be bought for prices that ranged from a few hundred to a few thousand yen.[17] The small collector movement began in 1956 at the national Sōbi seminar, and sales often took place in conjunction with Sōbi events. The aim of the movement was twofold. The first goal was to give regular people access to art as purchasers, with the idea that when people participated directly in buying and selling art, their relation to the work and to art more generally was different from passive absorption of masterpieces in museums and magazines. Because the artists participating in this movement were genuinely promising, purchasing one of their works gave the purchaser a stake in a cultural process from which they were usually disenfranchised. The second aim was to support artists languishing in obscurity because they were "not properly recognized in art journalism."[18] This helped artists live by their art and created a readily observable patronage link between the small collectors and the artists.[19] In this way, Kubo created opportunities for art educators and contemporary artists to meet and support each other. Kubo firmly believed that art was not a dead subject to be taught by rote, nor was it something available only in museums, but was rather a collective, ongoing project that grew from the participation of many stakeholders.

Sōbi and/as Minkan Kyōiku

As a movement of art educators, Sōbi undoubtedly had a special concern for creativity and aesthetics in education. But this appreciation went beyond Sōbi. Saitō Kihaku, one of the most prominent leaders of the *minkan kyōiku* movement, wrote, "Regardless of how precisely and scientifically one carries out research about teaching materials, it will not in and of itself further the aims of instruction; only when teachers invest the richness of their individuality, their knowledge, their sensitivity as total human beings . . . will it be possible to more fully develop the ability to give instruction." Saitō referred to the melding of research and teaching that occurred through the judgment of the individual teacher as art. "When the creative attitude of artistic endeavors is brought to bear on education, the teacher becomes an artist. To the extent that teachers do not approach their work with the creative touch of an artist, children are not extended their proper due as students."[20] Creativity and artistry, according to Saitō, were not simply expressions of an inner drive, but developed through fully present and engaged interactions between people and the world around them.

Article II of the Fundamental Law on Education points the way to a more robust understanding of the role of these groups in the early postwar. The article states, "The aim of education shall be realized on all occasions and in all places. In order to achieve the aim, we shall endeavor to contribute to the creation and development of culture by mutual esteem and co-operation, respecting academic freedom, having a regard to actual life and cultivating a spontaneous spirit." The proposition that education is to be realized "on all occasions and in all places" is radical. If taken literally, it would undo the division of labor between teaching and research and undermine hierarchies of learning and expertise. Teachers and students would always already be acting in a process that emerged from and returned to "actual life." By contrast, pedagogies that conceive education as a way to impart established bodies of fact or technical skill to students make the classroom an antechamber to the real world. In this type of pedagogy, students must master preparatory behaviors before their work becomes "real." This both degrades and empowers the teacher: while the classroom is diminished as the not yet real, the teacher assumes near-absolute authority as the sole representative of the real world.

For Sōbi members, the classroom was not separate from the real world. Both the student, through a fully engaged playing out of experience through art, and the Sōbi teachers, through their self-conscious and creative development of their own pedagogy, were learning from and developing through their experiences in the classroom. The classroom was a place where teachers could both guide children and self-consciously study their own pedagogy. The results of this research would be shared, critiqued, expanded in the context of the study group and seminar, and then reapplied in practice. This emphasis on education growing out of experience and of research being constantly in dialog with practice, is interestingly echoed by the Sūgaku Kyōiku Kyōgikai (Math Education Conference), which Ōtsuki quotes as representative of the 1950s *minkan kyōiku* groups: "Math education must not be chased and harassed by experience, but must . . . start from experience and organize it, instilling it into rational thinking and a critical stance."[21]

If this statement is representative, experience was both a starting point for classroom practice and a principle of the *minkan kyōiku* self-study movements themselves. The teacher's task was not to protect children from experience, but rather to protect the unpredictable space of experience itself from parochial ends that might intervene to short-circuit the process of learning. The underlying concern was similar to that of the reportage artists: the living memory of how teachers had let themselves become tools of the military state during the war redoubled the sense of urgency in the 1950s as they faced the postwar state's attempt to reinstitute centralized, top-down administration. The task of securing a space for free development inverted the position of the teacher from one who protected the child from the outside world to one who protected a child's right to the outside world from state organs that might pervert that unpredictability into something more bounded and usable.

There were, however, substantial disagreements among the *minkan kyōiku* groups.[22] Sōbi was the most influential of the art education movements in the 1950s but it had many critics.[23] Two other groups were of particular importance: the Zōkei Kyōiku Sentā (Center for Education in the Plastic Arts) and the Atarashii E no Kai (Society for New Pictures). The Zōkei Kyōiku Sentā was founded in 1950, inspired by a visit to Japan by former Bauhaus director Walter Gropius. Their mission was to research and promote material design and the plastic arts in education.[24] The Atarashii E no Kai stated its mission in a way that also helpfully maps out the rest of the field. "The Atarashii E no Kai has dedicated itself to the work of connecting children's consciousness with their creativity through a movement to depict daily life [*seikatsuga undō*]. Of course, we have opposed the outdated 'copying' mode of art education, which hinders children's growth. But we have also been critical of Sōzō Biiku's 'liberation pedagogy' that thinks it can psychoanalyze and treat [the symptoms of] the postwar, as well as the formalized 'modernism' of the Zōkei Sentā."[25] According to the pedagogy of the Atarashii E no Kai, creating art based on one's immediate social surroundings would be an exercise in coming to terms with them by objectifying them and making them conscious. The Atarashii E no Kai was close in spirit to the Writing Daily Life Movement. Its members were frequent and trenchant critics of Sōbi because they believed that the latter's ideas allowed too little room to address the specifics of the lived social world. The process of the child's self-overcoming was too abstracted, and the associated political assertions too idealistic. They argued that Sōbi's classroom practices were neglectful: students needed more active help in coming to understand a complicated world. For the Atarashii E no Kai, Sōbi's child-centeredness drifted into "hands-off-ism" (*hōnin shugi*).[26] The Japan Teacher's Union regularly echoed these criticisms in its annual reports.[27]

This having been said, we should not overemphasize these differences among the *minkan* art groups. Although the Atarashii E no Kai was critical of Sōbi, their position was based on actual study. E no Kai members attended the Sōbi seminar in 1955, resolved to "objectively investigate the strong and weak points" of the movement.[28] The greatest testament to the possibility of thinking of these varying approaches as a coherent field of complements is the 1956 book *Sōzō Biiku o koete* (Beyond creative aesthetic education), which showed how the three main strands of art education could be brought together in practice. The author, Kawaguchi Isamu, a professor from

Kansai University, researched curriculum development in public schools. His research at Yamataki Elementary School in Kishiwada, Osaka, showed that teachers were applying aspects of each flexibly. Kawaguchi concluded that Sōbi's emphasis on liberating the child from inherited repressive forms was an important first step, but one to move beyond. One example of the cross-disciplinary curriculum at Yamataki was a group project to draw and paint local folktales. This combined drawing from imagination and fantasy (a technique used in Sōbi), and goal-directed group work (associated with Zōkei Kyōiku), with a firm basis in local cultural history (an Atarashii E no Kai concern). The project also incorporated lessons in Japanese language and history. Here one can see the kind of experiment that was possible under decentralization. Kawaguchi believed that such principled eclecticism demonstrated that the *minkan* education movements were not destined to fall into intergroup feuding and that principles from each movement could be used in cross-disciplinary school projects.[29] This kind of local innovation and creative engagement became increasingly difficult after the late 1950s.

Throughout the 1950s, conservative lawmakers and bureaucrats worked to roll back the liberalizing reforms that had been instituted under the occupation. Following the abolition of locally elected school boards in 1956, the Courses of Study (*gakushū shidō yōryō*) issued annually by the Ministry of Education were made legally binding documents in 1958. While the 1947 Course of Study opened with a statement that encouraged teachers to "build a variety of things from the bottom up," the 1958 version stipulated that local entities did not have the authority to alter the rules therein.[30] All textbooks now had to conform to the Course of Study and the severity of the Ministry of Education's textbook screening was stepped up. In 1955, eighteen publishing companies produced twenty-one art textbooks for elementary schools. By 1961, ten companies were producing ten textbooks.[31] In 1961, the ministry instituted a scholastic achievement test that tested students according to the standards in the Course of Study and it began to develop its own approved courses in professional development (*kenshū*). Teacher evaluation and advancement became increasingly tied to centrally determined achievement standards.[32] Whereas Sōbi was a movement of teachers who were actively seeking out their own education and encouraging their students to do the same, the system the Ministry of Education aimed for sought to replace that active experimentation with a model of passive acquisition for both teachers and students.

The reforms of the late 1950s were also controversial for rearranging educational priorities. Nothing was more controversial than the reintroduction of moral education in schools, which critics saw as a return to wartime ideological education. The new push for moral instruction was paired with an emphasis on consolidating basic skills and expanding math and science education as a way to improve science and industry, on the one hand, and revamp technical and home economics training for people who might leave school at the end of mandatory education, on the other.[33] Thus, along with increased centralization and standardization, the new curriculum focused on practical training, paired with a separately conceived subject of moral education. Art education suffered. The two main networks of art teachers in Japan, the Nihon Bijutsu Kyōiku Rengō and the Zenkoku Zuga Kōsaku Kyōiku Renmei, joined forces in late 1957 to make the case to the Ministry of Education that art education should be protected. Sōbi joined the movement.[34] The effort failed, however, and the time allotted to art classes was reduced.[35]

Sōbi protested these changes, and their newsletter carried reactions and discussions over the next two years. One objection was straightforward: that the reduction in class time made teaching impossible.[36] Another focus was the teacher evaluation system (*ninmu hyōtei*). One teacher who was in charge of the Sōbi seminar in West Japan in 1959 wrote a piece about the difficulties teachers were having in his home prefecture of Ehime. The prefectural board of education had decided that teacher training should be run by the board itself and refused to give other parties access to schools or other public buildings for that purpose. In the face of this pressure, the ranks of the teacher union had dropped by almost half, and the teacher from Ehime wrote that "union and circle activity felt almost like being in an underground movement."[37] Some also criticized the plan for separate instruction in moral education, arguing that Sōbi had always been a form of moral instruction.[38] In general, the concern was that streamlining and standardization were incompatible with Sōbi's vision of liberating the human spirit. In her keynote address to the 1958 summer seminar, Hani Setsuko said, "Creativity cannot be divorced from people. Right now we are in the middle of a reverse course that restricts people so that they cannot freely exercise their creativity. . . . The Ministry of Education is trying to reform education [but] the important thing to remember is that before skill, ability, and scholastic aptitude, there is the human being. . . . Everyone possesses the power of creativity, and right now is the time to show it."[39]

Sōbi was in an unusual position, however. At the same time its members struggled against the reforms, key aspects of their philosophy began to appear in ministry guidelines. Arai Tetsuo writes that "allowing for a certain amount of fluctuation depending on the year, all of the Courses of Study written after 1958 are fundamentally rooted in the philosophy of creative art education."[40] Ōtsuki Takeshi points to this as a key difference between *minkan kyōiku* movements of the 1950s and those of the 1960s. While in the 1950s the groups carried out their research and practice independently of or in perceived opposition to ministry policies, starting in 1958, the ministry began to incorporate the work of these groups into its guidelines. This made the claim of radical liberation of the individual through art much more difficult.[41]

CHAPTER 9

Sōbi's Philosophy and Pedagogy

In this chapter I introduce Sōbi's philosophy as Kubo Sadajirō understood and promoted it. In his writings on education Kubo combined his own ideas with a pastiche of references to intellectuals and educators he took inspiration from. His writing relied so heavily on the ideas of others that some articles are composed almost entirely of quotations.[1] Whether consciously or not, his approach succeeded in portraying a broad intellectual community of shared values and beliefs, one whose key works were available in Japanese translation by the end of the 1950s, often thanks to the work of Sōbi and its fellow-travelers. Given how decentralized Sōbi's organization was, there was a lot of variation in the way that individuals and local study groups interpreted the body of knowledge that Sōbi welcomed into its intellectual universe. What follows is an introduction to Sōbi's philosophy through the lens of Kubo, that concludes with a set of critiques lodged against Kubo's philosophy by Kitagawa Tamiji, who had been an early supporter of the movement.

The foundation of Kubo's project was laid during his nine-month tour of the United States and Europe in 1938 and 1939. Kubo had a paradigmatic encounter during this trip when a member of a PTA in New York challenged his observation that child art in America generally lacked refinement. The PTA member objected passionately that "nevertheless, they show an intense desire to draw, and a sound overall grasp of their work." Kubo related this incident in a 1939 article that he wrote immediately after he returned to Japan. "Why does the artwork of western children affect us so strongly? Common to all of their pictures is an expression of a basic confidence that almost makes one envious. They are overflowing with a spirit of independence." For Kubo, the art of these children was "joyful" (*tanoshii*), "accomplished" (*senren sarete iru*), and "bright" (*akarui*), all signs of the child's healthy "desire to draw" (*egakō to suru seishin*). In contrast, the art of Japanese children was "skillful" (*kiyō*) but "lonesome" (*sabishii*), "intellectualized" (*gainenteki*), and "formalized and unemotional" (*keishikiteki muhyōjō*). While western children showed an enduring interest in drawing human figures, Japanese children's figures became mere outlines after about the fourth grade—"mere portraits," not "living humans." Kubo concluded that the most fundamental goal for art education in Japan should be to foster the child's "creative spirit" (*sōzō seishin*).[2]

This early article already contains many of the points that Kubo would expand upon in his later writing: a hostility to technical skill; an attraction to the values of confidence, independence, directness, and expression; a method of analysis that hinged on the overall emotional impact of a work; a belief that a child's art was an index of his or her psychological state; and a conviction that child development and education were deeply related to a society's health. For Kubo, the goal of art education was not to create artists. Instead, art was the activity where the drive to create played out in its rawest form. Aesthetic education was thus the theater where this creative energy could be set free with the fewest impediments and encouraged to blossom most openly, making it a model for full, uninhibited actualization of the individual and their fully responsive immersion in a shared present. Aesthetic sensibility was the highest capacity of human being, which should rightly inform all other endeavors, most especially education.

The following introduction to Sōbi's philosophy begins with the most straightforward and concrete aspects of the pedagogy and moves toward the more abstract and far-reaching. Before beginning, however, the most important word in Sōbi's lexicon should be addressed: creativity. Kubo's thinking on creativity was influenced greatly by Homer Lane (1876–1925), an American progressive educator who has since largely been forgotten. A. S. Neill introduced Kubo to Lane when Kubo visited Neill's Summerhill School in 1939. Lane's book of posthumously collected writings, *Talks to Parents and Teachers*, was one of the first to be translated for the Sōbi movement, appearing in Japanese in 1949.[3] Lane theorized that human being consists of two needs or drives: the possessive and the creative.[4] The possessive drive finds pleasure in safety, repetition, and predictability, making security the source of happiness. While this is a fundamental form of happiness, Lane argued that modern society overemphasized it. In modern society, children are motivated almost entirely by fear of punishment and humiliation, and insofar as the cessation of fear is the driving pleasure, children become pliable and lose the ability to explore and experiment for themselves. In contrast, creative pleasure comes from a fearless engagement with the world. It is the drive to experience the new. Although creative pleasure involves risk, danger, and error, it is how children grow: without it, contact with new elements of the world—that is to say, learning—would never be possible.

For Lane, however, the opposition of autonomy and heteronomy was arguably more important than the binary of creativity and possession. Lane's writing is full of aphorisms such as "Freedom cannot be given. It is taken by the child," "A conscience cannot be imposed," and "Fear . . . has never yet made anyone good."[5] He sometimes described the effort to value the native instincts of children as simply facing reality: the organic force of growth cannot be stopped, only twisted by adult attempts at control. But ultimately Lane's emphasis was grounded in a beatific vision of human nature. "Human nature is innately good; the unconscious processes are in no way immoral. Faults are not corrected by, but brought about by, suppression in childhood. If the child is allowed to express himself at different stages without restriction, he will himself eliminate the unethical, and, as altruism begins to unfold from the unconscious mind at adolescence, will develop into an ethical being."[6] Creativity was therefore a force of growth that would tend toward the good if it were not constantly interrupted by self-serving adult behavior. It was in the name of this force that Lane and Kubo fought.

The Child-Centered Classroom and Franz Cižek

Sōbi's basic aim was to overturn the hierarchy between student and teacher, to make the student's development—from the inside out—the primary mover of education and to reconfigure the teacher as a minimally invasive, facilitating presence. The problem was that this was not happening; even in postwar Japan, the child remained material upon which to impose an ideal of service that would best serve adult society and the nation.

Kubo recalls some of his visits to schools in the late 1940s, when he asked teachers what they took to be the goals of art education. The answers he received were "to instill a correct sense of form and color," "to foster the ability to create beauty," "to cultivate the ability to appreciate and understand beauty." Teachers seemed to judge the work of their pupils according to preexisting, inherently adult standards—"something like an adult picture, only smaller."[7] Kubo continued. "When the creative spirit of the child encounters intellectualized [*gainenteki*] adult guidance, it experiences it as repression and is obstructed, which then leads to regression and stasis at a lower level of development."[8] He therefore called on teachers to destroy intellectualized form (*gainen kudaki*) in their students' thinking and in their own thinking.

The classroom techniques were deceptively simple. Don't criticize. Don't give direct advice about what or how to draw. Avoid talking about visual fidelity. Don't give students any artwork to imitate. And most important, encourage students relentlessly. Though these prescriptions seem generic, they had a specific source: the Viennese art teacher Franz Cižek (1865–1946), who began his career as an artist and a member of the Secessionists but became best known for his later work in developing what at the time was one of the most extreme versions of noninterventionist teaching practice. Cižek's approach sought to stimulate the child's innate drive rather than direct children towards mastery.[9]

Cižek assumed that life was at base a movement, an energy, that pressed through matter, shaping it into new forms. Artwork was a particularly direct index of that energy. At first the energy appears as scribbles. Then, around age two, scribbling gives way to rhythmic production. "Rhythm is the origin of all art (music, dance), rhythm is life (breathing and pulsating, day and night). . . . And here again a parallel in language. '*And* he did this, *and* he did that, *and* . . .' It is rhythm."[10] Following this was the abstract symbolic stage. For Cižek, maturation was a process of increasing differentiation.[11] It was not a matter of becoming more accurate or skillful, nor a matter of the child's relationship to an independent external world. It was a matter of the child refining and expanding a set of creative possibilities. The process slowed and stopped with age. Cižek was so pessimistic about people retaining their creativity into adulthood that he refused to accept students over the age of 14. Though skill and realism would continue to develop, they were essentially noncreative in adulthood: they functioned as generally accepted crutches so one did not have to create for oneself.[12]

Cižek's practice was based on removing whatever crutches children might find to use. He forbade students to use models, photographs, or pictures and discouraged children from copying one another. He even avoided using natural models and would send children outside to look at things only as a last resort. When a child asked for assistance, Cižek might reply that the child already knew how to do it. To one student trying to draw a horse he said, "If I wanted to draw a horse, I would know how to do it. But I don't want [to]; you want [to]. So you must draw it."[13] To another child who asked what a meadow looked like, he answered, "Lie down in a meadow and close your eyes."[14] He would never provide a tool that might interfere with the child confronting their own desire to express something—the moment of reaching out, attempting "blindly," was precisely the moment that was most formative and valuable. The teacher's role was to recognize and encourage.[15]

Cižek stayed with his own self-run school until he retired in 1938.[16] His pedagogy gained fame in Europe through lectures, demonstrations, and shows of his students' artwork. By the end of his career, many artists and teachers were making the pilgrimage to observe his classroom. Viktor Lowenfeld, Marion Richardson, and Herbert Read were heavily influenced by Cižek's approach and went on to make expressionist, child-centered education the dominant force in art education between 1945 and 1970 in the United States and Britain.[17] Kubo and Sōbi can be seen as a parallel movement in Japan.

Kubo, like Cižek, preached that the creative spirit of children was the most basic life force and could not be restricted without negative consequences. In order to "return young boys' and girls' hearts to them," it would be necessary first to "liberate them from the authoritarianism of the teacher."[18] Like Cižek, Kubo advocated using stories and games to spark children's imaginations. One of the model lessons he wrote about begins on a snowy morning with the teacher telling the students Hans Christian Andersen's tale "The Snow Queen."[19] One difference, however, was that Kubo emphasized exposing children to the real world in order to give maximum room for learning and growth through experience. "Raising all boys and girls through the encouragement of their creativity means encouraging them to learn through their own experiences. The more alive and true [*chūjitsu*] they are to their own experiences, the better they will be able to regulate the desire that wells up inside them for themselves."[20] For Kubo, an encounter with an actual train, as opposed to a picture of a train, would stimulate the child and his or her natural excitation would flow from the experience directly into the moment of creation, bursting the banks of established categories of fidelity or skill.[21] Direct experience put much more at stake in the creative flow—the question of how to communicate and pass on the full moment of excitation—and Kubo argued that teachers must do nothing that might get in the way.

Seeing Creativity, Understanding Creatively

The proposition to liberate the classroom and school from the authority of the teacher invited questions that were difficult to answer. If teachers were to relinquish direct control, in what sense were they teachers? Most critics of

Sōbi—and even many members—voiced confusion and concern about the lack of a clear answer to this most pressing of questions. The answer was complex and context specific, but the child-centered classroom was not one where the teacher was absent. Rather the teacher was required to leave their position of authority and place themselves alongside the students to see and feel the world from their position. Standing on the side of the child meant empathizing with the child's present situation and having both the wisdom and the courage to allow the child to grow from there. Empathizing with children had two separate moments: understanding the child properly and then helping the child grow.

Kubo's claim that Japan's twenty million schoolchildren were unhappy as a result of psychological repression had been occasioned by a visit to an exhibition of children's artwork in Tokyo in February 1949. To Kubo, the paintings seemed "painted by fettered hearts, lacking freshness, nondescript, gloomy, withdrawn, noncommittal, stuck in form."[22] And if these were the paintings of 1,000 hearts, they stood for the hearts of millions not represented in the show.

> The activities of children as they change with the . . . stages of their mental development are subject to the parents, adults, and teachers who impose restrictions, force them into adult forms [of behavior], and forcibly make them conform to an extraneous "high culture." Adults do this out of notions of common sense foreign [to the child's situation] or out of their own adult complexes. For the child, this is repression. The repression comes to touch everything, shutting the child forever into a prison with no bars, sequestering them in a cavern of unhappiness, continuing to build them up possessively [*shoyūtekini*].[23]

The term "possessively" is almost certainly a reference to Homer Lane. It has a double meaning that gets at how repression propagates. In one sense, teachers and parents want to possess children as well-behaved homunculi who serve adult interests. In another sense, children who are forced into adult patterns develop self-possession, a form of being that finds pleasure only in the cessation of danger. As this receives reinforcement, the child becomes ever more dependent on others for affirmation and safety and is eventually unable to break out of the invisible prison of that dependence. It was the transfer of adults' own self-interested values to the child's behavior that Kubo saw as being the greatest danger. Behind the technical achievement of the "model child" (*yoi ko*) was the shadow of the adult's hand and the scar of a child's repression.[24] Taken to its logical end, it indicated "a conservative attitude, a dangerous caution, a mental state of the greatest concern."[25]

This is one example of Kubo's approach to looking at children's art. For Kubo, artwork was a sign that indicated multiple layers of association, from the individual child and his or her family to the wider society and the nation. Sōbi teachers had to learn to see this in their students' art and to reinforce and encourage creativity when they saw it. One effect of this was to overturn the usual criteria for judging children's art. Kubo enjoyed thumbing his nose at the usual hierarchy of talent and taste. Skill, verisimilitude, and control were values founded on a lack of respect for a child's creative, experimental force. Sōbi teachers had to learn to look with eyes that were not concerned with finding the adult in the child, not concerned with rewarding the child who did things *for* adults. Though one might object that this simply replaces one regime with another, there was an undeniably anti-authoritarian and non-conformist project at stake that questioned the "model child" (*yoi ko*), and spoke up on behalf of children who didn't conform so readily.

At its best, Kubo's reading approached a hermeneutics. Being on the side of the child meant unifying the horizons of teacher and student, allowing the teacher to see the artwork emerging from the child's own time in the world; that is to say, the child's own growth. The best example of this is in the February 1951 issue of *Mizue*, where Kubo spends almost three pages analyzing a series of drawings done by a six-year-old girl over a period of one month. He examines the drawings and notes what the girl said about them and what was happening generally in her life. The picture drawn on the 25th shows much greater force being used: a series of lines that the child identified as rain nearly obscure the rest of the figures. This, according to Kubo, was the climax of her crisis, which, we learn from a conversation with her father, was anxiety about where babies come from. After the father explained where they come from, the crisis passed and her drawing returned to a calmer style. Kubo argued that far from being attempts to represent a visual reality, the elements in a child's picture have a highly specific relationship to the child's mental state and social situation and that this relationship is constantly changing.

Saying that Kubo's interpretation of child art was hermeneutic, however, does not present a full picture. This example from early 1951 was one of Kubo's most involved interpretations, and the level of care he took in it was more the exception than the rule. It might always be the case that hermeneutics is haunted by the specter of psychologism: the effort to understand a work as it engages with the world according to its own time can harden into yet another explanatory model. But Kubo seemed unaware of this danger, and the project of "seeing from the side of the child" often devolved into a binary style of argument in which "good" paintings were compared with "bad" paintings: Kubo's corresponding Ur-categories were "creative" and "intellectualized/formalistic" (*gainenteki*). Over the course of numerous writings on child art, he dealt with many artworks using this simple notation. In 1956, the Aichi branch of Sōbi published one of the most popular handbooks for reading children's artworks, *Yoi e to yokunai e* (Good pictures and bad pictures).[26] Although the analyses of children's art in this book are more nuanced than the title suggests, they do not escape the general problem. Artworks were carefully selected to provide an illustrative key to things like developmental stages, personal qualities, and how pictures relate to life events (such as the birth of a brother or being scolded by one's mother).

Liberation into the Flow: A. S. Neill and Homer Lane

While a deep, intuitive understanding of children's attempts to work creatively with the world around them was one goal, the second major role for the teacher was to help the child continue to exercise that creativity. Although the creative drive was fundamental, it was also extremely malleable: easily bent in the process of its self-shaping. Kubo wrote that "children are subject to all kinds of repression at home, in society, in school. Repression blocks off the child's creative capacity. . . . Yet on the other hand, children are spurred on by their unconscious urge to extend their creative capacity. Drawing this out is the teacher's duty."[27] The key was a creative atmosphere in the classroom.[28]

For Kubo, the established approach to education relied on constantly reinscribing the authority of the teacher at the expense of the child. A deep-seated dislike of the creative potential of children lurked at the root of such authoritarianism.[29] Creativity was unsightly and dangerous.[30] Indeed, following A. S. Neill and Karl Menninger, Kubo theorized that what lay behind the teacher's need for authority was their own insecurity and fear.[31] Controlling children with formal exercises repeated the teacher's own hard-learned exercise of repressive self-control. Unless the teacher was liberated to explore their own creativity, they would not be able to admit its appearance in others. A creative classroom atmosphere was ultimately one in which the children would *want* to make new things. Kubo often used the term direct, or candid (*sotchoku*), to describe that atmosphere, meaning one that was free of fear or embarrassment.

Kubo suggested some whimsically concrete ways of creating a creative atmosphere, such as always smiling and wearing bright clothes. He once proposed that all local governments provide their teachers with one brightly colored scarf and sweater to change the atmosphere of schools.[32] Bright clothing might seem inadequate to such a task, but the point was that in the end, it would be *something like this* that would precipitate change. As with the handshakes and red caps at the Sōbi seminars, these were small things. But what change required was simply an opportunity for it to emerge. Giving a lecture to describe the desired atmosphere would be useless: a change in atmosphere could be generated only from within the collectivity of people participating in it, through gifts, deviations, and moments of humor, in an endless, small loosening of authority. If the faculty room at your school had an oppressive atmosphere, Kubo's advice was not to talk to your fellow teachers about it, but to arrange a day trip somewhere, or to have a *samisen* party. If that didn't work, then try something else, or something else.

It is clear that this demanded a great deal from the Sōbi teacher. A creative atmosphere required creativity. Teachers had to find pleasure in taking risks. The highly context-specific nature of actual interventions (bright scarves, finger painting, outings to the riverside, etc.), meant there could be no handbook for successful creative teaching. It was necessarily done in real time, in the uniquely developing dynamics of each classroom. Contrary to critics of Sōbi, who claimed that it was a kind of "hands-off-ism," the Sōbi teacher had to be so fully engaged in his or her teaching that it could not be summarized. Nevertheless, one can sympathize with teachers who complained that this gave them little practical understanding of how to proceed in their own classrooms.[33]

Intuition was the basis for Sōbi's teaching. The psychological and social theory that underlay this came from a number of radical reform educators, the most important of whom were Homer Lane and A. S. Neill. Neill was an early follower of Lane. After spending time at Lane's Little Commonwealth in 1917, he founded his own self-governing school, Summerhill, in 1921. The school still operates and A. S. Neill became a guru of sorts in the field of child-centered education. He frequently entertained guests and reporters at his school and gave lectures around Britain and Europe. As was the case at the Little Commonwealth, students at Summerhill were mostly "problem children" and everything related to the running of the school was settled by a vote of all the students at a weekly general meeting.[34] Summerhill became (in)famous as the school where children did not have to attend classes, and most students underwent a period of adjustment until they decided to go to classes of their own accord. In 1928, Shimoda Seishi visited Summerhill for two weeks and became the primary translator of Neill's works into Japanese.[35] Kubo visited in 1939.

One thing that underlay both Lane's and Neill's approach to schooling was a deep commitment to psychoanalysis, especially the belief that repressed energy would find expression in (self-)destructive forms. Both became interested in psychotherapy in the early stages of its development as a movement. Both had undergone therapy and practiced it as amateurs. Neill was close friends with Wilhelm Reich and corresponded with him for twenty years.[36] Although people today tend to use Freud's theories to analyze texts and behaviors, the psychoanalysis Lane and Neill encountered was part of an emancipative practice. A passage from Lane captures the profound liberation of energies it promised.

> For the adult who is properly "synthesized," there is no overcoming of unconscious resistances, no nervous strain, no wasted energy. . . . When this integration is complete, each constituent factor will have passed out of its originally limited and particular aim and will have become a fluid element in the whole energy of adult life, and the whole of this energy will without strain be available for the needs of the moment. . . . Thus, for example, where the synthesis is satisfactory, sexual abstinence is not only practicable but need bring no unhappiness; for no part of the energy will be tied inevitably to any single or particular aim, whether this aim be professional, or sexual, or social or recreative.[37]

For Lane, Neill, and many others in the 1920s, psychoanalysis promised to open doors to entirely new dimensions of being by unbinding energies locked up in neuroses.

The Sōbi teacher had to become something of a therapist, finding ways to help their students engage their creative drives, dissolving complexes (ingrown energy) in the process. Intuition was the crucial mechanism for understanding how and when to do this. When Neill found a new arrival at Summerhill breaking windows with stones, he joined in and began throwing stones himself. This not only deflated the rebelliousness of the child but enacted a form of sympathy for the child's anger at the world. By stepping out of the position of authority, he created situations where both obedience and rebellion ceased to be sufficient motivations for action.

In order to maintain a creative atmosphere in the classroom the teacher had to become one of the class so that they could see how they might intervene to change its direction. In Lane's unnerving formulation, the teacher needed to become the "brain" of the class.

> The policeman is more scientifically trained in psychology than the teacher. . . . He is taught that when there is a street accident, he must never rush in waving his baton of authority . . . He must first slip quietly into the crowd and appear to be one of them, and gradually,

> through understanding the emotion of the crowd, become its brain, and so control it. . . . Individual policemen vary greatly in their powers. Some go through the most dangerous experiences and are never hurt, others are always getting knocks.[38]

Although this passage reminds us that power differentials between student and teacher survive, its basic point is that one cannot directly oppose the flow of life within the individual or the group. One can shunt it, nudge it, encourage it, but attempts to control it end only in violence to both the teacher and the student. The flow can only be grasped intuitively, and to grasp it intuitively one must be inside it looking out. Embracing the flow promised positive freedom, attainable by surrender to the larger force of life.

Aesthetics and Morality: Herbert Read

Creative aesthetic education had a wider purview than art classes. Kubo wrote that the art education he advocated was simply "creative education taking place through art," and he saw the structures that shaped education as being microcosmic reticulations of the totality of Japanese society in the 1950s. "[Japanese art education at present] is like a Henry Ford–style system of parts—the mass production of pictures all in the same pattern. The Japanese education world is a gloomy place with an atmosphere of half-feudal traditionalism where we all still look at painting with a barbaric technical training mindedness and a formalism stuck in repeating patterns. . . . Beneath our heels, we grind the hearts of . . . children. As they try to reach out, we bind them and shut them inside a prison without bars."[39]

But while the political stakes went beyond the conduct of art classes, Kubo argued that art and the aesthetic constituted the "most central field" for creative education.[40] Why? The answer goes to something at the heart of Sōbi's intellectual heritage: a reaction against the overvaluation of the rational/intellectual faculties in industrial modernity and, perhaps even more fundamentally, a critique of the splitting of human knowledge into separate spheres that developed without the benefit of being tempered by the other. Although this critique was not new, it had special importance in the aftermath of fascism. Herbert Read was one of the strongest voices to assert that modern warfare and fascism were a result of human capacities having been split apart. In 1942, in the epilogue to his book *Education through Art*, he recounted that he had written the book against the background of

> hundreds of armored vehicles . . . manned by technicians carefully educated for constructive work, churn[ing] through the dust and torrid

> heat [of Libya] in a fury of mutual destruction. . . . I have been reminding the reader of 'the importance of sensation in an age which practices brutalities and recommends ideals' and I have built up a theory which attempts to show that if in the upbringing of our children we preserved, by methods which I have indicated, the vividness of their sensations, we might succeed in relating action to feeling, and even reality to our ideals."[41]

For Read, the aesthetic seemed to be the last and only hope in the face of a rationalism that had run to such disastrous extremes by uprooting humankind's ability to regulate itself morally.

Read's understanding bears a striking similarity to the reportage artists' concern that rational values always failed to connect with people's sensate being, always failed to motivate them. The aesthetic, for Read and Sōbi and for the reportage artists, was the key to that motivation, the joint that locked them fully into the present.[42] It was through the aesthetic that a morality that emerged from the situated body was felt and understood. For Read, what underlay this was a conviction that patterns of energy flow and growth existed within nature and that these patterns also ran through human beings.

> Aesthetic laws are inherent in the biological processes of life itself; they are the laws which guide life along the path of ease and efficiency . . . Balance and symmetry, proportion and rhythm, are basic factors in experience: indeed, they are the only elements by means of which experience can be organized into persisting patterns, and it is of their nature that they imply grace, economy and efficiency. What feels right works right, and the result, as measured by the consciousness of the individual, is a heightened sense of aesthetic enjoyment.[43]

Things feeling right and working right is a source of aesthetic enjoyment because it shows that the person is acting in harmony with an unconscious pattern of being. For Read, the aesthetic sense was how humans intuitively grasped the patterns of nature, and for that reason, it was the starting point for education.[44]

It was through the balance, proportion, and scale conceived as aesthetic sensations that the liberated creativity so important to Sōbi could claim to avoid a Hobbesian state of nature. "Discipline," Read wrote,

> does not have to be imposed by the schoolmaster or the drill sergeant. . . . It is a faculty within the child which responds to sympathy and love, to the intelligent anticipation of impulses and trends in the

> individuality of the child. For this reason the teacher must be primarily a person and not a pedagogue, a friend rather than a master. . . . The pattern of creation is in nature, and we discover and conform to this pattern by all the methods of artistic activity—by music, by dancing and drama, but also by working together and living together, for, in a sane civilization, these too are arts of the same natural pattern.[45]

The aesthetic would regulate the creative society and make that society visible to itself. But unlike law in the rational society, the aesthetic emerged from within lived experience.[46]

It is worth pausing over a connection that runs between Kubo and Henri Bergson, although it involves a few degrees of separation.[47] One can see that Sōbi's conception of the aesthetic resembles Bergson's idea of an intensive manifold. As Hulme explains in *Speculations*, the extensive manifold is any "complex [thing] which can be resolved into separate elements or atoms." Explanation, or the unfolding and laying out of the manifold, is the method by which people come to understand it.[48] "Suppose, however, that there existed certain finite things whose parts interpenetrated in such a manner that they could not be separated or analyzed out. The intellect would then be unable to understand the nature of these things, for it persists in forming a diagram, and in a diagram each part is separated from every other part."[49]

For example, one can examine the flow of a river from above by diagramming its currents and eddies, or by submerging oneself within the river with eyes closed, which will render a different understanding of its flow. As Hulme described, "If you put yourself in this position with regard to your own inner life—and this is what Bergson means by intuition—then you will realize that it is composed not of separate things but of interpenetrating tendencies."[50] Being on the side of the child similarly means submerging oneself in the lived experience of children as it unfolds in their own time. The child's experience, all the dynamics of his or her emotional, physical, and intellectual existence, along with the dynamics that flow through the classroom as a group are things whose complexity cannot be unfolded and analyzed but can only be felt from within using faculties beyond rationality. "One could express the same idea in a different way. . . . If the child has to fit together a jig-saw puzzle, it can learn to do it quicker and quicker. Theoretically indeed it requires no time to do it, because the result is already given. But to the artist who creates a picture, time . . . is one with the invention itself. It is the actual living progress of the thought, a kind of vital process like *ripening*."[51]

This seems abstract when thinking about Sōbi as a movement, but it need not be so. Bergson's appeal for the reality of such things as intensive manifolds could be read as a cry for local autonomy. What if we were to take the school or the school district as an intensive manifold? In their own conduct as professionals and as advocates for a new approach to education, Sōbi members attempted to embody many of the same ideals that they encouraged in their students. While they encouraged students to take risks by expressing themselves, they took similar risks in expressing their ideas to administrators and parents. While they discouraged students from imitating and relying on established form, they too spent their evenings learning new approaches that came into being only through their own practice. While encouraging their students to experiment, they reached out across disciplines to come up with new curricula. While they hoped that the creativity of their students would continue to burst in small revolutions throughout their lifetimes, they continually accessed their own creativity to find new ways out of restrictive situations. While they stepped down from the front of the classroom to create the space for their students to flower from the inside out, they too needed such a space for their own teaching. But they and the other *minkan kyōiku* groups did not succeed in fending off the Ministry of Education's reassertion of control, which brought with it homogenization and standardization enforced by authority. There was no place for the aesthetic within this.

Kitagawa Tamiji's Dissent

Although Kitagawa Tamiji was an early figurehead for Sōbi, he became critical of the movement early on. His ideas provide a counterpoint to Kubo's vision of emancipatory education, and his points correspond to common criticisms of Sōbi. Kitagawa developed his ideas about art education primarily through practice as a teacher. He was born in 1894. After dropping out of school, he traveled to the United States in 1914. Although he was from a well-to-do family, Kitagawa supported himself abroad. He worked as a set builder while taking night classes in New York. After journeying to Mexico in 1922, he worked as a tutor and then as an itinerant peddler of religious icons. In 1924, after entering the National Academy of Arts in San Marco, he was invited to participate in one of the revolution's educational experiments: the open-air schools of painting (*escuelas de pintura al aire libre*).

The first of these schools was founded in 1913, originally as a haven for art students who had been influenced by nineteenth-century French painting. David Craven writes that "teaching a variant of post-impressionism [was] a way to [de-academicize the academy] by directly appreciating the 'Mexican-ness' of the landscape.'"[52] About the time that Kitagawa joined the Churubusco school in 1925, a generation of artists who had grown up through that school was beginning to expand the schools and change their mission to that of serving people from lower economic classes and from traditionally excluded racial backgrounds.[53] By the late 1920s, there were eight such schools.[54] Kitagawa became an assistant to the superintendent of the Tlalpan school in 1925 and in 1932 he became superintendent of the school in Taxco, where he remained until 1936.[55]

Soon after he returned to Japan, Kitagawa introduced his ideas on art education, some of which were similar to those Kubo would begin to advocate postwar. He argued that art education was unique for two reasons. First, whereas the teacher-student relationship in other subjects was like that of state to citizen or father to child, in art education the teacher-student relationship was more like that of "friends or fellow travelers." Art education was more "encompassing," more "personal," and more "active" than subjects that analyzed their subject matter in order to make it more digestible for students. Second, the content and technique of art education was always variable and changing: what was needed for one student would not be appropriate for another and what had worked one day might not work the next. It was a constant process of adjustment, where "everything was connected dynamically from bottom to top."[56] Apart from writing a few articles and serving as an occasional judge at Kubo's children's art exhibits, however, Kitagawa had little involvement with education until after the war. Instead, he devoted himself to his art, entering the Nika Kai in 1937.

Kitagawa's reentry into education started with an experimental summer school he held each summer from 1949 to 1951, on the grounds of the Nagoya City Zoo. When he introduced his summer school experiment in an essay in *Mizue* in 1950, Kitagawa framed the issues using language that was in tune with the developing Sōbi movement, even going so far as to say that he and his three assistants were simply putting Kubo's and Cižek's ideas into practice: removing all repressions that would block a child's creative growth.[57] The experiment enjoyed a high profile regionally through coverage in the *Nagoya Times* and nationally through the *Mizue* feature.

Kitagawa chose the zoo as a site because he believed that children needed to be taken out of their school and home environments in order for them to be able to reclaim their "dreams."[58] Although it took time for the children to stop looking to him as teacher, he considered the experiment a success. Even at this early stage, however, Kitagawa pulled back from a full endorsement of Kubo's ideas, warning that "what we've done so far is pre-educational work. Real education should start from here. And to begin that real education, I believe we must invite the children out of the zoo and into an actual social situation for them."[59] Underlying this reticence was Kitagawa's conviction that art education for children under age ten had little significance because the aesthetic sense of young children was unconscious. Although the Japanese press always labeled him a child educator, he opened one article about his experience in Mexico with the caveat that the students he had taught were from 10 to 18 years old, hardly "children" (*jidō*).[60] Art was particularly important during puberty, Kitagawa argued, because puberty was "filled with suffering under a variety of conflicts. There is the turbulence of one's inner life, and both nature and everyday life become vexed. Perhaps that is the reason that the roots of visual expression . . . become stronger."[61] Whereas Kubo approached child art as testimony to the creative energy of human growth, Kitagawa believed that art was more important as a document of the conscious but nonverbal struggle to come to terms with the physical and social world. Kitagawa insisted that art was a way to grasp the reality of one's lived life.[62]

Kitagawa's position on creativity and freedom also differed from Kubo's. In "Jiyū e no kikyū no seishin" (The spirit of longing for freedom), an article he wrote in response to Kubo's seminal "Jidōga no mikata," which had appeared a few months earlier in the same journal, Kitagawa began by criticizing the paintings of American children that Kubo held so dear.[63] He objected that they were the work of "fortunate children, gazing languidly upon goodness and beauty alone." "[These children] should struggle more. . . . No matter how far you have gone, the human condition is one of struggle." Mexican children, who faced greater adversity, created art that was testimony not to their freedom per se but to their struggle to attain it. Instead of looking for freedom as if it were an identifiable quality, Kitagawa argued that the energy of the struggle was more important, both for the children who were growing up into the social world and for the art they produced. To be fair, Kubo's thinking was also based on a process theory that resisted reification, but his practice of judging tended to attach freedom to a predictable set of visual demonstrations and he was prone to emphasizing brightness and happiness. Kitagawa's formulation found a place for dark, pathos-filled work. Struggle was a necessarily "bloody" (*chimidoro*) process.

Finally, Kitagawa opposed the psychoanalytic tendencies of Kubo's approach as well as the practice of publicly judging children's art in exhibitions.[64] The exhibitions were particularly important to Kubo's goal of popularizing Sōbi and its values. In a paradigmatic early essay, Kubo listed the qualities of a "creative picture" this way:

1. Not intellectualized/formalistic
2. Resolute and brimming with confidence

3. Lively and energetic
4. Fresh, free
5. Brimming with a compelling power, or a bright happiness[65]

These are not immediately visible qualities, and it would be fair to say Kubo did not *want* the creative spirit to be too easily attached to pictorial markers. But Kubo had his tastes. As Arai Tetsuo has shown, Kubo favored non-naturalistic representation that did not use perspective or significant molding or shading. He liked bright colors, as well as compositions that filled the entire frame and relied on masses of color rather than lines.[66] Most fundamentally, he did not like the appearance of skill or imitation, so even when he judged the work of older children, Kubo favored works that appeared clumsy and childlike. Kubo himself realized as early as 1955 that the new view of art he had been advocating had started to look like "a new style."[67] But Kitagawa's criticism was more radical. He was hostile to the way the exhibition and its judging introduced an element of competition into art, especially insofar as it was taken to reflect the success of the teacher. He argued that the business of teaching was helping students who aren't talented grow and develop. Having talented students was not a measure of good teaching.[68]

For Kitagawa, puberty was a time when children began to grow out of the relatively safe and unconscious realm of childhood. The transition almost unavoidably involved friction and conflict and demanded an energetic struggle on the part of the child to form and maintain him or herself in the social world. Kitagawa always wanted to insist on the reality of artistic activity, of art as a conscious struggle against the world as given; this was why he argued that psychological evaluations and judged exhibitions of children's art had no role to play. It was only when a person became an adult that his or her art could be said to begin to engage with the world. Kitagawa's position helps us see that Sōbi's approach was in danger of creating a ghetto of noble savages: of affirming the virtue and power of young children's art to such a degree that it would divorce those values from adult society, limiting the scope of both art and education. If one took this approach to its extreme (as Cižek had), it would make true creativity impossible beyond puberty. The result would be that art would become sealed off from the surrounding society—virtue and beauty possible only within its walled garden. For Kitagawa, children should not, and ultimately could not, be protected from the adult world.[69] The most important moments of education were those that came when children encountered the historical world and struggled against it, and education provided the tools children needed to work through that struggle.[70]

As the years passed, Kitagawa came to the conclusion that aesthetic education was failing to take the all-important step out of the classroom. His biggest complaint about his art school was that the students never stuck with it, something he interpreted as "abandoning the struggle of forming one's own character, defeated by the pressure of established morality fenced up around you."[71] In 1955, he returned to Mexico and stayed for over a year. By the time he returned, he had become disillusioned with Sōbi and with the governments of both Japan and Mexico. "[In Mexico], the zeal for national liberation and spreading democracy has cooled completely. In Japan it's the same. In the early postwar, everyone was overflowing with the desire to fully realize democracy and make a better Japanese people, but when you look at the direction the Ministry of Education has been taking recently, it feels like things are going in the opposite direction."[72] Kitagawa had very little subsequent contact with Sōbi or art education. Time only strengthened his conviction that a full-fledged revolution was necessary to liberate people from repression and restore some balance to their lives. In 1968, in a discussion about art education with another Sōbi member, when asked what he thought teachers should do, he replied "sabotage and boycott."[73] His position became more extreme later in the conversation: "Things are going this way all over the world. Education is controlled by nationalist governments. . . . There's nothing to be done short of revolution."[74]

Kitagawa's warning, first voiced in 1950, seems to have been borne out by the course of events. To the extent that Sōbi advocated the importance of creativity and the aesthetic as special capacities at odds with instrumental rationality, they always ran the risk that this structure would flip back against them. Protecting children from instrumentality simply put off the inevitable moment when children would have to find a place in an instrumentally organized society. Rather than facing up to this moment, Kubo's attraction to young children's creativity created an ark for which there was no promised land. As often happens, the aesthetic returned to its cloistered existence as a sphere of release from the everyday world and art became something *only* children do. The fact that Sōbi members provided so little concrete theorization of how creativity would affect the given social world meant that their words were quite easily incorporated into the Ministry of Education's Course of Study. In the end, Sōbi was at best a model for the society it envisioned, one that flourished within the decentralization of the early postwar.

Chapter 10

Hani Susumu and the Creativity of the Camera

In 1955, Hani Susumu and his crew began shooting the film *E o kaku kodomotachi* (Children who draw, 1956). The subject of the film was an art class in a public elementary school in Tokyo that was taught by Nonome Keizō, a young Sōbi teacher. This film is the most concrete connection between Hani and Sōbi, but I will show in this chapter that Hani's filmmaking shared an intellectual and historical connection with Sōbi that goes deeper than this single film. An examination of Hani's films and writings reveals that he was concerned with the same issues of change, growth and, most importantly, the idea that certain types of knowledge were possible only from within the intensity of complexly unfolding systems. He wrote in 1960 that universal thought has no reality. Impartiality is an illusion that "presents nothing more about people . . . than their submission." In contradistinction, Hani advocated prejudice. An "impartial" stance foreordained every development, robbing life of its uncertainty. Prejudice was needed to create "the *footing* to make reality actual" (*henken ga nakereba, genjitsu o jittaika suru 'ba' ga umarenainoda*). Repeating the metaphor of fireworks that Elise Grilli used at the 1956 Sōbi seminar, Hani wrote, "The footing from which we frame and grasp reality is dynamic, like bursting fireworks."[1] The conviction that a dynamic, open-ended prejudice was needed to apprehend reality had special significance for Hani's filmmaking practice.

Hani Susumu was born in 1928, son of Hani Setsuko, a hugely influential educator and activist for women's rights, and Hani Gorō, an equally influential Marxist historian. Susumu's grandmother, Hani Motoko, was the first female news reporter in Japan. She launched her own journal, the long-running *Katei no tomo* (Family companion), in 1903. She also founded a boarding school in 1921 that taught the Christian-inspired virtues of self-reliance, self-esteem, and a good work ethic.[2] The school, Jiyū Gakuen (Freedom Academy), was organized to mimic a home and family environment: in addition to classroom studies, students took care of their own daily needs, such as cleaning, cooking, and raising vegetables. When Susumu reached school age, he was enrolled at Jiyū Gakuen, which had begun to admit boys in 1935.[3]

Susumu met Kubo Sadajirō as a child, when he accompanied his parents to some of Kubo's prewar art exhibitions that his father had been asked to judge.[4] But the more significant connection came from his own experience of progressive education as a student at Jiyū Gakuen. Although Jiyū Gakuen was nowhere near as liberal as Neill's Summerhill, students there had to take responsibility for themselves. From the time he entered secondary school, Hani and his classmates lived in an on-campus dormitory and were responsible for cleaning the dorm, washing their clothes, and cooking their own breakfasts and dinners.[5] On the first day of class, the students faced an empty classroom: their first assignment was to design and build the desks and chairs they would use.[6] Because Jiyū Gakuen secondary schools were not certified by the Ministry of Education, Susumu's education in the 1940s was vastly different from what most others his age were exposed to. Growing up through this system while witnessing the effects of military rule (his father was arrested and tortured) undoubtedly gave Hani some sympathy for liberal convictions like those underlying Sōbi's pedagogy.

After he graduated from Jiyū Gakuen, Hani began work at the newly created Iwanami Productions in 1950.[7] Iwanami Productions, part of Iwanami Publishing, was a public relations (PR) firm that could be contracted by government or industry to make documentary films. Hani made publicity films for companies that sold tea, beer, and shoes, along with two films about plumbing (one inflow, one outflow).[8] Despite the potential limits imposed by contract work, some of the most innovative directors, producers, and cinematographers in Japan began their careers at Iwanami in the 1950s, including Hani Susumu, Ogawa Shinsuke, Tsuchimoto Noriaki, Kuroki Kazuo, Higashi Yōichi, Tamura Masaki, Iwasa Hisaya, and Suzuki Tatsuo, among many others.[9]

Abé Mark Nornes suggests three reasons why Iwanami was such a fertile environment. First, the Iwanami publishing house had a long-standing allegiance with progressive causes, and the film unit "became a haven for intelligent, left-leaning filmmakers, young and old, who had recently been purged from other sectors of the industry." Second, the combination of Iwanami's name recognition and its theatrical distribution agreement with Nikkatsu in 1955 meant that the films it produced garnered a wide audience. Finally, and most important, the leadership of veteran producers Yoshino Keiji and Kobayashi Isamu made Iwanami "one of the more egalitarian and nonsexist spaces in the Japanese film world."[10] Two female directors, Haneda Sumiko and Tokieda Toshie, began directing at Iwanami in the 1950s. Overall it was a place that supported experiment and creativity, and Hani was one of the people who led the way. His example attracted younger filmmakers, such as Tsuchimoto Noriaki, who would lead Japanese documentary in the 1960s and 1970s.

Three of Hani's early films deal prominently with children and learning: *E o kaku kodomotachi*, *Kyōshitsu no kodomotachi* (Children of the classroom, 1954), and *Furyō shōnen* (Bad boys, 1961). The first two are short documentaries, the third is a feature-length fiction film that is usually included in the New Wave canon. In all three, Hani used nonprofessional actors and full location shooting. While these practices may seem obvious for producing documentaries, they were not at the time. The norm, especially for children's documentaries, was to use child actors to stage scripted narratives. Some examples are *Kodomo gikai* (Child parliament, written and directed by Maruyama Shōji, 1950), and *Hae no inai machi* (A town without flies, written by Hani Susumu, directed by Yoshino Seiji and Mura Haruo, 1951).[11] All three of Hani's films, however, rejected the use of child actors, and structured a visual narrative out of the unscripted footage they were able to capture. Unlike earlier films' emphasis on problem solving, these films represented a fundamentally open-ended growth. Hani's observational style of shooting and his practice of structuring a story from the behavior of the filmed subjects meant that his camera and the film were "on the side of the child" in much the same way the Sōbi teacher tried to be.

Hani conceived of film as having two principle aspects, montage and duration, and he was an enthusiastic proponent of the latter. Duration, which Hani saw in its purest form in the uncut shot, was the mode in which reality pushed into the film with its greatest force and directness. Montage, by contrast, was the moment where the filmmaker exercised unilateral control over the image. Hani termed filmmakers who relied on montage "God-like" filmmakers because they acted in the name of ideas and interests external to the image, resulting in films that became "little universes (*shouchū*)," implying something internally coherent but for that very reason separated from a wider reality.[12] Again we might think of a parallel with Sōbi. Just as the traditional teacher assumed unilateral control over the little kingdom of the classroom in the name of an externally justified order, the director using montage arrogated a similar dictatorship over the growth and motion within the shot. A director working through duration, however, assumed the opposite stance before the change emergent in the image, foregoing direct intervention to let the change run its own course. Through duration, the motion of the filmed subject itself would structure the film.

For Hani, the fragments of film in which motion was fully embodied in the singularity of the filmed subject had a resistant power (*teikōryoku*). The dialectic engine of film worked not between shot and shot but in the tension between the resistant power of the uncut shot and the will of the editor. "The force exerted by the fragments upon the process of montage itself" was the tension that held the film together through time. Giving maximum play to the tension between the motion of the world and the internal motion of the filmmaker (and audience) could make the film "a firm joint (*kansetsu*) between human being and reality," a "dynamic balance within the historical situation."[13]

When Hani said that film established a joint between human being and reality, he did not mean the image granted unmediated access to reality or that the joint was anchored in a material trace on the film stock. The link was "technique" (*gijutsu*) in the widest sense: that by which "humans worked on their reality" and "correctly grasped their reality."[14] The reality of the film image sprang from an understanding of how to position and calibrate camera, lighting, crew, and so forth within (not outside of) the subject to be filmed. The most important tools were the camera and microphone (also the title of Hani's 1960 collection of theoretical writings). Far from passive receptors, the camera and microphone were the principle aesthetic tools of the filmmaker, like paint and a brush would be for a painter: the sometimes arbitrary material disciplines where potentiality condensed into actuality. The shot was not an unmediated registering of reality, but a space where the technology of the camera and the technique of the filmmaker made aspects of reality visible that might not be with other cameras, or indeed with the naked eye. Technique was successful when the director's knowledge and intuition were aligned with the possibilities of the instruments so that they would register reality with greatest sensitivity.

Achieving success was difficult. On the one hand, pure duration risked triviality if a film failed to capture the momentum and suspense of an enveloped experience. But this was part of a larger problem: the currency of the "reality effect" of fiction films which was so successful in calling forth emotional, rational, even kinesthetic responses in viewers. The problem was that the "reality effect" was produced by editing and production codes, not based in any actual reality. One of Hani's examples of such manipulation was the cut on action, which cobbled together a continuous motion that had never happened in actual space or time. Given the power of the reality effect, the shot could be at a considerable disadvantage.

If on the one hand duration risked triviality in the face of fiction films' reality effect, it also risked destruction in the practice of avant-garde montage. Literary and art critics such as Abe Kōbō, Nakahara Yūsuke, and Hariu Ichirō praised experimental montage, particularly that of Eisenstein, because it broke the reality effect of standard fiction film and demonstrated alternative relations among material. Hani pointed out, however, that although critical montage might destroy one facile version of reality, the result was simply another. An important corollary to that error was a resulting blindness to the most basic opportunity the camera and microphone presented. The "literary" approach took cameras and microphones to be neutral (*chūritsuteki*) receptacles, used to gather the ingredients of a film yet to be made. But for Hani, they were instruments that presented a never before available opportunity—to locate resistance to logic, rationality, and continuity storytelling in the emergent dynamics of reality itself. Capturing reality's own inherent excessiveness in the film was the most radical and empowering way to subvert the tyranny of argument or story.

Hani's film theory has considerable affinities with what Ian Aitken has called the "intuitionist realist tradition," consisting primarily of the work of John Grierson, Siegfried Kracauer, André Bazin, and György Lukács.[15] Although these four come from different traditions, they all "contend that film corresponds to certain aspects of reality. But . . . this correspondence is a homological one, and not affected by . . . assumptions about film's relationship to perceptual reality." Further, especially Bazin and Kracauer believed that "the dense, empirical richness of the realistic image enabled film to transcend ideological indoctrination and this, in turn, makes it clear that their theories of cinematic realism emerged in response to what was perceived to be an overarching context of instrumental socialization, and loss of individual freedom. Intuition is . . . preferred to reason, as the foremost means of effecting emancipation and insight." One corollary of this is that they, like Hani, generally disapproved of expressionist and avant-garde cinemas because the emancipatory potential was ruined by the director's intervention. Finally, the intuitionist realists all had a utopian streak. Kracauer's belief in the redeeming power of film has particular resonance with Hani's theory and practice. His "theory of realism was premised on the need to counter forces which . . . were transforming the modern subject into a functional, and alienated cog; and [he] is centrally concerned with film's ability to 'redeem' the individual from this fate."[16] It will be remembered that Sōbi teachers saw their primary function as protecting the space for individual experiment and creative growth, a stance that entailed a hands-off attitude toward their students. The reality of the present emerging into the future lay with *them*. The same stance infuses Hani's film theory.

Redeeming the Human Image

What interested Hani most intensely and what pulls together the three films I discuss is the problem of how film could represent the reality of human beings. As a subject, human beings were an obvious match for Hani's overriding conviction that the camera could open a window into the workings of the intensive manifold of human being in the world. The special problems of filming humans were the main subject of Hani's first book of film theory, *Engi shinai shuyakutachi* (Performers who don't act), which he begins with a few anecdotes. While shooting a shoe promotion, the crew decided to have an elementary school girl model the shoes. But when she walked in front of the test screen, her manner struck Hani as "so *abstract*. . . . There is no situation where people walk in such a generic way. It was just like when a wooden puppet walks . . . and looking at a child walking with such self-composure made me feel embarrassed somehow."[17] Humans are even more difficult than other subjects to abstract from their full existence. Just as Sōbi teachers were critical of the "model child" who did things because they understood what adults wanted, Hani knew that child actors would only produce a hackneyed image of childhood behavior.[18] Both of Hani's early documentaries about children in school, *Kyōshitsu no kodomotachi* (Children of the classroom) and *E o kaku kodomotachi* (Children who draw), were filmed in actual functioning classrooms with no sets or actors, and Hani's creative use of the camera allowed the film to capture images of children who were not acting for the camera. The results were strikingly new.[19]

Kyōshitsu, the first of the two documentaries, was filmed over one month in a second grade classroom. Hani and his crew set up their camera in full view of the students and simply waited for the novelty to wear off. Within a few days, the children began to ignore it. The crew wrapped the camera in a thick blanket to muffle its noise and hung additional lighting over the whole classroom so it would not distract the class.[20] Most important was the lens. They shot most of the film using a long-distance lens, focused closely on one or two children at a time. The crew was forbidden to move around while classes were in session, so once a class started the camera stayed put and the lenses could not be switched. The long lens was what enabled the filmmakers to get close-up shots of individual children's facial expressions and behavior. The finished film has many close-ups and few placement shots. Though the camera does not move, the film is extremely dynamic, creating the impression of having been thrown into the middle of a churning classroom.

This is not to say the film has no narrative. *Kyōshitsu* was commissioned by the Ministry of Education to be used as a teacher training film. It begins with a trainee teacher having her first experience in a classroom. She has much that she wants to teach but the students do not pay attention: one explores his mouth with his finger, one is karate chopping his book in the back row, one intently balances a piece of wire on the end of his pencil. The opening problem of the film is that the trainee doesn't understand how to harness each individual's energy. The remainder of the film is narrated by her host teacher, who is more experienced. The visual narration could be thought of as looking through the eyes of this more experienced teacher. What she and we see are individual children, each with different abilities and each living in slightly different worlds. Although the film was commissioned to explain how to deal with problem children it ends up showing that every child is a unique "problem."

The film helps the audience see children in a new way. The long-distance lens picks out the surprising complexity and fluidity of children's behavior, which would be invisible without the intervention of the camera. It establishes a perspective sympathetic to their full embodiment and struggle with their environment, vividly portrayed in their gesture and expression. The boy balancing the strand of wire on his pencil goes through incredible expressive changes in the space of a single take. Having successfully balanced it once, he suddenly looks up, eyes wide and forehead creased in apprehension (he is in the middle of a Japanese language class). Seeing he's safe, he picks up the wire and balances it again, this time moving the pencil in the air as if it's flying. His concentration suddenly breaks again and he snaps his eyes forward to check on the teacher. Hani writes:

> [As I was shooting the film], I understood that the overflowing fresh curiosity and vitality fairly bursting out from inside the children, even if it was expressed in mischief, was something that people in the teaching profession shouldn't ignore. Guidance that could grasp the bodily and physiological condition of children would be able to raise that energy into an actual power to seek things out. The telescopic lens

> turned out to be very effective in creating an index to show that. If we had shot the scenes in the usual scale, [the activity] would have simply looked like mischief. In close-up, though, something *from inside of them* came through in their expressions.[21]

Though the boy sailing his wire through the air might have been a troublemaker from the standpoint of Japanese class, the problem was not that he lacked concentration or curiosity.

There are other instances of redemption. One sequence focuses on the children raising their hands, vying to be called on. Rather than shots of teacher, class, teacher, class, the sequence is mainly shots of the children. One boy with his head on his desk raises his hand excitedly, but when someone else is called on, he slumps back down. A student named Aoki raises his hand but struggles to answer. Public hesitation is always uncomfortable, and Hani lengthens the moment through editing. In the end, Aoki is overwhelmed by a chorus of other students, but the film continues to focus on his face after he sits down. A conscientious student named Tanigawa sits in the front row, but the teacher/narrator feels that some part of her is "being held in reserve." The problem comes out on the playground in a sequence that is quietly excruciating. Tanigawa hovers a few feet away from the other girls, looking on as they play. She seems eager to join in but wavers, physiologically, about how to make the move. The sequence ends with a cut to a long shot of her standing in the middle of the playground by herself.

All of these examples concentrate on a single child for long enough that they pass through major changes of bodily and emotional attitude. Further, because they are not aware of the camera, their bodies and faces become incredibly expressive, trembling with all the precariousness of an experience that does not know the future. By lingering for so long on individual children, the shots subvert the typical, synoptic narrative of classroom behavior. One boy is *not* paying attention, one raises his hand and is *not* called on, one who is called on does *not* answer the question, and a girl on the playground *fails* to join in a game. All of these children are portrayed in a vivid fullness that, partly because they are children, elicits a powerful sympathy while ultimately facing the viewer with the extended experience of children as they move within their own dynamic worlds, *not* satisfying immediate pedagogical desires and, indeed, not fully satisfying their own desires.[22]

If the shots of the film became places where the embedded complexity of individual children's lives can be glimpsed unfolding from the inside, Hani saw the corresponding technique of making a film from them in terms similar to those Sōbi theorists used to talk about teaching. The Sōbi teaching approach was based on an intuitive understanding of the whole classroom, something notoriously difficult to quanitfy and generalize. Especially since the crew could not move the camera, they had to anticipate who and what they would need to be aiming at before anything happened. Hani compared it to "weather forecasting." The key was for the filmmakers to immerse themselves in the dynamic system of the classroom. "When we became aware of the psychological waves that were constantly rippling through the classroom, all the different behaviors necessarily began to register in our own feelings. Or rather, whatever it was within us that responded dynamically to this calling began to move of its own accord, becoming happy, disappointed, anxious, distracted. . . . When we became participants in the class, suddenly things that we hadn't been able to see became visible."[23] Short of actually being there, film was the only way to represent the internal complexity of these events. *Kyōshitsu no kodomotachi* might be thought of as the purest example of Hani's filmmaking theory.

While *Kyōshitsu*, which was filmed over one month, was a snapshot of a classroom, the ambition of *E o kaku kodomotachi* was to capture growth over time. Hani and his crew again visited a classroom in a working-class public school in Tokyo, but this time they stayed with the class for six months.[24] The film, which was partially sponsored by Kubo, had a much larger budget than *Kyōshitsu*.[25] The primary audience potentially included anyone interested in art education. Focusing on a class of first grade students, the film attempted to portray the classroom as well as disseminate the Sōbi philosophy. Partly for that reason, it is not as daring an experiment as *Kyōshitsu* was. In *E o kaku kodomotachi*, the excessive energy of the children that is such a central part of *Kyōshitsu no kodomotachi*, is tamed by the need to explain the relationship between this excess and the children's drawings.

Whereas in *Kyōshitsu* the creative resistance of each individual is registered in the film directly in the embodied behavior of the child, in *E o kaku kodomotachi*, the hermeneutic challenge, the invitation into another horizon of experience is located less in the children's behavior than in their artwork. As Nornes has observed, "representations of the children's inner worlds [in their artwork] is accompanied by an astounding shift from black and white to brilliant color."[26] The artwork is also shot with some camera motion, starting with a close-up of one detail, then revealing other elements slowly as the narrator offers interpretations. This makes it hard to find the edges of the artwork and slows the eye down, forcing us to see the picture as a semi-autonomous world. We are brought inside the dynamics of the drawing, and the image unfolds according to its own logic. The issue for the film is how to represent the connection between the artwork and the real world.

As the Sōbi approach indicated, the drawings themselves were ways for a child to process their bodily and mental immersion in the world. Hani's editing creates provocative parallels that encourage the audience to consider the vitality and seriousness of children's art. When the class goes to the riverside to play in the water and make sculptures in the mud, the camera captures one boy pushing a wooden board over the surface of the water and trying to ride it. A cut takes us to a drawing of a boat. The camera pans down the boat to stop on a close-up of the wake, which the child has drawn in an emphatic blue flare. One can see the traces of kinesthetic absorption wherein the motion of the child's arm mimicked the force of the boat against the water. The film argues that the pictures are embodied explorations of the world just as other kinds of play are.

Hani had hoped to use his film to record the children's growth over the six months of shooting. In his writing about the production process he focuses on how difficult that was. He and his crew tried to pick out a few "characters" at the beginning of the shooting whose journey would carry the narrative. But the changes those children actually underwent took them in unexpected directions, destroying the filmmakers' attempts to ground a consistent narrative. For Hani it was another illustration of how reality, especially in the form of people, always exceeds expectations. However, the back story of the filming is only available through Hani's writing. It is not apparent in the film. As a film, *E o kaku kodomotachi* foregrounds the problem of psychologism that also haunted Sōbi. For example, a girl named Tagawa who has been left behind in a race begins to cry. Art class immediately follows the race, so we can observe how her misfortune comes out in her drawings. She begins with crayons, pressing very hard on the paper. She draws the ground, a single red flower, and then covers the rest of the paper with purple. The narrator tells us that "purple is a color often used when a child has failed at something, is unhappy, or unwell."[27] Tagawa's next drawing is three red flowers against a blue sky with no purple. The narrator ventures that her feeling has improved. The implication is ambivalent. A generous reading would say that the film has captured and the narrator has explained how Tagawa grappled with and overcame her upsetting experience through her artwork. A different reading might point out that the narration appears to make the process inevitable: an upset child uses purple, which, it turns out, is a color we now know upset children use. Is Tagawa's experience simply an illustration?

Acting, or People Behaving Badly

Hani's *Furyō shōnen* was released in 1961. It was one of only two fiction films produced at Iwanami, the other being Hani's *Kanojo to kare* (She and he, 1963).[28]

Furyō shōnen was voted the number one film of 1961 in the annual poll conducted by Japan's most prominent film journal, *Kinema Junpo*. The story follows Asai Hiroshi, who is arrested for robbing a jewelry store. The film opens with him being taken to a juvenile processing center in a police van while the backstory of his life is told in flashback. He was born in 1942, his father died in the war, and he was eventually abandoned by a mother who couldn't support him. He doesn't have a home, and his street crimes are in part a way to support himself. With no family to collect him from the police, Asai is sent to a reformatory. The reformatory is divided into three segments: the first month of "boot camp"; his transfer to the laundry unit, where he rebels against the unit hierarchy; and his transfer to the woodshop unit, where he finds meaningful work and a welcoming community. It is in this final section that we witness Asai's transformation from someone who casts himself as an outsider and trusts no one to a person who can listen to and learn from others. The climactic sequence is a conversation with his friend and mentor Debari. Knowing that Asai will soon be released, Debari pulls him aside to tell him about his own road to the reformatory in a series of flashbacks. The point of the story is to impress upon Asai that the hustler lifestyle is self-defeating and will rob you of the love and connection you need. The final shots of the segment are idyllic: the boys have reached a deep understanding of the dangers of the outside world and the need for friendship. The film ends with Asai leaving the reformatory.

Although it is a fictional narrative, *Furyō shōnen* has many similarities to Hani's documentaries. Like the others, *Furyō* is concerned with how people see things. It represents the experience of people who are normally invisible in a way that goes beyond established bureaucratic-analytic categories in order to understand the full experience of their struggle. When Asai arrives at the processing center near the beginning of the film and an official reads his confession, which contains the information about his parents, we hear his inner voice sighing, "When will this shit end?" As the segment progresses, he undergoes a battery of psychological tests: he is hooked up to an ECG, psychologists mutter about his Rorschach performance in a darkened room, the proctors of an IQ test wear white lab coats. Intercut with this extravagant testing, however, Asai recalls his street life with his two buddies: a penniless life, but one infused with adventure, ingenuity, and enterprise. The boys spy on a police officer, speculating he must be pretty poor himself because he's so thin. Asai gets his gang into a movie theater by bloodying his own face and claiming that the man who attacked him is inside. In this scene, it is the onrush of Asai's dramatic acting that allows him to push past the guard. The sequence ends with Asai by himself, parading down a brightly lit Asakusa street with his jacket slung over his shoulder, doing spins as he walks. When this reverie dissolves into him trying to complete a pattern of hexagons on his test sheet, the point seems clear: analytic psychology cannot begin to understand the complexity of people's motion through life.

The affirmative presentation of this sequence is important because it creates a parallel to the flashbacks that narrate Debari's life before incarceration, which come at the end of the film. Debari's crime was more serious than Asai's: he and his fellow gang members mugged two people at knifepoint. The visual narration of the events is striking for its lack of visual momentum. Although both victims give up their money, it does not come easily. The gang takes the wallet from the first victim, an office worker, and finds little money in it. They press him for more. He hasn't got anymore. They take his watch and he begins to protest. It means a lot to him. He wants them to leave it. They refuse. He finds some more money and tries to trade it for the watch. They get angry and rough him up. They leave with the money and the watch. At the end, he's kneeling with his hands in prayer begging for the watch. The second victim, a night student walking home with his month's earnings, also resists. One gang member accidentally cuts the student's hand. It's not a serious wound, but it creates a pause in the action: the student isn't struggling anymore and the assailant is taken aback at having cut him. The student shakes his head in bewilderment and asks, "You take my money and then have to go and cut my hand too?" The scene ends with the student staring them down, eyes full of contempt. The sloppy, quotidian negotiations deflate any sense of romance or power. This is the lesson that Asai is now capable of hearing and seeing. While the first street life sequence was picaresque, he now sees that such a life works against the grain and will be a hard, gritty slog. The fact that it is narrated as a difference in filmic momentums is key: life is a matter of attuning to the transfer of energies. Like Homer Lane's policeman protecting himself by working *with* the crowd, Asai learns that he cannot resist everyone around him.

What happened to bring about this change? Focusing the discussion on acting will be helpful. Asai has not only learned how to behave differently, he is also given the space and the supportive community to begin to act for himself. After a month of boot camp, which emphasizes the authoritarian organization of the reformatory, the boys are assigned to work units that consist of about a dozen other boys who live and work together. The laundry, where Asai is first sent, has a strong hierarchy. Asai rebels against the hierarchy, causing two fights. This causes him to be transferred to the woodshop unit, which has a more open and supportive culture. It is there that he finds the space to begin to spread his wings. The contrast between the two units is represented is spatial terms. In the laundry unit, newer boys must massage the older boys' shoulders and give them their food. The older boys pass around a pornographic magazine, but instead of letting the new boys look at it, they shove the magazine into their faces. The words between them are mostly expletives and enjoinments, the verbal equivalents of pushing and prodding. The invasion of space continues in the workplace, where Asai's first attempt to fold a pair of trousers is interrupted repeatedly by a senior boy. This leads—inevitably—to the first fight, which is shot as a paradigmatic example of the inescapable physical relationships among the boys. Fighting is the only role they *can* play within this situation.

The woodworking unit is drastically different. The shop is capacious, almost a barn. When Asai meets the teacher, Ōkuma, the encounter contrasts with the treatment he got from the laundry group. The teacher asks him if he's had any experience working with wood. Asai remains defiantly silent. Ōkuma ignores the bait, saying anyone can pick it up. The dynamics show how Ōkuma simply moves around Asai instead of confronting him and begins to gesture outside the circle of their initial encounter to the cribs he will be building. Asai is pulled along, as if in his wake, his energy moving away from the teacher toward the world around them. Not only is this a model shot, it is a demonstration of something that underlay the Sōbi philosophy as well as Hani's film theory: each moment is equally meaningful in its own present. Teaching and learning are not matters of accumulating material or progressing through steps. Each moment is an opportunity for the full energy of the student to flourish. This moment between Ōkuma and Asai is not really Asai's first step toward reform, it is his reform already achieved: it only needs to be repeated. Because these moments are so subtle and fleeting, however, the camera is that which can help us see them in a nonanalytic way.

Following Asai's entry into the woodshop, the boys' creativity and initiative begin to appear. Perhaps the most remarkable scene in the film comes right after the woodshop, when Debari lights a cigarette. Although it is hardly a momentous event, it lasts for five minutes as Debari demonstrates how to construct a lighter out of pieces of cotton and a wooden board. There is little dramatic motivation for the scene, but through duration it registers an appreciation of the sophisticated competence, even in disobedience, of the imprisoned boy. It is not that this action signifies something else—the significance is the action unto itself. The final scene before Asai's release is the reformatory's annual festival. Some boys hold a mock demonstration to demand more pork that includes papier-mâché pigs stuck on the ends of oversized forks. There are costume dramas that include a parody of the Japanese army and a recreation of a Roman or Egyptian scene that includes boys dressed up as ancient queens. The festival is where the boys' creativity and imagination get free reign, and they express themselves with humor, playful display, and physical action.

The fact that these scenes have been acted, however, makes them different from Hani's documentaries. At least one would think so. In his writing about the films, Hani emphasizes the continuity among them and claims that *Furyō shōnen* was largely documentary. His reasoning is rooted in his idea that long duration always contains resistant documentary moments within it. The boys playing the roles of the juvenile delinquents were nonprofessional actors who themselves had recently been juvenile delinquents. Hani had written a script for the film but he soon realized the young actors did not like reading it. He decided to leave the specifics of the performance up to the boys, letting them improvise the scenes as they thought best. To draw them into the process, Hani and his assistant, Tsuchimoto Noriaki, would act out a scene and then let the boys correct them and show them how to do it properly. Although the story was a fiction, the boys were acting as their former selves, which raises interesting questions about how acting relates to authentic behavior.

The fictional progression of *Furyō shōnen* presents a case where Asai is given the space and the support to begin to act for himself. But it is typical of Hani's theory and practice that the shift is not reasoned: there is no *bildung* montage to convince us of change and no internal monologues that account for the transformation. The change is registered in long takes and long sequences of the boys acting for themselves. From a traditional narrative standpoint, the change is undermotivated and underdetermined. There is no triumphant breakthrough. What might be considered breakthrough moments are extremely banal. But herein lies a point: the boys' actions exist apart from our desires and can only come into themselves for themselves.

Hani argued that the making of the film also offered a lesson in the importance of performance and the power of film to capture it. His concept of performance (*engi*) was extremely broad: a process of experimentation that formed the basis of all human and animal being in the world. "Living, insofar as one is reciprocally engaged [*aikakawatte iru*], doesn't admit of any truth that can be pinned down and stopped. Because [that truth] only ever presents itself in the already living moment. The process by which humans subjectively engage with that moment is precisely what we mean by performance."[29] This did not mean that everything always went smoothly. Performance was not an aesthetic moment of perfect "fit." Hani, like Kitagawa Tamiji, placed highest value on the process of struggle rather than on its achievement. That is why Hani was so concerned with capturing the moments of hesitation and apparent failure: the performative "stuttering," as Hani called it, revealed the moments when an individual grappled with a new environment or grappled with it in a new way. Automatic, habitual activity could not be considered performance. Performance was a process by which people brought themselves into a new form.

A common thread running through these three films is bearing witness to moments of experimentation and struggle. For younger children, art is one arena where the progression of trial and error can be seen. For the untrained actors of *Furyō shōnen*, it was the process of acting and being filmed. Being able to perform in front of the camera reopened the space for experiment as such. Adult reality insists on a basic character (*hontai*) against which the processes of experimentation and performance are taken to be inauthentic and untrue (*uso*). While Hani recognized the social power of this construction, he sought to revalue performance as proposing a "hypothetical form [*kari no sugata*]. This hypothetical form is not to be taken lightly because in life there can never be anything more than hypothetical personae."[30] Thus, although social convention might insist on stable roles (which is paradoxically read as basic character ex post facto), the actuality of life unfolding occurs only through provisional positions and forms of behavior.

Performance begins at the moment the subject begins to alter established patterns of behavior, exploring their own actions as they should be: as hypothetical forms. According to Hani, acting empowered the boys vis-à-vis their own behavior in a way that couldn't happen anywhere else in the adult world. Although they themselves had been juvenile delinquents, the process of reenacting their behavior *as an enactment* made the non-identity between them and their actions obvious and opened the possibility for change. It loosened their actions from the gravity of character and reopened the future as something not yet set. Hani argued that just as his fiction film portrayed the possible reformation of a boy through his process of discovering himself within new patterns of behavior, the making of the film gave the same chance to the "actors" who were playing the boys. He recalled the transformation that occurred when the actor playing Asai was assured that he could do the robbery sequence with no fear of arrest. In the film, the boys could fight off bullies in the reformatory with no fear of getting hurt and muscle their way into movie theaters with no fear of reprisal. In a way, it was a bad boy's dream.[31] However, instead of encouraging further bad behavior, the loosening of the bonds of "basic character" allowed the performance to come to the fore and be recognized as hypothetical. Read against this idea, the final shot of the film that shows the fictionalized Asai "behind bars" as he walks away from the reformatory gate might suggest he is returning to the prison of basic character that he had managed to escape inside prison.

Film was important to Hani's claim of redemption because it made possible a reanimation of a unique, indeterminate moment—a moment when the subject is completely absorbed in a contextualized passage of time. "Even if the same thing were repeated, its meaning, its effect, the reaction to it, would be different."[32] With film, however, a nonrepeatable performance can be replayed over and over. Hani related that when the boys were faced with the image of their actions when they were doing the overdubbing for the soundtrack, they began to criticize their own behavior. In the mugging scene that Debari relates in flashback, the boys were able to see the victims in the scene from a third-person position. They could come outside of the tunnel vision of violence and see the whole scene from outside the momentum of being part of it. Film alone could provide this feedback, this doubling of perspective that demonstrates so clearly that we are not the same through time. Abstracting this idea from the case of the juvenile delinquents gives a good sense of Hani's belief in the redemptive power of film: it alone could provide the way to understand the uniqueness of our actions within a richly embedded world. The vision it made possible reopened the possibility of each moment so that it again could become performance, and demonstrated the open-endedness of any historical present. This was also the ideal of the *minkan kyōiku undō* and the attitude of the Sōbi teachers toward their pupils: that all of life would be learning, change, and growth.

The common intellectual concerns between Sōbi and Hani are evident. They also shared political concerns and commitments to certain courses of action. The golden age of Sōbi was the 1950s, a period when in education, as in so many other areas, there was intellectual and institutional space for the active involvement of many. Hani was a part of this period as well, and although his field of activity was film, his attempt to take hold of and transform the present he lived through was characterized by a commitment to the egalitarian principle that each person should be afforded equal space to live a life of their own learning. His film practice was a self-conscious attempt to realize this.

Like Bazin, Hani was aware of the resurgence of the deep field and the long take in filming as a revolution that he was living through. The revolution began in earnest with the Italian neorealists, whose films also used amateur actors and location shooting, deep focus, and long takes. Italian neorealism is a fixture of Japanese film culture of the 1950s: its visual freshness understood as a faithful imprint of the moment of liberation it was born of.[33] Hani's respect for neorealism rested on the belief that non-hierarchical framings and motion that emerged from within shots had both a reality and a complexity that pulled viewers out of their seats and engaged them in the progression of that reality perceptually and cognitively. The structure and effect of the films became homologous to those of liberation: though uneven, abrupt, and sometimes violent and confusing, they drew everyone out to participate.

Hani's films followed similar convictions toward similar ends. The two classroom documentaries attempted to redeem the subjective growth of children, taking as their central subject matter the struggle to grow into oneself and one's world. Their form also challenged the top-down view of the child and called the audience into attempts at understanding the classroom, family, and neighborhood, from each child's perspective. In *Furyō shōnen*, the redemptive power of film became literal, at least according to Hani's account. The former juveniles learned from their participation. Some of them went on to star in other films. Film became a space for change in the world. While the guise of fiction allowed the boys the social space to reenact themselves, the film makes these performances available to reflection in a way that no other technology could: capturing individuals throwing themselves out in the world when they are that moment and no other, while at the same time demonstrating in the very distance between image and viewer that that was not the *only* possible moment. With time, change comes into the world. Children are but the best teachers of that.

Conclusion: Opening Open Doors

The Sōbi movement and the early works of Hani Susumu share a constellation of beliefs and commitments: that human beings are biologically and sensually involved in the world, that a certain moral balance springs from that understanding, that each person is equally able to create for themselves when given the space and time, that one must be committed to looking at life from the inside out, that each person's future is fundamentally open, and, finally, the conviction that the most important task facing them was to find social relations and modes of representation that would be founded upon these insights. There is no small degree of contradiction in these commitments, particularly the last one. By way of closing this chapter and providing final thoughts, I will pause over the contradiction while introducing some of the artists closest to Sōbi whose work also speaks to it.

Many of the artists most closely related to Sōbi were members of the Asocio de Artistos Demokrato (Association of Democratic Artists), which was founded in 1951 by the avant-garde artist Ei Kyū (1911–1960), a close friend of Kubo's since the two met at a gathering of Esperantists in 1935.[34] Kubo was a patron for both Sōbi and Demokrato, and he invited Demokrato members Ei Kyū, Izumi Shigeru, Katō Tadashi, Ay-O, and Hosoe Eikō to the Sōbi summer seminars to teach workshops on art production and appreciation. Some also submitted their works to his small collector sales.

Ei Kyū formed Demokrato with the express intention of opposing the cultural hierarchies of the established exhibition societies. For Ei Kyū—as for many of the modern and avant-garde artists that appear in this study—these societies were implicated in wider political and social structures of authoritarianism.[35] In choosing the word Demokrato in the name of their group, the members espoused an ideal of democracy that resembled an ethic of shared creativity and self-overcoming. They understood that choosing this particular word in the early 1950s was risky. In his opening essay for the first issue of *Demokurāto*, Fukushima Tatsuo wrote, "The word 'democracy' [*demokurashii*] passes among us like a papal indulgence. Everybody knows how this convenient word, in dressing up any injustice, can put a person's conscience to sleep, turn lies into truth, and conceal all undemocratic [*himinshuteki*] intentions from proper criticism. . . . We must take this word, made filthy with bad intentions, and throw it back once more into the faces of our enemies."[36] Democracy had clearly become degraded as a word. The group's response was to redeem it through action, making it more than a word through their activities and relations with others.

Members of Demokrato did not want to become just another exhibition society. They wanted to pioneer a new form of organization that would never harden into a creativity-blocking structure. There was no hierarchy among members, no apprenticeship, no antechamber to the real world: Ay-O remembers how surprised he was as a young artist to be invited to exhibit with the group immediately after he joined.[37] In the debut issue of the *Demokurāto* newsletter, Ei Kyū opened his article with the proposal that "freedom of exhibition is something all artists must desire equally."[38] Much like members of Sōbi, members of Demokrato assumed that everyone could be creative if they were only afforded the space. The Demokrato group was an open platform that came to include painters, printmakers, graphic designers, dancers, photographers, and critics. Demokrato took openness and equality to greater lengths than many other artists' groups; its members worked in truly disparate styles. While that may have been the truest embodiment of the group's values, it was also a liability: the variety of media and styles makes it difficult to apprehend Demokrato as a coherent artistic group.

Because of the difficulty in apprehending a group coherence in the artwork of Demokrato members, I have decided to focus on the work of two artists who would later join Fluxus. The humility of Fluxus artworks, the underdetermination of Fluxus events, the gentle but clear invitation to do something outside the usual course of habit but with no clear instruction as to what, all evoke connections with child-centered pedagogy. Hannah Higgins has made this argument with great clarity in her book *Fluxus Experience*. She finds conceptual connections between Fluxus and John Dewey's experience-based pedagogy, pointing out that they shared the aim of stimulating all the senses to suggest a mode of fuller engagement with the physical and social world.[39]

Ay-O (b. 1931; given name Iijima Takao) joined Demokrato in 1953, where he became close with Kubo. He was also briefly an art teacher in a public school, but he found that he was unsuited to teaching.[40] Following the dissolution of Demokrato in 1958, he left Japan for New York City to follow his dream of becoming an artist there. He fell in with the Fluxus artists in 1961 and became an important part of that group. One of Ay-O's most famous works are his *Finger Boxes*: small hollow cubes made of wood, each with one hole large enough to stick a finger through. Each box contains a different textured material, such as sponge, cotton, or nails, that can be explored by touch but not seen (fig. 10.1). Sōbi did not rely on any specific collection of practices to provoke students' engagement, leaving that experiment up to individual teachers. Like Fluxkits, we sense that the red caps and bright sweaters do not refer to any definite desired outcome. Rather, they function as what Hannah Higgins terms a "metarealistic trigger," shunting the ordinary toward significance, reorienting the foregone toward presence.[41] Fluxus events also share something with Sōbi and Hani's films—the conviction that time cannot be compressed or abstracted from lived situations. While Sōbi's pedagogy revolved around a humility before the internal logic of each child's development, John Cage's compositions demand a similarly rigorous respect for open-endedness.[42]

The connection between Sōbi and Fluxus is historically interesting because, although Higgins's analysis finds illuminating resonances between Fluxus and John Dewey's ideas about education and democracy, there are not many direct connections between the two, apart from Robert Filliou, an educator who took inspiration from Fluxus in developing a child- and play-centered pedagogy.[43] Ay-O and Takako Saitō provide at least two examples of people coming out of experiences with child-centered education and bringing that to Fluxus.

Takako Saitō was a member of Sōbi from 1953 until she left for New York in 1963.[44] She taught Japanese, and used creative classroom techniques that echo Neill's. She asked her students to write their own stories—whatever

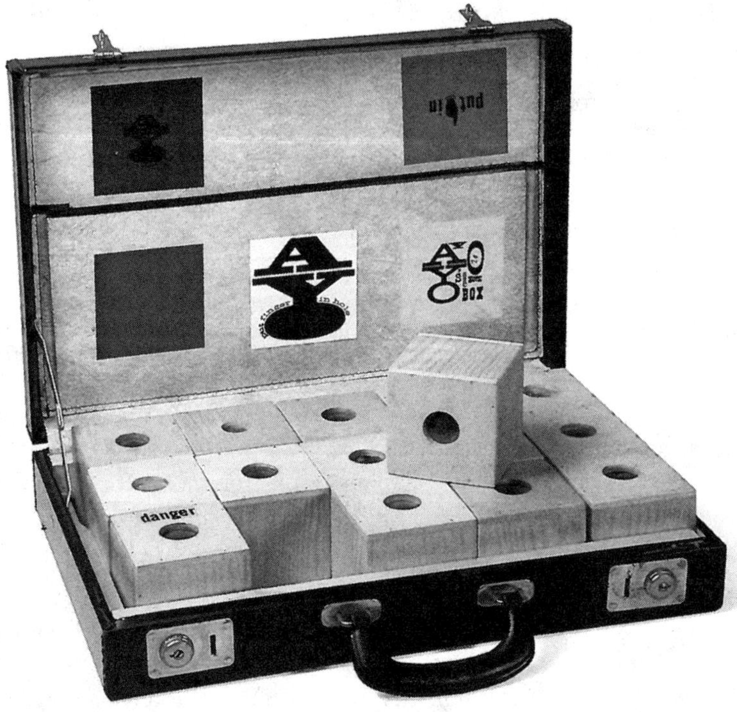

FIGURE 10.1 Ay-O, *Finger Box-Kit*, 1963. Mixed media. Artist's collection. Image from Kiyoshi Kusumi, ed., *Niji no kanatani Ay-O kaiko 1950–2006* (Over the rainbow: Ay-O retrospective, 1950–2006) (Bijutsu Shuppan-Sha, 2001), 45.

they wanted—and allowed them to skip class and play baseball until they began to write of their own accord. Once they started writing out of their own interest, they wrote so much she could barely keep up with correcting it.[45] Through Sōbi, she met Ay-O, who introduced her to Fluxus when she arrived in New York. Saitō's artistic career is one that models a constant learning process. She constantly experimented with new genres such as games, events, and performance, and she devoted correspondingly little energy to honing her public image, to forming herself into a stable "character," to borrow Hani's word. She simply continued her aesthetic explorations for their own sake. It is largely because of this that her work remained understudied until Yoshimoto Midori's research.

Many of Saitō's works are based on games and invite participation. Her chess series is one of the earliest and most well-known examples. Although some of her chess sets simply replace the usual pieces with other objects, some seem to confound the game itself. *Weight Chess*, *Sound Chess*, and *Smell Chess* use pieces that are differentiated by the invisible qualities of weight, sound, and smell (fig. 10.2). Like Ay-O's *Finger-Boxes* and the work of many other Fluxus artists, they demand the engagement of all senses and an integration of touch and smell with memory, cognition, and logic. It would not be impossible to play a game of chess with one of these sets but the player would have to keep reacquainting themselves with the pieces, sniffing or weighing them as they moved around the board, and would have to know the opponent's pieces also. The dynamics of the middle game, when most pieces are engaging with each other, would break down under the unseen idiosyncrasies of each piece. You could not rely on an instantly apprehensible order the same way you would by vision but would have to begin letting the pieces move without full knowledge of the system. In this respect, they

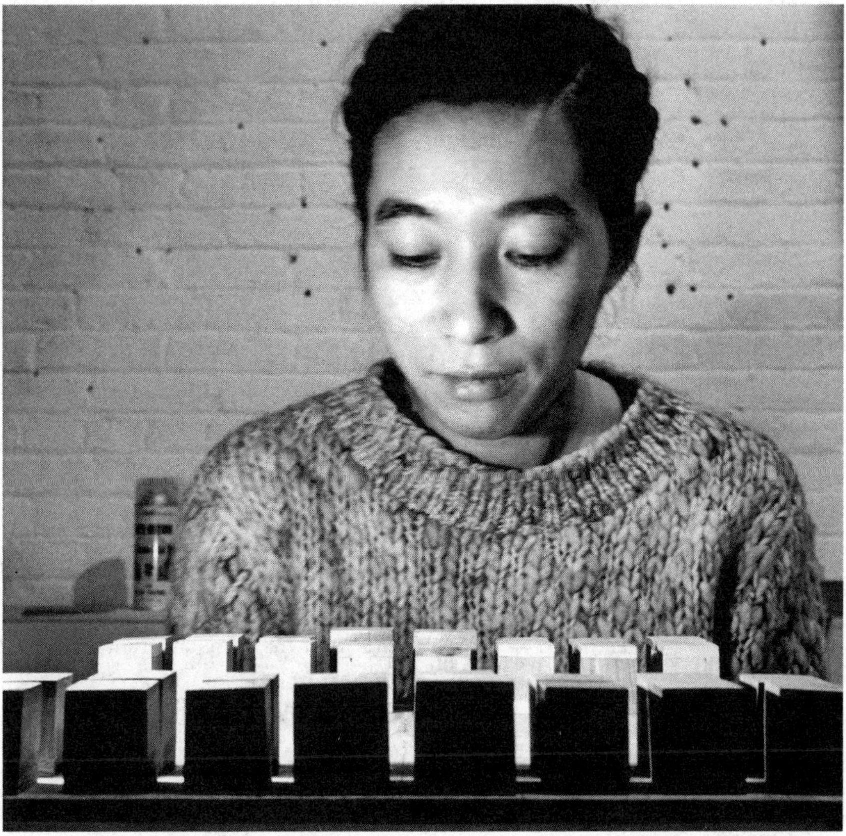

FIGURE 10.2 Takako Saitō with *Weight Chess* or *Sound Chess*, ca. 1965. Mixed media. Photo by George Maciunas. Gilbert and Lila Silverman Fluxus Collection, Museum of Modern Art.

might be like a class of children, their future open—in a game that begins and develops, but whose collective end no one can see.

What Sōbi, Hani Susumu, Democrato, Ay-O, and Takako Saitō all share is a conceptual and ethical commitment to the principle that every individual ought to be thought of and treated as if they each had a present and future unique to them. As an idea this is almost trite. But it becomes immensely difficult, if not contradictory, when people attempt to realize it in social structure or representation. It is precisely for the attempt to do that that these cases are most interesting and valuable.

Surely we should be suspicious when filmmakers, particularly documentary filmmakers, claim that they are simply letting reality speak for itself through their films, or when artists imply that we the viewers are really the artists. How can we take *teachers* seriously who claim to be the emancipators of children? Such claims too often hide power imbalances and manipulation. The suspicions must be acknowledged: it is, in the end, a paradox that people can be shown what they can already see and can be led to do things that only they can do. But short of quitting the teaching profession (and thereby ceding their classrooms to others), Sōbi teachers do seem to have avoided directing or coercing their students or each other to a great extent. For better or for worse, they attempted to create a space that was free from the matrix of inherited adult expectations and let their students explore their own experiences and desires to the maximum extent. They seem to have embodied an attitude that they did not know the individual futures of their charges and their own process of self-education enacted their belief that learning could happen everywhere and on all occasions. With no administrative or institutional advantages, their primary tactic was a direct demonstration of their ideals, showing them to be possible in the immediate present. Whether or not others followed was ultimately up to them.

In Hani's case, we must recognize that the films are, in the final analysis, arguments and messages about children. If the task is to represent the openness and indeterminateness of actuality happening, the most rigorous and precise technique would be to relinquish all attempts at representation. Hani would not be interesting if he did this. Though his films are narrative and polemical, there is an undeniable intensity to watching people acting in such proximity, but not for the camera or viewer. The kinesthetic and emotional resolution of certain movements, even quite small ones, are the most important engines of interest that keep the viewer watching the film present and engaged. Further, the fact that the film crew had to work within a functioning classroom is important. The film was possible only because of an actual relationship between the filmmaker and the filmed, something that is not infinitely pliable and certainly could not be made prior to the filming. The practice of filmmakers sharing the life space of the filmed would have to wait for Hani's younger colleagues Tsuchimoto Noriaki and Ogawa Shinsuke to reach its most developed form, but the view of young children made possible by Hani's adoption of a position where he could capture behavior from alongside its happening, was a significant first step along this trajectory. If we take the films as a whole, it is reasonable to say that they *suggest* or *indicate* an understanding of others that rests on the realization that they are inhabiting worlds whose fullness and complexity we cannot know and that this understanding implies certain ethics or types of practice. As a representation, of course, the films are necessarily partial, partisan, and contradictory.

One cannot deny the fundamental paradox of leading a liberation or of representing indeterminacy. But while this point is logically undeniable, it offers no way to begin to understand the vast record of attempts at such things that in the process of their inevitable partial failure have nevertheless produced shared cultures. One might even venture that *all* culture exists in this field somewhere shy of success, eternally falling short of identity and surety. Revealing a thing's construction, showing that it is partial and contingent, is a critical task that risks nothing because it is obvious from the outset. What is more difficult is indicating ways that people might *practice* or *show* the non-identity of such constructions and the possibility of their change. Here Hani, Sōbi, and Fluxus present some possibilities, specifically in their failures and imperfections.

While it is something of a mannerism in writing about the politics of representation to resolve the issue by claiming that the responsibility for actualizing the potential of a representation rests with the audience or the reader, that is the only fitting way to end a discussion of the political, social, and aesthetic work of the groups I have discussed here. The works of Ay-O and Takako Saitō do not involve the same extended interaction and expectation of responsibility as embedded documentary, much less teaching. But as artworks they concentrate a basic point. Their very modesty is an encouragement not to become too caught up in this particular embodiment of a possibility. They are highly aware of the risk of idolatry, whereby the work or the experience of it might be taken to stand in for emancipation itself. Do not get caught up with the pointing finger, or indeed with the finger box: it is more about the hole, which just needs some kind of framing.

Against the history of postwar Japan viewed from the present, the shared principle of every individual's future being open seems to harbor an improbably faint reality. But it is against this improbability that the work of these people in the name of such a fundamentally democratic ideal is important.

Although we might see their attempts as unlikely, they were not so isolated, and in fact it would be a mistake to confuse Sōbi's or Hani's specific trajectories for the possibilities of the early postwar in general. Sōbi itself is certainly not the key to democracy. To the contrary, the larger issue is that people could drop out of Sōbi and join the Atarashii E no Kai, or ignore both altogether. Although one can find many imperfect examples of democracy, its reality is not quite in any example, but in the realization that it is not the only one.

Part Four

Kyushu-ha Tartare

Anti-Art between Raw and Haute

Chapter 11

The Grand Meeting of Heroes

We will begin with the dark noon of Kyushu-ha—a group performance called The Grand Meeting of Heroes that left a beach charred, two chickens dead, and a group of female mannequins severed at the waist, their heads punctured with nails. The Grand Meeting unfolded through the night of November 15–16, 1962, five years after the founding of Kyushu-ha, and well past the high point of 1958–1960. By the time of the Grand Meeting, Kyushu-ha was coming apart: people had entered, left, and returned to the group, and subgroups had grown up around its edges. Tokyo-based critics were starting to move on to more novel acts. The Grand Meeting was a last-ditch effort by Sakurai Takami, Kyushu-ha's central personality and binding force, to reinvigorate the group and recapture its dynamism. He had brought Kyushu-ha together in the first place, and the Grand Meeting was his final attempt to bring it together again. It can be thought of as a microcosm of Kyushu-ha, striving for millenarian, untimely dreams just on the dawn of failure.

Kyushu-ha was from Kyushu, the southernmost large island of the Japanese archipelago, an eighteen-hour train ride from Tokyo at the time. Known for coal, steel, and farming, Kyushu was not a place one would expect to find a radical avant-garde art group. But there they were. Their work on the night of the Grand Meeting was true to form. They performed a series of happenings on a deserted beach outside the regional capital of

Fukuoka, composing what they called a "festival of darkness" (*yami no shukusai*). Itoi Kanji, making a guest appearance, opened the events by handing each participant small assemblages he had constructed. Ōyama Uichi moved the performance outside, burning down a tower of wood and empty bottles that he had labeled, "a symbol for old art," and rolling around in the embers while they burned on the ground. A group visiting from Tokyo performed a piece of experimental music. Obata Hidesuke, wrapped completely in bandages and working over a white canvas, killed two chickens by inserting a pin into each one's head and then covered them and the canvas with black paint. Tabe Mitsuko began a performance driving nails into the heads of mannequins, but finding it difficult to get them in, dismantled the mannequins and dressed the lower halves in women's stockings. Sakurai Takami and Chō Yoriko performed a collaborative piece using an installation covered with eggs. Sakurai handed an instruction to the participants: "Eat eggs that fill up the hole. When you've eaten them, I'll be here." When the participants had eaten all the eggs, Chō was revealed sitting motionless inside the structure. While the other members took turns doing their performances, Miyazaki Junnosuke worked alone down near the waterline, digging a series of holes in the sand that filled in and disappeared when the tide came in at midnight.[1]

None of the twenty or so members of Kyushu-ha were trained as artists. Most were wage earners in full-time jobs who worked on their art in their "free" time.[2] Yet in that free time they were able to create an art movement that forged a place in Fukuoka for avant-garde, contestatory art where none had existed before. Their work overturned the time of the daily round of work and measured recovery. It also challenged the space of Fukuoka, expanding the places and possibilities for art. They brought art out onto the street, organized independent exhibitions where anyone could display their work, and attacked the standards of established exhibition societies that dictated what could and could not be seen as art. Sakurai's vision for the group was of a truly mass art movement that anyone could join regardless of training or talent, so long as they were passionate. Much to the consternation of more ambitious members, he invited anyone to join, inflated membership lists, and tried to look past all differences, just so that he might expand the group a little further: to make it a movement in which "anyone [could] become a god."[3] Even as Kyushu-ha itself disintegrated in the early 1960s, other groups were forming out of its body. Its example spread, providing a model for small-group organizing and activist exhibition.

Kyushu-ha also managed to carve a place for itself in Tokyo-centered art history as one of the most important and irreverent practitioners of Anti-Art (*hangeijutsu*). Anti-Art is a term used to label the eruption of junk assemblage in the Japanese art world in the late 1950s, a phenomenon that happened nearly simultaneously in the capitalist west: paralleled by *nouveau réalisme* in France and proto-pop art in the United States. Kyushu-ha held group exhibitions once a year in Tokyo and participated in the annual Yomiuri Independent Exhibition, which was open submission and a hothouse for Anti-Art, spawning most of the experimental artists who would go on to make their mark in the 1960s and beyond. Kyushu-ha was notorious for earthy and uncanny works made of paint, reed mats, wood, rope, wire, springs, nails, cardboard, mannequin parts, cement, and, of course, their trademark material, tar. They used tar instead of black paint, they used it for its gooey sculptural properties, they used it as an adhesive, they used it for its *smell*. They have the dubious distinction of being the first art group to have had one of their works rejected from the open-submission Yomiuri exhibition: a mass of junk left behind after a marathon group production session. Kikuhata Mokuma recalls that they decided to submit it because they thought it would be easier to do that than throw it away.[4]

It all sounds like good fun, but in fact it wasn't. Few former members of Kyushu-ha look back positively on this episode in their lives. It left grudges, betrayals, scars, and embarrassments. It also left few works: about 10 percent of the original work survives. Some of it was simply abandoned or burned in Tokyo after the Yomiuri Independent every year because it was not worth paying to ship it back to Fukuoka. But much of it was victim to slow decay and loss. Museums and collectors did not acquire the works, so the artists had to find storage space in their own homes, something made more difficult by their outlandish size. Until 1988, the year that the Fukuoka Art Museum held a retrospective exhibition, it was widely thought that the group had left no surviving work. Kuroda Raiji, the curator of the 1988 exhibition, found works moldering in backyard sheds and beneath the eaves of houses. He also found artists unwilling to talk.

To find out why, let's revisit that seaside in late 1962. The Grand Meeting itself had grown out of a critical failure. On the occasion of their 1961 group show at the Ginza Gallery, in Tokyo (what would turn out to be their last show there), they were criticized in the art press for seeming to have "forgotten their real work." The show looked like they had "upended a box of toys and gone wild with them."[5] A meeting at the end of 1961 to reflect on this turned nasty, leading to the group's second breakup. In 1962, Sakurai began, one more time, to pull it back together: the Grand Meeting was in part a desperate last stand for him. On the night of the Grand Meeting it was raining and cold and, other than the Heroes themselves, the beach was deserted. There was no audience. It is hard to imagine how desolate this must have seemed as the participants performed their works in turn, behind them the shadows of the mountains that surround Fukuoka, in front of them the blackness of the November sea. As if a symptom of this darkness, only a handful of photographs of the event survive, of Ōyama hurling fire against the night (fig. 11.1).

But more than just the night was cool. A group of artists and musicians had made the journey from Tokyo to participate: Tone Yasunao, Kosugi Takehisa, Kazakura Shō, and the activist and critic Yoshida Yoshie. Tone, Kosugi, and Kazakura were experimental musicians and performers who explored highly conceptual, atonal music that verged on instruction-based performance art. They could not have been more temperamentally distant from Kyushu-ha's earnest artistic and social interests, and they arrived in Fukuoka just one month after John Cage and David Tudor's first live performances in Japan, which had been held in Tokyo. The performances sent shockwaves around Japan's music and art world, becoming known as the "Cage shock."[6] Although the young performers had already been experimenting with found sound and the objecthood of musical instruments, they were impressed with Cage and Tudor's aleatory approach to composition and performance.[7] This led to almost immediate disagreement with Kyushu-ha over the schedule of

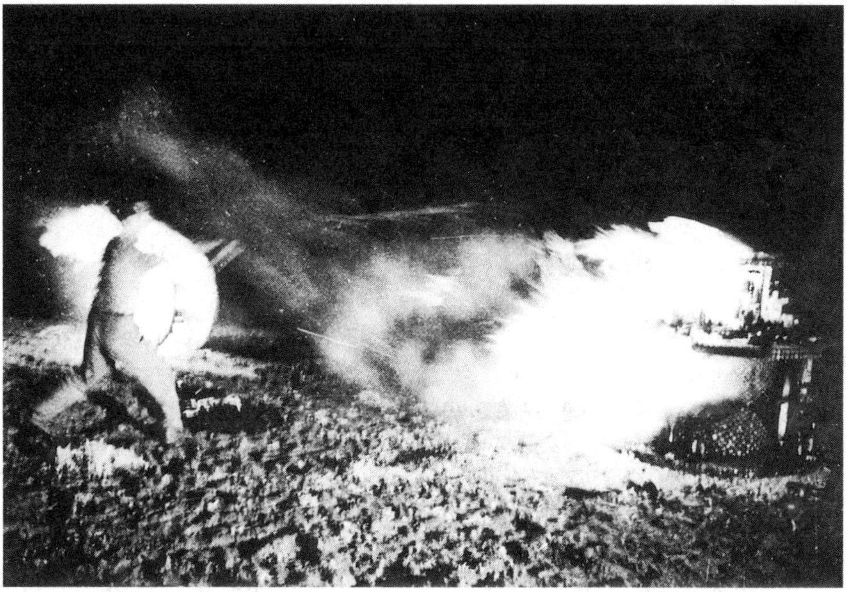

FIGURE 11.1 Photograph of Ōyama Uichi's performance at the Grand Meeting of Heroes, November 1962. Photographer unknown. Courtesy of the Fukuoka Art Museum.

performances that Kyushu-ha had drawn up for the Grand Meeting. Kyushu-ha's premeditated structuring of performance necessarily implied a clear beginning and end to each artist's work, and this conflicted with the musicians' interest in chance and steady-state everydayness.

A few months later, Yoshida Yoshie wrote an insightful but ultimately critical piece about the Grand Meeting in the small art journal *Sansai*. He explained the objection of the Tokyo group as being that "[a performance] isn't something you can do from time A to time B." The performance had already started on the train down from Tokyo: "We'd already started what we were doing, and we weren't going to stop doing it when the next morning came."[8] The problem was that Kyushu-ha's performances, no matter how destructive they might have been, were governed in the last instance by a "dramaturgy in which a predictable outcome is resolved in a climax." In other words, the Grand Meeting was a piece of theater, a drama, whose "optimistic fighting spirit" created dissonance between the two groups. Yoshida implied that this optimism was no longer appropriate to art and its community by contrasting it to what he argued was a new kind of performance: the Happening. "The Happening has sprung up against a background of despair, to capture apathy, desire, humor, nonsense in their everyday register . . . not a performance, but a precise doing of what one is already doing."[9]

Yoshida's critique is symptomatic of a larger shift underway in the world of contemporary art at the time: performers on a stage (and John Cage and David Tudor were most definitely on a stage) would eschew dramaturgy and representation to realize a "precise doing of what [they were] already doing." Kyushu-ha had formed in 1957 and the Grand Meeting was in late 1962, a five year period that saw immense political and social change in Japan. The "background of despair" that Yoshida invokes is most likely the failure of the the Anpo protests of 1960 to block the renewal of the Treaty of Mutual Cooperation and Security with the United States. Yoshida is arguing that the toned down, non-climax-oriented Happening was one more element in the emerging consensus that direct political confrontation was doomed to failure. Many doomsayers saw the end of the avant-garde (*zen'ei*) in this period and the consolidation of another paradigm, the contemporary (*gendai*).[10] At stake was a replacement of historically, narratively articulated social movements (of a mostly left wing variety), with a spatially expansive, nondeveloping flux of international contemporaneity (*kokusaiteki dōjisei*).[11] Kyushu-ha, in aiming for revolution, in even planning their events, was simply falling behind the times, and their days in Tokyo were numbered.

What I propose in the following chapters is to turn this upside down. Kyushu-ha's poster for their fateful 1961 exhibit at the Ginza Gallery read

"In the Tokyo provinces: Kyushu-ha makes a surprise appearance!"[12] They imitated a poster format used by itinerant theater troupes to advertise their shows, poking fun at themselves and also pretending to overturn the usual hierarchy between Tokyo and the provinces, by referring to Tokyo itself as a province. Of course they could never succeed in doing that. But here I want to take its challenge seriously. For the moment let us consider Tokyo and, more importantly, New York, to be provincial and benighted. Let us consider the hierarchies of taste that structure inclusion and exclusion from art as things built primarily on ignorance. Let us recognize that Kyushu-ha is an undoubtedly minor group, one that just barely made it into the history of contemporary art, but consider it a rare opportunity to examine a movement which shouldn't have survived the tidiness of purported paradigm shifts. Although there were dozens of small modernist and avant-garde art groups scattered around Japan at this time, few managed to reverse the gears like Kyushu-ha did, coming back up the cultural hierarchy to lodge something in the throat of its history.

Kyushu-ha does not fit anywhere easily—it is between three worlds, as I argue in the next chapter. But we will use this position to shed light on, and question, the worlds themselves rather than the other way around. In this book so far, I have discussed two other movements that in their own ways did not flourish during the 1960s: the reportage movement, which used their art to create a community of visibility—bringing to light the economic injustices and moral failings of the Cold War in an attempt to realize a different future outside of the American umbrella; and Sōbi, whose idealistic vision of a society that celebrated individual exploration and creativity was undermined by bureaucratic demands to administer education and democracy. Kyushu-ha is slightly later than these two groups and has one foot in two eras. It was born partly out of the communal, enlightened spirit of popular participation that was so characteristic of the 1950s, but it was also subject to the emerging field of contemporary art that would structure the art world of the 1960s and later. It is this position that makes Kyushu-ha important for this book: they are a concrete example of a group on the edge of two formations of culture, with little hope of becoming a mass movement, but also unable to adapt itself to an increasingly professionalized and internationalized art field.

This project will proceed in three stages. Chapter 12 is an examination of Kyushu-ha's emergence and cultural activism. It will explain the three worlds Kyushu-ha found itself between: circles, established art societies, and the emergent field of contemporary art. Each world was an institutional ordering of creative work, each with its own way of establishing artistic value and of accounting for art's relationship with its communities. In the final part of the chapter I consider Kyushu-ha's art as part of a project of activism that revolved around this very question of art's proper relationship to different communities. The chapter that follows examines four Kyushu-ha artists: Sakurai Takami, Tabe Mitsuko, Kikuhata Mokuma, and Miyazaki Junnosuke. These treatments introduce a selection of artworks, while demonstrating concretely how diverse and ultimately incompatible the group was as a collection of individuals. Finally, I revisit the issue of contemporary art as an institutional paradigm. Though I do not deny the reality of the large-scale shifts that took place in the late 1950s and early 1960s, I will take them down a peg. Change does not just happen: people are party to it, some benefit, others don't. Though only a partial account of how and why contemporary art developed as it did, this chapter will focus on journalism, in particular, on journalism's role in shaping the phenomenon of Anti-Art. From that we will be able to see why Kyushu-ha seems destined to have been the "avant-garde that got left behind."[13]

Chapter 12

Kyushu-ha: Between Three Worlds

Although the word "independent" may be overused, consider Kyushu-ha. Its members had no art education. They had no contacts in the Tokyo art world or internationally—their first contact with a Tokyo critic occurred when Sakurai Takami showed up uninvited at Hariu Ichirō's house to beg him to look at the group's work.[1] They had very little money. Their shared workspace was an off-season beach cabana where they held the Grand Meeting of Heroes (Kuwatori Minoru's family ran a business renting the cabanas in the summer). The money that Kyushu-ha used to ship its works to Tokyo and secure exhibition space came from a high membership fee, 10,000 yen, which members paid annually.[2] Being wage workers also meant they had to balance their time. To this list of handicaps we must add what was probably the biggest drag on their success: the fact that their self-conception as a group was not defined solely in terms of national or international fame. Sakurai Takami in particular wanted Kyushu-ha to include as many people as possible, regardless of talent or style. As a result, the group never achieved a stylistic unity and lapsed into many battles over its identity. Hataraki Tadashi, a late-joining member and insightful critic, likened it to running a "three-legged race."[3]

Here lies one of the great contradictions of Kyushu-ha. Although the reportage artists similarly believed in the democratization of art, they were for the most part formally trained and, though poor, came from families rich enough to cope with their artistic careers. When they involved themselves in worker culture they were unmistakably going *down* to the masses to help them attain a creative subjectivity. But the members of Kyushu-ha were themselves members of the working and clerical classes. They were all interested in art but had little technical knowledge, cultural capital, or actual capital. And yet Sakurai and others insisted on opening the group even more: starting with the masses and staying with them. And yet further, they worked not in an amateur Sunday-painting style, but on the sharp edge of avant-garde irreverence. The assemblage artists in California during the 1950s provide a rough parallel though they are not an exact fit.

This chapter locates Kyushu-ha among three overlapping art worlds among which it tried to hold together a workable group: poetry circles, established exhibition societies (*kōbo dantai*), and the system of contemporary art. Each of these worlds had a more or less coherent account of art's value, its place, and its proper audience and mode of enjoyment. Kyushu-ha drew from but also rebelled against each of these worlds, never completely identifying with any one of them but retaining elements of all three. Different members measured their distance from those art worlds quite differently, creating an antinomy at Kyushu-ha's core, around which countless arguments, splits, and resentments swirled. The group's major splits occurred over the organizational identity of the group rather than over artistic differences, suggesting that members' strongest and most rigid investments had something to do with the questions of what publics it should be addressing, how it should position itself in relation to other groups, how it should measure its success, and who it should include. It was through an unstable, in-between space that Kyushu-ha navigated its independence. Their wavering road could appear erratic to outsiders and the push and pull of varying loyalties eventually tore it apart, but that tense field is also what enabled members to experiment with new modes of publicness for art and with new ideas about who could create it. As a group, Kyushu-ha was not directly involved in political activism (although individual members were extremely active, especially in labor movements). Where they *were* consistently active was around questions of art's placement and visibility and, more generally, questions of who could participate in creating culture and on what terms. In this Kyushu-ha itself was much like a circle, though one that demonstrates the chaos that such open organizations can entail and one that was incompatible with the market-oriented collectivism of contemporary art.

This chapter is organized chronologically. The first three sections, on poetry circles, exhibition societies, and contemporary art, provide a narrative account of how Kyushu-ha formed. The destination of the narrative is

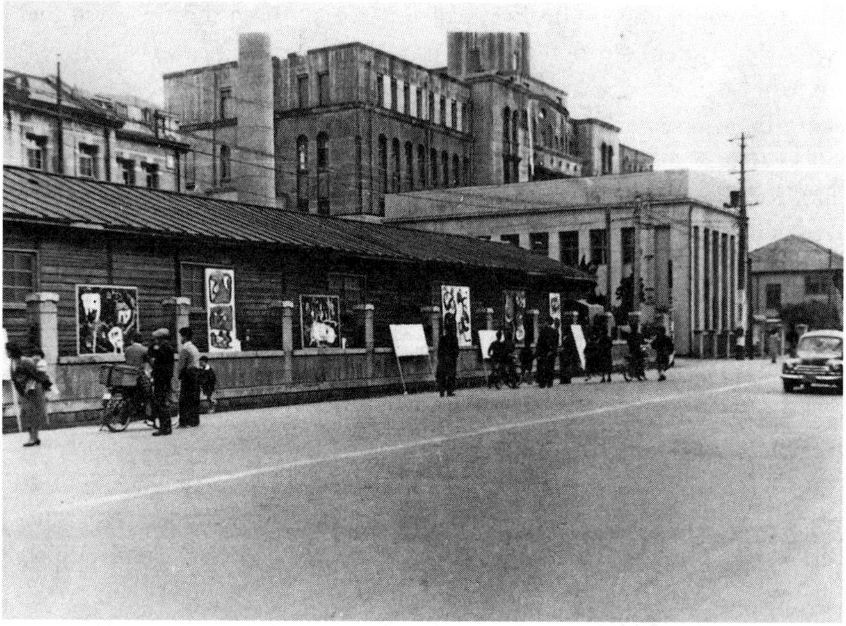

FIGURE 12.1 Photograph of the first Perusona-ten, November 1956. Photographer unknown. Courtesy of the Fukuoka Art Museum.

the Perusona-ten (Persona exhibit), an outdoor exhibition along the outer wall of the Fukuoka prefectural offices that took place in November 1956 (fig. 12.1). This groundbreaking exhibition raised a flag that attracted other young artists in the region who came together to form Kyushu-ha. The final section examines the cultural politics of Kyushu-ha in its peak years, between its formation in 1957 and the Grand Meeting of Heroes in 1962.

Poetry Circles

The first route to the Perusona-ten is through poetry and poetry circles. A key person connecting Kyushu-ha with poetry circles was Matano Mamoru. Born in 1914, he was the oldest member of Kyushu-ha by more than a decade. Like Tokyo, Kyushu teemed with poetry circles. One of the most important of them, Boin, formed in the town of Kurume, just south of Fukuoka City in 1947. The group was led by poet and physician Maruyama Yutaka and produced the journal *Boin* (*Vowel; Mother Sound*), which Kuroda Tatsuya, a leading historian of Kyushu poetry, has called "the most noteworthy poetry journal in Kyushu" for that period.[4]

Matano Mamoru (b. 1914) was among the founding members of Boin and he served as a secretary and organizer for the group.[5] Many in the group had returned to Japan from horrible experiences on the front lines of defeat, not least Maruyama, who was stationed as a military doctor near the border of Thailand and Burma when the war ended. Born in part of his disillusionment, Maruyama's two brainchildren, the Kurume Bunka no Kai (Kurume Association of Culture), and the Boin circle, both demonstrated hostility to centralized cultural authority. Maruyama's words on the leaflet insert that accompanied the first issue of *Boin* give us some insight into his commitments.

> For the moment, all of the members of Boin are connected in some way to the rural city of Kurume, but the purpose of our group is nothing so narrow as to rise in the ranks of the Kyushu poetry hierarchy [*shidan*]. . . . First, more important than anything else is the hope that each poet develop their own original work individually, to become outstanding poets, and more than that, to become poets who use poetry as a whetstone to enrich and temper their humanity. These opinions, however, are only those of one Boin member, Maruyama Yutaka, and don't represent the wishes of all the poets in Boin.[6]

One can see Maruyama's care around issues of representation and leadership and his hostility to established cultural authority. Thus, although the original group of poets favored romantic, pastoral poetry (*jojō*), as the group changed over the years, Maruyama never made a move to control it. One major change occurred when Tanigawa Gan and Morisaki Kazue joined the group. Their poetry and criticism featured forthright social critique and both were members of the Communist Party (JCP). The disagreements this introduced did not threaten the existence of the group itself, however, because it was founded as a forum open to thoughtful and committed poets.[7]

Matano left Boin and Kurume in 1954. He began working in the Fukuoka offices of the *Nishinippon shinbun* (West Japan news), the Kyushu regional newspaper, where he met Sakurai Takami. Matano is significant for the development of Kyushu-ha for several reasons. It was he who, in 1957, urged the group to adopt the name Kyushu-ha and to put out a journal of its own.[8] He was also the person who wrote the manifesto for the cover of the first issue and the introductory essay for the group's first exhibition in Tokyo in February 1958. It is interesting to note the ways that Kyushu-ha's manifesto resembles Maruyama's manifesto in *Boin*.

> We stand at this moment at the start of a new art movement. We have attached the name "Kyushu-ha" to our art movement, but this is nothing more than a designation of the place where we practice our production. Our most basic tenet is rejecting all established ways of

thinking and exploring the possibilities of art to their outermost limits. The range of problems assembles mountain-high around us, from contemporary science and society to the problem of individual and nation. In terms of method: realism, abstraction, Informel. We must confront all of these issues through our art. We, Kyushu-ha, will create our own truly unique art while involving ourselves in these issues and trying to solve them.[9]

Matano's and Maruyama's manifestos both invoke location as an arbitrary but enabling factor, both exhibit a hostility to established cultural hierarchies, both insist that the question of artistic style be left open, and both emphasize the practice of poetry and art as an approach to bigger tasks: for Maruyama, the elevation of the poet's individual humanity, for Matano, the betterment of society. Although the avant-garde is often associated with a thoroughgoing rejection of established norms and a strong destructive impulse, Matano offers a more constructive vision.[10] Whatever threat might come with rejecting "all established ways of thinking" is immediately recuperated into the urge to solve problems.

Boin was a relatively elite group, a coterie with an air of public duty. But another poetry circle, Shika (Poetry Section), which was intertwined with Kyushu-ha's formation, attempted to establish exchanges between coterie journals (*dōjinshi*) and workplace circles (*sākuru*).[11] Sakurai was a member of Shika, and ten poets from Shika exhibited their poems along with four artists who would become the core of Kyushu-ha at the Perusona-ten in November 1956. Shika's name still featured prominently in the banner for the second outdoor street exhibition, held in 1957 (see fig. 12.2).

In the mission statement in the first issue of the journal *Shika*, the group's patron, Itabashi Kenkichi, a prefectural official, proposed thinking of Shika as a "place of art" (*geijutsu no ba*) that existed somewhere in between the everyday and the elevated, both connected to the present and moving toward the future. "Undeniably, any activity that deserves to be called a 'place of art' [*geijutsu no ba*] will include a sense of play—an intellectual and sensuous enjoyment, a creative, inaugurating hope, an unrepentant joy that burns with the momentary significance of life together in sympathy with the masses [*taishū*]. If that is play, it is an extremely elevated play."[12] It is unclear whether Itabashi was able to realize his wish for a joyful reunion with the masses in practice. In the wish, however, we can find some commonality with Sakurai's vision for Kyushu-ha as a movement with as wide a membership as possible. The ideal of the group with no boundaries or hierarchies, where anyone would be welcome (so long as they paid the membership fee) and where everyone could participate equally comes largely from the organizational inheritance of poetry circles.

More than simply openness, however, circle organization entailed certain ideas about what the artist or poet should be doing. Sākuru Mura (Circle Village) is a poetry circle that many commentators mention in parallel to Kyushu-ha. Sākuru Mura's connection to Kyushu-ha is less direct than to the Boin and Shika circles, but the two groups share some points of resemblance.[13] They were geographically close and also contemporaries: Sākuru Mura was active from 1958 to 1961. The most important connection, however, lies in a shared attitude toward the place of art and the artist in daily life. As discussed in chapter 2, the coal mines were a mixed community in terms of cultural capital, something that began with the great leveling at the end of the war and remained as an ideal even after the differentiated economy had returned. The poets who sought to realize this communal ideal together with non-professional, working poets, were not capitalizing on a liminal, daring experience, but aiming to provide a conduit that went both up and down the cultural field. Tanigawa Gan referred to these in-between figures as *kōsakusha* (cultural activists, cultural agents). "A band of 'agents' [*kōsakusha*] that would stand in fierce opposition to both the masses and the intellectuals. . . . They will implode the silence of the masses and repudiate translation by the intellectuals. In other words, these agents will follow a hypocritical path by exposing the face of resolute intellectuals to the masses and turning the face of the cunning masses toward the intellectuals."[14] *Kōsaku* was also the name for the work Katsuragawa Hiroshi did in Shimomaruko. It denoted the contradictory work of building communities of cultural producers, often across class lines.

Tanigawa gives an idea of what such communities might look like in a manifesto in the inaugural issue of *Sākuru mura* (Circle village), titled "Further deepening the meaning of the group [*shūdan*]."

> Right now the creative culture movement in Japan is experiencing a sharp turn. It is showing us that in order to stem the drift of the last two or three years toward dismantlement [of the circle movements] and score settling, and to break the extreme view that takes culture as the creative product of individual persons, we have to summon up a new collective that will become the bearer for it. We can only overcome the steep divisions and fissures between workers and farmers, intellectuals and masses, older and younger, center and periphery, men and women, one field and the next, through a disruptive and spirited collision, a union founded in opposites, an exchange [*kōryū*] on an

> enormous scale. There is nothing to do but deepen that exchange, fearing no antagonisms and jealously preserving the space [*ba*] we have in common. What is the new subject of creation? It is the circle that seals its group formation around the axis of creativity.[15]

Tanigawa imagines the circle first and foremost as the creative subject of culture, poetry, and art. But it is also a model for an inclusive and communicative community in general. This resembles a public sphere, but with two crucial differences. First the circle does not assume rationality; indeed, the major vector of exploration for both Kyushu-ha and Sākuru Mura was downward, to the depths of the earth, society, and the psyche, to release a dark, unpredictable energy. Second, whereas Habermas can claim little familiarity with actual group organizing, the people in Sākuru Mura had been operating within culture movements, unions, and party cells for a decade before endorsing the above words.

Kyushu-ha was not modeled specifically on Boin, Shika, or Sākuru Mura. The relationship I am suggesting was more diffuse: the groups shared a historical background in which this type of organization flourished, with numerous variations. Coteries and circles were implicitly and sometimes explicitly a reaction to wartime centralization of cultural production and the perceived postwar reconstitution of that concentration in the form of various hierarchies: the *shidan* (poetry establishment), *bundan* (literary establishment), and *gadan* (artistic establishment, as represented in the large exhibition societies and the Nitten salon). Through their organizational work, groups such as Boin, Shika, and Sākuru Mura struggled to create autonomous expressive communities that would rebuild culture, its production and reception, in a more democratic fashion, as discussed in chapter 1. The participants in these experiments were well aware of how much effort and planning was necessary to maintain cultural autonomy.

Another element of the poetry circle model of organization was the avoidance of a leader and a principled agnosticism regarding style. In Boin and in Kyushu-ha there was no leader who could decide who was in or out of the group, or what direction other members should take. The effect of this in Kyushu-ha was that the group's direction was less a unification than an agglomeration. This was both the realization of an associational ideal and a curse: verbal and physical confrontations were not uncommon. In its early years (until about 1960), Kyushu-ha held group critique sessions in which members commented on each other's works, true to the ideal of Tanigawa's "disruptive and spirited collision." They also occasionally engaged in group production, submitting some works to the Yomiuri Independent as "Kyushu-ha," rather than as individual artists. Though Sākuru Mura and Kyushu-ha had only sporadic contact, I would argue that Kyushu-ha, especially Sakurai's version of it, developed as a response to some of the same concerns that motivated Sākuru Mura: the desire for a community that would bridge increasingly deep social divisions, for art as a space for creativity that anyone could access and participate in, and, most important, for art itself as a generative social force that would build new relations between people by serving as a place for aesthetic and intellectual exchange. Sakurai had a fervently populist vision for Kyushu-ha that was probably closest among Kyushu-ha artists to that of Tanigawa Gan. As he wrote in 1961, "I realize that now art may only be . . . a high class sleeping pill or a toy for grown-ups, but it's also possible to set the conditions for revolution if one could set up some other, enormous organization against this. . . . A single picture can't put up any resistance, but it comes to have a powerful meaning when it is the one on the flag of Joan of Arc. . . . Haven't the red flag and the color red already begun to function this way all across the world?"[16] The question was how far other members of the group were ready to follow this idea and how far the institutions of art were ready to recognize it.

Art Societies

The second institution that Kyushu-ha was working both from and against was the art society. The Perusona-ten in 1956 was staged by the artists and poets close to the Shika group, but it attracted artists from around Fukuoka, many of them young aspirants on the fringes of the art societies.

Art societies, more properly called open-call societies (*kōbo dantai*), are an institution that might be unique to Japan. As Reiko Tomii has shown, art societies were, at their core, salon-based exhibition societies.[17] But in the prewar period, when both the institutions and stylistic modes of modern art were in the process of being established in Japan, they fulfilled a range of important functions. Their exhibitions were tremendously popular and played a leading role in popularizing modern art for a middle-brow audience. The judging of works created legibility in a diverse and unfamiliar field, while the affiliated study groups, research institutes (*kenkyūjo*), and publications carried out an ongoing educative function. Over the first half of the twentieth century, art societies combined three art-institutional roles: that of critic, dealer, and curator. Over time these roles would become professionalized and would be removed from the remit of the societies, but in the first half of the century, art societies were the primary builders of the field of modern art in Japan.

Because of these multiple roles, art societies became the primary institutions of cultural authority, making them perennial targets of criticism from artists who wanted to push the boundaries of expression. Indeed, the first open-call society, the Nika Kai (Second Section Society), came into existence when a group of painters split off from the state-sponsored Bunten salon to "create a new separate section for artists with fresh approaches."[18] This was but the first in a long, intermittent process of splintering, in which artists rejected an established art society and went on to form their own group. Some of the larger groups include Dokuritsu Bijutsu Kyōkai (Independent Art Society, founded in 1931), Jiyū Bijutsu Kyōkai (Free Art Society, founded in 1937), and Kōdō Bijutsu Kyōkai (Action Art Society, founded in 1945). The recurring problem was that although a group would break away due to the perceived conservative hegemony of one organization, they would adopt the same institutional structure and soon become cultural authorities themselves. The mechanism that established and maintained that authority was, first and foremost, the system of judging.

In postwar Fukuoka, these established societies (primarily Nika, Dokuritsu, and Jiyū) and the annual Prefectural Exhibition (Fukuoka Kenten) were the only avenues for an artist to achieve recognition among his or her peers and to receive national attention. Anyone could submit work to a society's annual exhibition (it is for this reason they are referred to as "open call"). Judges would then select the works to be included in the exhibition, which was held in Tokyo. After a particular artist had been selected for a few years running, they might be invited to join the organization as an associate member (*kaiyū*) or official member (*kaiin*). As an example, Terada Ken'ichirō, a member of Kyushu-ha, first exhibited with Nika in 1951 and was invited to be an associate member in 1962.[19] Generally speaking, judging panels were composed only of full members, giving the elder members a monopoly over access to publicity. This encouraged the growth of a patronage system in which aspiring artists would affiliate themselves with an established member, usually by studying under them. The payoff was a stable standing that guaranteed a certain level of income. Especially for an artist based outside Tokyo who had no exhibition alternatives, membership in an established art society lent a cultural cachet that translated directly into higher prices for one's work and educational services.[20] Because of this system, the art societies were frequently criticized for conservatism and academism, and for fostering a system of value based on parochial rather than public concerns.

There is merit to those criticisms, but they are only half the story. As Tomii argues, the organizational stability of the art societies "serv[ed] certain public interests."[21] It was through them that the Japanese public first encountered a wide variety of modern artistic styles. Although they are often portrayed as static, art societies did incorporate new styles, though not as quickly as in the west. Also, unlike the structuring of modern art in the west, new styles did not displace older ones, so that by the 1950s, most of the major societies exhibited works in styles from naturalism and impressionism to surrealism and abstraction in a gradually expanding pluralism. In addition, because the exhibitions of the various societies traveled around the country, they brought modern art to the provinces. Finally, although older members dominated the selection of works for the exhibition, the shows also included large numbers of works by nonmembers and newcomers who were working in new styles.

Until Kyushu-ha formed in 1957, there were no venues that exhibited modern art in Fukuoka other than the annual art society exhibitions and the prefectural exhibition. Kyushu-ha could not help but have some relationship with them. Although Kyushu-ha is often understood as rebelling against the art societies, its creation was made possible by networks that had been built partially through them. The annual exhibitions were places young artists could meet and learn about each other's work. Subgroups sprang up within the societies, especially around particular geographical areas. Itō Kenshi and others in Nika Kai who lived in northern Kyushu, for instance, formed a subgroup called the Nika Seijinsha (Nika Company of Westerners [western Japan]).[22] Terada Ken'ichirō and Kuroki Yōji, protégés of Itō, formed another subgroup in the early 1950s, together with two other artists, Yonekura Toku and Nakagawa Yasutaka. It was called the Ao no Ie (Blue House), a reference to the tiny shack the young artists built with some financial support from their Nika patrons.

This was the hangout where future Kyushu-ha members Kinoshita, Yamauchi Jūtarō, and Kikuhata Mokuma met with Terada for the first time. Kikuhata Mokuma remembered the Ao no Ie this way:

> In those days, even right downtown, there were still open areas left in ruin from the bombings. In most of them tiny drinking dens popped up, red lanterns hung outside. There were four or five of these around the [Blue House], and they were piled up so tightly that the lanterns on either side of the narrow alley knocked against each other when the wind blew. Right at the end of the alley there was a big garbage heap, and . . . right next to that stood the studio. A couple yards wide, a couple yards deep, a dirt floor. But it did have a roof. . . . And a door, mounted on hinges made from old tires. After I read about this

> "Blue House" in the local newspaper, I was suddenly seized as if by a compulsion, a conviction that things would never open up for me unless I could get the strange artists living in just such a place to have a look at my work.[23]

Kikuhata's account, filled with vivid detail and a certain nostalgia for the rough-and-tumble days of youth, also shows ambition: these were young, bohemian artists who were beginning to succeed in the Nika Exhibition. While Kikuhata found his way to the Ao no Ie through a newspaper article about them, Sakurai met them through Shika: Kuroki and Terada designed the covers and graphic inserts for the group's journal.[24] It is not clear why Sakurai began painting—until his death he identified himself as a poet, not an artist. But already at this point he had some canvases stacked up at his home and he dragged Kuroki and Terada to see them. Kuroki remembered that when he saw the paintings he sensed "a black aura that he had never experienced from a painting before."[25]

The final element that precipitated the formation of Kyushu-ha was a meeting between Sakurai Takami and Ochi Osamu that happened through Nika Kai. Ochi is generally recognized as the most inspired experimentalist of Kyushu-ha.[26] Although both Sakurai and Ochi had works selected for the 1955 Nika Exhibition, they did not meet until six months later, when Sakurai found himself sitting next to Ochi at a party Itō Kenshi had organized for the Nika participants in Fukuoka. He then dragged Ochi to his house to show him his work. Ochi confessed years later how embarrassed he had been on the train on the way there, with Sakurai talking loudly and gesticulating as everyone in the carriage stared at them.[27] Ochi was overflowing with ideas about how to expand art by using materials such as soot, sand, strawboard, glass, and asphalt.[28] This meeting was the creative spark that led to the Perusona-ten exhibition a few months later.

Not only was the Persona the first outdoor art exhibition in Fukuoka, but it took place in one of the most public places in the city, along one of the largest and most redeveloped streets in the city, right in the governmental center. The participants brought together ten poets from Shika, including Matano Mamoru and Sakurai, and the artists Ishibashi Yasuyuki, Kuroki Yōji, Ochi, and Sakurai, all of whom had exhibited in Nika. But the relationship between the Perusona-ten and Nika was double-edged. Just two months earlier, Ochi had submitted works for that year's exhibition but the judges had rejected them, despite the fact that Ochi had been nominated for the New Artist award the previous year. The significance was clear for young artists around Fukuoka: the Perusona-ten was a public riposte aimed at the local art establishment. The exhibition was covered in the local newspapers and artists around Fukuoka saw a banner being hoisted as a new group of artists struck out on their own.[29] Most of Kyushu-ha's core members came together over the next year, and the three subsequent years, 1957, 1958, and 1959, were the group's most productive.[30]

To sum up, the art societies provided some of the social network that allowed Kyushu-ha to form. Once Kyushu-ha had formed, however, this origin left a tension within the group between those who were participating in Kyushu-ha as just another art group and those who saw Kyushu-ha as a specifically anti-art society group. In December 1959, Kyushu-ha's first split occurred when Ochi Osamu, Yamauchi Jūtarō, and Kikuhata Mokuma, criticized Sakurai's tolerant attitude toward the art societies and left to form their own group, the Dōkutsu-ha (Cave School). According to Hariu Ichirō, the reason was "dissatisfaction that [Kyushu-ha] had begun to put up with a lot of artists from the established art societies in northern Kyushu, meaning that the significance of the group as something different from those societies had progressively faded."[31] Conflicts over what Kyushu-ha was in relation to the exhibition societies was thus the cause of its first major split and would be a point of contention afterward as well.

Informel, the Yomiuri Independent, and the Beginnings of Contemporary Art

1956 and 1957 were watershed years in the Japanese art world. One of the most important changes was brought about by the importation of Art Informel. The critic and promoter Michel Tapié coined the term *informel* to describe a certain body of work produced in the late 1940s and early 1950s by French and American artists, and the word was soon picked up by other French critics. Ming Tiampo has summarized the term's intellectual underpinnings:

> Influenced by Maurice Merleau-Ponty's writing on painting and Jean-Paul Sartre's writing on Giacometti, Tapié conceived of Un Art Autre/Informel as the core of an existential struggle to rebuild society after the war. From Merleau-Ponty, Tapié developed a theory of expression that privileged gesture and texture over linear description, and from both authors, the idea of rejecting *a priori* structure to seek, above all, authenticity. To this combination of intellectual perspectives, Tapié also added his own utopian internationalism.[32]

This internationalism led Tapié to Japan. In November 1956, Japanese audiences got their first major introduction to Art Informel and abstract expressionism in an exhibition titled Sekai Konnichi no Bijutsu (Art of the World Today).[33] The exhibition started in Tokyo before touring regional cities, including Fukuoka. It was such a success that Tapié and associated artists Georges Mathieu, Sam Frances, and Imai Toshimitsu toured Japan in 1957. This, combined with a campaign to publish Tapié's writing in Japanese, created what is known as the "Informel whirlwind."[34]

The whirlwind decisively reoriented both art practice and art criticism in Japan. It exploded the abstraction/figuration debate that had shaped much of art criticism for a decade. Sakurai and Ochi helped set up the exhibition in Fukuoka in 1957. It was there that Sakurai recalls hearing an older-generation modernist, Sagaya Itoku (1918–1995), declare that the age of the exhibition societies was over.[35] Although such proclamations are a perennial phenomenon, Informel overturned the hierarchy of skill and knowledge so thoroughly that Sagaya's concern is understandable. Some members of Kyushu-ha embraced the new style, but more important than the Informel style itself was that it opened a space for young artists by bestowing artistic legitimacy on expressive work that could be done quickly, often without a great deal of finish. Art's meaning and value could be found in the authenticity of its execution and the intensity with which the finished work demonstrated it. This was a leveling moment that threw open the door to the surge of rough experimentation that was Anti-Art. Kysuhu-ha was one of the groups to storm into that space.

The Yomiuri Independent is equally important in the formation of the field of contemporary art (*gendai bijutsu*) in Japan. If Informel provided intellectual and critical space, the Yomiuri Independent was the literal space that supported the new generation of Anti-Art experimentalists. The exhibition was established by the Yomiuri Shimbun in 1949 as an annual event that would have no juried selection of works. The man most responsible for creating and running the Independent was Kaidō Hideo, who "had a longstanding commitment to theoretically sophisticated and politically committed art."[36] Although Kaidō undoubtedly had progressive hopes for the Independent, it was attractive to the newspaper company because it drew attention away from a rightward shift in the newspaper's policy and management in the wake of a series of major strikes.[37] The Yomiuri Independent also displaced the Independent exhibition organized by the left-wing Nihon Bijutsu Kai (Japan Art Society) by using the same name as their exhibition which had started a year before. There were two "Nihon Andepandan-ten" (Japan Independent Exhibition), until the Yomiuri changed its name a few years later.[38] The Yomiuri Independent thus colonized the name and exhibition format of the Nihon Bijutsu Kai's exhibition, which had been conceived explicitly as a vehicle for socialist cultural revolution.

At first many artists exhibited in both the Yomiuri and Nihon Bijutsi Kai Independents, but by 1955 a certain polarization had become evident and by 1957 it was clear that the Yomiuri had become the preferred venue among young artists exploring new ideas. The combination of the open-submission Yomiuri Independent and a newly opened artistic and critical landscape was the initial institutional foundation for contemporary art. Just as Kyushu-ha drew from but did not fit into the forms of the poetry circle and the art society, I argue in chapter 14 that it did not fit into the institutions of contemporary art either, and more than any other, this was the failure that eventually tore the group apart.

Exhibition and Community: Kyushu-ha as a Movement

Kyushu-ha was not directly involved in political activism, at least not as a group. Where they were active was around the question of art's placement and visibility, and more generally around the question of who could participate in creating culture and on what terms. I will introduce this in two steps, looking first at Kyushu-ha's work in Fukuoka and then at what Kuroda Raiji calls their "Tokyo strategy."[39]

Kyushu-ha held several major exhibitions after the Perusona-ten of 1956. The Perusona-ten was repeated at the same location in November 1957 and 1958. In August 1957, they had their first true group exhibit, the Group Q Exhibit. Kyushu-ha also held its own independent exhibition in 1958, the Kyushu Independent, in the assembly hall of the Nishinippon Shimbun. Modeled on the two big independents in Tokyo, it was open submission and included artists who were not members of Kyushu-ha. They held the independent exhibition again in 1959. After that, the next big outdoor exhibition was the Grand Meeting of Heroes in 1962. Kyushu-ha exhibited as a group in Tokyo in two major exhibitions each year: the Yomiuri every March from 1957 and a summer show at the Ginza Gallery that was held four times, 1958–1961. In addition, members participated in many other exhibitions as individual artists and in one-, two-, and three-person shows at galleries in Tokyo and Fukuoka.[40] After 1960, the number of Kyushu-ha's group exhibitions decreased and the number of individual shows increased, a trend that was by no means random.

Because there is little direct evidence of what Kyushu-ha's members thought about exhibition, we must look at the exhibitions themselves. What relationship were the exhibitors trying to establish with the community in the first two street exhibitions, in 1956 and 1957? They lasted for three days each and were held along a downtown boulevard of Fukuoka, on the outside wall of the prefectural offices (figs. 12.1 and 12.2). The paintings were large to better fit the space, and poems were written on placards and hung along the wall beside the paintings. The local newspaper published photographs and short reviews of the first two exhibitions, and some of the participants published longer reviews in *Shika*. There was no charge for viewing; passersby were free to linger, look, read, and conceivably converse with the artists and poets who were there to watch over things. The photographs that survive show that the installation created a steep differential between the artworks and the formality of their surroundings. By contrast, the whimsical artworks and the setting of the park in Gutai's outdoor exhibitions in Ashiya in 1955 and 1956 combined to create an ethereal overall atmosphere. Those exhibitions created an immersive environment, prefiguring strategies of installation art. Kyushu-ha's street exhibitions were more conventional in their artworks (which take the form of hanging canvases, albeit large ones), and more incongruous with their surroundings (the site of local government being a space people traverse with a serious purpose rather than to play, relax, or ponder). Rather than experimenting with dematerialization, these exhibitions juxtaposed art and daily life in a way that left both categories clearly distinct. The exhibition creates maximum access, but does not attempt to suppress the distance between

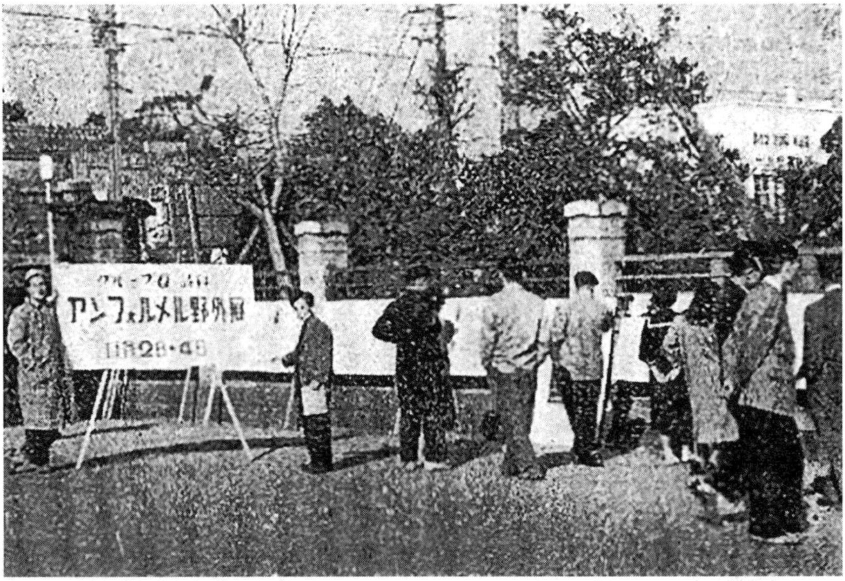

FIGURE 12.2 Photograph of the second Kyushu-ha/Shika street exhibition in downtown Fukuoka, November 1957. The title of the exhibition was Gurūpu Q/Shika Anforumeru Yagai-ten (Group Q/Shika Informel Outdoor Exhibition). Photographer unknown. Image published in *Shika* 15 (January 1958).

artworks and the people passing by or the everyday processes going on around them.

One possible explanation for why the groups' activity took this form is that it emerged from the model of the poetry circle. Poetry has a relative luxury when compared to visual art or theater in that it can be intimately enmeshed in daily life. It can be written and read on the fly, it does not require a space for performance or production, and its content can be about everyday activities. The fact that the words people may be reading (or writing) could easily have direct correlations with the world in front of them marks an important spatial difference between poetry and theater or exhibition. Poetry is also potentially present at any time in the songs people sing in their heads. Of any medium, poetry should suffer the least anxiety about a separation between artist and audience, and this is doubly true for amateur poetry circles of the 1950s. Following this, we might imagine Kyushu-ha's experiments with the institutions of art as something of a similar impulse: that is, not suppressing a real difference between art and life by evaporating or attenuating poesis, but acknowledging its underdetermining relationship to reality, letting words be words, letting art be art, but trying to bring as many people as close to it as possible, as producers or onlookers or both.

Kyushu-ha's two independent exhibitions in 1958 and 1959 also expanded the space for art and attempted to find new relationships between creators and the community. These exhibitions were nonjuried: members of Kyushu-ha organized and produced them but anyone could exhibit. Kyushu-ha organized the exhibitions as an explicit attack on the stifling lack of spaces and opportunities for exhibition in Fukuoka. According to Kikuhata, members of Kyushu-ha deliberately scheduled the registration days for their exhibits to coincide with the registration days of the Fukuoka Prefectural Exhibition and lay in wait outside the prefectural exhibit's submission area to poach artists for their own exhibition.[41] Each independent exhibit featured just over 100 works,[42] displayed in the assembly hall of the Nishinippon Shimbun.[43]

A few months after its first independent exhibit, Kyushu-ha formalized its objections to the Fukuoka Prefectural Exhibition by submitting a letter of protest about the composition of the judging committee. The letter, which was signed by twenty-three Kyushu-ha members, demanded that the entire selection committee for the *yōga* (western art; modern art) section be replaced and that art critics (*bijutsu hihyōka*) be included among the new members. They also demanded that the selection process be made public, so that anyone could listen to the judges' conversations.[44] Kyushu-ha's demands aimed to correct a parochialism that they believed had more to do with the judges' individual tastes and the internal politics of the art society than with the value of the artwork.

Photographs of the Kyushu Independent show that it was a conventionally installed exhibition. The location and presentation of artworks were not unusual or incongruous in the way the street exhibitions were (fig. 12.3). There are some innovations: Ochi Osamu's works are placed on the floor, a display format he would experiment with for a few years, culminating in his masterpiece, *Deguchi nashi* (No exit) (1962). The first Kyushu Independent was also the only venue where Kyushu-ha could show the enormous collaborative junk assemblage the Yomiuri Independent had rejected a few months before.

The question of how and when art is allowed to be visible and who is allowed to access it arises in many discussions of public art and institutional critique. Kyushu-ha's effort to organize their own exhibitions stemmed from similar dissatisfaction with the rules governing who was allowed to show what, where. But whereas latter-day guerilla artists engage in episodic actions, Kyushu-ha was trying to create something more permanent and more straightforward. Although their critique was not entirely systematic, they took the lack of access that resulted from the art society and the prefectural exhibit oligopoly to be a de facto form of censorship. As with the

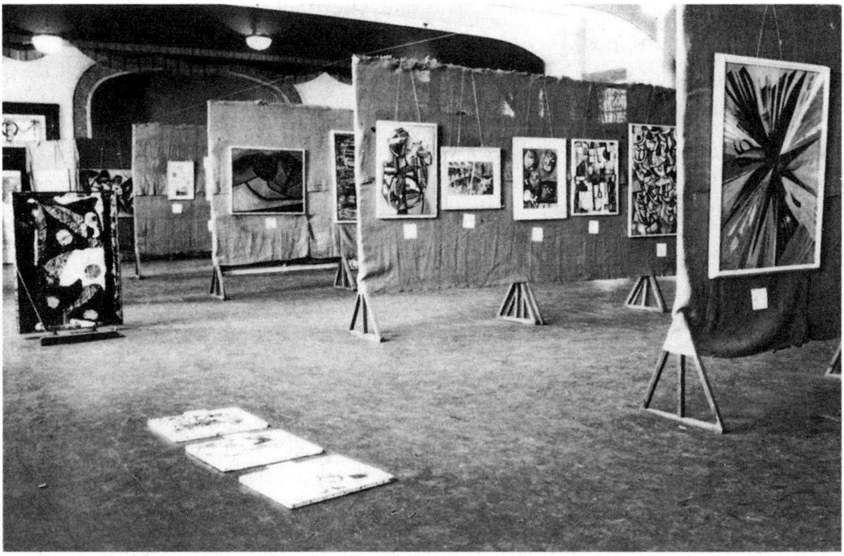

FIGURE 12.3 Photograph of the Kyushu Independent Exhibition, Fukuoka, 1959. Photographer unknown. Courtesy of the Fukuoka Art Museum.

Nihon and Yomiuri Independents, the Kyushu Independent created a more democratic way of deciding what would be visible and what wouldn't, by letting as many people contribute to the mass of visible culture as wanted to. From the late 1940s through the 1950s, at least nine other independent exhibitions appeared around Japan.[45] Kyushu-ha's was part of this dispersed and uncoordinated movement toward democratic access to visibility.

That having been said, there is ample room to question how far Kyushu-ha succeeded in opening art up to new participants and publics. Acknowledging their failure to become a focal point for a mass movement of artistic producers, Kuroda Raiji writes, "The response of the masses, the group's primary target audience, was far from enthusiastic. In 1962, in the notice of *A Grand Meeting of Heroes*, Sakurai went so far as to say, 'People hate us so much that we are on the cutting edge of local hostility.'"[46] Part of the problem undoubtedly lay in the grotesque and outrageous character of their works, as well as with the barrier to participation created by the difficulty of producing and storing works of visual art. But I would argue that Kyushu-ha *itself* was a circle, specifically because it brought together artists, largely untrained, some with art career ambitions, some without, and provided a context for their shared artistic development where none had existed before. Though the group was far too small to constitute a mass in itself, somehow, through Kyushu-ha, these copyeditors, store clerks, piecework painters, schoolteachers, train conductors, printers, and weavers were able, at the same time, to be avant-garde artists, exhibiting in both Fukuoka and Tokyo. In this respect it functioned like a circle: it created a place for cultural value to erupt out of the collision of many individuals, it made that work public, it made a public issue out of publicity itself, it welcomed the uninitiated, and, largely at the insistence of Sakurai, it tried to remain autonomous from external structures of value.

Just as Tanigawa said he would applaud only what "rose from the corpse" of the *kōsakusha*, many experiments in small, independent artist groups grew out of Kyushu-ha as it began to falter. In late 1959, two such groups were born: Dōkutsu-ha (Cave School) and Gurūpu Nishi Nihon (Group West Japan). Dōkutsu-ha included the most promising contemporary artists, Yamauchi Jūtarō, Ochi Osamu, and Kikuhata Mokuma, but it broke up within a year and Ochi and Kikuhata returned to Kyushu-ha. Gurūpu Nishi Nihon included Kawakami Shōzō, Saitō Hidesaburō, Surusumi Seiryō, Taniguchi Toshio, Nakanishi Kazuko, Hataraki Tadashi, and Minashima Mansaku. This group was centered in the city of Ōmuta, located one hour south of Fukuoka and home to the Mitsui-Miike coal mine. Many members of this group, such as Taniguchi and Hataraki, remained in both groups at the same time.

Gurūpu Nishi Nihon evolved into another group in 1962, called the Shingenjitsu Shūdan (New Reality Group), also centered in Ōmuta. Like Kyushu-ha, this group held outdoor events and published a journal. The activity of these small organizations blossomed into a number of major exhibitions in the late 1960s and early 1970s: the Kyushu Gendai Bijutsu no Dōkō-ten (Trends in Kyushu Contemporary Art Exhibition), which was held annually from 1967 to 1971; the Gurūpu Rengō ni yoru Geijutsu no Kanōsei-ten (Potential for Art in Group Alliance Exhibition), held in 1968; the Kyushu Shinsei Gaka-ten (Kyushu Leading Artist Exhibition), also held in 1968; the Konnichi no Bijutsu-ten (Art of Today Exhibition), held in 1969; and the Gensō to Jōnen-ten (Fantasy and Emotion Exhibition), held in 1974. These exhibitions not only featured many works by former Kyushu-ha members but were also organized by them, with the help of the arts editors at two local newspapers, Fukano Osamu at *Fukunichi* and Taniguchi Harumichi at *Nishinippon*.[47]

In addition to these exhibitions, the late 1960s was a time of happenings, festivals, and demonstrations, which almost always overlapped with the expressive politics of the day: the student movements, the 1970 Anpo demonstrations, the demonstrations against the 1970 World Expo, and, long familiar to Kyushu-ha, demonstrations against established art institutions in Fukuoka. Former Kyushu-ha members were involved most heavily with the latter two. In a situation that might have come straight out of the late 1950s, former members disrupted a new juried art exhibition, the Asahi-sponsored Seibu Bijutsu-ten (Asahi West Art Exhibition), by appealing to jury members to boycott it. The efforts of Tabe Mitsuko, Sakurai Takami, and two groups of younger artists—Shūdan Kumo (Spider Collective) and Shūdan He (Toot Collective)—persuaded two out of the five jurors not to participate. In a final example of their continued involvement in the politics of public art and expression, members of Kyushu-ha, including Hataraki, Tabe, and Sakurai, supported members of Shūdan Kumo when a public indecency case was brought against them after they paraded down the street with a banner featuring a large painted penis.[48] In this way, Kyushu-ha's example—its efforts to find as wide and free a public space for its artwork as possible through direct action, agitation, and by building its own organization—were projects that carried on after Kyushu-ha itself had dispersed. These efforts continued into the late 1960s and early 1970s, affecting the shape of the public sphere in Fukuoka. Tabe Mitsuko argues that Kyushu-ha still survives today insofar as it represents a movement that is adamant about maintaining art's independence from established institutions and cultural hierarchies.[49]

What can we say about Kyushu-ha's efforts to overturn the hierarchy of center and periphery in their relationship with the Tokyo art world? To answer this, we need to expand the discussion of the avant-garde and its relationship to various communities.

As argued so far, the claim that the avant-garde can overcome the division of art and the everyday cannot be taken at face value: the dynamic between avant-garde art and the everyday is often closer to selective gentrification than it is to bridging. Thomas Crow is well-known for having argued that the avant-garde is the research and development arm of the culture industry.[50] Avant-garde artists are rarely untrained or ignorant of the institutions of art and rarely lack a connection with the wealthy: their "umbilical cord of gold" in the words of Clement Greenberg.[51] In contrast, the subcultures from which they draw ideas, material, and an aura of authenticity, rarely see any direct or timely acknowledgement for their "participation" as stand-ins for the abject or the everyday. From the cubist use of African's art, to the surrealist flirtation with anthropology, to Andy Warhol's reliance on New York subcultures, to Murakami Takashi's capitalization and nationalization of *otaku* culture, the avant-garde leverages differentials of knowledge to realize value within hegemonic cultures, in a form of cultural arbitrage.

As the Murakami example illustrates, artists from "exotic" countries around the world regularly leverage their own culture in a bid for success in the global art world. Often there is little choice. To what extent did Kyushu-ha use its own provincial status in its bid for attention in Tokyo? Kuroda argues that the naming of the group was highly strategic.[52] Certainly the name Kyushu-ha loudly proclaims the group's geographical origin. But there is a question about what function that proclamation was meant to serve. Matano's proposed name for the group carried the day, but some younger members, notably Tabe Mitsuko and Surusumi Seiryō, supported an alternate name, "Group Q."[53] In Matano's opening manifesto in the group's journal, he seems to invoke Kyushu as an arbitrary factor, not as anything with a prescriptive content. As shown above, he was the member of Kyushu-ha most deeply engaged in poetry circles. The issue of how regionalism was articulated in the circle movements is complex, but in general, the value structure of circles and their networks was more horizontal and dispersed than the system of contemporary art as it was developing midcentury. Circles developed their own accounts of value autonomously, and although recognition from other circles and major cultural figures was surely encouraging, it was not a necessary condition.

In assessing the regionalism in Kyushu-ha Hariu Ichirō has argued "[Kyushu-ha] was not looking toward the center [Tokyo] or abroad [for approval]. Rather, the group challenged Tokyo, venturing into the territory of Tokyo art, while embracing its Kyushu origins."[54] This seems to capture Matano and Sakurai's posture in relation to Tokyo: the Tokyo art world did not define success for them. Even Kikuhata Mokuma, who is usually regarded as the most cosmopolitan among Kyushu-ha members, had a period of only a few years in the mid-1960s when he was very active in the Tokyo art world and even then he remained based in Fukuoka. Kyushu-ha's artwork also rarely takes up Kyushuesque themes.[55] Although the works are connected to Kyushu as a specific historical location, that connection is not readily visible. For the group's first exhibition, Matano wrote, "What I want [people in] Tokyo to understand most is that our group rejects the traditional focus on formal matters in its ardent desire to infuse a new image of humanity into painting."[56] This does not suggest particularism.

Nevertheless, we can immediately see how contradictions were bound to arise when the circle model of center-periphery relations encountered contemporary art. Members who wanted to achieve success in the art world could not afford to be indifferent to centrally mediated standards of value. Although criticism of established value is a refrain of the avant-garde, Crow insists that we must come to grips with the entire circuit through which peripheral cultural forms are moved up the chain of value, rather than trying to hold onto one part of that movement as authentic while rejecting the other as compromised and co-opted.[57] Along similar lines, John Roberts has pointed out that

> in direct contrast to the early avant-garde, the production of art since Conceptual art has derived the internal and external relations of its social identity from a primary critique of the art *institution*. This is very different from the early avant-garde's critique of the academy and museum. Whereas the academy and museum were judged to be in a joint state of decrepitude and were thus assumed to have been surpassed in practice by revolutionary artists, in contemporary culture institutional critique has become the *frame of practice*.[58]

Which is to say that what passes as critique in contemporary art must be carefully staged within the orbit of the museum. *Actually* ignoring the institutions of contemporary art, or developing a substantial critique in the form of wholly alternate accounts of value, results in being ignored. Within Kyushu-ha, this tension between autonomous value and a more knowingly staged negotiation with trends set by critics generated what many refer to as Kyushu-ha's "Tokyo complex": a back and forth between a claim that the group renounced Tokyo and the apparent need to have Tokyo recognize that renunciation. The point to be made, however, is that this "complex" was not the result of personal failing or misapprehension, but of an antinomy between two accounts of where and what culture should be, each of which was coherent on its own. Kyushu-ha's Tokyo strategy was indeed doomed to failure or, I would rather say, an unresolved in-betweenness, insofar as both of these commitments ran through the group.

Their position might be analogous to the position of California artists in the 1950s who, Thomas Crow writes, "lacked any stable structure of galleries, patrons, and audiences that might have given them realistic hopes for worldly success." Compared to California, northern Kyushu had far less infrastructure for contemporary art and the Kyushu audience was at least as conservative. California artists were often untrained and developed their own form of assemblage art that brought elements of rusticity and folksy mysticism together with a hybrid urban culture that was brimming with waste from postwar reconstruction. As Crow points out, "The small audience they did possess, particularly in San Francisco, tended to overlap with the one for experimental poetry, and in both, the majority was made up of fellow practitioners."[59] This has parallels in Kyushu-ha, including in its relationship to the metropole. In the early days of the American avant-garde's rise, there was cross-pollination between the New York and California art scenes. Visionary curator Walter Hopps held the first Duchamp retrospective in the United States at the small suburban Pasadena Art Museum (now the Norton Simon Museum), while Andy Warhol's first major show was at the Ferus Gallery in Los Angeles.[60] But as momentum developed, the early innovations in California became increasingly irrelevant to the exploding market for pop art in New York. The junky, homely, perverse, and political assemblages of the late 1950s had only a marginal place in that market. Kyushu-ha found itself in a similar position—it was instrumental in the early ferment of assemblage, but too gauche and too committed to have ever made it far up the ladder of contemporary art.

Chapter 13

Kyushu-ha's Art

The previous chapter assessed Kyushu-ha as an organization. But the group did not organize for the sake of organization. It was, always and for everyone, an effort to make art production and exhibition possible. Each member had a unique style and a different idea about what type of organization Kyushu-ha should be. Examining members as individuals will show what a "disruptive and spirited collision" of opposites, to use Tanigawa Gan's words, looked like and what its effects were. In Kyushu-ha's case, the collisions eventually tore the group apart and made it appear erratic to audiences. Most former members look back on the group with some reservations. In one of the first attempts to historicize the art movements of the 1960s, Kikuhata Mokuma opened his essay on Kyushu-ha by saying that "the only thing it managed to do was to shoot itself in the foot in a fit of indignation."[1] Tabe Mitsuko recalled the infighting as reflecting a "first union, second union, us or them" mentality.[2]

Kyushu-ha was split by incompatible conceptions of cultural value. Each of those conceptions of value entails a different approach to history. The dominant historiographical mode for understanding Kyushu-ha has been that of contemporary art, which habitually relies on the episodic timeline as its foundation: a succession of two- to three-year slots that a handful of groups fit into, resulting in a smorgasbord of groups that appear and disappear across time.[3] The problem with that historical mode, however, is that it is itself part of contemporary art's system of value, founded in periodic novelty. In order to show the complexity of Kyushu-ha's relationship with that value system, we should set aside its historical mode. The alternative that I pursue here is to assess artworks with reference to a temporality that is more closely related to artists' whole lives and with greater appreciation for the differences among their goals and values.

The artists I have chosen to concentrate on—Sakurai Takami, Tabe Mitsuko, Kikuhata Mokuma, and Miyazaki Junnosuke—are four of the most prominent and influential former members of the group. They are also artists whose works and ideas are among the most accessible, be that through their own writing, through writing about them by other researchers and critics, or, with the exception of Miyazaki, through their continuing availability to talk about their work. The selection, therefore, is partially shaped by the relative success of these four artists. It is less easy to access artists who did not remain as productive or did not publish as much about their experiences. But those quieter presences are arguably the more important to understand. Little has been written, for instance, about the group Kuroda Raiji has called the "purists." They include Terada Ken'ichirō and Taniguchi Toshio, Saitō Hidesaburō, Surusumi Seiryō, and Funaki Yoshiharu. The latter four constituted Group Nishi-Nihon, which split off from Kyushu-ha in late 1959. As a group they were less interested in art with a social mission than other Kyushu-ha members were. Therefore my approach is at best a first step toward understanding the true scope of the diversity that was the group's lifeblood and downfall.

Sakurai Takami

Sakurai Takami (1928–2016) was by all accounts the driving force behind Kyushu-ha. He held the members of Kyushu-ha together as a group and he was, from the beginning, a thorough-going experimentalist, indifferent to any form of careerism. Sakurai was eccentric, but also charismatic and compelling, with a gift for gathering people to him and motivating them. This carried through from his years as a union organizer, to Kyushu-ha, to the Konnyaku Commune (Jellied Yam Commune) which he started in San Francisco in the early 1970s. Although he did not explicitly lead people or devise clear plans of action, it was the force of his personality, his innocent intensity, that held groups together.[4]

It is not clear why Sakurai started painting. He trained as a teacher but quit teaching after just a few weeks. He then became a pigeon handler for the regional newspaper *Nishinippon*, which still used carrier pigeons to shuttle messages between offices around Kyushu. He had apparently had his heart set on the job, and after a long period of cajoling the old man who was in charge of it, he finally moved to Fukuoka in the late 1940s to take up his position atop the roof of *Nishinippon*'s head office.[5] He was eventually transferred to the Corrections Department in 1954, where he worked as a copy editor. It was there that he met Matano Mamoru for the first time. "He had just finished editing Tanigawa Gan's poetry collection, *Daichi no shōnin* [The earth's merchant]," Sakurai recalls. "The smell of the sweat from this work got right into me and got my blood pumping. This had a large role in creating a youth filled with absurd dreams about communes of politics and art."[6] Sakurai also had a significant effect on Matano. Though Matano had never painted before, the pair staged an exhibition in a café near Sakurai's house less than two years later. It was the first nonaffiliated exhibition any Kysuhu-ha member held.[7] Even at this early stage of his career, Sakurai was following an unusual path, one that succeeded through his personal powers of persuasion and did not rely on established career or professional patterns.

Sakurai's early artwork was figurative; it drew upon reportage painting in its use of montage and deformation to comment on the difficulties and injustices of the early postwar. Matano's paintings from this period are also essentially reportage art. One huge work, *Sugo jiken* (*Sugo Incident*), commemorates an incident where communist party members were framed for a dynamite attack in rural Ōita Prefecture and were subsequently acquitted in trial. Another huge work, *Uragiri no imēji* (*Image of Betrayal*), depicts a man holding his own head out, as if as a trophy. The title could be a reference to the problem of loyalty in union struggles. The late 1950s and early 1960s witnessed a major shift in the relationship between labor and management in Japan. While in the early postwar, vigorous unions saw to it that "workers gained 'citizenship' in the enterprise and a measure of control over . . . the workplace," they began to face concerted pushback from management in the late 1950s.[8] The most common tactic on the part of management was to whittle away union solidarity by encouraging the more conciliatory, less combative members to divide off and form a "second union (*daini kumiai*)." Second unions appeared in workplaces all over Japan, and were generally more pragmatic and sympathetic to management's need to rationalize operations. Betrayal of the first union was a common theme in film, poetry, and prose of the period; it was a common experience that split whole communities in company towns.

The life of work and union membership was a reality for most of the members of Kyushu-ha, and for Sakurai it was quite central. The splits in the *Nishinippon* union were so grave that by the early 1960s there were six separate ones, all competing for advantage.[9] Newspaper companies feature complex vertical integration: editors and journalists are close to public intellectuals, whereas typesetting, printing, and delivery are between craft and manual labor. Sakurai maintains that his union was one of the strongest because it represented all the various levels of labor in the company; he put off his departure for San Francisco for a year in the early 1960s because the union needed him as an organizer.[10] Sakurai's vision for Kyushu-ha may have been close to his idea of a union: stronger in numbers and in diversity. His utopian vision of a revolutionary artistic community that would control its own means of production and thereby its own destiny surely provided Kyushu-ha a great deal of daring and energy. But the model flew in the face of all types of artistic careerism and left little room for compromise. Especially after 1962, following two major breakups, Sakurai became increasingly embittered and critical of other members and began to demand ever more loyalty from them. What Tabe refers to as the "first union, second union" dynamic of Kyushu-ha can be read as quite precise: something that arose when a faction that valued solidarity above all became more intransigent and demanding in response to a faction that preached compromise and pragmatism in the interest of success in the contemporary market.[11]

Although Sakurai's artwork and organizing demonstrate a keen awareness of social and political issues that affected the working classes, most of his work is not classifiable as reportage. As the first stirrings of Anti-Art began to appear at the Yomiuri Independent and as he began to be influenced by Ochi Osamu, whose innovative work incorporated "reed screens, paper lanterns, *fusuma* screens, stands for Hakata dolls, and shopping baskets,"[12] Sakurai began to incorporate more and more everyday objects into his work. The gruesome *Rinchi* (*Lynching*) (1958) is an excellent example (plate 14). Mounted on wire netting, it is less a canvas than an assemblage: a lumpy mass of asphalt, nails, bits of plastic, wire, and metal tubing. The shape of a face is barely recognizable, swimming up out of a pit of junk. This work also features the theme of betrayal and mob justice. An irregular ring of nails closes in on the face yet also gives the impression that the face has been taken over by its own sharp-toothed maw.

The work is an assemblage of objects and materials that would have been familiar from everyday life. Peter Boswell argues that "because of the ties of the component objects to the society that produced them, 'what you see' in found-object art is never just 'what you see,' but is inevitably tied to 'what you know,' 'what you think,' 'what you remember.'"[13] Rusty nails, wires, and tar are ubiquitous, and although they would not usually excite any particular association when in their familiar disposition, when they are encountered in a work like *Lynching*, they can generate an uncanny effect. By tugging at deeply matted associations and memories in unfamiliar ways, the assemblage warps the fabric of emotional association, potentially pulling the viewer into an uncomfortably personal relation with the work. The inherent vulnerability of that position makes the estrangement of the objects all the more violent. The gothic and voyeuristic effect of much assemblage is

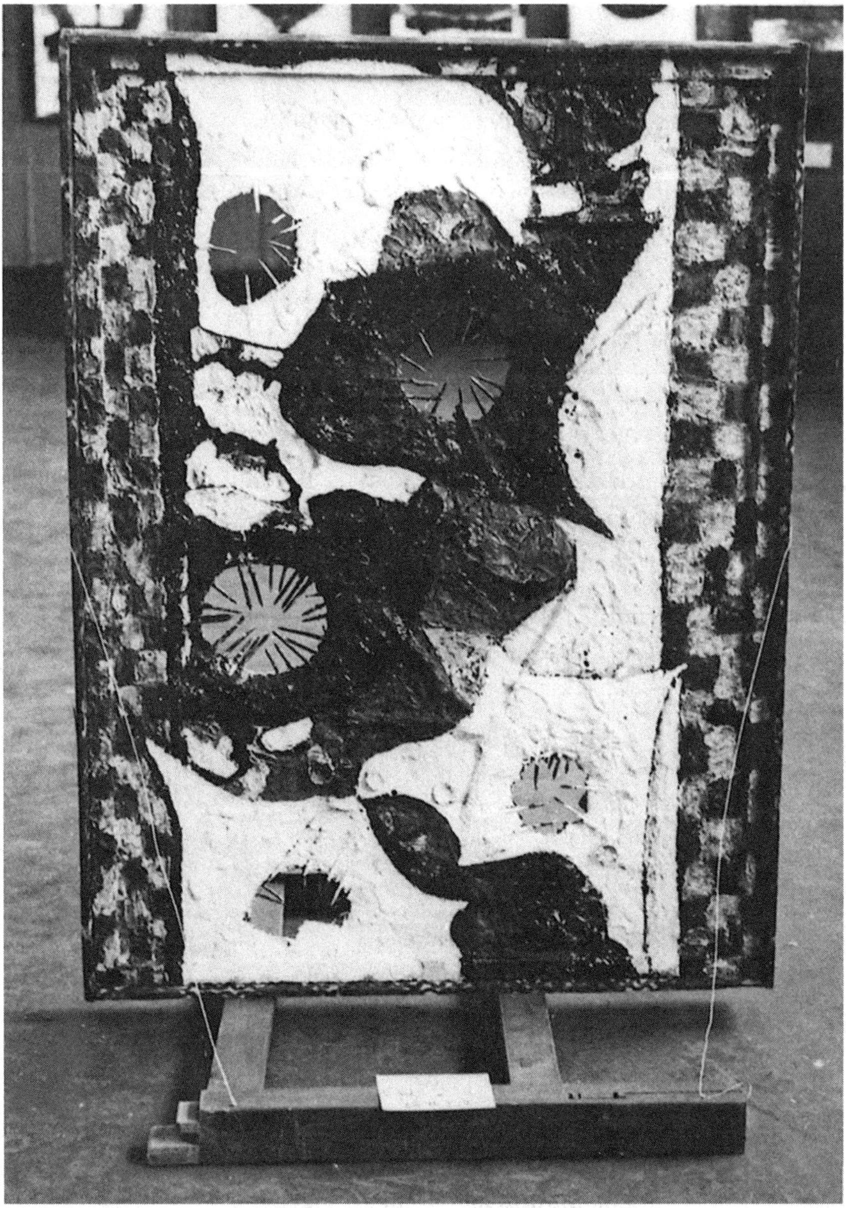

Figure 13.1 Sakurai Takami, *Dokuritsu* (*Independence*), 1959. Mixed media. Photographer unknown. Courtesy of the Fukuoka Art Museum.

in part a result of this resonance with things and feelings half-forgotten or buried, a sudden exposure of umbilical connections that one might prefer to cover or cut loose. Sakurai portrayed the abjection inherent in the process of individuation in works like *Dokuritsu* (*Independence*) (fig. 13.1), which is a free-standing work but bears the internal wounds that are the inevitable price of independence—wounds that then fence themselves off from investigation or tender advance (fig. 13.1). The awareness of the contradictions and violence attendant to independence, along with an appeal to a homely intimacy in the face of it, is something common to both Sakurai's works of art and works of organization.

Assemblages often celebrate the raw, low, excessive, unformed, dark, irrational, and occult. They bring together the seemingly opposite poles of squalid realism and mysticism.[14] Sakurai's works also suggest a dark romanticism for the occult power of the the soil, the sun, and the popular. Kuroda Raiji writes that Kyushu-ha's use of tar "was pregnant with historical and social implications. . . . Its black color could symbolize the coalmining industry that sustained the economy of Kyushu and its shiny materiality, the energy of the [lumpen] masses."[15] But because romance with the marginal and the vanishing is such a common trope throughout modernity, it is important to distinguish among variations. In the late 1950s in Japan, there was a groundswell of interest in traditional Japanese arts and aesthetics that spanned from things like Okamoto Taro's explorations of Neolithic Jōmon civilization to a renewed avant-garde interest in calligraphy and ikebana.[16] But in an essay titled "That Which Surpasses Tradition," Sakurai rejected this reinvigoration of a specifically Japanese heritage:

> People are sometimes fearful of the strange forms of animals. . . . With such warped forms and colors these strange things nonetheless *live*—that, in itself, sends a shudder through you far more artistic than what you get from the cheap painting that's so popular now. The world of animals has a rigor that makes a mockery of . . . the patterns carved into Jōmon pottery, or [Ogata] Kōrin painting, or religion. Animals are supported by the strict rule of survival [*seizon*]. Ugly or beautiful, each animal in the animal world lives on. . . . For this very reason we have to throw away tradition in the sense of things that only Europe has, or tradition as a narrow monopoly on Japaneseness, . . . and be able to flop down and live anywhere in the world, recognizing no barriers between countries, realizing a kind of human being that has never existed before, and finding innocent wonder at ourselves as humans, as things, breaking ourselves down into our most minute elements, seeking through to the mysteries of the atomic.[17]

More than a return to the past, Sakurai advocated a plunge to the depths: to a shared humanity beyond borders, to a shared biology beyond species, all the way to an atomic level of interpenetration and enamourment. This is where we can begin to glimpse the mysticism that goes hand in hand with

Sakurai's use of the grotesque. The natural world he envisioned was fundamentally inspired, alive with the motion of its own renewing. Thus the marginal life that Sakurai invoked as the abject other of civilized life took the form of a biological flux undivided from itself, something that he believed could be accessed in the present in both art and society.

The aim of realigning human existence along a deeper natural axis is a common theme of romantic poetics and ethics. Realigning human forces with the natural promises to unleash great waves of creativity, a more vital art and a better way of life. But as a theory of art it means that the artistic sign must partake directly of the natural sign in a relationship of synecdoche: not representing, but incarnating powers that are latent in the world.[18] This leads almost inexorably to a sacralization of the creative act, as something so primordial that it creates nature itself in its own motion. In just one ecstatic example of many, Sakurai writes, "We must attempt to establish the stage of a completely different type of existence [*seizon*], by sheer force at first, as an enormous assumption, take painting itself, human life itself and throw them open anew, not nature as it is, but as it should be, as it must be, we must achieve a completely man-made mutation."[19]

This poetics is similar to the account of creativity that underlay Informel. But Sakurai was probably already committed to it before Informel arrived on the scene; it was a major element of poetry in postwar Kyushu, practiced by, among others, the poets of Boin and Sākuru Mura. In his famous essay "Genten ga sonzai suru" (An origin exists), Tanigawa Gan presented his own account of this darkly mystical poetics. "There is nothing else to do than go down and down. . . . Down to the base, down to the root, where flowers don't bloom, where darkness overflows, for there is our universal mother. There is an origin of existence. There is a first moving energy. . . . A poet is one who captures . . . the energy that sets form to the flowers, branches, and leaves—but the poet catches it and makes people aware of it while it is still nebulous and of unsettled shape, while it is a bud, an infant."[20] In this way, the tar and the junk in Kyushu-ha's assemblage works can be read as having a lyric element: they access an ambivalent, metamorphic energy that infuses both biological and social reality. Although this aesthetics is broadly similar to the aesthetics of Informel, the latter was undeniably high art and was practiced by some of Japan's most venerable artists. Sakurai and Kyushu-ha brought that down, to insist on an origin in the present and in anybody's everyday life.

Yamauchi Jūtarō's works are the best examples of the haunting beauty that can be achieved with base and discarded materials. His *Sakuhin 5* (*Work 5*) (1958) is made from tangles of string stuck to a wooden board with asphalt (plate 15). Yamauchi punched a hole in the middle of the board and then he covered the entire piece with kerosene and set it on fire. The fire scorched some of the exposed string and left a dull patina on the pigment and asphalt, making it look ancient or haunted. The string is matted and bunched. Unlike muscle, it is not arranged in striations—its implied motion is in the form of slow growth or decay. The coloring and arrangement of material focus attention on the hole in the middle, something that is very simple but rich in meaning. The hole in this work is not an assault on the institution of the picture plane, but suggestive of the hole we are all born out of and will fall back into. Likewise, setting fire to the work is an action that is more elemental than anything in abstract expressionism or in Dadaist uses of junk. The junk here is the life force itself in a vegetable mode, a tangled flux that things rise from only to fall back into.

Sakurai's ethic and aesthetic thoroughly opposed differentiation and division. Organizations worked only through his presence and had no articulated structure that would outlive his involvement. His ideas, as written in the journal *Kyushu-ha*, were based on a radical continuity between mind and nature that required ecstatic artistic action to realize. The difficulty in achieving this, the constant specter of failure, the need for greater exhortation toward rapture are almost unavoidable results. Although his approach had a warm and generous side, Sakurai's intensity could become tiring. In a last-ditch effort to recover Kyushu-ha's momentum, he took over office duties and the publication of *Kyushu-ha* in 1961. During 1962, he sent out countless postcards and announcements and held meetings to build up to the Grand Meeting of Heroes, cajoling, persuading, sometimes bullying, insisting that the Grand Meeting would "hail a new tomorrow" (*ashita no kokuji*). "Revolution. There are none among the young who don't dream of seizing political power from the ruling classes and causing a sudden revolution in the social structure. Even in the biological imperative of living, even in the most basic biological sense of growing from a child into an adult, we are implicated in an unavoidable process of resistance . . . and so cannot but wish for revolution."[21]

Although a desire for permanent biosocial revolution characterized Sakurai's wanderings through the subcultures of the world, it was not something other members of Kyushu-ha were interested in. In volume 7 of *Kyushu-ha*, published almost a year after the Grand Meeting, Sakurai wrote a long piece exhorting the members to prepare for another Grand Meeting, this time to be held in New York. It was accompanied by a long piece by Hataraki Tadashi that objected to the idea and criticized Sakurai for always wanting to rush on to the next thing without reflection. There was only one more major group exhibition before the group dissipated.[22]

Sakurai departed for San Francisco in March 1965. He lived there until October 1967, at which point he came back to Fukuoka for about two years. During his time in Fukuoka in 1968 and 1969, he participated in protests and happenings, together with Shūdan Kumo (Group Spider) and Zero Jigen (Zero Dimension). One can see from his beard and his penchant for nakedness during this time that he was exploring the counterculture that thrived in both California and Japan. He wrote a series of articles for the *Tokyo shinbun* (Tokyo news) on hippie subculture, accompanied by images of artwork he had created while on LSD. When he returned to San Francisco in 1970, he started the Konnyaku Komyūn near the traditional Japanese and Filipino districts. About a dozen artists lived and worked there. Though he meant it to be for anyone, in practice it became a stop-off point for young Japanese trying to find their way in the United States. During his stay, he became friends with poet and activist Al Robles, a third-generation Filipino who fought with activist Bill Sorro for the housing rights of the Filipino community in San Francisco.

His next move was to a suburb of Paris, where he lived from 1974 to the late 1980s. He claims that he moved to San Francisco to find Alan Ginsberg; when he moved to France, he began to track down Gilles Deleuze. It seems fitting that Sakurai, whose life constantly moved from the next to the next to the next, was attracted to the theorist of the ceaselessly conjunctive schizophrenic personality. Sakurai's later work, in the 1980s and 1990s, involved books: books made of concrete, metal books, large folding screens. These returned to a junk aesthetic, as things keep latching themselves onto the edge of surfaces, forming hinges that unfold into the next, then the next, then the next. His most recent production was a series of collage-like volumes of his and others' writings. Each volume is huge, between 1,100 and 1,200 pages; there are thirteen, totaling over 15,000 pages.

Tabe Mitsuko

Former members of Kyushu-ha each have their own memory of what it was and what it meant. Tabe Mitsuko (b. 1933) believes it was, at its core, a resistance movement (anti–prefectural exhibit, anti-Nika) that went hand in hand with other resistance movements of the 1960s (anti-war, anti-Anpo, anti-Expo). For Tabe, Kyushu-ha meant always being on the outside, displaced, defeated, but becoming all the more substantial for that. "I had intended to live defeat from the very beginning. An aesthetics of defeat is the only way to achieve that completely, and this is the way work continues to be produced. For me."[23] Whereas Kikuhata soon began to seek his fortune in Tokyo and Sakurai went to San Francisco a few years later, Tabe points out that she stayed with Kyushu-ha all the way through, even down to the present day, "wandering the wasteland of obscure art in Fukuoka."[24] From the beginning, Tabe's stance and artwork were not caught up in a romance about unalienated life or concern for Kyushu's working classes. She was, however, the most tenacious fighter for artistic freedom in the group, and more than any other member she can claim to have built a public place for her art with her own hands.[25]

Tabe was born in 1933 in Taiwan.[26] Her family returned to Fukuoka to ancestral farm holdings that had been reduced by the occupation land reform. She had enjoyed drawing all her life, and when she began working at the Iwataya Department Store in downtown Fukuoka in 1953, she joined the company's painting circle. It was a committed group that met a few times a week with a regular teacher and a nude model so students could practice sketching. Tabe must have shown talent because one of her paintings was selected to appear in the Prefectural Exhibition in 1953, the same year she joined the company. Her development thus falls slightly outside both the poetry circle and the art society. She was not involved in poetry circles and was cool toward the exhibition societies: she turned down invitations to exhibit at the Jiyū Exhibition, for example.[27] She recalls that even in the company's painting circle, she had little respect for her teacher because he had the habit of adding his own painterly touches to his students' work in the process of teaching. The most interesting people were the other "crazies" in the class and the model who came to pose.[28]

In 1957, Tabe took a decisive step away from both the department store and the prefectural exhibitions. That was the year Kyushu-ha formed. It was also the year of a long strike at Iwataya during which management locked out employees for fifty-three days.[29] The strike slightly preceded Kyushu-ha's formation and left Tabe suddenly without work and without a painting circle. She did not believe in the necessity of the strike and identified more with the management than the strikers. She had little trust in the union, writing a few years later that she saw little difference between the placards of the right wing and the placards of the labor movement.[30] Instead of participating in the strikes she went to hang out at Terada Ken'ichirō's atelier.[31] Thus Kyushu-ha coalesced for Tabe at a moment when she was free from work, fed up with union organization, and, we can imagine, seeking more than what her painting circle could provide.

Some of her earliest work takes up marine themes: *Gyozoku 1 & 2* (*Fish 1 & 2*, 1957), *Umi de no hanashi 1 & 2* (*Conversation by the Sea 1 & 2*, 1957), and *Gyozoku no ikari* (*Anger of the Fish*, 1958–1959). In *Kysuhu-ha* 2, she discussed her interest this way: "I've made fish a theme of mine. It's something that started when I began to feel a fascination with a biology, an ecology, other than the human one. The forms of fish and shells, when you really concentrate on them, don't make any single stable form. In their wet sliminess we can receive and feel them in any way we choose. They're also full of irony and humor. My aim is to capture what is so hard to capture, swimming around freely."[32] Tabe's goal was indeed a difficult one, the task of capturing a motion that is alien and fickle. Like Sakurai, she is inspired by the fecundity of nonhuman ecology but she differs from him in that her interest is explicitly focused on representation. There is more play in her aesthetics.

But anger soon entered her work. In *Anger of the Fish* (1958–1959), colors and hexagonal grid lines explode out from the center and a black strip grounds the composition on a left-right axis (plate 16). Although it is an abstract work, it seems tied to place. The red and the white have been raked over the rough surface of the paint and board underneath, creating stippled edges, as if they have been brushed over sandstone. The radiation from the center is in straight lines, suggesting that something has been crushed from above by a great force. Although the white and black are strong, the red is rusting, the blue is pale, and the green is mixed with brown in a recalcitrant organicism. On top of this are tiny rings that Tabe made from cross-sections of a bamboo broom handle and stuck to the canvas with tar. Gathered in two clumps, their tiny self-containedness seems superfluous, almost petty, against the blast of colors under them, like organisms on the outer surface of a vast biological memory.

The theme of the swarm developed in another of Tabe's series, titled *Hanshoku suru* (*Propagating*). There are four canvases in this series, all painted in 1958 (fig. 13.2). The small rings of tar-coated bamboo form the central figure. Their groupings suggest the fluid formations of living things: fungi, swarms of insects, herds of prey animals, and crowds of people. The propagation of manmade objects is a theme other Kyushu-ha artists explored. For *Q-shi no fukaki* (*Mr. Q's Incubator*, 1963) Taniguchi Toshio welded large woks together to make disks that he decorated with metal scrap. He installed these on the walls and floor of galleries to suggest a flock of alien presences. Kikuhata Mokuma's *Sōsōkyoku No. 2* (*Requiem No. 2*, 1960) uses dozens of pottery shapes to suggest a progression of ghosts or souls.

In Kikuhata's case, however, the elements of the flock are clearly humanoid and the composition lacks the disjuncture between the propagating entities and the ground that characterizes Tabe's work. Taniguchi's work or, in a similar vein, Nakanishi Natsuyuki's *Sentaku basami wa kakuhan kōdō o shuchō suru* (*Clothespins Assert Agitating Action*, 1963) imagine mass produced conveniences overwhelming the individual subject with an unexpected demonstration of herd intelligence. The formulation, however, does not undermine the

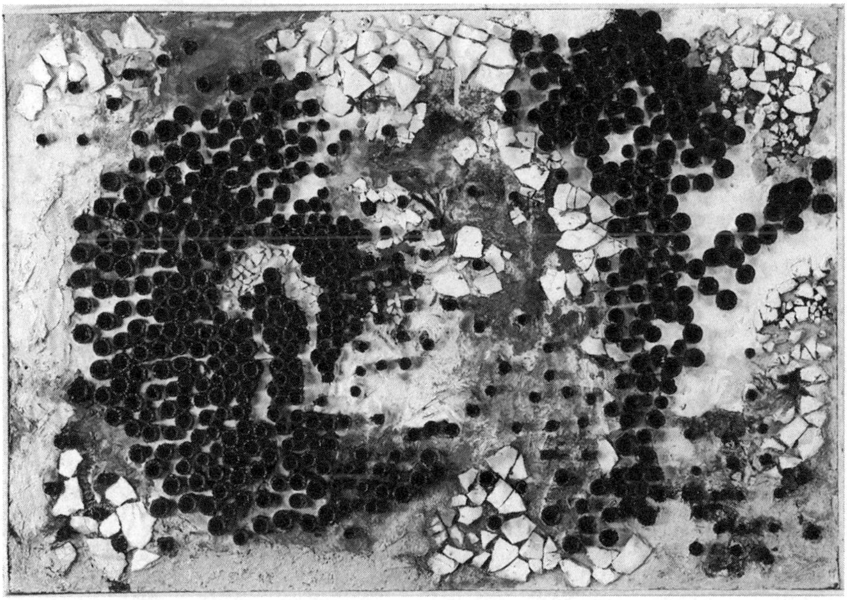

Figure 13.2 Tabe Mitsuko, *Hanshoku suru 2* (*Propagating 2*), 1958. Asphalt, plaster, and bamboo on board. 92 cm x 130 cm. Courtesy of Tabe Mitsuko / Fukuoka Art Museum.

centrality of the human, no matter how vexed he or she may be by runaway clothespins or pots. The ironic, playful bite rests on the assumption of a relatively competent, sentient individual who retains an expectation of dignity in order to make the mass-produced affront meaningful. The human subject is not displaced but remains at the center of the drama.

Tabe's work allows fewer presumptions. *Jinkō taiban* (*Artificial Placenta*, 1961) is one of her most powerful assemblage works, many of which take up themes related to gender (fig. 13.3). It consists of five mannequins: three adult females that have been cut at the torso and thigh and placed upside down, and two children that hang above them. The female mannequins have been cut open where the womb would be. Ping-pong balls line the edge of the opening, and a vacuum tube is placed inside each womb. The torsos of the children have been cut down the middle and ping-pong balls placed inside. Tabe left little writing about the work other than the statement, "Women will only be truly free when there is an artificial placenta."[33] The statement goes to the heart of the tension between childbearing and the ideal of a liberated, modern subjectivity. The ideal subject is free from attachments that might hinder the exercise of rationality but is, in concept and practice, always male. Children are attachments that cannot be denied, but as long as the labor of childrearing is regarded as a private, familial one, it will always be in tension with

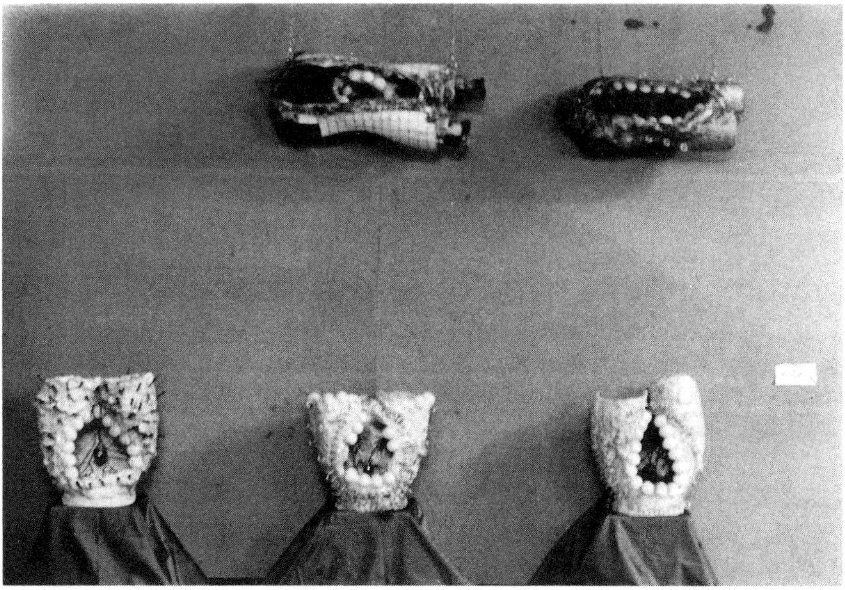

FIGURE 13.3 Tabe Mitsuko, *Jinkō taiban* (*Artificial Placenta*), 1961. Mixed media. Photographed at Group Kyushu Exhibition at Ginza Gallery, 1961, by Taniguchi Toshio. Courtesy of Tabe Mitsuko / Fukuoka Art Museum.

the demands of the public sphere. Japan was thoroughly divided along gender lines in the 1960s: men held nearly all positions of institutional authority (as they still do). Female artists faced a particular burden because art is second only to politics in its appetite for publicity. Unlike industries that may offer parents leave from work to reduce the pressure of work and family, contemporary art has no such system. Before she married in 1958, Tabe had wanted to go to Tokyo to try to make it as an artist, but that wasn't possible after she married and started a family in Fukuoka.[34]

Artificial Placenta was exhibited in 1961 at the annual group show in the Ginza Gallery. Tabe was five months pregnant with her first child when she and the other members of Kyushu-ha made the eighteen-hour train trip to Tokyo for the show. She was also holding 200,000 yen in cash, wrapped into a sash tied tightly around her waist. This was money the whole group would need for their trip and it was a huge responsibility: her husband's monthly wage at the time was 15,000 yen.[35] Taking care of the family accounts is a duty traditionally assigned to the wife in Japanese households, so it was not random that Tabe had to shoulder the responsibility (she was also in charge of collecting membership dues). With all of this demanded of her, we can appreciate the urgency of the statement that "women will only be truly free when there is an artificial placenta." This call for liberation, however, is hard to reconcile with the assemblage itself.[36] The work is ambivalent and seems to communicate anger more than an optimistic wish for the future. One possibility is that the sculpture itself is the absence of an artificial placenta, the contradiction and violence of women not yet liberated. Tabe's statement about liberation insists that the problem cannot be resolved by reanimating a version of the natural community (as may have been Sakurai's instinct). Predictably, the ideological challenge of the *Artificial Placenta* was ignored by art critics. The only coverage it got was in a weekly magazine that was eager to play up the scandal of a female artist making a sculpture of genitalia.[37]

During the 1960s, Tabe balanced her artwork and her work as a mother and wife without seeming to sacrifice either. She recounted her activities in the last half of 1967:

June—San Francisco / Kyushu-ha Exhibition at Tokyo Gallery.
July—Poetry and painting exhibition at BOBO, a nightclub in Fukuoka. Tabe and Obana Shigeharu perform together, covering a nude model in soap bubbles. The intended message was that the media made women as ephemeral as bubbles.
September—Women of Kyushu-ha Exhibition (Kyushu-ha Josei-ten), at Tokyo's Kunugi Gallery. Tabe, Ōguro Aiko, and Chō Yoriko exhibited on the theme of marriage.

In the months leading up to these exhibits, Tabe stayed up nights to prepare, and in the middle of the preparation her second son was born. She continued nonetheless, "nursing with the left hand, painting with the right."[38] In 1968 and 1969, she participated in the anti–World Expo demonstrations that spread through northern Kyushu and it was she who penned a public letter to artists living in Fukuoka to join her and other members of Kyushu-ha in protesting the judging panel of the Seibu Bijutsu-ten (Asahi West Art Exhibition) that Asahi sponsored.[39] In the 1970s and 1980s, her artistic production slowed, but she continued to organize new exhibition forums. She founded, for example, the Kyushu Joryū Gaka-ten (Kyushu Women's Art Exhibition), which was held every year from 1974 to 1984 and, in conjunction with the exhibition, held classes for aspiring female artists.

Describing Tabe's work as being concerned with politics and gender seems too flat.[40] One might be tempted to say her awareness is something born of lived experience, but that would discount her respect for books. She is not only a voracious reader, she has written a book on gender in medieval

Japanese art in the series Onna to otoko no jikū: Nihon joseishi saikō (Time and space of gender: Redefining Japanese women's history).[41] But her ability to forge a path for herself and for others—organizing independent exhibitions with Kyushu-ha in the 1950s, protesting the corporatization of art in the 1960s, managing an exhibition for women in the 1970s, while producing works like *Artificial Placenta* around which there were no interlocutors for decades—her work to find these avenues outside an art world that is still stubbornly dominated by men, must not be confused with the ease of accounting for it by recourse to an available label. Labels imply that there is something already there, waiting to be labeled. That would miss the point of her achievements. Tabe created her artworks at the same time that she was creating the possibility for them to exist, making time bloom so as to be able to work on them amidst her other duties and building spaces where they could be seen even when there was no audience yet to see them. While I argue in chapter 2 that interpersonal engagement was critical to sustaining the creative energy of autonomous, democratic culture, Tabe managed to build her autonomy largely as a movement of one.

In 1988, Tabe "submitted her retirement notice" from her job as housewife.[42] Since then, her career has steadily gained momentum. She has had multiple exhibitions each year since 1991, in Fukoka; Tokyo; Paris; Washington, D.C.; and New York. She has worked over the past two decades in collage and assemblage, always in the form of large, open-ended series. Some of the major ones are the *Apple Series*, *Sign Language Series*, *One Hundred Notebooks*, *Fun with Non-Art*, and *Universal Gravitation*. Most of the works are bright; many use gold and silver leaf. They are awash with clippings and references to present-day popular culture and to art history. They are full of motion, color, and associations that range from the funny to the deeply thoughtful. Figures that recur are apples ("they're so sexy—they're symbols of everything")[43] and plaster hands cast from the hands of her friends and relatives. The assemblages often take the shape of boxes that, when opened, reveal small worlds overflowing with meaning. One is a tea box in homage to Mishima Yukio that opens to a small chamber filled with sequins, as if treasuring him and his erotic excesses. Another is a bookstand crowned with a golden book. In back of the stand is a model of a still life that is transfigured by an explosion of tiny colorful objects. As Jeffrey Wright notes, "Tabe probes the twin desires of creating a vessel and filling it—or fashioning a pedestal and crowning it."[44]

Kikuhata Mokuma

Kikuhata Mokuma (b. 1935) is the most well-known artist to come out of Kyushu-ha. Partly because of this success, he is sometimes taken to represent

Kyushu-ha in historical accounts. From the time the first historical accounts of contemporary art appeared in *Bijutsu techō* in the late 1960s, Kikuhata was the go-to person to represent Kyushu-ha in Tokyo-based journals. A decade later he published an autobiographical account of his career.[45] Partly because Kikuhata is a highly engaging writer and partly because there was little else available, accounts of Kyushu-ha before the 1988 retrospective exhibition tended to rely on these writings.[46]

Kikuhata was born in Nagasaki. His father, grandfather, and grandmother all died before his first birthday, which sent the family fishing business into bankruptcy. His mother struggled to support him through weaving and waitressing. But she succumbed to cancer in 1947, leaving Kikuhata, at age twelve, with no home or relatives. He made it through junior high school and high school with the help of teachers and the families of his schoolmates. Despite his precarious situation, but perhaps also because of it, his ambition to become a successful modern artist was clear from an early age. After graduating from high school in 1953, he began doing piecework as a painter of souvenir plates in the Iwataya Department Store. That same year, he took his first paintings to the Ao no Ie (Blue House), looking for recognition and success as a modern artist. His artistic debut three years later can only be described as meteoric. His work *Futari* (*Couple*) was accepted into the 1956 Dokuritsu Exhibition and became one of the small proportion of such exhibition works to be commented upon by a critic, Hariu Ichirō. A small picture of the work was carried in the leading journal for avant-garde art trends, *Bijutsu hihyō*.[47] Despite this rare recognition, the Dokuritsu Exhibition rejected Kikuhata's submission in 1957, an event that set the stage for his entrance into Kysuhu-ha.

Kikuhata and Ochi Osamu were the two members of Kyushu-ha whose works were most frequently mentioned in the Tokyo press. They were also the ones who were chosen to participate in high-profile, specially curated exhibitions in the early 1960s. Although Sakurai was undoubtedly the main force behind Kyushu-ha, his near-total lack of interest in the prevailing hierarchies of taste has relegated him and his work to obscurity. Kikuhata, Ochi, and Yamauchi quit Kyushu-ha in December 1959 to form Dōkutsu-ha (The Cave School). Their new group excluded artists who submitted to open-call exhibitions in order to focus on artists with greater ambitions. Though both Kikuhata and Ochi drifted back to Kyushu-ha within a year, Kikuhata's career in Tokyo always exerted a stronger pull on him than Kyushu-ha did. He never shared Sakurai's vision of a mass movement, and as his career prospects in Tokyo developed, he drifted away from the group.

It should be noted that Kikuhata was not hostile to Kyushu-ha or collectivism *per se.* But he had a clear idea about what kind of group Kyushu-ha would need to be to warrant his participation. Before leaving Kyushu-ha for the last time in 1961, he tried to convince Sakurai to form a group with a more coherent organization and goals. In a letter to Sakurai that was later published in *Kyushu-ha*, he outlined what he called a "promoter system."[48] The promoter at the center of the system would have full responsibility for planning, budgeting, and admitting members to the group. The budgets and expenditures would be transparent but the members of the group would not have any say in them: they would only have a yes/no vote on the final plan. Further, there would be no fixed group name: the group would go by the name the promoter chose. Kikuhata's promoter was what today might be called an independent curator. One of the most important sources of value in the system of contemporary art in Japan at the time were critics and journalists who spotted or seeded new trends. Trends, mediated through art journalism and themed exhibitions, were what organized shared public values. Kikuhata was responding to this new reality, which demanded clearly themed exhibitions, and his proposal to Sakurai reveals that he hoped Kyushu-ha could continue to be an innovative force. But Sakurai was not interested.

Like other members of Kyushu-ha, Kikuhata began exploring a heavy, material painting style after Informel, and subsequently shifted into assemblage. While he approached collectivism pragmatically, his artworks also demonstrate his ability to establish an operative intellectual distance from his subject matter. While many Anti-Art works revel in the moment of expression and rely on the impact of the mass and curiosity of certain materials, Kikuhata's work retains a level of articulation and authorial comment that cannot be reduced to the material or to elemental gestures. His general refusal of a poetics of identity creates a space for structural and semiotic manipulation which, while increasing the impression of control, is also liberating in that it makes sophisticated explorations possible. Kikuhata would not be tied to anything so general as a life force unfolding, and in his work we can see the benefit of insisting on a space for critical intellectual engagement.

Because so much has been written about Kikuhata, I limit myself to a series of works titled *Dorei keizu* (*Slave Genealogy*). These were Kikuhata's breakout pieces; his success with them opened the way for a number of private shows in the 1960s, ensuring him a profile in Tokyo. The first work in the series was exhibited as part of a specially curated show at the National Museum of Modern Art in 1961 titled Experiments in Contemporary Art (fig. 13.4). The exhibit featured a selection of Japan's most noteworthy contemporary artists, including Ochi Osamu. The second work in the series was shown at Kyushu-ha's final group exhibition at the Ginza Gallery (fig. 13.5). It was the

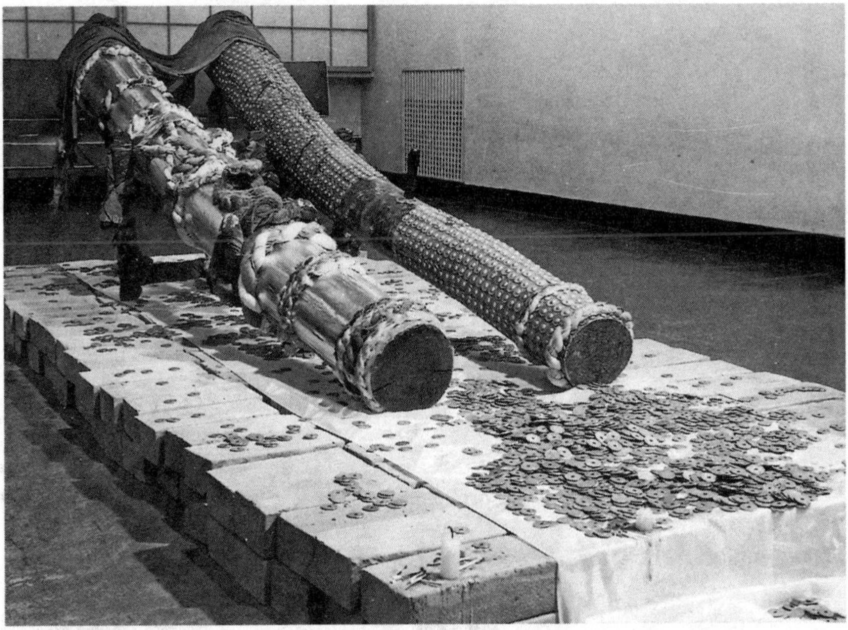

FIGURE 13.4 Kikuhata Mokuma, *Dorei keizu* (*Slave Genealogy*), 1961. Mixed media. Photographed at Gendai Bijutsu no Jikken-ten (Experiments in Contemporary Art Exhibition) at the National Museum of Modern Art, Tokyo, 1961. Remade in 1983. Museum of Contemporary Art, Tokyo. Courtesy of Kikuhata Mokuma / Museum of Contempory Art, Tokyo / Fukuoka Art Museum.

unfavorable reception of this exhibition that led indirectly to Kikuhata leaving the group again at the end of 1961. The final installment in the series was a solo exhibition held at the Minami Gallery in Tokyo (fig. 13.6). Patronage from the Minami Gallery helped Kikuhata cement his standing in the art world over the next few years. The venues for these three works appear to have been decisive: the first and final works in the series prompted write-ups in major art journals, while critics ignored the second, exhibited at the Kyushu-ha group exhibition.

The series references rural life, folk religion, and superstition. Few Kyushu-ha works reference Kyushu specifically or even the countryside generally. Kikuhata's works in this period are the exception. But Kikuhata invoked rusticity critically, not as a badge of his identity. Even the title of the series, *Dorei keizu* (*Slave Genealogy*), can be taken as deeply scornful. The first in the series features two large logs with a natural bend in the middle mounted in a reclining position on a bed of bricks. The "female" log is swaddled in rope, with a circle of rope near the middle, indicating her genitalia. The "male" log has been armored with hundreds of five-yen coins. He is adorned with a

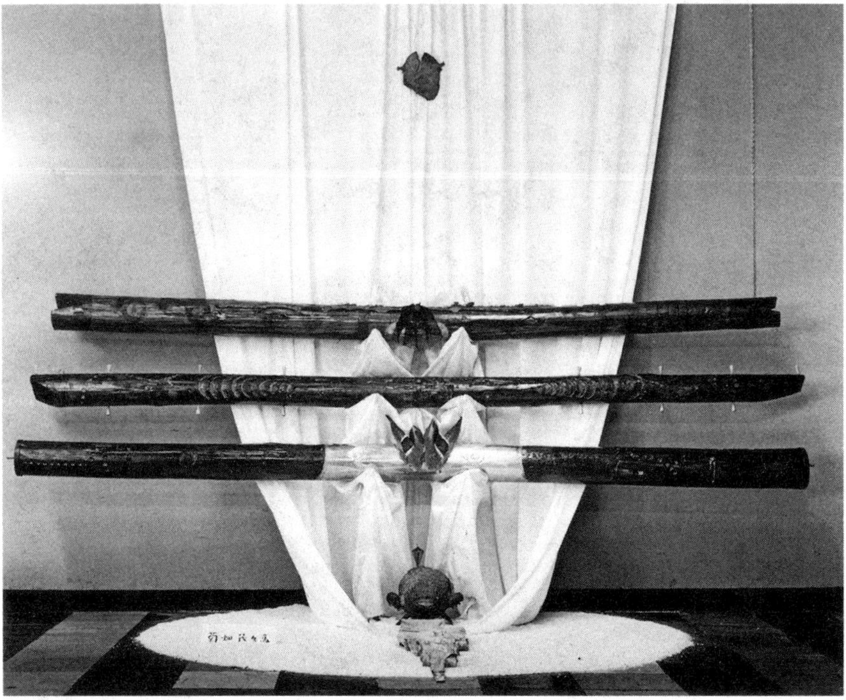

FIGURE 13.5 Kikuhata Mokuma, *Dorei keizu* (*Slave Genealogy*), 1961. Mixed media. Photographed at Group Kyushu Exhibition at Ginza Gallery, 1961. Courtesy of Kikuhata Mokuma / Fukuoka Art Museum.

phallus, and the area around it has been stamped repeatedly with the Chinese character for "hair." The cloth draped over the tops of the logs, along with the candles and white sheeting below them, suggest a ceremonial marriage bed: a setting where sex is an act of public and sacral interest. Five-yen coins scattered at the foot of the "bed" look as if they have been left by well-wishers who have tossed the coins as they would on a visit to a shrine or temple. On the one hand, the work suggests identity between human and nature: the people are logs and they are there to reproduce themselves and continue the community. It is important to note that the work's aura derives largely from its massiveness and the ceremonial setting: elements that might well be present in an actual ceremonial religious display. Yet, while indulging the latent power in the material and iconography, Kikuhata resists identity with these. The clean cut ends of the logs, the token appearance of the phallus, and the replacement of hair with stamps that say "hair," suggest a farcical interpretation is equally valid, one that invites criticism of a pre-modern social system where reproduction was of critical community importance, where

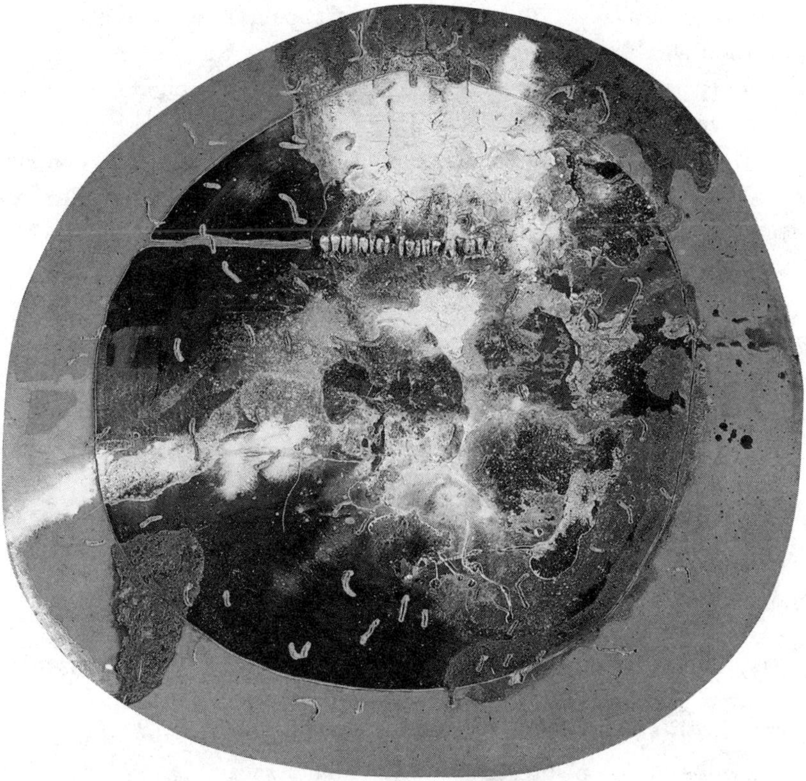

FIGURE 13.6 Kikuhata Mokuma, *Dorei keizu: enkyō ni yoru no. 13* (*Slave Genealogy: Disc Mirror No. 13*), 1962. Mixed media on plywood. 95 cm x 85.1 cm x 1.5cm. Courtesy of Kikuhata Mokuma / Tokushima Modern Art Museum.

the bare mechanics of reproductive capacity and its success, become objects not of lurid, but of flinty material interest. By stripping the scene down to a rude caricature of itself, Kikuhata outs a sexual economy in which sexual relationships are a moment of voyeuristic accounting, dressed up as something sacred.

In the second work in the series, Kikuhata continues to use a ceremonial motif, using flowing white cloth and a stand of horizontal logs. The logs are symmetrically decorated—the middle one with a series of flutes cut along each side and the bottom one with metal leaf. An important element of the sculpture is the small fragment hanging above the stand, which has the image of a mouth on it: a tiny, shrunken reference to a face, suggesting that the whole piece is a human body. As with the first work the body is reduced to a few arcs. The motion in this piece is downward, down the flow of the sheets, through the suggestive decorations on the logs, to a legged fish crawling out of the base along a rumpled tongue of papers. This assemblage is also concerned with the linkage between the sacred and the profane, across the terrain of the human body. The body itself is almost ephemeral, barely a breeze, while the weight of the work comes through the dark, heavy bars hung across the lower half: like enormous ceremonial piercings lodging the skin to its eternal duty of reproducing itself. The formal beauty, however, effectively frames whatever uncanniness might inhere in the motif, leaving the viewer in an ambiguous position. We are confronted with the attraction and beauty that is attendant upon culture's traffic with nature. While Sakurai's works tend toward a binary between the natural and the civilized with an absolute elevation of the former, Kikuhata's works insist that nature and civilization are collaborators. He does not idolize the natural, but shows how it is just as compromised and hybrid, indeed just as "dirty," as any cultural formation. Kikuhata does not exempt the viewer: the beauty of the work foregrounds the way we, the viewers, are bound by the farce even when we can see it. In the end, the double-edged critique leaves only the author unscathed.

As Yamane Yasuchika has argued, the final work in this series is a transitional piece.[49] More than a piece, it is a collection of pieces along a theme, titled *Dorei keizu: enkyō ni yoru* (*Slave Genealogy: Disc Mirror*). The pieces are a series of irregular wooden discs. They lack the complexity of address in the previous works and present a more straightforward approach to the grotesque, using materials such as plastic, cashews, mannequin eyeballs, and real human teeth. The next few years in Kikuhata's career demonstrate how quickly he was able to adapt his production to the trends of the contemporary art world. His *Roulette* series, begun in 1963, combined folksy material and found objects with immediately recognizable pop art motifs and arrangements, while the *Botanical Picture Book Series* continued with the same basic structure of geometric arrangement on wood while incorporating a new interest in body castings. Coupled with this adaptability and productivity was greatly increased exposure. After 1962, Kikuhata participated in a number of important exhibitions. In 1964, his work was included at the Yangu Sebun (Young Seven) Exhibition, a second solo show at the Minami Gallery, and the Gendai Bijutsu no Dōkō (Trends in Contemporary Art) Exhibition held at the National Museum of Modern Art. In 1965, he participated in the New Japanese Painting and Sculpture Exhibition, which toured seven museums in the United States, including the Museum of Modern Art and the Staempfli Gallery in New York.

This exhausting schedule and incredible artistic metamorphosis did not last for long. Kikuhata wrote a fascinating piece for a special issue of *Bijutsu techō* on body art in 1965. It was as much about the state of the contemporary art world as about body art.

> Recently my life has turned into the life of a transparent person. But strangely my skin alone carries on like before, wandering in search of a master. A foolish human wisdom [prevails] at the present moment that skin is the strongest and that it alone survives. . . . But there must be a limit to how far this skin (my shadow) can support its form (me) on its own. Herein lies the reason why bands of shadow warriors have emerged in the art world recently. But [the situation] has made me reach the opposite conclusion, that the problem for art today is how to find another master that will inhabit this cast-off skin.[50]

Although Kikuhata succeeded in accessing the international world of contemporary art during this span of about five years, he did not stay with it for long. Perhaps not unlike his decision to leave Kysuhu-ha, Kikuhata was ready to leave contemporary art, insofar as it got in the way of his ability to engage deeply with specific things.

After this period, Kikuhata continued to produce artwork. His subsequent work includes a series of small, disciplined assemblages that he created in the 1960s and 1970s and a long-running series of minimalist works on canvas that he began in the early 1980s. Kikuhata has also made major contributions to the field of art history. His pioneering book on war paintings, *Tennō no bijutsu: kindai shisō to sensōga* (The emperor's art: War paintings and the idea of modernity), laid out the provocative thesis that war paintings are the purest example of modern art as it has been institutionalized in Japan and remains a standard reference work on the subject.

Miyazaki Junnosuke

Miyazaki Junnosuke (1930–1989) first encountered Kyushu-ha when he saw the group's publicity parade for its second street exhibition in 1957. He soon became a member and participated in most of the shows and group meetings. But because he lived in Kokura, about two hours north of Fukuoka by train, he did not attend all the drinking parties and informal gatherings and was able to keep some distance.

He was the only person in Kyushu-ha with artistic training; he had studied sculpture at Kyoto Gakugei Daigaku (Kyoto University of Arts and Sciences). After he graduated in 1956, he began working as an art teacher at Kokura School for the Deaf, where he stayed until 1973. Several Kyushu-ha members were teachers. Taniguchi Toshio operated an art school for children in Ōmuta and was a devotee of Sōbi pedagogy. When Taniguchi moved to Fukuoka in the mid-1960s, he started another school there and Hataraki Tadashi took over his Ōmuta school. Kikuhata Mokuma sometimes helped out at Taniguchi's school in Fukuoka. In 1970, Kikuhata became a guest instructor at the experimental arts school, Bigakkō, where he continued to work until 1992. Miyazaki's work as a teacher focused on sculpture and crafts: clay and paper sculpture, pottery, woodcut, design, and wood carving. Though the reasons for his interest in wood must be complex, he claims his first inspiration came when he was working with his students on a totem pole project in which they all collaborated to fashion a single log.

The work he is best known for as a member of Kyushu-ha was his performance at the Grand Meeting of Heroes. While the other participants in the Grand Meeting performed their works one at a time while the other participants looked on, Miyazaki chose to work on his own project through most of the night by himself. Armed with a shovel, he dug holes along the shore in the strand between the low and high tide marks. He began as the tide went out at 7:00 in the evening. When he reached the water table in one hole, he began the next one, digging to a depth that was about the height of a grown person. He managed to dig six or seven rectangular holes before the tide came in around midnight, filling them in. By the time the tide had receded again, there was no trace of the holes or the piles of sand he had created.[51] Based on his subsequent work, this may be less a demonstration of futility than an exploration of rhythm and cycle: the cycle of the tide, of the digging hand, of moving from one hole to the next. Each of these cycles leaves its marks as it passes, and whether or not we attend to the mark of the shovel that is obliterated by the shovel's next strike or the holes the tide washes away or the tide that washes its own traces away is a matter of our own position and interest. One can always find passings to mark and arrivals to anticipate. In this case, Miyazaki's work of nested rhythms gave itself over to the arrival of the tide and the daybreak, a human scale that characterizes much of his work.

Miyazaki is known best for his wood sculptures, which he started making in the mid-1960s, a few years after the Grand Meeting. His earliest work is a series of egg shapes, many of which are carved with runes (fig. 13.7). They are made from single pieces of wood and are sanded soft. The elliptical shape and size is such that if a person hugs one of them it fits perfectly in the curve of the body's embrace. There are a few dozen pieces in this series, which Miyazaki produced slowly over years, using hammers, chisels, and sandpaper. When a few of them are arranged together they take on a human

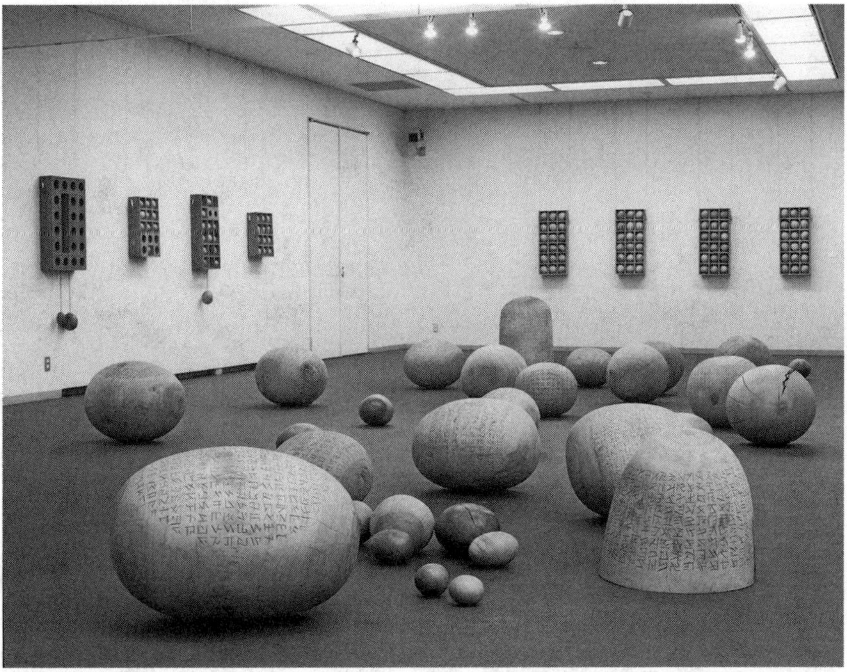

FIGURE 13.7 Miyazaki Junnosuke, *Kinotama ni yoru teiji shiriizu* (*Presentation by Wooden Balls Series*), 1966–1967. Wood. Photographed as exhibited at the Miyazaki Junnosuke Exhibition, Fukuoka Prefectural Museum of Art, 1998. Courtesy of Miyazaki Kōji / Fukuoka Prefectural Museum of Art.

presence, seeming to converse very quietly or very slowly. The time taken to produce them seems appropriate to their shape: such eggs would mature slowly over months. The unhurried, determined chiseling and sanding is the exact inverse of that growth, the two seeming to equal each other out or call each other into being.

The number and grouping of objects sometimes suggests small villages. His *Ware wa denpu* (*I Am a Farmer*) could be a village if we take the wooden shapes to be the farmers (fig. 13.8). They could also be fruits laid out to dry. We might be the farmers—the elliptical shapes so perfectly suggest our hands picking them up. Other works also invite audience manipulation. Starting in the 1970s, Miyazaki began to make simple, oversized vehicles. Wheelbarrows first, then pulleys and levers, all evoking simple machinery used in premodern farming but gradually becoming more playful. One is a wheeled platform with two oars to row it. Another is a seesaw. The retrospective exhibition at the Fukuoka Prefectural Museum of Art in 1998 included an area where children could play with some of his smaller sculptures. These

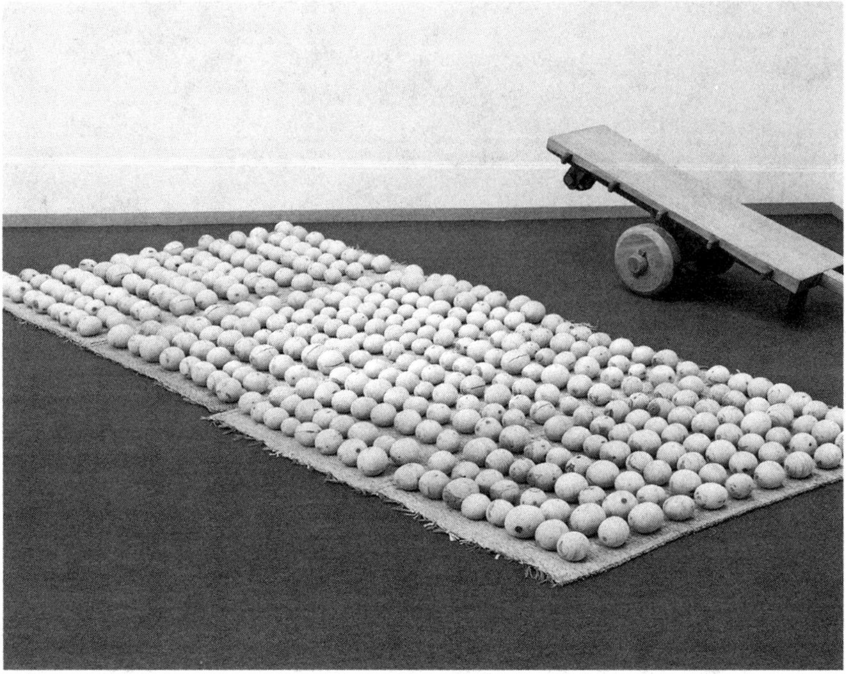

FIGURE 13.8 Miyazaki Junnosuke, *Ware wa denpu* (*I Am a Farmer*), 1979–1982. Wood. Fukuoka Prefectural Museum of Art. Photographed as exhibited at Miyazaki Junnosuke Exhibition, Fukuoka Prefectural Museum of Art, 1998. Courtesy of Miyazaki Kōji / Fukuoka Prefectural Museum of Art.

movable sculptures are also realized around a cycle, turning or rocking according to a principle of dynamic balance. But the cycle is never closed: the wheel moves as it turns and the seesaw comes back down to a world that is slightly altered. Each movement moves only a small distance, but the meaning of the mechanism as a whole gathers in the accumulation of small efforts.

All work must return to earth eventually however. One of Miyazaki's seesaws was installed outside in a garden, under a tree where children and adults could use it. In a photograph from 1998 we can see that it was already quite weathered. It might not be there anymore. But one wonders if, in all of his digging of holes and sculpting of eggs, Miyazaki might not have dug a hole somewhere in this or another garden and buried one of his large, engraved eggs without telling anyone. If he had, it would still be there, slowly decaying, never to be found.

Chapter 14

A Cruel Story of Anti-Art

The term "contemporary art" (*gendai bijutsu*) had been used since before the war, but in the late 1950s and 1960s it began to take on a more specific meaning. It came to denote a new kind of art and a new cultural formation of art that was becoming increasingly well-defined over the same period. The work of art critic Miyakawa Atsushi, which appeared near the end of the process, has had a large role in ensuring that "contemporary art" would survive as the term for the formation.[1] Contemporary art does not (and did not) denote all recently produced art, but refers to "a field of practice unto itself, evolved and institutionalized."[2] How did contemporary art develop, what was it, and why is it important? Art historians Reiko Tomii and Mitsuda Yuri have both pointed to the importance of internationalization as a spur which drove the development of the new institutional formation. Mitsuda traces the seeds of the formation back to the early 1950s.[3] When U.S. occupation ended in 1952, Japan found itself back on the international art stage after more than a decade of war and occupation. Japanese artists began to be invited to the major biennials (Venice, Sao Paolo) and to the Salon du Mai in Paris. Three museums devoted to modern art also opened in Japan in 1951 and 1952, where there had been none before (the Kamakura Prefectural Museum of Modern Art, the Bridgestone Museum, and the National Museum of Modern Art). The question of what should be put in these museums and international exhibitions suddenly became urgent. What was modern art supposed to be? How could it be appraised and selected, how could value be assessed? In 1950, the only institutions that assigned cultural value to modern art were the large exhibition societies, but as discussed in chapter 12, those societies were built around a process of slowly expanding pluralism quite different from the ruthless innovation that features in accounts of American and European modern art.

When Imaizumi Atsuo, the first director of the National Museum of Modern Art, toured the major international exhibitions in 1952, he quickly discovered that the artwork coming from the Japanese art societies was not relevant on an international stage. He came back feeling defeated, and through a series of self-flagellating articles and lectures about the state of modern Japanese art, he caused what is known as the "Imaizumi whirlwind," the first of many such whirlwinds and shocks that would hit the Japanese art world over the coming years.[4] The origins of the formation that would come to be called contemporary art was born out of this need to make Japanese art internationally competitive, to find a way to assign and foster an internationally public value in modern art, and Tomii's work shows that the idea of international contemporaneity (*kokusaiteki dōjisei*) continued to play a decisive role in discussions of contemporary art throughout the 1960s.[5]

Following Mitsuda's work, I will introduce the role of art criticism and journalism in building the field of contemporary art. Starting from the early 1950s, both art journalism and popular journalism played an increasingly prominent role in establishing trends and identifying artists, in essence carrying out a powerful curatorial function. Curation in the print media often went hand in hand with exhibition curation, as prominent critics began to assemble young artists into thematically organized shows in the early 1960s. Though journalism is only one piece of the puzzle, it was vital in establishing value publicly. The opening stages of this new form of art criticism appeared in the pages of the journal *Bijutsu hihyō*, which ran from 1952 to 1957. Over this short period, the journal fundamentally transformed art criticism in Japan by making art part of a larger intellectual discourse that included literature and poetry, philosophy, history, and contemporary society and politics. Articles took up both Japanese and western modern artists: the western artists were mostly twentieth century, while the Japanese artists had mostly become active post-1945. Criticism covered film and theater, photography, design, architecture, music, and *manga*, and introduced these alongside the ideas of Andre Breton, Paul Eluard, Tristan Tzara, Herbert Read, Jean Paul Sartre, Maurice Merleau-Ponty, Hanada Kiyoteru, Okamoto Tarō, Takiguchi Shūzō, Noma Hiroshi, Takei Teruo, and more. Discussions were informed by the social and cultural politics of the day, including the place of leftist art, the role of the masses, and the impact of mass culture. It was fundamentally a debating magazine, with debates between critics stretching across multiple issues and an active letters section at the beginning of every issue. *Bijutsu hihyō* was the birthplace of a public, intellectually sophisticated criticism that played an important part in establishing the field of value for contemporary art. In the process, it launched the careers of the four critics whose work defined art criticism through the mid-1970s: Hariu Ichirō, Nakahara Yūsuke, Segi Shin'ichi, and Tōno Yoshiaki.[6]

Although *Bijutsu hihyō* stopped publishing in February 1957, the work of this group of critics continued to grow in importance thereafter. Nothing since ever rivaled its ability to focus critical debate. With its closure, art criticism lost an important platform that constituted a forum rather than a tapestry of competing voices. After *Bijutsu hihyō*, the big four critics, who were joined a few years later by Miyakawa Atsushi, pursued their careers in media that included mass circulation newspapers (especially the *Yomiuri*), other art journals (especially *Mizue* and *Bijutsu techō*), and a variety of semi-academic literature, art, and culture publications. Though they still had to argue their positions, this institutional arrangement made those positions as much a development of individual voice and career as a debate. As this shift was taking place, Japan's media environment—particularly in the realm of modern art—was becoming ever more closely tied to trends that developed across the capitalist world nearly simultaneously.

The paradigmatic example that brings internationalization and nascent careerism together is the introduction of Informel to Japan in 1956 and 1957. Informel was a movement brought together by the enterprising critic Michel Tapié in the early 1950s. Its introduction into Japan was engineered by Tapié, artist Imai Toshimitsu who was living in France, Gutai's leader Yoshihara Jirō, renowned *ikebana* master and avant-garde impresario Teshigahara Sōfu, and the young critic Hariu Ichirō. The impact of Informel on the Japanese art world can be understood by realizing that it was not simply a collection of paintings, but a multi-platform media campaign that included panel discussions and round tables, lectures, tours by the artists, demonstrations of art-making, collaborations with Japanese artists, and timely introductions of Tapié's own writing in Japanese. One of the most important elements of the campaign was back-to-back special issues of the premier art journal *Mizue,* timed to coincide with the Sekai Konnichi no Bijutsu (Art of the World Today) exhibition. The two *Mizue* issues introduced Informel artworks in photographs and essays, along with Tapié's theory of *un art autre*.[7] What came to Japan in 1956 and 1957 was a fully articulated cultural unit.

An important part of the story, however, is that just as Tapié and the Informel artists were touring Japan in 1957, the young critic Segi Shin'ichi was touring France. During the tour, he discovered that Tapié's stock in France was considerably lower than the presentation he was receiving in Japan. Jean Fautrier, one of the most important Informel artists, even referred to Tapié's promotional activity as a circus.[8] This scoop proved extremely valuable to Segi. When he returned to Japan he reported his findings in a series of articles on "The Scandal Surrounding Informel," which created a cloud of suspicion over the legitimacy of Informel and undermined the status of Japan's art establishment by raising the possibility it had let itself be talked into buying into this art movement that was being disowned in its home country. This is the first moment where we can see that increased mobility meant that no single cultural authority or conduit controlled the definition of the "contemporary." Though a network of elite critics and artists had engineered Informel's introduction to Japan, Segi's individual intervention put it all into question. While Informel was undeniably appealing and enabling to many Japanese artists, the fact that it also became a potent symbol of Japan's lack of autonomy in the international art world has meant that to this day many artists are reluctant to admit they were ever influenced by it. Segi's "Informel scandal" showed that critics (and artists) could compete to introduce new trends, leveraging valuable but increasingly short-lived differentials in information.

Although Informel undoubtedly affected Kyushu-ha, the trend that involved them most directly was Anti-Art (*hangeijutsu*).[9] Anti-Art appeared as an artistic phenomenon around 1958.[10] The first use of the term "*hangeijutsu*" was in the title of a series of three performances by Kudō Tetsumi in 1957–1958.[11] The two groups most associated with Anti-Art were Kyushu-ha and Neo Dada, while the most prominent individual artists include Kikuhata Mokuma, Ochi Osamu, Arakawa Shūsaku, Yoshimura Masanobu, Shinohara Ushio, Akasegawa Genpei, and Kudō Tetsumi.[12] These artists began to submit assemblages (both hung and free-standing) to the Yomiuri Independent in 1958, and with each passing year the works got larger, more daring, and more confrontational. The common characteristics of Anti-Art that critics picked out in the late 1950s were expressiveness, interest in material, youthfulness, iconoclasm, and lack of finish. The most common association was with energy. Not only were the assemblages exploding with all kinds of junk, but the artists themselves relished rambunctious public performances. They often took pride in how fast they could lash their works together and were indifferent about what happened to them after exhibition. Almost none of the larger assemblages survive.[13]

Although Kudō had used the term "anti-art" in the title of his performances in 1957–1958, the term did not catch on immediately: in 1959 critics were discussing the phenomenon in familiar generational terms such as "new talent" (*shinjin*), and "second generation" (*dainisedai*). Hariu compared their work to Dada in an article in early 1959. But it was Tōno Yoshiaki's use of the phrase "anti-art" in early 1960 that ended up making it catch on as a label for the movement. The term appeared on the front page of the *Yomiuri shinbun* in the caption of a photo that accompanied Tōno's short review of that year's Yomiuri Independent.[14] The photo was of Kudō Tetsumi's sculpture, *Hanshokusei rensa hannō B* (*Propagating Chain Reaction B*). The caption read "Junk Anti-Art" (*garakuta no hangeijutsu*). "Anti-art" is a catchy phrase, both intuitive and flexible. But there are other reasons why Tōno's usage might have stuck while others' didn't. Tōno had gone on a tour of Europe and the United States in 1959 that had brought him into contact with the *nouveau réaliste* artists in France and the proto-pop art of Robert Rauschenberg and Jasper Johns in New York. The commonality in artistic approach must have struck Tōno immediately. Indeed, even from the standpoint of the present, it is amazing how three such similar art movements developed contemporaneously with no contact among them. They would soon come into contact, however, partially through Tōno's work of introducing the European and American trends to Japan. One of his earliest articles appeared in the *Yomiuri*, where he referred to the work of Rauschenberg and Johns, as "apathetic anti-art [*mukanshin no hangeijutsu*]."[15] Although Tōno repeatedly claimed in subsequent years that he had never intended "anti-art" to be more than a casual label, it is understandable why his usage of the term gained currency. He was the critic who, through his articles on Euro-American assemblage art in 1959, was emerging as the leading interpreter of the phenomenon.

As Tōno introduced the American scene to Japan over the subsequent year, however, the coolness and dryness of American proto-pop began to influence the Japanese discourse and practice of Anti-Art: the energy and expressiveness of Anti-Art's early years began to be replaced. One of Tōno's most important pieces appeared in *Mizue* in March 1960, the same month the Yomiuri Independent was being held and the same month his caption "Junk Anti-Art" appeared on the front page. The article was titled "Yangā zenerēshon no bōken" (Adventures of the younger generation) and introduced New York proto-pop and French *nouveau réalisme* at length, including photos of the art and the artists and a substantial critical piece by Tōno. What he highlighted was the emotional distance of their work: it was "cool," had a "dry anti-lyricism," "a completely deadpan insanity," a "dry spirit of adventure," it rejected "sticky self-expression."[16] "Dry" and "wet" were common affective markers used by cultural critics in Japan at this time. "Wet" connoted sentimentalism, emotion, and irrationality and was to some extent a national and generational marker: Japanese people, especially older Japanese people, were wet. "Dry," on the other hand, evoked emotional distance, calculation, and cool-headedness and had a certain cosmopolitan air. It was also attached to the *après-guerres* generation, particularly the *taiyōzoku* (sun tribe), because of their perceived immunity to sentimentalism. Thus, in addition to introducing the artworks and their relationship to their own cultural backgrounds, Tōno located them on a Japanese cultural-affective field.

Tōnō's writing on Duchamp in 1961 and 1962 also shifted the reception and development of Japanese assemblage art along increasingly cerebral paths. Whereas energy and expressiveness had been the markers of Anti-Art until about 1960, Anti-Art cooled after this point. A clear example of Tono's and Duchamp's influence, which Mitsuda points to, is Shinohara Ushio's work, *Shikō suru Maruseru Dyushan* (*Marcel Duchamp Thinking*), in which the artist used fragments of Tōno's articles on Duchamp to form part of his collage. This was a significant shift from the Neo Dada performances of 1960. Many Neo Dada artists, including Shinohara, Arakawa Shūsaku, and Akasegawa Genpei, moved into conceptual, generally non-expressive work. Arakawa and Akasegawa had always worked in this mode, but as the critical landscape shifted, it was this work that became more prominent.

Anti-Art is therefore a term that covers two different bodies of work: expressive, accumulative, uncanny junk assemblage that is most pronounced in the early part of its history, and emotionally cooler, more conceptual work that became more prominent after 1960 through the mediation of contemporary currents in the United States and Europe. The "John Cage shock" of 1962, mentioned in chapter 11, was part of this shift. Happenings, as Yoshida Yoshie used the term in his article about the Grand Meeting of Heroes, denoted non-dramatic, non-cathartic, highly disciplined and concentrated continuations of everyday activity. Happenings renounced the avant-garde pretense of leading historical development, replacing its heroism with irony. Location certainly matters: contemporeneity is never actually a fact, and the distance between Kyushu and Tokyo was enough that the John Cage shock had not reached Kyushu-ha by the time they staged the Grand Meeting. But even if it had, I would argue that Kyushu-ha would have had difficulty incorporating this new aesthetic and political ethic.

Although Kyushu-ha and Neo Dada are accepted as two representative examples of Anti-Art, and although, interestingly, many Neo Dada members also hail from northern Kyushu, the two groups were quite different. Neo

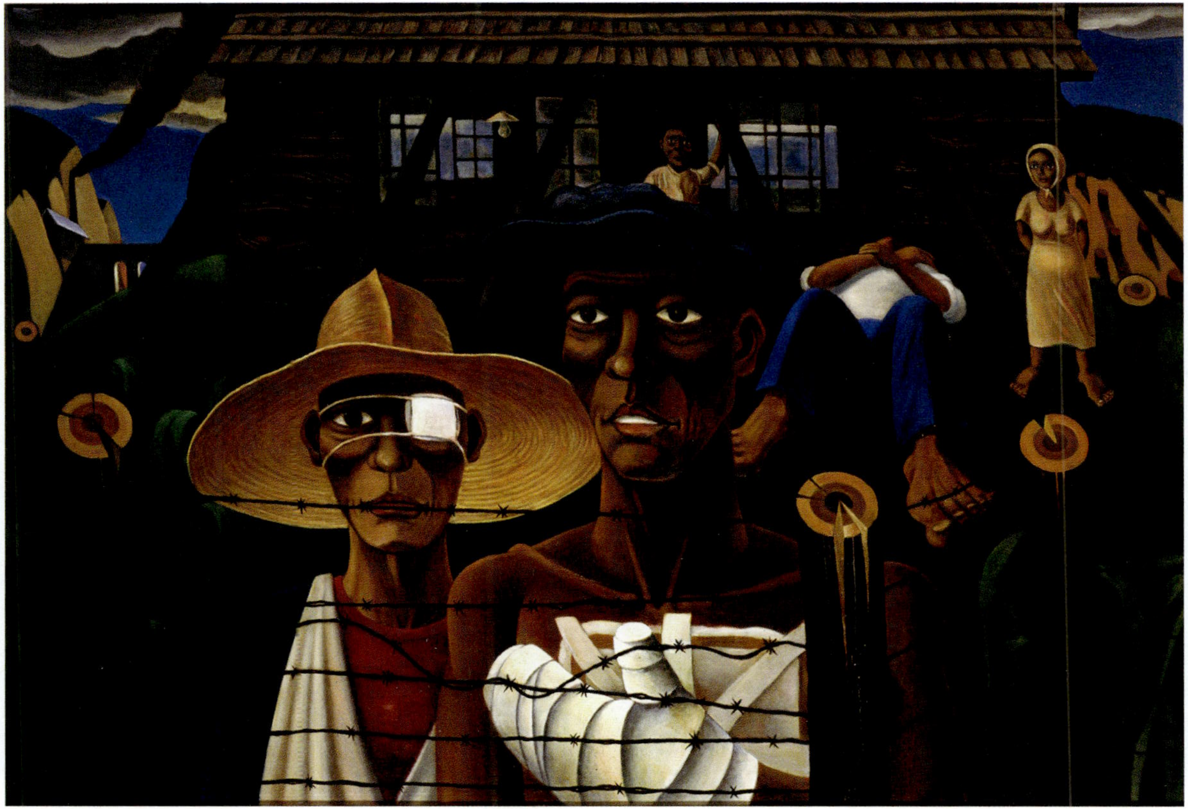

9. Katsuragawa Hiroshi, *Ogōchi mura* (*Ogōchi Village*), 1952. Oil on canvas. 97 cm x 145.5 cm.
Courtesy of Katsuragawa Jun / Katsuragawa Akane / Itabashi Art Museum.

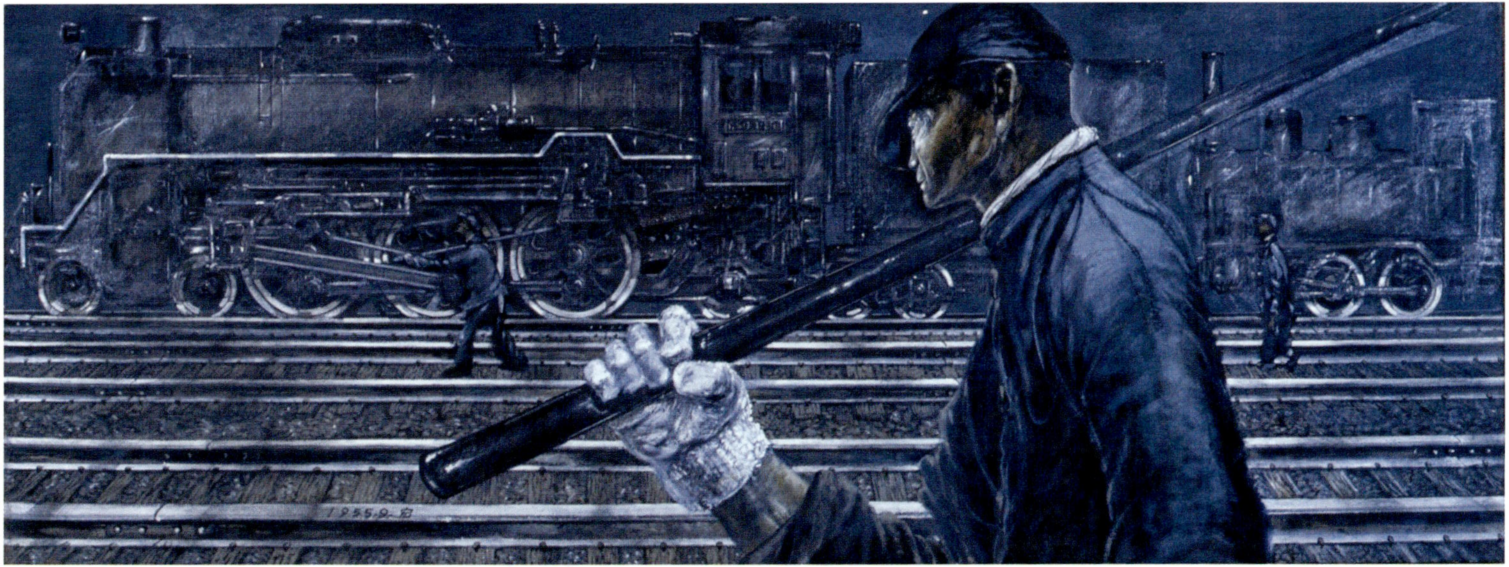

10. Nakamura Hiroshi, *Kokutetsu Shinagawa* (*JNR Shinagawa*), 1955. Oil on canvas. 37.5 cm x 101.5 cm.
Courtesy of Nakamura Hiroshi / Hamamatsu Municipal Museum of Art.

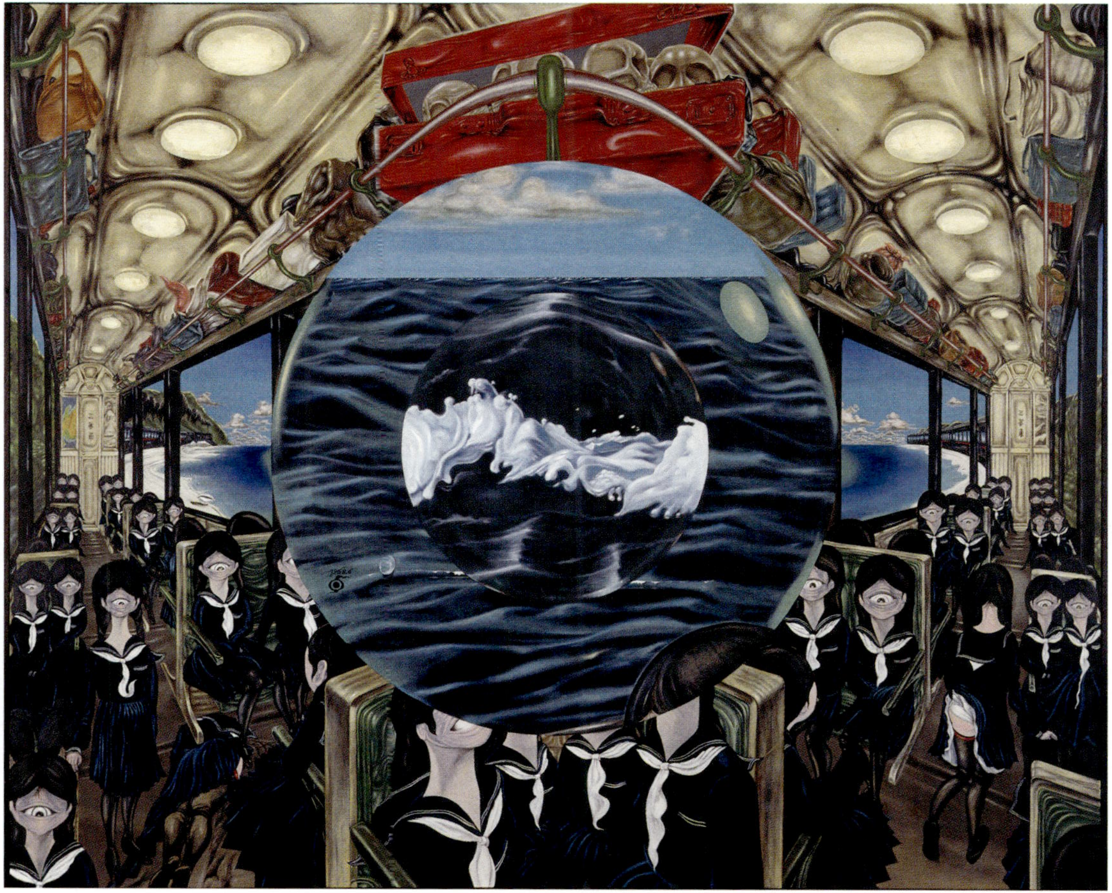

11. Nakamura Hiroshi, *Enkan ressha A—bōenkyō ressha* (*Circular Train A: Telescope Train*), 1968. Oil on canvas. 185 cm x 240 cm. Courtesy of Nakamura Hiroshi / Museum of Contemporary Art, Tokyo.

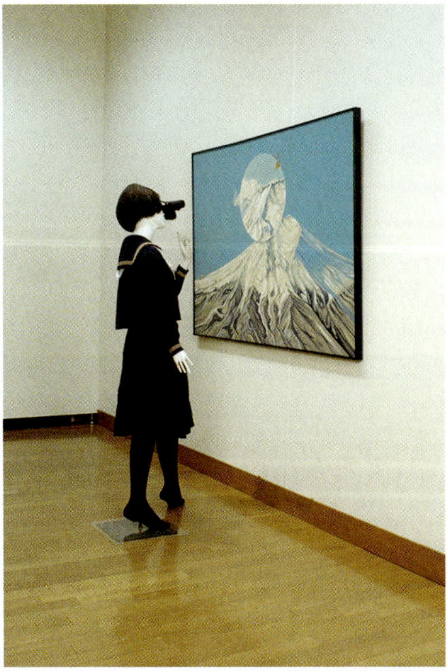

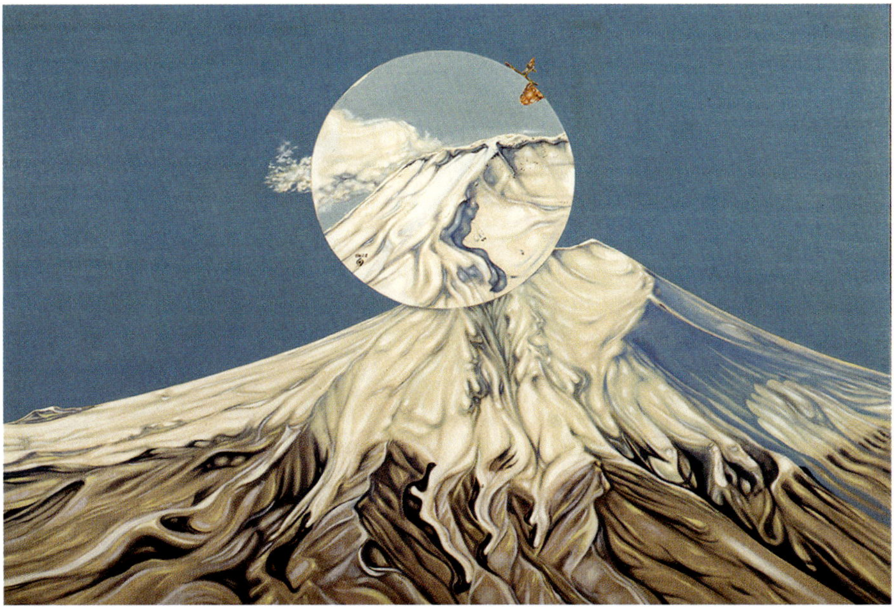

12. Top image: Nakamura Hiroshi, *Jogakusei ni kan suru geijutsu to kokka no shomondai* (*Problems of Art and Nation as They Relate to Schoolgirls*), 1967. Oil on canvas, mixed media. Installation at the Urawa Art Museum. Photograph by Uchida Yoshitaka. Courtesy of Nakamura Hiroshi / Takamatsu Art Museum. Bottom image: detail.

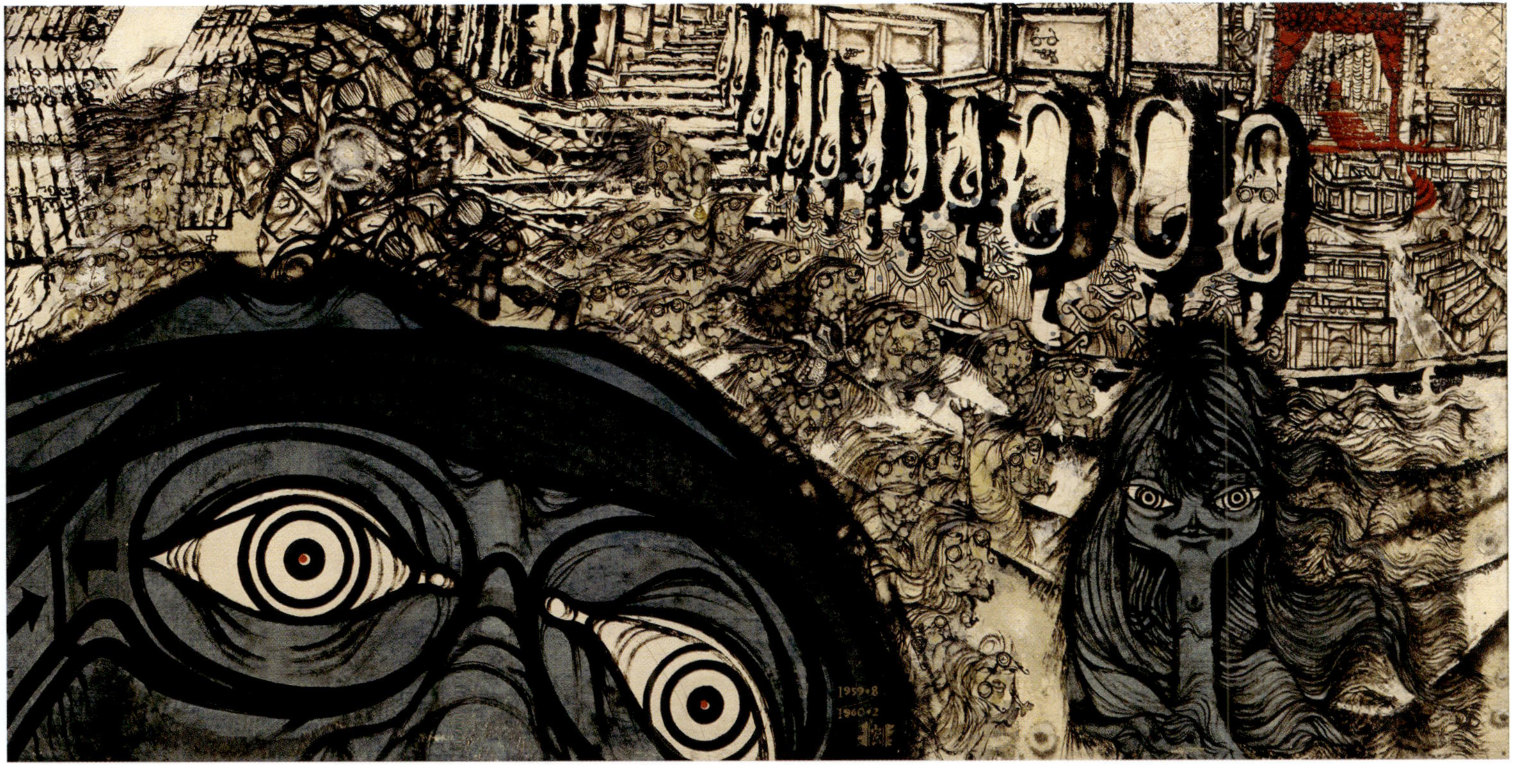

13. Nakamura Hiroshi, *Kaidan nite* (*On the Steps*), 1959/1960. Oil on plywood. 90.5 cm x 181.5 cm.
Courtesy of Nakamura Hiroshi / The Miyagi Museum of Art.

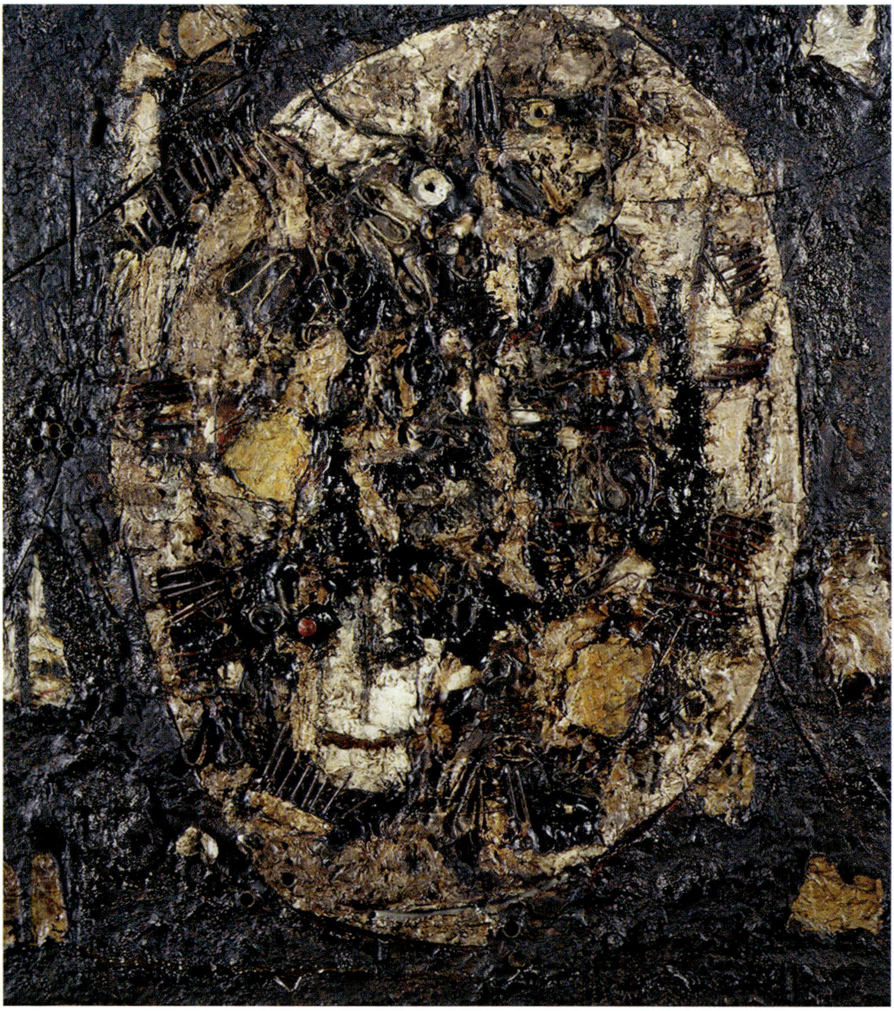

14. Sakurai Takami, *Rinchi* (*Lynching*), 1958. Asphalt, nails, and other scrap on metal mesh. 91.5 cm x 80.5 cm. Courtesy of the Fukuoka Art Museum.

15. Yamauchi Jūtarō, *Sakuhin 5* (*Work 5*), 1958. Asphalt, pigment, and string on board. 117 cm x 91 cm. Courtesy of Oshajima Momoko / Fukuoka Art Museum.

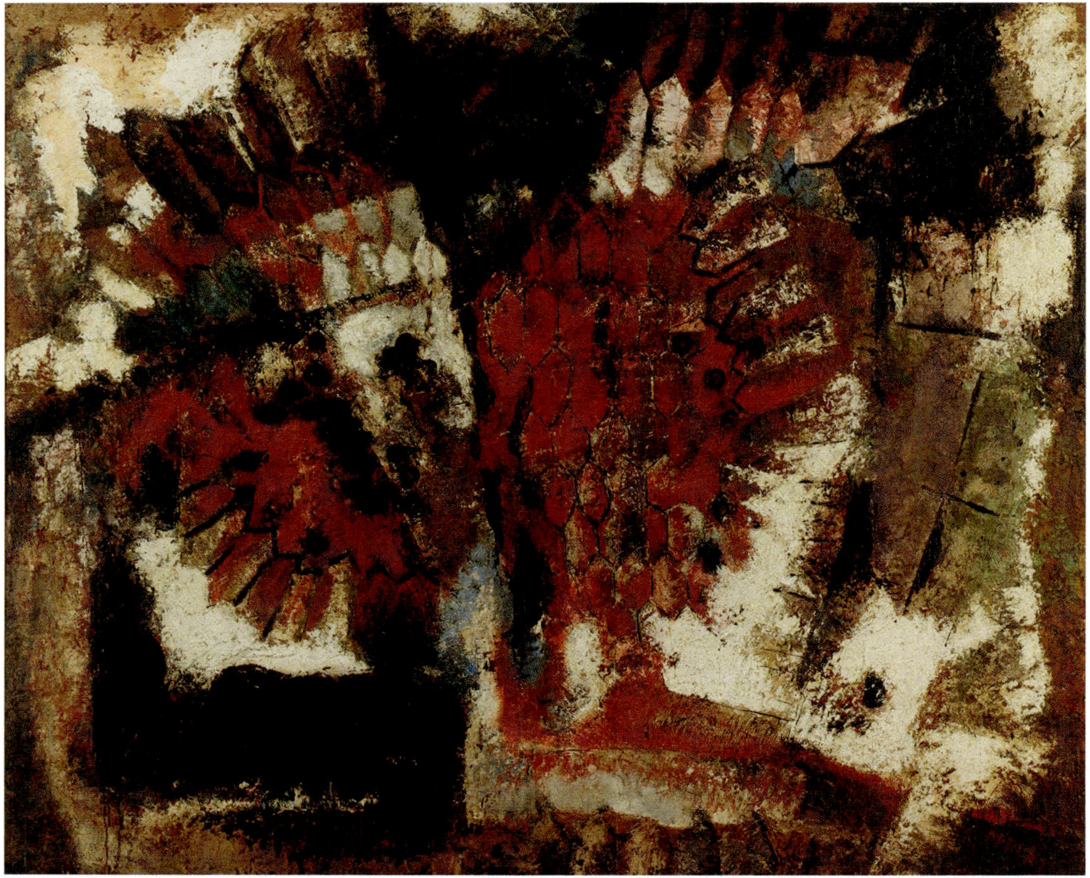

16. Tabe Mitsuko, *Gyozoku no ikari* (*Anger of the Fish*), 1958–1959. Oil, asphalt, and bamboo on board. 128 cm x 161 cm. Courtesy of Tabe Mitsuko / Fukuoka Art Museum.

Dada was younger, its members born mostly after 1935. In contrast, Sakurai was born in 1928, Tabe in 1933, and Matano in 1914, giving them a different perspective on war and defeat as well as the experience of coming of age artistically within the more self-sufficient and localized culture of the early postwar. Almost all of Neo Dada's members came to Tokyo to attend one or another of the three most prestigious art schools in Japan and dropped out before graduating. They did not have ties to career-track jobs and enjoyed the patronage of fellow member Yoshimura Masanobu, who provided them with a private atelier and meeting space in Shinjuku.[17]

These differences are more than simply logistical: for people painstakingly carving out their own space and time for their art, it is understandable that the whole project becomes a shade more serious. Though members of Kyushu-ha did attempt to adopt Happenings, the result was, as Yoshida said of Ōyama's performance at the Grand Meeting, "terribly sentimental." What might be a more important difference between the two groups, however, is a result of their location and their relation to the local cultural field that that entailed. Neo Dada was a collection of artists living in Tokyo, some of whom had met at art university, others through the Yomiuri Independent. Once formed, the group proper stayed together for less than a year. But their breakup did not mean the artists split away from each other: they went on to form a patchwork of other short-lived groups in a sort of mixing and matching under different banners. Broadly speaking, these were collectivities of artists working in similar ways on similar issues who came together for as long as their collaboration remained productive. Keeping the group together was not the main goal. This kind of organizational existence was possible because of the quantity of talent and the rapidity of exposure that a new group could count on in Tokyo. No particular group bore the burden of having to serve as the first and final route to visibility because the cultural environment of critics and exhibitions, along with the momentum built by the artists themselves, did so much of that institutional work.

Fukuoka was different. It did not have a wide pool of artists working in the style of Anti-Art. Kyushu-ha was unavoidably uneven, and that unevenness created two problems. First, it was a liability in a contemporary art scene that was structured around increasingly focused trends. The group's 1961 Ginza Gallery show was criticized because the group seemed to have "upended a box of toys and gone wild with them."[18] But the critic, Ebara Jun, went on to compliment the work of individual artists: Tabe Mitsuko, Taniguchi Toshio, and Ochi Osamu. The critique could be interpreted, then, as a critique of the show's curation: it did not have a coherent theme or tone. But there was little Kyushu-ha could do about this problem. Although Kikuhata proposed a solution in the form of the promoter system, it is unlikely to have worked for long. Artists could not leave the group lightly because there was no wider field to support them in Fukuoka. If Kikuhata's promoter deemed a particular member not relevant to the show at hand, excluding that member could have long-lasting repercussions because there were no other options for that artist. This brought a pressure to bear on Kyushu-ha that Tokyo-based groups did not face: it had to serve as the only channel for success in the system of contemporary art. That was a liability in a system of value that was fast-changing, relatively homogeneous at any one moment, and beyond their control to define.

Although contemporary art and criticism opened up new possibilities for some, it was an institutional formation that could be as restrictive, arbitrary, and closed as any other. Though the playfulness, vigor, and talent of the artists who flourished within this institutional form understandably lead it to be associated with freedom, iconoclasm, independence and an anti-institutional stance, we must not confuse this general atmosphere of the artwork with the realities of how the field operated. Kyushu-ha as a group of individuals who failed to navigate the developing institutions of contemporary art is a corrective to the idea that contemporary art had suddenly freed itself from cultural hierarchies of taste built on exclusion. It is also worth considering that Kyushu-ha's gauche directness can be seen as a corollary to the movement of building the ground of their art's visibility themselves. Maybe it was precisely because of their need to balance the demands of family, work, and art and their need to establish their own spaces for visibility that their claims about what they could do through their art were correspondingly grand.

Kuroda Raiji has proposed another way of thinking about Anti-Art, particularly Neo Dada: that is, in their relationship to the burgeoning popular media culture of the late 1950s. He argues that it is precisely through photographs (not recreations of lost works) that we can come into contact with the "true" Neo Dada, because "Neo Dada was historicized when photographed, and it was socialized when reported in the mass media." The group, especially its media star Shinohara Ushio, employed shock, violence, and instantaneity because "these elements . . . satisfied the demand of the quick moving and newfangled media—i.e., television and weekly magazines—which endeavored to instantaneously transmit the news of sensational and scandalous events to an eager and impatient audience." Neo Dada thrived on the mass media. In addition to their embrace of the media, the group embraced materialism and American capitalism more broadly. "When Yoshino Tatsumi called his group . . . an 'occupation culture,' this youthful member meant no criticism of the US as an imperialist or political oppressor; rather, typical of his generation, he openly acknowledged America as the origin of mass production and mass consumption, music, fashion, and new art."[19] Emblematic of this is Shinohara Ushio's early appearance in the weekly magazine *Shūkan Sankei* as the "Rockabilly Artist."

Both rockabilly and weekly magazines are tightly tied up with the mass-mediated youth and image culture of the late 1950s. Ann Sherif has analyzed one aspect of this *après-guerre* mass culture, the phenomenon of the *taiyōzoku*, or sun tribe. Many characteristics of that phenomenon can be seen in the work of Neo Dada: the cult of speed and energy, a rough-and-tumble masculinity, an aesthetics of plenty, and a cavalier humor and cheerfulness. Even boxing seems to connect the two. The protagonist of *Taiyō no kisetsu* (*Season of the Sun*), the work that sparked off the *taiyōzoku* fad, is an aspiring boxer, and although Shinohara's *Boxing Painting* may or may not be inspired by *Season of the Sun*, it provides a similar demonstration of strength, plenty, and casual mastery.

Kyushu-ha did not have the same access to the Tokyo-based mass media that Neo Dada did, and perhaps it did not have the same panache to manipulate it. But more important, most of Kyushu-ha's oeuvre was earnest: it was not given to celebration and did not embrace American culture. One of the first critics to try his hand at naming what became Anti-Art was Kawakita Michiaki, in 1958.[20] He used the term rockabilly, describing the artists as the "rockabilly faction" (*rokabirii-ha*). Kawakita's rockabilly faction put Kyushu-ha and other artists at the 1958 Yomiuri Independent together in the same category with the "dancing cult" (*odoru shūkyō*) of youth and rock and roll. His understanding of rockabilly, however, was more redemptive than Sherif's. Opposed to the rockabilly faction, for Kawakita, was the predictive intellectual faction (*yosokuteki chisei-ha*), which represented administered society—a "dry" place where reality is always already covered by a thin membrane of anticipatory rationalism, taking every move into account in advance. Kawakita saw the "cathartic energy" of the rockabilly faction as an understandable reaction to the spread of administration in the everyday world. Their energy insisted on something vital that could not be contained or predicted. Although this romantic mode of Anti-Art would not survive, it might be the view that got closest to Kyushu-ha.

Conclusion

Kyushu-ha was a circle. Almost without exception its members were untrained, though they all had a clear desire to create and express themselves artistically. Their access to the local arbiters of cultural value (the open-call societies) was unreliable, and at first Kyushu-ha was a forum for the display and discussion of members' work. Its members could make *anything* and know that within their circle they would find engaged (often extremely critical) interlocutors and a chance to exhibit their work, either in the Kyushu Independent or Yomiuri Independent. In an environment where there were so few opportunities to share and display work, this was no minor thing. Kyushu-ha's incredible activity from 1957 to 1960, achieved when almost all its members were full-time wage earners, is testament to the creative liberation and stimulation this forum generated. Although a good number of Kyushu-ha's members were aiming for larger forums, such as success in the art worlds of Tokyo or Fukuoka, surely part of the bravado that colored their performances in Tokyo, their fun in playing the edgy hicks storming the capital, came from a pride at being a group that had created its own terms of value and that was in fact self-reliant as they brought their vision to a public.

The problem for Kyushu-ha however, was that its self-reliance was not enough for most of its members. Terada Ken'ichirō, who was a rising star in the Nika Kai, left Kyushu-ha when he was forced to choose between the two. Kikuhata left when it became clear Kyushu-ha wasn't going to be coherent or selective enough to serve his needs. The people who formed Gurūpu Nishi Nihon got tired of Kyushu-ha's (particularly Sakurai's) populism and preferred to concentrate on art production as such. Kyushu-ha was not exceptional in this respect: this book has not been about the successful union of artists with the mass of amateur producers in circles. It has been more about a relationship that is always troubled and unstable. Artistic labor is different from other kinds of productive labor, and although circles testify to how widely accessible artistic labor can be and how broadly embraced it was in early postwar Japan, they do not dissolve a gap between people who do artistic labor professionally and those who do not. One thing that is so interesting about the case of Kyushu-ha is that we can see this tension playing out as a problem that emerged from within a single group rather than in a relationship between different groups (such as artists and workers or filmmakers and those they film).

Kyushu-ha's case also poses a question about the formation of contemporary art in postwar Japan and about some of the assumptions of contemporary art more generally. That question concerns the status of everyday life. It is orthodox to think of the avant-garde project as aiming to meld art and everyday life and of the neo-avant-gardes as disrupting everyday life. But as shown, the field of contemporary art in Japan grew out of professionalization. A relatively small group of critics established trends and problematics within a wide field of artistic production. While it was artists' work that drove this, artists had to adjust their production regularly so their work would remain valuable and, by extension, visible. Certain trends through the 1960s clearly addressed issues of daily life, such as the material homogenization of consumer culture. But even as artists explored these issues in provocative ways, their explorations are ultimately thematic. This is equally true of Kyushu-ha's work. What is different about Kyushu-ha is that the group itself was, from the beginning, a place where art was deprofessionalized and decentralized. It was precisely for these reasons that it failed. The conclusion then, is that while the themes and content of many works of contemporary art in the long 1960s address daily life repeatedly, such thematic interest in the topic should not lead us to conclude that contemporary art played any part in relocating artistic production within the production of daily life or in expanding artistic authorship to the uninitiated. This was the work of other, predictably less well-known groups. Kyushu-ha, for its part, is somewhere in between.

Epilogue

Hope in the Past and the Future

Yes, we can change the world because we have many times before. You row forward by looking back, and telling this history is part of helping people navigate toward the future. . . . The past is set in daylight, and it can become a torch we can carry into the night that is the future.

Rebecca Solnit

The main goals of this book have been to reframe the history of the period 1945–1960 in Japan and to demonstrate a method of examining the relationship between art and politics that approaches art as a mode of intervention, but insists artistic intervention move beyond the idea that the artwork or artist unilaterally authors political significance, to trace how creations and expressive acts may (or may not) actually engage the terms of shared meaning and value. By way of summary, let us look at the second of these first.

Art was central to all of the movements I have examined and was taken to be central to their political interventions. Yet equally, their aesthetic and political engagements entailed forms of labor that operated in milieus and media that they at the time did not call art: passing out leaflets, attending study meetings, organizing classes, teaching, going to rallies, transporting artworks, hand-printing, mailing things, negotiating, researching unexpected subjects, setting up and tearing down exhibitions, interviewing, and so on. Though these activities have become approachable as art in recent decades it is often in the mode of "singular examples," to use Tyrus Miller's characterization of the interventions of the neo-avant-gardes: "special, 'singular' attempts to provide examples of alternative ways to think, act, feel, and be [by means of experimental presentations] that *anticipate* the context or conventions that would clarify what they intend to persuade us to be or do."[1] For the groups in this study, however, the activities that might be re-imagined as a singular example in the work of a neo-avant-garde artist would never have been considered meaningful as singularities. Mailing a self-printed publication, for instance, was not exemplary as a single act. To the contrary, it was only in repetition and extension that such activities could become additionally significant. Miller's theory hinges on the idea that the singular examples "*anticipate* the context or conventions" that might eventually redeem them by making them less singular, more broadly shared, more conventional. In other words, the singular act gains exemplary significance only when we assume that the desired context is absent in the present. In early postwar Japan, however, an exemplary context was not beyond the horizon. It was within reach, in the multiple engagements that collectively form what I have called the democratic culture of the time: characterized by movements to spread practices of authorship, to build collaboration and audience across lines of class and geography, and to increase access to the means of production and publicity. Democratic culture was also characterized by egalitarianism at the level of the small group, fluidity in organization among them, and finally, by an open disposition toward the breadth of the unknown and the scale of possibilities, both good and bad, in things yet to come. This openness, both to the future and to others, was the necessary condition of the ad hoc, experimental conjunctions of art and social movements. It is what made people's evolving engagement with each other possible, as "producers, possessed of power and vision, in an unfinished world."[2]

This situation means, however, that there is no necessary formal or logical continuity between artworks and social engagements. Although both artworks and social engagements were inflected by an experimental search for new ways of seeing and doing, there was not a prescriptive unity to their execution. That means that our method of understanding interventionism in the early postwar cannot rely on asserting such unities, by reducing art to a political tool or politics to an artwork or performance. One might then assume that they were not connected. But all the evidence in the foregoing pages runs counter to that. They *were* connected, in the form of ongoing activity. They were simultaneously necessary: they could not but be related. But the nature of that relation was not subject to a singular will to enclose, complete, or to make rigorously coherent. It is in that sense that art and social movements were in a free relation, but a freedom that allowed neither to be dropped or overstepped: incongruous yet inescapable engagements forced together, but with no script to say how or if cultural enjoyments or theoretical insights were to manifest in social relations and vice versa, no assumptions about who was an artist, an audience, a proper subject to politics, no faith but also no lack of faith in the reach of art and action, and a driving intuition that transformations were everywhere afoot but no agreement that they tended to the good.

Freedom under these conditions was not a luxury or a capacity to be exercised but a challenge, inasmuch as it declared unforeclosed potential—something which, I believe, is a key to the incredible, and incredibly broad, creative activity of the period. Production that is snatched from punishing workdays yet exudes peace, or appears pained or desperate but in being so required daunting leaps of faith that new ways into the future could be found. Many pursuits appear to have been infused with this clash of crisis and possibility, mission and joy—poetry, theater, history writing, networking, simply speaking and standing in certain places at certain times. Artwork was crucial, uniquely crucial, but far from alone in being so. Insofar as we make the egalitarian assumption that change is equally everywhere, art as a material/institutional practice will not be a privileged sphere for generating "singular examples." Work that generates change can take place anywhere and through any medium, but it will only do so in actuality, in action, and therefore only ever in plural, partial, incomplete ways. To adapt a phrase from Merleau-Ponty, the work will never be evident at the center of itself: "we never see our ideas or our freedom face to face."[3] Notionally then, the collective, spontaneous assumption of being engaged with change—the recognition, nurturing, and sharing of its significance—is the common "medium" of the particular material practices of democratic culture, be those art, politics, or what have you.

The full picture of democratic culture was not fully visible in its own present: it was not, after all, a thing. But the idea that something important was happening in the dispersed and numerous movements was discussed regularly, in the debates over the "small group" and the research of the Shisō no Kagaku Kenkyūkai (Institute of the Science of Thought) in the mid-1950s, in Tanigawa Gan's faith that there was a "village" of circles to be discovered among the mines, kitchens, and harbors of Kyushu and Yamaguchi, in Abe Kōbō's idea of a map being created in the process of speaking and acting. Abe wrote in the mission statement that appeared at the back of every volume in the Nihon no Shōgen Ruporutāju Shirīzu (Testimonies of Japan Reportage Series) that "it is now our task to set out into the depths of the land of our ancestors to recapture the future that has been taken from us. We slip into our shoes of language—words that fly and words that crawl. It is still dark where we go. Invisible walls have been thrown up, between factory and factory, town and town, person and person, soul and soul. Into this darkness we cast our torch of light, and we draft a map for this place that has none."[4] In Abe's metaphor, the map in not a page in an atlas, but a map in the way a road or a path is a map: crossing real distances between here and there but existent only because it is among people and has the power to beckon. In their wake, the words and movements might leave a new map of connection but it would be created only out of actions and poetic work.[5] Artworks did not represent futures, destinations, or things finished, nor did they model ideal modes of walking, but tried to illuminate and further drive the process of everything happening together: a type of naming, or midwifery, simultaneously instigating and designating.

The work of the reportage artists kept the moment of metamorphosis open, especially in its most disturbing aspects. They depicted the human body and landscape as being torn and reaggregated. The present for them was deeply unsettled and the questions of inner vulnerability and outer political failure remained perilously unexamined. Facing the abjection at the core of human being in history was the only way to break the ghastly repetition at work under the surface of "peaceful and democratic" postwar Japan. Actual movement was integral to the process of defamiliarization: sites of struggle were where the wounds of the historical moment could be found cutting across people's bodies and livelihoods. These sites were the crucibles that turned the inside out and the outside in, opening the participant to the heteronomous energies of history's force—the very force that was to come across in their artwork. Presenting this artwork in as many media and as many locales as possible—most especially the less accustomed ones—was their expansive and ambitious form of publicizing. We can say, then, that dismantling the familiar so that change could do its work most powerfully is a basic feature of the reportage artists' work, in both movement and artwork. But their activism and organizational work was at odds with the abjection of the visual. With hindsight, it seems obvious that their transgressive artworks did not flatter the people involved in struggle or create a context that would encourage those outside the struggle to participate. That logic, however, did not diminish the energy they poured into mapping the arduous road they saw as necessary. The primary reason for their distrust of their elders was the elders' unwillingness to investigate the painful question of their past political and personal inadequacies. The young reportage artists pursued that investigation fearlessly, even recklessly. Their work did not promise salvation, only relevance: if the country was ever to rid itself of the corruption that bred war, the way forward could only be through unremitting openness to the failures of the past and the uncertainty of the future.

The case of Sōbi and Hani Susumu's documentaries appears at first glance to be less contradictory: the modes of social action and film practice are homologous. Sōbi's pedagogy and organization and Hani Susumu's documentary theory and practice spring from similar insights about the instability of identity in time, the ethico-political implication that being subject to change makes everyone equal in non-identity, and the paradoxical work of building structures to frame that ever-open future and make its openness shareable. The patience of the Sōbi teacher in allowing each student's growth to play out parallels Hani's object-centered shooting and tendency to make resolutions unsatisfactory and climaxes non-climactic. Hani's filming was less interested in resolution than in the ongoing tense minutiae of individual, embodied movement or the swell and momentum of the full field in motion. In a similar way, the Sōbi teacher was attuned to the collective motion of the classroom atmosphere on the one hand and to myriad "extraneous" details such as a child's use of color or habits of afterschool play on the other. Both opened up an enlivened future through attention to scales below and above the habituated focus on the "student" or "juvenile delinquent." But both did so amid rampant contradiction. Sōbi liked to stage debates at its annual gatherings by assigning antagonistic roles to different parties. This made the comfort of going along with the crowd more difficult and highlighted the permissibility of clashing ideas, but it did so only to the extent that people submitted to playing their assigned roles. While Hani demeaned editing and elevated duration as the vital source of instability in the process of filmmaking, it is often through careful editing that Hani creates the most powerful extended moments in his films. Instability, it appears, must be constructed. Opening doors that are claimed to be open already is surprisingly painstaking work. This is the most concise example of how the conjunction of art and social movements is constitutively, necessarily impure—mutually stymied by a need to persist and prevail on the one hand and to be unbounded and fluid on the other. Bringing them together is a work of contradictions, entirely satisfactory to neither.

Kyushu-ha is an example of a circle that realized the "disruptive and spirited collision" of opposites that Tanigawa Gan referenced in his manifesto for Circle Village and it was able to build a platform for part-time artists to pursue their artwork and gain visibility where none had existed before.[6] Here also we might detect a homology in the way Kyushu-ha's work tapped into the alien power of discarded objects by reassembling them in ways that revived their poetic force and the way the group fashioned a platform for collective presence from the rogue energies of an unlikely band of young artists and poets around Fukuoka. However, while drawing such a parallel may be gratifying, the fault lines are much more illuminating. The unpredictability, unevenness, and incompleteness that was at the heart of the group—in other words, its very flexibility and open-endedness—constituted a fatal flaw in a system of art that valued greater finish, in all senses of the word. Kikuhata Mokuma's idea of a "producer system," which he proposed in the hopes of making the group more successful in that system, was essentially a rotating dictatorship. Only such unified control would be able to martial Kyushu-ha's collective being into a more palatable object—something more like a finished work of art. And Kikuhata was right. The most open collectives are always the most hybrid and least object-like. Apprehending such groups is challenging; my own work, in fact, participates in homogenizing Kyushu-ha. Sakurai, Tabe, Kikuhata, and (arguably) Miyazaki are among the most compatible with the field of value that is global contemporary art: they are a relatively homogeneous cohort within the group. Concentrating only on the most artistically radical members tames the group as a whole, domesticating it for the house of contemporary art. As Kyushu-ha fell apart in the early 1960s, it is remarkable how predictably its members took up their "proper" places in separate art worlds. What allowed Kyushu-ha to come together and flourish for a time was a formation of culture where such differences were welcomed, where localism was not a form of identity but something that forced extreme diversity in taste and talent. There was a time when such diversity could be the spark of discovery. From that perspective, contemporary art, although it tends to claim diversity, enforced a distinct narrowing of possibilities.

My conclusion from this research is that those who would track artistic intervention beyond the relatively safe zone of artistic or critical intent must be able to countenance contradiction and compromise. Messy translations are more telling than models. While it is commonly asserted in discussions of art and politics that avant-garde and contemporary art have a valuable destabilizing effect on cultural and social order, it is less common to hear valuations of disruption in the opposite direction: that politics and social change can and should destabilize assumptions about art. Understandings of the relationship between art and politics are limited to the extent that they do not countenance the mutual interference that occurs when different fields of endeavor cross. A corollary to this that is more tentative is that the work of aesthetic judgment may play a more important role in assessing the messiness of incomplete transitions and unexpectedly generative interference patterns than in evaluating works already framed as art, no matter how expanded that frame is claimed to be.

Now I return to the first goal, that of reframing the significance of the period 1945–1960 in Japan. My comments go beyond the scope of my research and should therefore be taken as speculative, but it is necessary to address diachronic questions in order to suggest how the early postwar democratic culture relates to periods before and after the early postwar. To begin, I invoke a crooked lineage of organizational practice and social, economic, and cultural creativity that appears episodically in Japan's modern and early modern history, at small scales and in humble milieus, outside the purview of state administration. A number of recent English-language studies have brought to light other instances of this self-reliant local form of organization. Eiko Sakaguchi's *Bonds of Civility: Aesthetic Networks and the Political Origins of Japanese Culture* examines nonstate networks of the early modern period (roughly 1600–1868) from a perspective that resonates deeply with the democratic culture of the early postwar. As she argues, culture and aesthetics formed a language for the practice of civility, which in turn was the lifeblood of the horizontal networks that developed and thrived beneath and across the strict social divisions imposed by the Tokugawa state. Aesthetic civility included what Raymond Williams might call the "common" aspects of culture such as gesture and speech pattern as well as more "elevated" aspects like poetry composition and calligraphy. Thus, while the aesthetic was not instrumentally useful in the substance of specific artistic practices, the social capital (in the form of networks) and cultural capital (in the form of adaptive frames of language use and posture) of the aesthetic came to mediate the nonscripted, unofficial interactions among commoners when they operated outside their immediate geographical or class position.

Tetsuo Najita's *Ordinary Economies in Japan: A Historical Perspective, 1750–1950* shows how commoners, generally merchants and village leaders, pooled and organized economic surpluses to be used for large investments or as insurance against hard times. Such organizations were built on complex contractual relationships completely outside the official domain. Najita shows how these practices and the ideas that informed them survived into the modern period in altered forms such as insurance companies, mutual banks, and cooperatives. More than simply surviving, Najita argues that these ordinary economies are what made it possible for ordinary people to weather the wrenching hardships of modernization. Sho Konishi's work, discussed in chapter 1, explores the activities of improvisational, self-reliant networks of culture and learning in Meiji Japan, showing how the most vibrant and forward-looking elements of that period's intellectual and cultural ferment developed in niche networks, not state institutions.

Ordinary economies, practices of aesthetic civility, and cooperatist anarchism appear only faintly in the historical record. They are episodic and fugitive presences, especially when compared with the footprint of the state. When they do appear clearly, it is often in the form of mavericks who seemingly spring from nowhere, such as Ninomiya Sontoku (1787–1856), a peasant-born moralist and economist whose Hōtoku movement worked to ensure the economic stability of farming villages through a cosmologically inscribed ethic of husbandry and mutual aid, or Tanaka Shōzō (1841–1913), a visionary environmental activist and ecological thinker. It is a lineage invoked in the minority labor farmer (*rōnō*) school of Japanese Marxism that stood for a united people's party of urban workers and rural farmers. It often forms the subject and perspective of *minshūshi* (people's history) and *seishinshi* (history of popular consciousness), and was invoked in postwar debates under the banner of "cooperative democracy."[7] The efflorescence of cultural and political activism in early postwar Japan was not, therefore, a unique occurrence and it cannot be adequately understood solely as a reaction against wartime restrictions. It appears to be, rather, the surfacing of a pattern of organization and self-determined progress that comes to the fore in moments when the power of the state is in dispute. As the state gradually reasserted control over postwar civil life—reassuming the role of the "activist state" as Susan Pharr describes it—the scope for such self-determined forms of social life narrowed.[8]

Casting the 1960s and beyond as a time of narrowing civic possibilities, however, puts my interpretation at odds with common understandings of postwar civil society, according to which true civil society (*shimin shakai*) consolidates in the 1960s with the birth of citizen movements (*shimin undō*). Simon Andrew Avenell's *Making Japanese Citizens* takes this view. But, it is difficult to see any basis for arguing that the movements of the 1960s were more developed than those of the 1950s. In terms of breadth of participation, variety in modes of participation, organizational and intellectual adaptability, and effect on state policy, the movements of the 1950s are at least equally significant, and arguably more so. During the 1950s there were pitched battles over police powers (twice), the terms of the relationship with the United States and the world (ongoing), gender law (twice), war/peace and the military (ongoing), education (ongoing after 1955), food safety (1954–1955), rights of due process (intermittent), and worker/union rights (ongoing). These battles brought together intellectuals, opposition political parties, labor unions, and large and varied networks of "regular" people who came to the movements through various interests and connections—often through participation in a culture circle of some kind.

Avenell shows that the "*shimin* idea" that he associates with the 1960s endorsed "nonhierarchical, ideologically plural, small-scale, voluntary mobilizations . . . legitimated spontaneous political action, encouraged autonomy and self-reliance, promoted active engagement in the public sphere . . . and, most important of all, . . . infused individual and social action with significance far beyond the specific issues at stake."[9] But all of these traits are at least equally on display in the democratic culture of the early postwar years. Apart from the notable exception of the environment, it is difficult to find any area in which the citizen movements of the 1960s were broader, more diverse, or had greater impact than those of the 1950s. And, indeed, in their ability to link broad-based activism with oppositional politics in the Diet and in sustaining a global-scale horizon for local problems, the movements of the 1950s seem to avoid the shortcomings that are sometimes ascribed to post-1960s movements. It seems that the *shimin* idea was alive and well in the 1950s (although the word *shimin* itself was not).

Avenell references the circle movements of the 1950s with care but fails to show why they are not proper citizen movements. He implies at certain points that the 1950s movements were directed by political parties as if that might raise questions about whether they deserve the mantle of *shimin*, but the cases in *Kyōdō kenkyū: shūdan* (Collaborative research: The collective) that he uses do not back up that claim.[10] Further, political parties in postwar Japan are private, voluntary organizations which devise their own platforms: it remains to be argued why membership in a party would make one *less* of a true citizen. Using the example of the Midori no Kai (Green Association), which was cowed by state investigations to tone down its politics in the late 1950s, Avenell argues that grassroots groups before 1960 tended to be politically weak, that they degenerated into apoliticality or became complicit with state projects.[11] But these reservations are at least equally applicable to later movements. Indeed, the intellectual and political ambition of the Midori no Kai *before* official harassment began is precisely what makes the movements of the 1950s so compelling: the 1950s was a time when the radical and idiosyncratic dream of the group's leader Terashima Fumio of melding Ninomiya Sontoku's ethics with Maoism could sustain many hundreds of local chapters around Japan.

If the early postwar might reframe assumptions about the decades following it, it also reaffirms a break with the social structures of total war. Beginning in the 1970s, transwar approaches to history began to call attention to the acceleration of modernization during the period of militarism, from the early 1930s to 1945.[12] Transwar historians argued that many elements we might think of as definitive of modernization and the postwar "miracle" were a result of war, not of liberalization. As these arguments relate to the organization of industry and elite rule, they are strong. But the approach has been less successful when applied to other aspects of culture and society. Sheldon Garon's *Molding Japanese Minds* is a case in point. Garon shows that a drive to modernize and rationalize daily life continued throughout the twentieth century, bringing state administrators and Japan's middle classes into consensus. Regarding the early postwar, Garon frames his argument as a counterweight to the usual narrative in which, he writes, "the 'conservatives,' who struggled to restore the bedrock of the prewar order [battled with] 'progressives,' who steadfastly resisted conservative governments' 'feudalistic' efforts to tighten control over the people." For his part, Garon argues, "if one looks beyond a few controversial issues . . . such as the role of the emperor or the status of the postwar military, we discover many areas of consensus between the progressive and conservative camps."[13] But this framing is problematic. The "few controversial issues" that Garon urges us to look beyond include the military, the emperor, public education, and the structure and scope of police power. These are institutions of fundamental importance to state-society relations, not simply controversial issues.

Controversy itself is also not trivial. As Garon's work itself shows, women's groups in the mid-1950s defied conservative opposition to pass an Anti-Prostitution Law and blocked a 1954 attempt to return to the *ie* system of patriarchal household law, while in the late 1960s and 1970s they were instrumental in bringing pollution onto the national agenda. In a minor but telling example, a youth organization in Kōchi decided to turn down the local Board of Education's co-sponsorship of an event after the board tried to block certain speakers.[14] These examples raise possibly the most important consideration in state-society relations: the degree of autonomy civil society groups enjoy vis-à-vis the state. Although the postwar state's ability to co-opt civil society groups is legendary and although the state tilts the regulatory and financial field to serve its own ends,[15] that is different from sanctioning or imprisoning problematic parties on a discretionary basis. Women's groups were not able to get a prostitution law passed in the 1930s, and they would not have been able to resist changes to their legal status had the state tried. Leaders of prewar youth groups who flouted state guidance would have been arrested if they persisted. The public controversies surrounding the police and the military would clearly have been impossible before 1945. The controversies and struggles that characterize the early postwar demonstrate not only that it was possible for people to participate in civil society on a more equal footing with the state but that many people actually did so. The fact that these actions had local, national, and international effects makes it difficult to brush them aside.

Looking at some of the characteristics of democratic culture as I've laid them out, one might argue that amateur-elite interaction and connection between culture and political movements were also principles of the wartime imperial assistance movement, which integrated local cultural activities into the war effort. When the war ended, many of those local organizations remained intact, switching their mission from imperial assistance to building a nation of culture (*bunka kokka*). In those cases, it is reasonable to argue that cultural associations merely switched one statist objective for another. Such cases, however, do not account for the whole field. Kitagawa Kenzō has researched local cultural organizations during and after the war. He shows that in Fukushima Prefecture, for example, there were twenty local cultural organizations during the war, all connected to Imperial Rule Assistance. By the year 1950, however, the number of such organizations had grown to 322, a sixteenfold increase.[16] It is difficult to see how that could be considered a continuation of a wartime state structure. Kitagawa also investigates the publications of such groups, demonstrating a whole range of reactions (both intellectual and institutional) to democratization.[17]

In the realm of visual art, my own research affirms the value of such contextualization.[18] The Mitsubishi Bibai coal mine in Hokkaido had a company-sponsored art circle that formed in early 1945 to provide cultural activity for wartime industrial workers. The circle continued relatively unchanged until 1949, when a group of young artists who were chafing under the company's control of the circle split off to form a new circle under the aegis of the union. Under the union, the circle gained the autonomy to choose who they would invite as instructors and obtained access to permanent studio space. The union circle thrived for a few years before its core members "graduated" to regional and national venues. From the perspective of the young artists, both the company circle and the union circle seem to have served as resources in their pursuit of art. Though the Mitsubishi Bibai company circle did continue from war to postwar, and though the union circle, with some important differences, had structural similarities with the company circle, it is difficult to imagine the entire phenomenon of worker-artists moving from one to the other and then moving away from both as they found other associations to support their work existing during the war. While comparisons between the wartime state and the postwar developmental state have some basis, the assertion that that entails *continuity* can be maintained only by excising the inconvenient controversies of the early postwar years.

While this book has been about early postwar Japan, its insights also relate to the present. It did not feel that way when I began my research in 2005, but since then there has been significant diversification in ways of thinking about art and politics that has allowed new histories to be told. Whatever comfort that might bring, however, is overshadowed by the increasing desperation of the political situation in Japan, the United States, and many places around the world. In Japan, the most explicitly reactionary government since the late 1950s is pushing constitutional reform that would undermine civil liberties and limits on the use of military force. In the United States, the presidency is only the latest major public institution to be undermined by a virulent hostility to even the most timid of progressive ideals. In both countries, endemic bullying on social media and occasional state persecution raise the personal costs of speaking out, while leaders are increasingly fixated on war as a way to build their own power.

The sense that our lives and our world are at a precarious moment of major historical change grows ever more intense and discomforting. The intensity and scale of the crisis now approaches what I imagine people in the 1950s saw themselves confronting. I wonder, however, whether we will have the resources to recognize that scale. In early postwar Japan, two decades of war and occupation produced, I imagine, a certain clarity about just how bad things could get and a certain realism about the limited power of any one individual, no matter how strong his or her beliefs might be. Most people living at the time were painfully aware that change was not always for the better. Yet they were not bereft of hope, in the sense that Rebecca Solnit understands the idea: "We don't know what is going to happen, or how, or when, and that very uncertainty is the space of hope." For the artists and activists in this study the future was dark, but the darkness was "as much of the womb as the grave."[19]

It is easy to lose sight of hope's importance as a historical force. While Cold War modernization theorists were eager to write off Japanese fascism as an aberration in order to frame the story of Japan's capitalist modernization as a success, many among those who have criticized them seem equally eager to write off signs of democratic dispute and civic engagement as aberrations in an otherwise unbroken pattern of state-centered managerialism. In the fields of contemporary art and critical theory, many claim to renounce dogmatic Marxist understandings of history yet compensate with an equally religious faith in the purifying rupture of the event as the only legitimate appearance of change.[20] All of these theories claim to know how the world will change or, more importantly, how it will *not*.

I imagine those living in the early postwar as being less prone to such assumptions. It is a characteristic that potentially makes them unsightly: sadly insecure in failing to see that capitalism and technology would soon rescue them or sadly earnest in their attempts to change the world through conscious collective action. Their lack of assumptions, however, left them well prepared to act. At present, in contrast, unlearning such assumptions may be a long process for those who have not yet seen just how little the future owes them.

> How do we get back to the struggle over the future? I think you have to hope, and hope in this sense is not a prize or a gift, but something you earn through study, through resisting the ease of despair, and through digging tunnels, cutting windows, opening doors, or finding the people who do these things. They exist.
>
> Rebecca Solnit

Notes

Introduction

1. The title of this series of works is usually translated as *Hiroshima Panels*. "Atomic bomb" is closer to the Japanese title. All of the panels are displayed on the Maruki Museum website: http://www.aya.or.jp/~marukimsn/index.htm.

2. See Kozawa Setsuko, *Genbaku no zu: egakareta "kioku," katarareta "kaiga"* (Tokyo: Iwanami Shoten, 2002); and Okumura Yukinori, *Genbaku no zu zenkoku junkai* (Tokyo: Shinjuku Shobō, 2015).

3. Both Kozawa Setsuko and John Dower point this out. Kozawa, *Genbaku no zu*, 119–128; John Dower, "War, Peace, and Beauty: The Art of Iri Maruki and Toshi Maruki," in *The Hiroshima Murals: The Art of Iri Maruki and Toshi Maruki*, edited by John Dower and John Junkerman (Tokyo: Kodansha International, 1985), 9–26.

4. Kozawa, *Genbaku no zu*, 138.

5. Martin Jay, *Downcast Eyes: The Denigration of Vision in Twentieth-Century French Thought* (Berkeley: University of California Press, 1994).

6. Ibid.

7. Kozawa, *Genbaku no zu*, 148–149.

8. Yoshida Yoshie, *Kaitaigeki no makuorite* (Tokyo: Zōkeisha, 1982), 50.

9. Shannon Jackson, *Social Works: Performing Art, Supporting Publics* (New York: Routledge, 2011), 125.

10. See the epilogue to this book, including notes 12–14, for further discussion of these issues.

11. Grant Kester, *The One and the Many: Contemporary Collaborative Art in a Global Context* (Durham, NC: Duke University Press, 2011); Shannon Jackson, *Social Works: Performing Art, Supporting Publics* (New York: Routledge, 2011); Doris Sommer, *The Work of Art in the World: Civic Agency and Public Humanities* (Durham, NC: Duke University Press, 2014).

12. William Marotti, *Money, Trains, and Guillotines: Art and Revolution in 1960s Japan* (Durham, NC: Duke University Press, 2013); Guy Debord, *The Society of the Spectacle*, translated by Donald Nicholson-Smith (New York: Zone Books, 1999); Tom McDonough, ed., *Guy Debord and the Situationist International* (Cambridge: The MIT Press, 2002); D. N. Rodowick, *The Crisis of Political Modernism: Criticism and Ideology in Contemporary Film Criticism* (Berkeley: University of California Press, 1995).

13. Rebecca Solnit, *Hope in the Dark: Untold Histories, Wild Possibilities* (Chicago: Haymarket Books), 22.

14. Yuriko Furuhata, *Cinema of Actuality: Japanese Avant-Garde Filmmaking in the Season of Image Politics* (Durham, NC: Duke University Press, 2013), 3.

15. Katsuragawa Hiroshi, "'Shūdan toshite no bijutsuka' wa nani o subekika?" *Konnichi no bijutsu* 1 (April 1953), 7–9, reprinted in Katsuragawa Hiroshi, *Haikyo no zen'ei: kaisō no sengo bijutsu* (Tokyo: Ichiyōsha, 2004), 154–57.

16. "On the side of the child" is a phrase made famous by A. S. Neill. See A. S. Neill, *A Dominie's Log* (New York: Robert McBride, 1915), 117, and *Neill! Neill! Orange Peel* (New York: Hart Publishing, 1972), 184. Also see William Ayers, *On the Side of the Child: Summerhill Revisited* (New York: Teachers College Press, 2003). A. S. Neill attributes the phrase to his early mentor Homer Lane.

17. Shirato Hitoyasu, "GHQ senryoka no *Genbaku no zu* Hokkaido junkai ten," in *Bunka shigen toshite no tankō ten: yoru no bijutsukan daigaku kōzaroku*, edited by Masaki Motoi (Tokyo: Meguro Art Museum, 2012), 276.

18. Jinushi Aiko, ed., *Tobenai tsubasa: Kurihama Shōnenin shukishū* (Tokyo: Rironsha, 1958).

19. Kikuhata Mokuma, *Hangeijutsu kidan* (Fukuoka: Kaichōsha, 1986), 28.

20. Raymond Williams, "Culture Is Ordinary" (1958), in *The Raymond Williams Reader*, edited by John Higgins (Oxford: Blackwell, 2001), 11.

21. Jacques Rancière, *On the Shores of Politics*, translated by Liz Heron (New York: Verso, 2007), 45–47.

22. See Takeyama Hiroko and Kokatsu Reiko, eds., *No ni sakebu hitobito: Kita Kantō no sengo hanga undō* (Utsunomiya: Tochigi Prefectural Museum of Fine Arts, 2000); Tomotsune Tamotsu, "Minshū hanga undō no 50-nendai," in *Jikkenba 1950s*, edited by Suzuki Katsuo, Masuda Tomohiro, and Ōtani Shōgo (Tokyo: The National Museum of Modern Art, 2012), 86–99; and Justin Jesty, "Hanga to hanga undō," *Gendai shisō* 35, no. 17 (December 2007): 152–161.

1. Participatory Culture and Democratic Culture

1. Carol Gluck, "The Past in the Present," in *Postwar Japan as History*, edited by Andrew Gordon (Berkeley: University of California Press, 1993), 69.

2. John Dower, *Embracing Defeat: Japan in the Wake of World War II* (New York: W. W. Norton, 1999), 148–154; Mark Sandler, ed., *The Confusion Era: Art and Culture of Japan during the Allied Occupation, 1945–1952* (Seattle: University of Washington Press, 1997). For the left-wing critique of *kasutori* culture, see Christopher Gerteis, *Gender Struggles: Wage-Earning Women and Male-Dominated Unions in Postwar Japan* (Cambridge: Harvard University Press, 2009), 30–64.

3. Dower, *Embracing Defeat*, 189.

4. The Gordon W. Prange Collection contains 16,500 newspaper titles and 13,000 magazine titles published in Japan in the period 1945 to 1949. Kitagawa Kenzō, *Sengo no shuppatsu: bunka undō, seinendan, sensō mibōjin* (Tokyo: Aoki Shoten, 2000), 18–20.

5. Dower, *Embracing Defeat*, 198–199. For a more in-depth look at this phenomenon, see Wesley Makoto Sasaki-Uemura, *Organizing the Spontaneous: Citizen Protest in Postwar Japan* (Honolulu: University of Hawai'i Press, 2001), 63–76.

6. One well-known example of this is the "Hitotoki" column in the Homelife (*katei*) section of the *Asahi shinbun*, begun in 1951. The column's popularity led other newspapers to imitate it. For a discussion of how contributors to the column

spontaneously formed their own independent writing groups, see Sasaki-Uemura, *Organizing the Spontaneous*, 127–132.

7. Narita Ryūichi, "'Sākuru undō' no jidai: 1950 nendai 'Nihon' no bunka no basho," in *Rōkaru hisutorii kara gurōbaru hisutorii e: Tabunka no rekishigaku to chiikishi*, edited by Kawanishi Hidemitsu, Namikawa Kenji, and M. William Steele (Tokyo: Iwata Shoin, 2005), 245–260.

8. Satō Yō, "Kyoto Kiroku Eiga o Miru Kai ni tsuite, sono zenshi," *Engeki eizōgaku* (2013): 41–55.

9. For a map of some of the best-studied circles in Japan, see Toba Kōji, "Chizu de miru sākuru bunka no bokkō," *Shūkan Nihon no rekishi*, May 25, 2014, 16–17. The map lists 393 circles, most of them literary.

10. Andrew Gordon, *The Wages of Affluence: Labor and Management in Postwar Japan* (Cambridge: Harvard University Press, 1998), 95–99.

11. For one such group, the Poets of Ōi, see Sasaki-Uemura, *Organizing the Spontaneous*, 81–111.

12. Narita Ryūichi, "*Heibon* to sono jidai," in *Sengo Nihon sutadiizu 1: 40, 50-nendai*, edited by Iwasaki Minoru, Ueno Chizuko, Kitada Akihiro, Komori Yōichi, and Narita Ryūichi (Tokyo: Kinokuniya Shoten, 2009), 219–243.

13. Gordon, *The Wages of Affluence*, 96.

14. Furukawa Sōichirō [Kurahara Korehito], "Puroretaria geijutsu undō no soshiki mondai," *Nappu* (June 1931), reprinted in *Kurahara Korehito hyōronshū*, vol. 2 (Tokyo: Shin Nihon Shuppansha), 109–136.

15. Mizutamari Mayumi, "1950-nendai kōhan no sākuru undō to shōshūdan ron," *Kokugo kokubun kenkyū* 128 (August 2005): 1–16.

16. Michiba Chikanobu, "Shimomaruko Bunka Shūdan to sono jidai," *Gendai shisō* 35, no. 17 (December 2007): 41.

17. Narita, "*Heibon* to sono jidai." Narita proposes that the *Heibon* readers' circles are paradigmatic examples of the leisure circle. One of the most popular magazines of the postwar period, *Heibon* encouraged a participatory readership through readers' columns, fan letters and contributions, contests, and the organization of a large number of readers' circles.

18. "Cultural democracy" is a related idea that is important to the fields of cultural activism, community arts, and social justice education, especially in the United States. Many commonalities can be found between the ideas and practices of cultural democracy and those of Japan's early postwar democratic culture. I do not set out to compare them here because there are also differences that deserve more attention than I can give them. See Arlene Goldbard and Don Adams, *New Creative Community: The Art of Cultural Development* (Oakland, CA: New Village Press, 2006); James Bau Graves, *Cultural Democracy: The Arts, Community, and the Public Purpose* (Urbana: University of Illinois Press, 2005); Lambert Zuidervaart and Henry Luttikhuizen, eds., *The Arts, Community, and Cultural Democracy* (New York: St. Martin's Press, 2000).

19. Raymond Williams, "Culture Is Ordinary," in *The Raymond Williams Reader*, edited by John Higgins (Oxford: Blackwell, 2001), 11.

20. Ibid.

21. Leslie Pincus, "A Salon for the Soul: Nakai Masakazu and the Hiroshima Culture Movement," *Positions: East Asia Cultures Critique* 10, no. 1 (2002): 173–194.

22. Ibid., 183–184.

23. Amano Masako, *'Tsukiai' no sengoshi: sākuru, nettowāku no hiraku chihei* (Tokyo: Yoshikawa Hirobumi Kan, 2005), 44.

24. Sasaki-Uemura, *Organizing the Spontaneous*, 55–80.

25. *Kyōdō kenkyū: shūdan*, edited by Shisō no Kagaku Kenkyūkai. Tokyo: Heibonsha, 1976.

26. Ōsawa Shinichirō, "Sākuru no sengo shi," in *Kyōdō kenkyū: shūdan*, edited by Shisō no Kagaku Kenkyūkai (Tokyo: Heibonsha, 1976), 68.

27. Sasaki-Uemura, *Organizing the Spontaneous*, 133.

28. Yoshimoto Takaaki, "Zensedai no shijintachi" (1955), in *Yoshimoto Takaaki zenchosakushū*, vol. 5 (Tokyo: Kinsō Shobō), 38–55.

29. I discuss generation further in chapter 4. Generations are important discursively but do not always correspond consistently with birthdays. Yoshimoto Takaaki, who was born in 1924, was an intellectual leader for a series of younger generations.

30. See Yoshimoto Takaaki, "Gisei no shūen," in *Minshushugi no shinwa*, edited by Tanigawa Gan, Yoshimoto Takaaki, Haniya Yutaka, Morimoto Kazuo, Umemoto Katsumi, and Kuroda Kanichi (Tokyo: Gendai Shinchosha, 1960), 43–76.

31. Justin Jesty, "Tokyo 1960: Days of Rage and Grief," *MIT Visualizing Cultures*, n.d., https://ocw.mit.edu/ans7870/21f/21f.027/tokyo_1960/anp2_essay01.html, accessed November 9, 2016.

32. Scott Richard Mehl, "The Concept of Expression in Modern Japanese Poetics: Thought, Consciousness, Language" (PhD diss., University of Chicago, 2013).

33. Fukushima Tatsuo, "Izon shinai hito ni kyōryoku dekiru hito ni, kimi ni soshite wareware ni" (1953), in *Kaihō sareta sengo bijutsu: Demokurāto*, edited by Takano Akihiro, Yasugi Masahiro, Okubo Shizuo, Morimoto Shigeharu, and Teraguchi Yoshiaki (Miyazaki Prefectural Art Museum; The Museum of Modern Art, Wakayama; The Museum of Modern Art, Saitama; The Yomiuri Shimbun; and The Japan Association of Art Museums, 1999), 152.

34. I include work that has been published since 2000 by Amano Masako, Adam Bronson, Chaen Rika, Curtis Anderson Gayle, Laura Hein, Kitagawa Kenzō, Ko Youngran, Kozawa Setsuko, Masaki Motoi, Michiba Chikanobu, Mizutamari Mayumi, Narita Ryūichi, Leslie Pincus, Wesley Sasaki-Uemura, Thomas Schnellbacher, Toba Kōji, and Tsuboi Hideto.

35. Sho Konishi, *Anarchist Modernity: Cooperatism and Japanese-Russian Intellectual Relations in Modern Japan* (Cambridge: Harvard University East Asia Center, 2013).

36. On this tradition, see Tetsuo Najita, "Civil Society in Japan's Modernity—An Interpretive Overview," in *Civil Society, Religion, and the Nation: Modernization in Intercultural Context, Russia, Japan, Turkey*, edited by Gerrit Steunebrink and Evert van der Zweerde (Amsterdam: Rodopi, 2004), 101–115.

37. Mutual aid is an umbrella term for a variety of early modern commoner practices that pooled and organized local resources to various ends: as a buffer in case of disaster, for improvements to the common good, as a form of venture capital, or to support schools of learning and religious observance. By the beginning of the 1800s, mutual aid was well established as practice and organizational consciousness in local communities all over Japan. The discourse, collectivities, and practices were not centralized and were separate from the state. Many remained that way well into

the twentieth century, although as Konishi argues, their history becomes occluded as western modernity became established as the organizing assumption of historical progress. See Konishi, *Anarchist Modernity*; and Tetsuo Najita, *Ordinary Economies in Japan: A Historical Perspective, 1750–1950* (University of California Press, 2009).

38. See Tsurumi Shunsuke, "Naze sākaru o kenkyū suru no ka"; and Itō Toshio, "Sākaru zenshi e no kokoromi," both in *Kyōdō kenkyū: shūdan*, edited by Shisō no Kagaku Kenkyūkai (Tokyo: Heibonsha, 1976).

2. Art and Engagement

1. Oguma Eiji, *"Minshu" to "aikoku": Sengo Nihon no nashonarizumu to kōkyōsei* (Tokyo: Shin'yōsha, 2002), 16.

2. For more on Senda and Ueno, see Justin Jesty and Tokunaga Keita, "Senda Umeji-ron," in *Bunka shigen toshite no tankō-ten*, edited by Masaki Motoi and Ishizaki Takashi (Tokyo: Meguro Museum of Art, 2009), 10–27.

3. For more detail on this group, see Jesty, "Hanga to hanga undō," *Gendai shisō* 35, no. 17 (2007): 152–161.

4. Reprinted in Ueno Eishin, *Oya to ko no yoru*, illustrated by Senda Umeji (Tokyo: Miraisha, 1984), 187–188.

5. Ueno Eishin, "Atogaki: watashi to tankō to no deai," in *Ueno Eishin shū: hanashi no kōkō*, vol. 1 (Tokyo: Komichi Shobō, 1985), 296.

6. See Ueno Makoto, *Seikatsu hanga* (Tokyo: Meiji Tosho Shuppan, 1956).

7. Michiba Chikanobu, "Ueno Eishin *Oya to ko no yoru* sono san," *Mirai* 474 (March 2006): 9.

8. On this process, see Toba Kōji, "Ruporutāju shiriizu: Nihon no shōgen ni tsuite," *Bungei to hihyō* 8, no. 10 (1999): 41–57.

9. Ueno Eishin and Tanigawa Gan, "Taishū keishiki to rōdōsha no kao: Ueno Eishin cho *Oya to ko no yoru* o megutte," *Sākuru mura* 2, no. 12 (1959), 8–12.

10. Paraphrase of Jacques Rancière, *Aisthesis*, translated by Paul Zakir (London: Verso, 2013), 64–68.

11. A recurring example is Auguste Blanqui's use of the word "proletarian." See Jacques Rancière, *Dis-agreement: Politics and Philosophy*, translated by Julie Rose (Minneapolis: Minnesota University Press, 1999), 37–39; and Jacques Rancière, *On the Shores of Politics*, translated by Liz Heron (New York: Verso, 2007), 45–47.

12. An excellent account of the consequences of Rancière's willful blindness to the role of logistics and planning in social movements is Meg McLagan and Yates McKee's critique of his analysis of Rosa Park's role in the Montgomery bus boycott in *Hatred of Democracy*. See Meg McLagan and Yates McKee, *Sensible Politics: The Visual Culture of Nongovernmental Activism* (New York: Zone Books, 2012), 9–28; Jacques Rancière, *Hatred of Democracy*, translated by Steve Corcoran (London: Verson, 2007), 61.

13. For a critique of this general tendency in relation to contemporary work, see Shannon Jackson, esp. her analysis of Mierle Laderman Ukeles in *Social Works: Performing Art, Supporting Publics* (New York: Routledge, 2011), 75–103.

14. Ernesto Laclau and Chantal Mouffe, *Hegemony and Socialist Strategy: Towards a Radical Democratic Politics* (New York: Verso, 2001), 125.

15. Michel de Certeau, *The Practice of Everyday Life*, translated by Steven Rendall (Berkeley: University of California Press, 1984), 29–30.

16. Grant Kester, *The One and the Many: Contemporary Collaborative Art in a Global Context* (Durham, NC: Duke University Press, 2011), 54.

17. Doris Sommer, *The Work of Art in the World: Civic Agency and Public Humanities* (Durham, NC: Duke University Press, 2014), 146.

18. Ibid., 143–146.

19. Friedrich Schiller, *On the Aesthetic Education of Man*, edited and translated by Elizabeth M. Wilkinson and L. A. Willoughby (Oxford: Clarendon Press, 1982), 12.

20. Jean-Paul Sartre, "Existentialism Is a Humanism," (1945), translated by Philip Mairet, first appeared in *Existentialism and Humanism* (London: Methuen & Co., Ltd., 1948); reprinted in *Existentialism from Dostoyevsky to Sartre*, edited by Walter Kaufman (Meridian Publishing Company, 1989), 210–226, https://www.marxists.org/reference/archive/sartre/works/exist/sartre.htm, accessed November 11, 2016.

21. Hariu Ichirō, "Viruherumu Teru no ringo," *Bijutsu hihyō* (April 1956), 30.

22. Although Bert Winther-Tamaki argues that Japanese art moved toward *dis*-embodiment in the late 1950s, embodiment seems central to art and aesthetics at least through the early 1970s in Japan. Two of the four registers he identifies continued to be important in the 1950s: the materiality of artistic practice and the way that that materiality was taken to index the bodily presence of the artist him/herself. Bert Winther-Tamaki, *Maximum Embodiment: Yōga, the Western Painting of Japan, 1912–1955* (Honolulu: University of Hawai'i Press, 2012), 14–21.

23. Raymond Williams, *The Long Revolution* (London: Chatto & Windus, 1961), 37.

3. The Tales of *The Tale of Akebono Village*

1. Ozaki Masato, "'Akebono mura monogatari' kara, soshite 'Akebono mura monogatari' e, 1950-nendai: kitarubeki Yamashita Kikuji-ten no tame ni," in *Yamashita Kikuji-ten/Yamashita Kikuji*, edited by Harada Hikaru, Egawa Yoshihide, Arikawa Ikuo, and Ozaki Masato (Kanagawa Kenritsu Kindai Bijutsukan, Tokushima Kenritsu Kindai Bijutsukan, Miyagi-ken Bijutsukan, Itabashi Kuritsu Bijutsukan, 1996), 146–151.

2. For the story behind the painting, see Yamashita Kikuji, *Kuzureru numa: gaka Yamashita Kikuji no sekai* (Tokyo: Subaru Shobō, 1979).

3. A selection of their journals and poetry collections are available in a reprint edition, *Tokyo Nanbu sākuru zasshi shūsei* (Tokyo: Fuji Shuppan, 2009). For an account of their activity, see *Sengo minshū seishinshi*, special issue, *Gendai Shisō* 35, no. 17 (2007).

4. Author's interview with Maruyama Teruo, March 17, 2007.

5. Author's interview with Maruyama Teruo, March 17, 2007; Yamashita Kikuji, *Kuzureru numa*, 48.

6. Yamashita, *Kuzureru numa*, 48.

7. See Suzuki Katsuo, "Shūdan no yume: gojū nendai o tsuranuku rekishiteki patosu," in *Jikkenba 1950s*, edited by Suzuki Katsuo, Masuda Tomohiro, and Ōtani Shōgo (Tokyo: National Museum of Modern Art, 2012), 23–31.

8. Yamashita, *Kuzureru numa*, 35–46, 53–60.

9. John Berger, "The Honesty of Goya," (1954) in *Selected Essays*, edited by Geoff Dyer (New York: Vintage, 2001), 57.

10. Ishikawa Kazuo signed a confession the police wrote for him while he was in custody. He soon recanted. His trial and conviction became a long-running cause for social activists. He was released from prison in 1994, but the movement to clear his name continues.

4. The Social Work of Documentary and Reportage Art as Movement

1. Toba Kōji has suggested that at least five types of documentary work flourished in the 1950s: the writing daily life and documenting daily life movements, which inspired a huge wave of popular self-writing; reports and testimonies from sites of political struggle; film and television documentaries; artistic reportage in literature, painting, and photography; and the people's history writing movement. See Toba Kōji, *1950 nendai: "kiroku" no jidai* (Tokyo: Kawade Shobō Shinsha, 2010), 9. To this we should add movements to document wartime experience: see Wesley Makoto Sasaki-Uemura, *Organizing the Spontaneous: Citizen Protest in Postwar Japan* (Honolulu: University of Hawai'i Press, 2001), 55–80; and David C. Stahl, *The Burdens of Survival: Ooka Shohei's Writings on the Pacific War* (Honolulu: University of Hawai'i Press, 2003).

2. Notable exceptions to this trend include Ozaki Masato at the Itabashi Art Museum, Masaki Motoi at the Meguro Museum of Art, and Yamada Satoshi at the Nagoya City Art Museum in the 1980s and 1990s and the pioneering *Reconstructions* exhibit of 1985, curated by David Elliott and Kazu Kaido and held at the Museum of Modern Art Oxford. Recent work that marks a shift away from the paradigm includes that of Kokatsu Reiko, Toba Kōji, and Suzuki Katsuo and, in English, Linda Hoaglund, Laura Hein, Rebecca Jennison, Doryun Chong, and Thomas Havens.

3. Ueno Eishin, "Atogaki: Akai jūjika," in *Chitei no shuki: Kunigami Nobuo ikōshū*, edited by Nittan Takamatsu Bungaku Sākuru (Fukuoka: Kunikami Nobuo Ikōshū Henshū Iinkai, 1958), 142–143. Reprinted in *Dokyumento Chikuhō: kono kuni no kashō ni ikite* (Tokyo: Shakai Shinhō Shincho, 1969), 92–94.

4. Shōda Akira, in Ueda Hiroshi, "Domon Ken no yūki to gosan," *Sākuru mura* (April 1960), 13–16 (Ueda Hiroshi interview with Shōda Akira).

5. Ueno Eishin, *Owareyuku kōfutachi* (Tokyo: Iwanami Shinsho, 1960), *Nihon kanbotsuki* (Tokyo: Miraisha, 1961).

6. Ueno Eishin and Chō Kunje, *Shashin manyōroku: Chikuhō* (Fukuoka: Ashi Shobō, 1984).

7. Senda Umeji, *Tankō shigoto uta bangakan* (Fukuoka: Urayama Shobō, 1990), 109.

8. Toba, *1950 nendai*, 9–10.

9. Ueda Seikichi and Gotō Shōjirō, *Ayamatta saiban* (Tokyo: Iwanami Shinsho, 1960).

10. A basic source on Matsukawa is Matsukawa Undōshi Hensan Iinkai, ed., *Matsukawa undō zenshi—taishūteki saiban tōsō no jūgonen* (Tokyo: Rōdō junpōsha, 1965).

11. In *Tokyo Nanbu sākuru zasshi shūsei* (Tokyo: Fuji Shuppan, 2009), supplement volume.

12. In Toba, *1950 nendai*, 169.

13. Matsukawa Bunshū Hensan Iinkai, ed., *Shinjitsu wa kabe o tōshite* (Tokyo: Getsuyō Shobō, 1951).

14. See Kathryn M. Tanaka, "Through the Hospital Gates: Hansen's Disease and Modern Japanese Literature" (PhD diss., University of Chicago, 2012).

15. In Toba, *1950 nendai*, 172.

16. See chapter 1 for more information on Kusa no Mi. On the Kokuminteki Rekishigaku Undō, see Curtis Anderson Gayle, *Marxist History and Postwar Japanese Nationalism* (New York: RoutledgeCurzon, 2003). Ann Sherif also discusses the discourse of establishing facts around the *Lady Chatterley's Lover* translation trial in *Japan's Cold War: Media, Literature and the Law* (New York: Columbia University Press, 2009).

17. In Toba, *1950 nendai*, 174.

18. John Welfield, *An Empire in Eclipse: Japan in the Postwar American Alliance System* (London: Athlone, 1988), 25.

19. See Takei Toshifumi, "Sunagawa tōsō to bijutsuka tachi," *Fuchū Bijutsukan kenkyū kiyo* 16 (2012): 19.

20. Ibid., 15.

21. Uchida Iwao, *Kaiga no rinri* (Tokyo: Shoshi Hitosugi, 1953), 36.

22. Shinkai Kakuo, "Riarizumu bijutsu ni tsuite," *Akahata*, November 14, 1955, cited in Takei, "Sunagawa tōsō to bijutsuka tachi," 13.

23. Shinkai Akashi, "Sunagawa Tōsō no jōkyō to nōmin no kao o egaku to iu sōdaina chichi no mokuhyō," in *Sunagawa Tōsō 50-nen: sorezore no omoi*, edited by Kiichi Hoshi (Tachikawa: Keyaki Shuppan, 2005), 89–91.

24. The photograph is included in Takei, "Sunagawa tōsō to bijutsuka tachi," 12.

25. Kiichi Hoshi, ed., *Sunagawa Tōsō 50-nen: sorezore no omoi* (Tachikawa: Keyaki Shuppan, 2005). This is an observation I have made elsewhere; see Justin Jesty, "Casting Light: Community, Visibility and Historical Presence in Reportage Art of the 1950s," *Quadrante: Areas, Cultures and Positions* 10 (2008): 233.

26. Mita Genjirō, "Atarashii E no Kai," in *Nihon bijutsu kyōiku sōkan sengo hen*, edited by Nihon Bijutsu Kyōiku Rengō, 324–329 (Tokyo: Nihon Bunkyō Shuppan Kabushiki Gaisha, 1966).

27. See Justin Jesty, "The Realism Debate and the Politics of Modern Art in Early Postwar Japan," *Japan Forum* 26, no. 4 (2014): 511–513.

28. Segi Shin'ichi, *Kūhakuki no sengo bijutsu* (Tokyo: Shichōsha, 1996); Segi Shin'ichi, *Nihon no zen'ei 1945–1999* (Tokyo: Seikatsu no Tomosha, 2000). Written as memoirs: Ikeda Tatsuo, *Geijutsu avangyarudo no senaka* (Tokyo: Chūsekisha, 2001); Ikeda Tatsuo, *Mu/gen/ki: ichi gaka no jidai e no shōgen* (Tokyo: Gendai Kikakushitsu, 1990); Katsuragawa Hiroshi, *Haikyo no zen'ei: kaisō no sengo bijutsu* (Tokyo: Ichiyōsha, 2004). For works that focus on the involvement of Abe Kōbō, see Margaret S. Key, *Truth from a Lie: Documentary, Detection, and Reflexivity in Abe Kōbō's Realist Project* (Lanham, MD: Lexington Books, 2011); and Thomas Schnellbacher, *Abe Kōbō, Literary Strategist: The Evolution of His Agenda and Rhetoric in the Context of Postwar Japanese Avant-Garde and Communist Artists' Movements* (Munich: Iudicium, 2004). For a useful chart of the groups and their relationships, see the insert in Suzuki Katsuo, Masuda Tomohiro, and Ōtani Shōgo, eds., *Jikkenba 1950s* (Tokyo: The National Museum of Modern Art, 2012).

29. Takeuchi Kingo, "Taburō hitei no ron," *Konnichi no bijutsu* 1 (April 1953).

30. Ōno Saiji, "Hitotsu no hanron," *Konnichi no bijutsu* 2 (May–June 1953): 7–8.

31. In Katsuragawa, *Haikyo no zen'ei*, 38.

32. The series includes Franz Kafka, *Kafuka Shōshinshū* [Kafka short story collection], translated by Hanada Kiyoteru, illustrated by Katsuragawa Hiroshi and Teshigahara Hiroshi; Suzuki Hidetarō, *Kamigire* [Scraps of paper], illustrated by Ōno Saiji; Piet Mondrian, *Amerika no chūshō geijutsu* [American abstract art], translated by Segi Shin'ichi, illustrated by Segi Shin'ichi; Abe Kōbō, *Mahō no chōku* [The magic chalk], illustrated by Abe Machi and Teshigahara Hiroshi; Abe Kōbō, *Jigyō* [The enterprise], illustrated by Katsuragawa Hiroshi; Sekine Hiroshi, *Sabaku no ki shishū* [Desert tree poetry collection], illustrated by Katsuragawa Hiroshi; Aleksandr A. Fadeyev, *Bungei hyōron no kadai ni tsuite* [On questions of literary criticism], anonymous translator, illustrated by Segi Shin'ichi. In addition to this series, the Seiki no Kai published the *Seiki gashū* [Seiki picture collection] in 1950 featuring the art of Abe Kōbō, Abe Machi, Katsuragawa, Ōno, Segi, Suzuki, and Teshigahara. Further volumes were also planned, but the group disbanded before they were completed. See Katsuragawa, *Haikyo no zen'ei*, 26–84.

33. Katsuragawa, *Haikyo no zen'ei*, 60–61.

34. For an overview of the Nippon-ten, see Jeong Hyeon-a, "1950-nendai riarizumu saikō: ruporutāju kaiga o chūshin ni," *Kyoto bigaku bijutsushigaku* 8 (March 2009): 99–135.

35. Katsuragawa, *Haikyo no zen'ei*, 112.

36. Author's interview with Katsuragawa Hiroshi, March 30, 2006.

37. Katsuragawa Hiroshi, "'Shūdan toshite no bijutsuka' wa nani o subekika?" *Konnichi no bijutsu* 1 (April 1953), 7–9.

38. Reiko Tomii, "Introduction: Collectivism in Twentieth-Century Japanese Art with a Focus on Operational Aspects of Dantai," *Positions: East Asia Critique* 21, no. 2 (2013): 225–267.

39. Ibid., 252.

40. See Ikeda Tatsuo, *Mu/Gen/Ki*, 212–216; Hirasawa Gō, *Andāguraundo firumu ākaibuzu* (Tokyo: Kawade Shobō Shinsha, 2001), 154–156.

41. Nishizawa Harumi, "Ikeda Tatsuo no datsuryōikiteki katsudō: 1950-nendai kara 60-nendai o chūshin ni," *Tsukuba Studies in Art and Design* 13 (2009): 87–97.

42. Ikeda, *Mu/Gen/Ki*, 12.

43. Segi, *Kūhakuki no sengo bijutsu*, 40–45. See also Segi, *Nihon no zen'ei 1945–1999*, 135–137, 373.

44. Ikeda, *Geijutsu avangyarudo no senaka*, 13–14.

45. Katsuragawa Hiroshi, "Kōyō to botsuraku no sedai 1950–1955," *Keishō* 4 (July 1960): 17.

46. See Robert A. Scalapino, *The Japanese Communist Movement, 1920–1966* (Berkeley: University of California Press, 1967); Schnellbacher, *Abe Kōbō*, 83–109; 173–206.

47. Narita Ryūichi, "Dansō no jidai," *Shisō* 980 (December 2005): 95–112; Michiba Chikanobu, "Shimomaruko Bunka Shūdan to sono jidai," *Gendai shisō* 35, no. 17 (December 2007): 38–101.

48. "Nihon Kyōsantō: tōmen no bunka tōsō to bunka sensen tōitsu no tame no wagatō no ninmu," *Zen'ei* (May 1952), reprinted in Minami Hiroshi ed., *Sengo shiryō: bunka* (Nihon Hyōronsha, 1973), 384.

49. Ibid., 374; Nanjō Tōru, "Bijutsu sensen ni okeru kokumin kōryō no gutaika no tame ni," *Zen'ei* (February 1954), 70–95.

50. Segi Shin'ichi, *Sengo kūhakuki no bijutsu* (Tokyo: Shichōsha, 1996), 107.

51. Schnellbacher, *Abe Kōbō*, 86.

52. Ibid., 108–109.

53. Nagai Kiyoshi, "Bijutsu o meguru hansei," *Bunka mondai to Nihon Kyōsantō*, special issue, *Zen'ei* (March 1957), 88–94.

54. Yoshimoto Takaaki and Takei Teruo, *Bungakusha no sensō sekinin* (Tokyo: Awaji Shobō, 1956), 16–17.

55. In "Zensedai no shijintachi," *Shigaku* (November 1955), reprinted in *Yoshimoto Takaaki zenchosakushū*, vol. 5 (Tokyo: Kinsō Shobō), 38–55.

56. His writings are collected in *Eizō no hakken: avangyarudo to dokyumentari* (Tokyo: Sanichi Shobō, 1979). Relevant passages to be found on 109–118, 185–193.

57. Katsuragawa Hiroshi, "Nihon bijutsu no dotai wa doko kara kawari hajimete iru no ka," *Bijutsu undō* (June 1954), 6–7. Many critiques of naturalist realism and of transwar continuity in artists' behavior appeared before this essay was published. But none made a strong claim that the logic of naturalist realism itself as a form of representation implies wartime complicity. In the context of the realism debate, for instance, although Hijikata Tei'ichi critiqued Nagai Kiyoshi's defense of naturalist realism (see, for instance, Hijikata Tei'ichi, "Rearizumu to moshasetsu," *Sōbi* 6–7 [August 1948]: 14–18), he did not target naturalist realism as a form. His critique focused on inadequate theorization and inadequate attention to the practice of artistic creation. His critique was not made in the name of a different account of reality, as Katsuragawa's was; it was a critique of naturalist realism's theoretical underdevelopment as a theory of art and the consequent inappropriateness of claims about its political significance.

58. "Teikō to zasetsu no kiroku," special issue, *Keishō* 4 (1960).

59. Nakamura Hiroshi, "Tenkanki no geijutsu ideorogii," *Keishō* 4 (1960): 24–31.

60. Ibid., 25.

61. Nakamura Hiroshi, "Fushin no 'jiko hihan'" (1957), in vol. 1, *Kaigasha 1957–2002* (Tokyo: Bijutsu Shuppansha, 2003), 14, my italics.

62. The article Katsuragawa refers to is Hariu Ichirō, "Sengo bijutsu no saikentō no tame ni," *Bijutsu undō* 53 (April 1957): 4–5, 21.

63. The Nanjō thesis, referenced above, was an attempt to create a movement around the idea of *kokumin bijutsu* (people's art). Such a movement had developed for literature (*kokumin bungaku*; people's literature) and history (*kokuminteki rekishigaku*; people's history) in the context of JCP-affiliated culture movements in the early 1950s. Nanjō Tōru, "Bijutsu sensen ni okeru kokumin kōryō no gutaika no tame ni," *Zen'ei* (February 1954), 70–95.

64. Katsuragawa Hiroshi, "Kōyō to botsuraku no sedai: ruporutāju undō to sengo no avangyarudo," *Keishō* 4 (1960), 16.

5. Avant-Garde Realism

1. Speaking generally, reportage refers to a production practice and pattern of reception that operates on the assumption that the writer or painter is representing an actual (and usually recent) place or event. The term "reportage" came from the

French word for news reporting. In the 1920s, Czech and German left-wing writers began to use the word to refer to a new kind of literature which they envisioned as a hybrid between reporting and established literary forms. This usage spread internationally through the proletarian movements of the 1920s and 1930s. In postwar Japan, literature brought the word reportage (*ruporutāju*) back into currency. The term was adopted in the visual arts in the early 1950s. Although some historians have claimed that "reportage painting" (*ruporutāju kaiga*) is an ex post facto art historical label, documents show that artists were beginning to use the term as early as 1952. See Ikeda Tatsuo, "Kaiga ni okeru ruporutāju no mondai," *Konnichi no bijutsu* 2 (May–June 1953): 12; Katsuragawa, *Haikyo no zen'ei*, 142–143; *Nakamura Hiroshi: zuga jiken 1953–2007* [Hiroshi Nakamura: Pictorial disturbances, 1953–2007], edited by Chinzei Yoshimi, Fujii Aki, Yamada Satoshi, and Iwata Taka'aki (Tokyo: Tokyo Metropolitan Museum of Modern Art, 2007), 17–18.

2. James Hyman, *The Battle for Realism: Figurative Art in Britain during the Cold War, 1945–1960* (New Haven, CT: Yale University Press, 2001), 2.

3. Jesty, "The Realism Debate and the Politics of Modern Art in Early Postwar Japan."

4. Reprinted in Nagoya City Art Museum, ed., *Sengo Nihon no riarizumu* [Realism in postwar Japan, 1945–1960] (Nagoya: Nagoya City Art Museum and Sengo Nihon no Riarizumu Jikkō Iinkai, 1998), 29.

5. The Tōhō strikes of the late 1940s were part of many large-scale occupation-era labor disputes. See Inoue Masao, *Bunka to tōsō: Tōhō sōgi 1946–1948* [The struggle for culture: The Tōhō strikes, 1946–1948] (Tokyo: Shinyōsha, 2007).

6. Mita Genjirō was a member of the Avant-Garde Art Society. He is a good example of how style is a more consistent way to understand avant-garde realism than group membership. Groups were usually eclectic.

7. Adachi Gen's research brought the importance of this work to my attention. Adachi Gen, *Zen'ei no idenshi: anakizumu kara sengo bijutsu e* [Memes of the Japanese avant-garde: From anarchism to postwar art] (Tokyo: Brücke, 2012), 263–269.

8. Takei Toshifumi interview with Nakamura Hiroshi, January 18, 2012.

9. Okamoto Tarō, Nagai Kiyoshi, and Hanada Kiyoteru, "Avangyarudo no seishin," *Sōgō bunka* (April 1948), 2–13.

10. Hanada's most complete collection of thoughts on art is *Avangyarudo geijutsu* (Tokyo: Miraisha, 1954). The basic concerns I introduce here, however, can be found scattered throughout much of his writing in the 1950s.

11. Hanada Kiyoteru, "Riarizumu josetsu," in *Atarashii geijutsu no tankyū*, edited by Yoru no Kai (Tokyo: Getsuyō Shobō), 145.

12. Originally published in *Ningen* 5, no. 9 (1950), 62–67. Reprinted in *Hanada Kiyoteru chosakushū*, vol. 4 (Tokyo: Kōdansha, 1977), 119–128.

13. Hanada, "Ringo ni tsuite no ichi kōsatsu," 124.

14. Hanada Kiyoteru, *Fukkōki no seishin*, reprinted in *Za Kiyoteru* (Tokyo: Daisan Shokan, 1986), 657.

15. Abe Kōbō, "Atarashii realizumu no tame ni: ruporutāju no igi," *Riron* 18 (August 1952): 29–36, reprinted in *Abe Kōbō zenshū*, vol. 3 (Tokyo: Shinchosha, 1997), 244–251.

16. Hariu Ichirō, "Kirokusei," *Bijutsu hihyō* (January 1955), 56–57.

17. Ibid., 54.

18. Hariu Ichirō, "Shakaiteki shudai to riarizumu," *Bijutsu hihyō* (January 1954), 9.

19. Hariu Ichirō, "Shin gushō no hōkō," *Bijutsu hihyō* (December 1954), 10.

20. Abe Kōbō, "Ruporutāju no igi," in *Ruporutāju to wa nani ka?*, edited by Genzai no Kai (Tokyo: Hakurin Shobō, 1955), 8–9.

21. Abe, "Atarashii realizumu no tame ni: ruporutāju no igi," 246.

22. Abe Kōbō, "Shūruriarizumu hihan," *Mizue* 525 (August 1949), reprinted in *Abe Kōbō zenshū*, vol. 2 (Tokyo: Shinchosha, 1997), 260–267.

23. Abe, "Atarashii realizumu no tame ni: ruporutāju no igi," 247.

24. Katsuragawa, "'Shūdan toshite no bijutsuka' wa nani o subekika?"

6. Katsuragawa Hiroshi, Ikeda Tatsuo, and Nakamura Hiroshi

1. Katsuragawa, *Haikyo no zen'ei*, 15.

2. Author's interview with Katsuragawa Hiroshi, March 30, 2006.

3. Schnellbacher, *Abe Kōbō*, 152–153.

4. For a history of the group, see Michiba Chikanobu, *Shimomaruko Bunka Shūdan to sono jidai* (Tokyo: Mizusu Shobō, 2016).

5. See Kido Noboru, *Tokyo Nanbu sengo sākuru undōshi nenpyō: haisen kara 60-nen Anpo tōsō made* (Tokyo: Me no Kai, 1992).

6. *Shishū Shimokaruko* (Tokyo: Shimomaruko Shūdan, 1951), 31–35. Reprinted in *Tokyo Nanbu sākuru zasshi shūsei* (Tokyo: Fuji Shuppan, 2009), vol. 1.

7. Xiaobing Tang, "Echoes of *Roar China!* On Vision and Voice in Modern Chinese Art," *Positions: East Asia, Cultures, Critique* 14, no. 2 (2006): 479.

8. The reason is that one of the cadres who had left before Katsuragawa arrived had organized a slide show and speech in the mess hall. When the crowd became unruly, the police came to disperse it. After that incident, the mess hall was surrounded by a barbed-wire fence and only workers were permitted inside. See Katsuragawa, *Haikyo no zen'ei*, 126.

9. Ikeda, *Mu/Gen/Ki*, 106.

10. Ikeda, diary entry for February 3, 1954, published in Ikeda, *Mu/Gen/Ki*, 191.

11. Ikeda Tatsuo, *Mu/Gen/Ki*, 192.

12. Ibid.

13. Ikeda, diary entry for August 11, 1952, published in Ikeda, *Mu/Gen/Ki*, 160–161.

14. Ikeda Tatsuo, Fukuda Tsuneta, Sudō Shinichi, and Yamano Takuzō, "Tachikawa Kichi," *Jinmin bungaku* (July 1953), 46–50.

15. Ikeda, *Mu/Gen/Ki*, 174. Many of Ikeda's pen drawings were made for exhibition. A partial list of his drawings done for printed works includes "Banchi no nai machi," *Kaizō* (April 1954) (with text by Sekine Hiroshi); "Kakuritsu no kuni: Jittainaki hiji no tanima," *Kaizō* (December 1954) (text by Sekine Hiroshi); "Chōchōsan fushinnin," *Kaizō* (February 1955) (text by Sugiura Minpei); and "Chōkai giin ichinensei," *Akahata* (January–April 1957) (text by Sugiura Minpei). *Genshiryoku* (text by Masaki Kyōsuke); *Tetsu: omocha no sekai* (text by Sekine Hiroshi); and *Mura no senkyo* (text by Sugiura Minpei), are each single volumes that are part of the Testimonies of Japan Reportage Series edited by the Genzai no Kai (Tokyo: Hakurin Shobō, 1955).

16. Children in base towns were the focus of a certain level of general public concern. In 1953, three well-known intellectuals, Shimizu Ikutarō, Miyahara Seiichi, and Ueda Shōzaburō, published *Kichi no ko: kono jijitsu o dō kangaetara yoika* [Children of the base: How can we think about this issue?] (Tokyo: Kōbunsha, 1953).

17. For more detail on this series, see Schnellbacher, *Abe Kōbō*, 190–207; and Toba Kōji, "'Ruporutāju shiriizu: Nihon no shōgen' ni tsuite," *Bungei to hihyō* 8, no. 10 (1999): 41–57.

18. *Akahata*, March 1, 1957.

19. Toba, "Ruporutāju shiriizu," 44.

20. Imaizumi Yoshihiko, "Nakamura Hiroshi no koto," *Kikan* 15 (1990): 5.

21. Ibid.; Nakamura Hiroshi, "Seiji, taburō, jiko hihan," *Kikan* 15 (1990): 20. This is an interview with Kikuhata Mokuma.

22. Author's interview with Nakamura Hiroshi, February 4, 2007.

23. Namiko Kunimoto, *The Stakes of Exposure: Anxious Bodies in Postwar Japanese Art* (Minneapolis: University of Minnesota Press, 2017), 90–91.

24. Hariu, "Shakaiteki shudai to riarizumu," 9.

25. Suzuki, "Shūdan no yume: 50-nendai o tsuranuku rekishiteki patosu," 18–23; Key, *Truth from a Lie*, 75–124.

26. Sasaki Ki'ichi, "Kiroku Geijutsu no Kai ni tsuite," *Gunzō* 12, no. 10 (1957): 262, quoted in Suzuki Katsuo, "Shūdan no yume," 23.

27. Key, *Truth from a Lie*, 75–124.

28. Ishii Shigeo, "Kindai geijutsu e no ketsubetsu," *Bijutsu hihyō* (January 1957): 21–23.

29. William Marotti, *Money, Trains, and Guillotines: Art and Revolution in 1960s Japan* (Durham, NC: Duke University Press, 2013).

30. Nakamura, "Fushin no 'jiko hihan,'" 15, reprinted in *Kaigasha 1957–2002*, vol. 1 (Tokyo: Bijutsu Shuppansha, 2003), 13–15.

31. Nakamura Hiroshi, "Kaiga senden 1: koritsu suru taburō," in *Kaigasha 1957–2002*, vol. 1 (Tokyo: Bijutsu Shuppansha, 2003), 21.

32. The book is a collection of individual accounts of the events and the subsequent trials of participants. It includes essays by Yoshimoto Takaaki, among others.

33. Steven Ridgely, *Japanese Counterculture: The Antiestablishment Art of Terayama Shūji* (Minneapolis: University of Minnesota Press, 2010), 99.

7. Touching Down at the Sōbi Seminar

1. The peak years for attendance at the summer seminar were 1955, 1956 and 1958, with 1,670, 1,441, and 1,064 attendees, respectively. For information on these seminars, see Sōzō Biiku Kyōkai, ed., *Sōbi nenkan* (Tokyo: Bunka Shobō Hakubunkasha, 1978), 79–144; Arai Tetsuo, "'Sōzō biiku undō' to sono konnichitekina imi," *Biiku bunka* 55, no. 3 (2005): 25–27; Hōkokusho Sakusei Iinkai, ed., "Yudanaka semināru hōkokusho," *Sōbi panfuretto* 6 (1956); Hōkokusho Sakusei Iinkai, ed., "Kamiyamada Togura semināru hōkokusho," *Sōbi panfuretto* 8 (1957).

2. Quote is attributed to Ōno Motoaki in Ichioka Hisako, "Gāden pāti," *Sōbi panfuretto* 8 (1957): 77.

3. The term *biiku* could be translated "aesthetic education" or "art education." The term is used as a standard shorthand for "art education" (*bijutsu kyōiku*), and given that Sōbi is a movement of art teachers, "art education" would not be incorrect. I use "aesthetic education" to emphasize that the horizon of the group's ideas went beyond the discreet subject of art education to include claims about fundamental aspects of human being. In addition to being an abbreviation, *biiku* functions as a word unto itself, forming one leg of a triad: intellectual education (*chiiku*), moral education (*tokuiku*), and aesthetic education (*biiku*). Previous translations do not provide a clear consensus. Okazaki Akio uses the name Society for Creative Art Education in "An Overview of the Influence of American Art Education on the Development of Japanese Art Education," *Journal of Multi-Cultural and Cross-Cultural Research in Art Education* 2, no. 1 (1984): 90. Kingo Masuda follows this usage in "A Historical Overview of Art Education in Japan," *Journal of Aesthetic Education* 37, no. 4 (2003): 10. Kaneda Takuya uses the name Society for Creative Aesthetic Education in "The Concept of Freedom in Art Education in Japan," *Journal of Aesthetic Education* 37, no. 4 (Winter 2003): 14.

4. Herbert Read, *Education for Peace* (New York: Charles Scribner's Sons, 1949), 27.

5. Preamble to the InSEA Constitution (1954). Quoted on InSEA home page, http://www.insea.org/insea/about, accessed July 3, 2014. InSEA was well known to Sōbi members through Read and through the writings of Muro Osamu, who attended the 1951 conference that inaugurated InSEA and wrote about it in the first Sōbi pamphlet, published in 1952.

6. Kubo Sadajirō, "Jidōga no mikata," in Kubo Sadajirō, *Jidōga no mikata* (Tokyo: Dainihon Tosho, 1954), 3–42; originally published in *6–3 Kyōshitsu bessatsu furoku* (June 1949), 1–30.

7. See the introduction, note 16.

8. In the paragraphs below I have combined elements from the 1954, 1955, and 1956 seminars. See note 1 for sources.

9. The keynote was given by Japanese art historian Elise Grilli. For a written account, see Elise Grilli, "Bijutsu kyōiku katei ni okeru sokkyō ni tsuite," *Sōbi panfuretto* 8 (1957): 34. Other keynote speakers included Hani Setsuko and Hani Gorō.

10. Ozaki Shōkyo, "Sōbi sentā," *Sōbi panfuretto* 8 (1957): 77.

11. *Sōbi panfuretto* 6 (1956): 16.

12. Irie Shōzaburō (1954), in *Sōbi nenkan*, ed. Sōzō Biiku Kyōkai (Tokyo: Bunka Shobō Hakubunkasha, 1978), 88–89.

13. Read, *Education for Peace*, 51–52.

14. See Ashiya Shiritsu Bijutsu Hakubutsukan, ed., *Biiku—sōzō to keishō* (Ashiya: Ashiya Shiritsu Bijutsu Hakubutsukan, 2000).

8. Sōbi as Organization and Movement

1. Sōbi members numbered 548 in 1953, 1,584 in 1954, 2,360 in 1956, 1,398 in 1957, 734 in 1961, 711 in 1963, 545 in 1967, 355 in 1971, and 250 in 1978. Sōzō Biiku Kyōkai, ed., *Sōbi nenkan*, 75–77, 261.

2. See Murata Masahiro's detailed timeline of Kitagawa's life in Murata Masahiro and Takahashi Shūji, eds., *Kitagawa Tamiji-ten* (Nagoya: Aichi Prefectural Museum of Art and Kitagawa Tamiji-ten Jikkō Iinkai, 1996), 193–212.

3. Laura Gonzáles Matute, "Kindaika e no michinori: nijūseiki Mekishiko bijutsu," translated by Hōjō Yukari, in Katō Kaoru and Laura Gonzáles Matute, eds., *Mekishiko nijūseiki kaigaten: Camino a la modernidad, maestros de la pintura Mexicana* (NHK Promotions, 2009), 43–44.

4. In honor of the 80th birthday of Kubo's father, the family donated a lecture hall to the local Mōka elementary school, a magnificent structure designed by Endō Shin, a student of Frank Lloyd Wright. Kubo planned to hold an inaugural cultural event but could not decide whether it should be an exhibition of reproductions of western masterpieces, a concert, a film screening, or a children's art exhibit. Input from Hani Gorō tipped the decision in favor of children's art. See Arai Tetsuo, "Kubo Sadajirō no bijutsu kyōiku (1): *Jidōga no mikata* to bijutsu kyōikuron no keisei katei," *Bijutsu kyōikugaku: Daigaku Bijutsu Kyōka Kyōiku Kenkyūkai hōkoku* 14 (1993): 14–15. For Kubo's account, see Kubo Sadajirō, *Watashi no deatta geijutsukatachi* (Tokyo: Keishōsha, 1978), 196–215.

5. See "Kubo Sadajirō nenpu," in Kubo Sadajirō o Kataru Henshū Iinkai, ed., *Kubo Sadajirō o kataru* (Tokyo: Bunka Shobō Hakubunsha, 1997), 2; and Kubo Sadajirō, ed., *Jidōga wa dō shidō shitara yoi ka: Chiizekku jidō bijutsu kyōiku no mondō* (N.p., 1952), first page of the introduction. I thank Shimazaki Kiyomi for giving me access to this volume from his private collection.

6. Teruhisa Horio, *Educational Thought and Ideology in Modern Japan*, translated and edited by Steven Platzer (Tokyo: University of Tokyo Press, 1988), 106–167.

7. Ōtsuki Takeshi, *Sengo minkan kyōiku undōshi* (Tokyo: Ayumi Shuppan, 1982). Ōtsuki arrived at the number fifty-four by including all organizations that were members of the umbrella group Nihon Minkan Kyōiku Kenkyū Dantai Renrakukai (Japan Federation of Non-Governmental Education Associations). Ōtsuki notes that some nongovernmental education groups didn't join the network. See 22 and 41n5. My estimate that the number could have been twice that is derived from a comparison of the number of art groups Ōtsuki cites (3) with the number of art groups (10) in a more complete list in Nihon Bijutsu Kyōiku Renmei, eds., *Nihon bijutsu kyōiku sōkan sengo hen* (Osaka: Nihon Bunkyō Shuppan, 1966), 308–332. If the same is true for other subject areas, there would be double or triple the number that Ōtsuki cites.

8. Ōtsuki, *Sengo minkan kyōiku undōshi*, 23.

9. For a map of the distribution, see Yamagata Hiroshi, *Nihon bijutsu kyōiku shi* (Nagoya: Reimei shobō, 1982), 878.

10. This account of Sōbi is based on my interviews with Shimazaki Kiyomi and Takamori Shun and my interview and correspondence with Shimazaki Kiyomi. Author's interview with Shimazaki Kiyomi, May 28, 2007; correspondence with Shimazaki Kiyomi, July 2009; author's interview with Takamori Shun, July 26, 2007. Both men have long been active in Sōbi at the regional and national levels. Both have been members of the standing committee, and Shimazaki headed the national office from 1957 to 1972. In addition to numerous publications of their own, they have also co-edited a two-volume collection of Kubo Sadajirō's writings on education: Shimazaki Kiyomi and Takamori Shun, eds., *Kubo Sadajirō bijutsu kyōiku ronshū* (Tokyo: Sōfūsha, 2007).

11. Aoyanagi Tamotsu and Ōno Motoaki, eds., *Sōzō shugi bijutsu kyōiku ni tai suru hantairon* (N.p., 1952). I thank Shimazaki Kiyomi for giving me access to this book from his private collection.

12. Sōzō Biiku Kyōkai, *Sōbi nenkan*, 21–23.

13. It is difficult to verify how much this happened. Kubo argued that this was one of the most important functions of national and international exhibitions and related an anecdotal example in "Rakusen to nyūsen" (1951), in Kubo Sadajirō, *Jidōga no mikata* (Tokyo: Dainihon Tosho, 1954), 49–58.

14. Kubo, *Jidōga no mikata*; Kitagawa Tamiji, *Kodomo no e to kyōiku* (Tokyo: Sōgensha, 1952); Kitagawa Tamiji, *E o kaku kodomotachi* [Children who draw] (Tokyo: Iwanami Shoten, 1952). The last book has no direct relation to Hani's film of the same title.

15. The newsletter started in December 1957 and was published until spring 1972. Regional offices also published newsletters.

16. Arai Tetsuo, "Kubo Sadajirō no bijutsu kyōikuron (2): sono sōzōsei no gainen o megutte," *Bijutsu kyoiku: Daigaku Bijutsu Kyōka Kyōiku Kenkyūkai hōkoku* 16 (1995): 13.

17. In Kubo Sadajirō, *Hanga shūshū no hiketsu*, vol. 9 of *Kubo Sadajirō: bijutsu no sekai* (Tokyo: Kubo Sadajirō Kankōkai, 1987), 230–231.

18. Ibid., 235.

19. These include Kimura Hidesaburō, Takeda Shinzaburō, Hirata Katsunori, Iizuka Kunio, Ōura Nobuyuki, and Kagoshima Ippei. See Kubo, *Watashi no deatta geijutsukatachi*, 228–236.

20. Saitō Kihaku, *Saitō Kihaku zenshū*, vol. 6, 20; *Saitō Kihaku zenshū* vol. 4, 117 (Tokyo: Kokudosha, 1969–1971), respectively. Both quotes in Teruhisa, *Educational Thought and Ideology in Modern Japan*, 267.

21. Ōtsuki, *Sengo minkan kyōiku undōshi*, 29–30.

22. Information about other groups can be found in Nihon Bijutsu Kyōiku Renmei, *Nihon bijutsu kyōiku sōkan*, 308–332.

23. Sōbi's preeminence can be deduced from the fact that the other main groups recognized it and took their differences from Sōbi's position as a starting point for describing their own movements. See Satō Yūko, "Zōkei kyōiku no genten o tashikametsutsu habahiroi shichō o kesshū suru," in "Minkan bijutsu kyōiku undō," special issue, *Āto edyukēshon* 2, no. 3 (1990): 10; and Nihon Bijutsu Kyōiku Renmei, *Nihon bijutsu kyōiku sōkan*, 325–326.

24. See Satō, "Zōkei kyōiku no genten o tashikametsutsu habahiroi shichō o kesshū suru," 10–13.

25. This manifesto was written when the group re-formed in 1959. From 1951 to 1959, the group was called the Atarashii Ga no Kai, but it changed its name when it reconstituted in 1959. Mita Genjirō, "Atarashii E no Kai," in Nihon Bijutsu Kyōiku Renmei, *Nihon bijutsu kyōiku sōkan*, 324–329.

26. A good collection of criticisms of Sōbi and Sōbi's responses can be found in Takimoto Masao, *Ningen kaihō no bijutsu kyōiku* (Nagoya: Reimei Shobō, 1976), 63–186.

27. Nihon Kyōshokuin Kumiai, ed., *Nihon no kyōiku* (Tokyo: Kokudosha, 1955), 246–249; Nihon Kyōshokuin Kumiai, ed., *Nihon no kyōiku* (Tokyo: Kokudosha, 1956), 191–193; Nihon Kyōshokuin Kumiai, ed., *Nihon no kyōiku* (Tokyo: Kokudosha, 1958), 241–244.

28. Mita Genjirō, "Atarashii E no Kai," 325.

29. Yamaguchi Isamu, *Sōzō biiku o koete* (Tokyo: Reimei Shobō, 1956), 206–210. For discussion of various curriculum experiments, see 156–205.

30. Yamagata, *Nihon bijutsu kyōiku shi*, 823–825; Nihon Bijutsu Kyōiku Renmei, *Nihon bijutsu kyōiku sōkan*, 55–66.

31. Nihon Bijutsu Kyōiku Renmei, *Nihon bijutsu kyōiku sōkan*, 92.

32. The legality of these administrative initiatives has been challenged in numerous court cases. See Teruhisa, *Educational Thought and Ideology in Modern Japan*, 171–294.

33. As announced by Naitō Yozō, the director of the Primary and Middle School Education Section of the Ministry of Education, in 1957. See Yamagata, *Nihon bijutsu kyōiku shi*, 826.

34. The first meeting was covered in the article "Sakanna zenkoku kekki taikai," *Sōzō biiku* 2, no. 2 (1958): 1. The movement is discussed in Yamagata, *Nihon bijutsu kyōiku shi*, 828–831.

35. See Nihon Bijutsu Kyōiku Renmei, *Nihon bijutsu kyōiku sōkan*, 58–66.

36. Sōbi submitted a demand to the Ministry of Education that this be changed. Published in *Sōzō biiku* 2, nos. 9–10 (1958): 9.

37. Matsukawa Tarō, "Kinpyō o kinpyō ni," *Sōzō Biiku* 3, no. 7 (1959): 1.

38. "Sōbi to Dōtoku Kyōiku," *Sōzō biiku* 2, no. 4 (1958): 8.

39. Hani Setsuko, "Sōzō no kyōiku," *Sōzō biiku* 2, nos. 11–12 (1958): 1. This quote is based on the notes of someone who had heard Hani's speech.

40. Arai Tetsuo, "Kubo Sadajirō: bijutsu kyōiku kanren chosaku nenpu," *Gunma Daigaku Kyōiku Gakubu kiyo* 30 (1995): 68.

41. Ōtsuki, *Sengo minkan kyōiku undōshi*, 27–37.

9. Sōbi's Philosophy and Pedagogy

1. See Arai Tetsuo, "Kubo Sadajirō: bijutsu kyōiku kanren chosaku nenpu," 73n4.

2. Kubo Sadajirō, "Ōbei no jidōga," (1939), in Kubo Sadajirō, *Jidōga no mikata* (Tokyo: Dainihon Tosho, 1954), 59–64.

3. It was translated by Kubo's younger brother, Okonogi Shinsaburō, as *Oya to kyōshi ni kataru: kodomo no sekai to sono michibikikata* (Tokyo: Hakubunsha, 1949).

4. Homer Lane, *Talks to Parents and Teachers* (New York: Hermitage Press, 1949), 29.

5. Ibid., 125, 148, 181.

6. Ibid., 147–148.

7. Kubo Sadajirō, "Kiso kyōiku toshite no zuga" (1948), in Kubo Sadajirō, *Jidōga no mikata*, 159.

8. Ibid., 164.

9. His actual classroom practice is a matter of some controversy: the sheer skill of so many of his students has raised questions about how free his classroom actually was. Efland proposes that we must realize that what was considered free in Cižek's time might not seem so free today. See Peter Smith, *The History of American Art Education: Learning about Art in American Schools* (Westport: Greenwood Press, 1996), 58–78; and Arthur D. Efland, *A History of Art Education: Intellectual and Social Currents in Teaching the Visual Arts* (New York: Teachers College Press, 1990), 195–198.

10. Wilhelm Viola, *Child Art* (Kent: University of London Press, 1942), 26, italics in original.

11. Ibid., 25.

12. Ibid., 25–34.

13. Ibid., 39.

14. Ibid., 45.

15. Cižek's advice to teachers was so important to Kubo that he repeatedly translated only two of the twelve chapters of Viola's introduction to Cižek, *Child Art* that focused on the role and technique of the teacher. Kubo self-published these two chapters as mimeographed pamphlets in 1950, 1952, and 1955. See Uda Hideshi, *Biiku bunka* 55, no. 3 (2005): 40.

16. Cižek started a private class in 1897. In 1903, it was incorporated into the state-run Vienna School for Arts and Crafts (Kunstgewerbeschule), which meant that he could offer his classes free of charge. It also meant that his class was never part of a larger school curriculum. There were no time schedules or inspectors, so he was free to conduct the class as he wanted. Viola, *Child Art*, 12.

17. Efland, *A History of Art Education*, 230–235.

18. Kubo Sadajirō, "Zukōka no dōtoku kyōiku," in Kubo Sadajirō, *Jidōga no mikata*, 172.

19. Kubo, "Ichigatsu no zukōka," (1950), in Kubo Sadajirō, *Jidōga no mikata*, 105–114.

20. Kubo, "Zukōka no dōtoku kyōiku," 177.

21. Kubo, "Zuga no shidō," (1948), in Kubo Sadajirō, *Jidōga no mikata*, 93–104.

22. Kubo, "Jidōga no mikata," 5.

23. Ibid., 18.

24. Ibid., 23.

25. Kubo Sadajirō, "Sekai no jidōga to Nihon no jidōga" (1947) in Kubo Sadajirō, *Jidōga no mikata*, 74.

26. Sōzō Biiku Kyōkai Aichi Shibu, ed., *Yoi e yokunai e* (Nagoya: Reimeisha, 1956).

27. Kubo Sadajirō, "Zuga kyōiku no hōhō" (1952), in Kubo Sadajirō, *Jidōga no mikata*, 146.

28. The phrase "creative atmosphere" originally comes from Cižek. See Viola, *Child Art*, 35.

29. Kubo Sadajirō, "Bijutsu kyōiku kaizen no hōhō" (1951), in Kubo Sadajirō, *Jidōga no mikata*, 125–126.

30. Kubo, "Sekai no jidōga to nihon no jidōga," 80.

31. Kubo Sadajirō "Kyōshi no sensu" (1953), in Kubo Sadajirō, *Jidōga no mikata*, 215; Kubo, "Zuga kyōiku no hōhō," 151–152.

32. Kubo, "Bijutsu kyōiku kaizen no hōhō," 123.

33. All of the educators Kubo was most drawn to—Cižek, Neill, and Lane—were by all accounts exceptionally gifted teachers. However, none of them succeeded in communicating how they did it.

34. See A. S. Neill, *Summerhill: A Radical Approach to Child Rearing* (New York: Hart Publishing, 1960); and Jonathan Croall, *Neill of Summerhill: The Permanent Rebel* (New York: Pantheon Books, 1983).

35. Croall, *Neill of Summerhill*, 228.

36. For an account of this relationship, see ibid., 250–264. There is also a collection of Neill's and Reich's correspondence; see Beverley R. Placzek, ed., *Record of a Friendship: The Correspondence of Wilhelm Reich and A. S. Neill, 1936–1957* (New York: Farrar, Straus, Giroux, 1981).

37. Lane, *Talks to Parents and Teachers*, 149.

38. Ibid., 128. Kubo recommends that teachers pay special attention to this passage in "Zuga kyōiku no hōhō," 149.

39. Kubo, "Zuga kyōiku no hōhō," 145.

40. Kubo Sadajirō, "Jidō bijutsu kyōiku no hōkō" (1951) in Kubo Sadajirō, *Jidōga no mikata*, 191.

41. Herbert Read, *Education through Art* (New York: Pantheon Books, 1942), 296. Read attributes the internal quotation to E. M. Forster's lecture on Virginia Woolf at Cambridge in 1942.

42. Uemura Takachiyo and Mizusawa Kōsaku translated Herbert Read's *Education through Art* into Japanese in 1953. More popular than this work, however, was his collection of essays, *Education for Peace*, which Sugo Hiroshi translated in 1952. The collection was devoted to making the connection between aesthetics, peace, and a nonrepressive society.

43. Read, *Education for Peace*, 127.

44. Although some of the more problematic elements of Read's theory are not central to Sōbi's reception of him, it is worth noting them. Read's belief that virtue was an extension of ideal patterns to be found in nature was based largely on Plato. For Read, modern discoveries in biology and psychology meant that Plato's concept of natural form could be rescued from idealism. Biology and psychology had begun to discover that ideal forms were real and material. For Read, the death of the Enlightenment subject was not disempowering: man was reinscribed as a part of nature in a way that could be empowering and positive. He wrote, for instance, that "harmony within the family, harmony within a social group, harmony within and among nations [are] psychophysiological problems, questions of pattern and practice, of adjustment to natural proportions and conformity to central harmonies." Read, *Education for Peace*, 150. This simultaneous faith in a moral universe and the right power of science to reveal it is a dangerous combination.

45. Read, *Education for Peace*, 152–153.

46. Kubo also made more specific arguments about the moral gains from aesthetic education in "Zukōka no dōtoku kyōiku."

47. The connection can be traced from Kubo to Read to Hulme to Bergson.

48. T. E. Hulme, *Speculations*, edited by Herbert Read (London: Kegan Paul, Trench, Trubner, 1936), 177.

49. Ibid., 180.

50. Ibid., 188.

51. Ibid., 196, italics in original.

52. David Craven, *Art and Revolution in Latin America, 1910–1990* (New Haven, CT: Yale University Press, 2002), 34.

53. Artists who were involved in the open-air school movement also formed the group *30–30!*, of which Kitagawa was a member. See Murata Masahiro, "Kitagawa Tamiji no kaiga: Mekishiko jidai o chūshin ni," in *Kitagawa Tamiji-ten*, 13–14.

54. The schools in mountainous areas served majority Amerindian populations in Taxco, Cholula, and Michoacan, and, later, in Xochimilco, Tlalpan, and Gudalup Hildago. See Ana Mae Barbosa, "The Escuales de Pintura al Aire Libre in Mexico: Freedom, Form, and Culture," *Studies in Art Education* 42, no. 4 (2001): 289.

55. Kitagawa's Taxco school was the last of the open-air schools to close. As early as the late 1920s the movement was coming under criticism, perhaps most vigorously from David Alfaro Siqueiros. Craven, *Art and Revolution in Latin America*, 34.

Kitagawa wrote about his experiences in the open-air school movement in *E o kaku kodomotachi*.

56. Kitagawa Tamiji, "Mekishiko no jidōga ni tsuite" (1938), in *Bijutsu kyōiku to yūtopia*, edited by Kubo Sadajirō and Shimazaki Kiyomi (Osaka: Sōgensha, 1969), 31.

57. Kitagawa, "Atarashii jidō bijutsu no jikken" (1950), in *Bijutsu kyōiku to yūtopia*, 77.

58. Ibid., 72.

59. Ibid., 89.

60. Kitagawa, "Mekishiko no jidōga ni tsuite," 29.

61. Kitagawa, "Mekishiko, Tasuko ni okeru jidō bijutsu kyōiku no keiken" (1937), in *Bijutsu kyōiku to yūtopia*, 21.

62. Kitagawa, "Watashi no bijutsu kyōiku" (1938), in *Bijutsu kyōiku to yūtopia*, 41.

63. Both in *6–3 Kyōshitsu*, Kubo Sadajirō, "Jidōga no mikata," *6–3 Kyōshitsu bessatsu furoku* (June 1949), 1–30; Kitagawa Tamiji, "Jiyū e no kikyū no seishin" *6–3 Kyōshitsu* (November 1949).

64. In one of his earliest essays, he says he was so suspicious of the popularity of the "mental test" (*mentaru tesuto*) movement in the United States that it was one of the three reasons he left New York for Mexico. Kitagawa, "Watashi no bijutsu kyōiku," 37. In another essay, he said that the task of the psychologist is to analyze illnesses and failures, while the task of the teacher is the opposite. Kitagawa, "Bijutsu kyōiku no michi wa kewashikute tōi" (1959), in *Bijutsu kyōiku to yūtopia*, 282–283.

65. Kubo, "Jidōga no mikata," 26.

66. Arai Tetsuo, "Kubo Sadajirō no bijutsu kyōikuron (5): Kubo Sadajirō no jidōga hyōka," *Gunma Daigaku Kyōiku Gakubu kiyo* 39 (2004), 81–113.

67. Kubo Sadajirō, "Jidōga būmu" (1955), in *Kubo Sadajirō bijutsu kyōiku ronshū*, edited by Shimazaki Kiyomi and Takamori Shun, vol. 1 (Tokyo: Sōfusha, 2007), 268–272.

68. Kitagawa, "Bijutsu kyōiku no michi wa kewashikute tōi," 203.

69. Kitagawa, "Mekishiko zuga kyōshitsu no gūkan" (1938), in *Bijutsu kyōiku to yūtopia*, 51–52.

70. Kitagawa, "Jiyū e no kikyū no seishin" (1949), in *Bijutsu kyōiku to yūtopia*, 67.

71. Kitagawa, "E o kaku Mekisho to Nippon no kodomo" (1953), in *Bijutsu kyōiku to yūtopia*, 133.

72. Kitagawa, "Atarashii bijutsu kyōiku e no kitai" (1957), in *Bijutsu kyōiku to yūtopia*, 180.

73. Kitagawa, "Bijutsu kyōiku to yūtopia" (1968), in *Bijutsu kyōiku to yūtopia*, 214.

74. Ibid., 240.

10. Hani Susumu and the Creativity of the Camera

1. Hani Susumu, *Kamera to maiku* (Tokyo: Chuō Kōronsha, 1960), 91–92.

2. B. Winston Kahn, "Hani Motoko and the Education of Japanese Women," *The Historian* 59, no. 2 (1997): 400.

3. Jiyū Gakuen Joshibu Sotsugyōseikai, ed., *Jiyū Gakuen no rekishi*, 2 vols. (Tokyo: Fujin no Tomosha, 1991).

4. Hani also had classes with Yamamoto Kanae, the leader of the Jiyūga Undō. Hani Susumu, *Jiyū Gakuen monogatari* (Tokyo: Kōdansha, 1984), 91–95.

5. Ibid., 172–173.

6. Ibid., 181–189.

7. For a history of Iwanami Productions, see Kusakabe Kyūshirō, *Eizō o tsukuru hito to kigyō: Iwanami Eiga no sanjūnen* (Tokyo: Mizuumi Shobō, 1980).

8. Hani Susumu, *Engi shinai shuyakutachi* (Tokyo: Chuō Kōronsha, 1958), 13.

9. Abé Mark Nornes, *Forest of Pressure: Ogawa Shinsuke and Postwar Japanese Documentary* (Minneapolis: University of Minnesota Press, 2007), 17. See also Takuya Tsunoda, "The Dawn of Cinematic Modernism: Iwanami Productions and Postwar Japanese Cinema" (PhD diss., Yale University, 2015).

10. Abé Mark Nornes, *Forest of Pressure*, 16–17.

11. Both of these films start out with a problem. In the first case, the children don't have enough rain gear among them, in the second there is a fly infestation. The films progress as the children discuss the problem and come up with a solution, which they put into action collectively. Both are models of democracy as a problem-solving device, while the second film additionally promotes the idea that scientific investigation contributes to good community hygiene. In the style of British documentaries, the second film also portrays the interconnection of the locality and the wider world.

12. Hani, *Kamera to maiku.*

13. Ibid., 68.

14. Ibid., 48.

15. Okada Susumu introduced Bazin in Japanese in 1960 and Hani was close friends with Okada. I thank Takinami Yuki for sharing this information with me.

16. Ian Aitken, *European Film Theory and Cinema: A Critical Introduction* (Bloomington: Indiana University Press, 2001), 191–192.

17. Hani, *Engi shinai shuyakutachi*, 9–10, italics in original.

18. Ibid., 15.

19. *Kyōshitsu* won top prize in the general education category at the Educational Film Festival (Kyōiku Eigasai). It was third place in *Kinema Junpo*'s top ten list of short films that year. It was also the first Iwanami film to be distributed to Nikkatsu theaters, through a distribution arrangement that was finalized in 1955. Kusakabe Kyūshirō, *Eizō o tsukuru hito to kigyō,* 50–51.

20. Kusakabe, 56–57.

21. Hani, *Engi shinai shuyakutachi*, 24–25, italics in original.

22. This must be balanced with recognition that the narrative of the film ends with the class's choral performance at the school festival. The chorus functions as a metaphor for each student finding their role in a productive whole, opening the classic question of whether the resolution defuses the lessons of the rest of the film. Hani admits that some of his colleagues complained that this was the least experimental part of the film, but he says his own feeling upon watching the scene during dubbing was one of happiness for the teacher and students. Ibid., 46.

23. Ibid., 33–34.

24. Since art class took place only two or three times a week for each class, this meant the actual filming was limited to the meeting times of the chosen class.

25. Hani, *Engi shinai shuyakutachi*, 51. The original idea for the film came from Hani. He proposed it to Sōbi and they decided to support it. See Shimazaki Kiyomi,

Kubo Sadajirō, and Nonome Keizō, "Taidan: Eiga *E o kaku kodomotachi* to Sōzō Biiku Undō," *Biiku bunka* 41, no. 5 (1991): 21.

26. Nornes, *Forest of Pressure*, 15.

27. The idea that purple signifies emotional distress may have come from Rose H. Alschuler and La Berta Weiss Hattwick, *Painting and Personality: A Study of Young Children* (Chicago: University of Chicago Press, 1947), which was included in many Sōbi bibliographies.

28. It was distributed by Shin Tōhō. Kusakabe Kyūshirō, *Eizō o tsukuru hito to kigyō*, 126–127.

29. Hani Susumu, *Ningenteki eizōron* (Tokyo: Chuō Shinsho, 1972), 123.

30. Ibid., 105–106.

31. Ibid., 111–112.

32. Ibid., 109.

33. Writing in 1960, Hani saw the New Wave as being borne along by the same pursuit of actuality that had animated neorealism. *Kamera to maiku*, 140.

34. "Kubo Sadajirō nenpu," in Kubo Sadajirō o Kataru Henshū Iinkai, ed., *Kubo Sadajirō o kataru*, 1. An authoritative biography of Ei Kyū (given name Sugita Hideo) is Yamada Mitsuharu, *Ei Kyū hyōden to sakuhin* (Tokyo: Seiryūdō, 1976).

35. See Masaki Motoi, "Demokurāto bijutsuka kyōkai sōron: bunken kirihari ni yoru shiken," in *Kaihō sareta sengo bijutsu: Demokurāto*, edited by Takano Akihiro, Yasugi Masahiro, Okubo Shizuo, Morimoto Shigeharu, and Teraguchi Yoshiaki (Miyazaki Prefectural Art Museum, The Museum of Modern Art, Wakayama, The Museum of Modern Art, Saitama, The Yomiuri Shimbun, The Japan Association of Art Museums, 1999), 16.

36. Fukushima Tatsuo, "Izon shinai hito ni kyōryoku dekiru hito ni, kimi ni soshite wareware ni" (1953), in *Kaihō sareta sengo bijutsu—Demokurāto*, 152.

37. Ay-O quoted in Fujimori Shigetsugu, "Miyazaki to Ay-O," in *Hiji no kanatani: Ay-O kaiko*, edited by Kusumi Kiyoshi (Tokyo: Bijutsu Shuppansha, 2006), 114.

38. Ei Kyū, "Kibō wa jiyū naru soshiki ni" (1953), in *Kaihō sareta sengo bijutsu—Demokurāto*, 153.

39. Hannah Higgins, *Fluxus Experience* (Berkeley: University of California Press, 2002).

40. Author's interview with Ay-O, August 24, 2007.

41. Higgins, *Fluxus Experience*, 62.

42. Ibid., 51–55.

43. Robert Filliou and John Cage, *Lehren und Lernen als Auffuehrungskuenste* (New York: Koenig, 1970).

44. Yoshimoto Midori, *Into Performance: Japanese Women Artists in New York* (New Brunswick, NJ: Rutgers University Press, 2005), 115–137.

45. Takako Saitō to the author, February 28, 2011.

11. The Grand Meeting of Heroes

1. Fukuoka-shi Bijutsukan, ed., *Kyushu-ha taizen sengo no Fukuoka de ubugoe o ageta kiseki no zen'ei bijutsu shūdan* (Tokyo: grambooks, 2015); Kawanami Chizuru, ed., *Miyazaki Junnosuke-ten* (Fukuoka: Fukuoka Prefectural Museum of Art, 1998),

18–21; Sakurai Takami, "Eiyūtachi no daishūkai ripōto," *Kyushu-ha* 7 (October 1963): 13–15; Tabe Mitsuko, *Nisennen no ringo: watashi no datsugeijutsuron* (Fukuoka: Nishinihon Shinbunsha, 2001), 202–222; Yoshida Yoshie, *Kaitaigeki no makuorite* (Tokyo: Zōkeisha, 1982), 147–158.

2. Sakurai and Matano worked in the copyediting department of *Nishinippon shinbun*, Tabe and Yutaka Yagara worked at the Iwataya Department Store, Kikuhata Mokuma painted souvenir plates at the same department store (though he wasn't a full employee), Taniguchi Toshio ran an art school for children, Miyazaki Junnosuke taught art at a school for the deaf, Ishibashi Yasuyuki was a conductor for Nishitetsu Railway, Hataraki Tadashi painted signs for movie theaters, Ochi Osamu worked at a printer, Yamauchi Jūtarō had inherited his father's small weaving business, Terada Ken'ichirō worked for a mannequin company, and Obata Eishin and Saitō Hidesaburō were schoolteachers. Perhaps the wealthiest among them was Oyama Uichi, who worked for an electronics company. None of the group members had formal studio training. Funaki Yoshiharu and Miyazaki Junnosuke studied art education and Owari Takeshi had studied design at a technical school. See Kuroda Raiji, "Kyūshū-ha as a Movement: Descending to the Undersides of Art," translated and edited by Reiko Tomii, *Josai University Review of Japanese Culture and Society* 17 (December 2005): 18; Yamaguchi Yōzō, ed., *Shirriizu Kyushu-ha zaihō 1* (Fukuoka: Fukuoka Art Museum, 2006), 3; and Tashiro Shun'ichirō, *Kakenuketa zen'ei* (Fukuoka: Kashoin, 1996), 34.

3. Sakurai Takami, "Meirei suru geijutsu: eiyū daishūkai Nyū Yōku ni tsuite," *Kyushu-ha* 7 (October 1963): 28.

4. Kikuhata Mokuma, *Hangeijutsu kidan*, in *Kikuhata Mokuma chosakushū*, vol. 2 (Fukuoka: Kaichōsha, 1993), 139–140.

5. Ebara Jun, "Garō kara," *Mizue* 679 (November 1961): 76. The story of how this led to the breakup comes from Sakurai Takami, "Shusseki sareru kata no tame ni," *Kyushu-ha* 6 (October 1962): 1. The listed author is the Kyushu-ha Jimukyoku (Kyushu-ha Office).

6. Katō Mizuho, Warashina Hideya, and Yamamoto Atsuo, eds. *Sōgetsu to sono jidai 1945–1970* (Ashiya Municipal Museum and Chiba Municipal Museum, 1998), 220.

7. See Yamamoto Atsuo, "Oto no jikken," in *Sōgetsu to sono jidai 1945–1970*, 217–218.

8. Yoshida Yoshie, "Eiyū izukoniowasu: Nippon Saijo no hantotachi," *Sansai* (July 1963), 62.

9. Ibid., 60–62.

10. For example, Hariu Ichirō, "Kiki no naka no zen'ei gun," *Bijutsu techō* (January 1961), quoted in Mitsuda Yuri, "Geijutsu/fuzai/nichijō—Hangeijutsu o meguru hihyō gensetsu," in *Bijutsu hihyō to sengo bijutsu*, edited by Bijutsu Hyōronka Renmei (Tokyo: Brücke, 2007), 153–154.

11. Reiko Tomii has linked the discourses of contemporary art and international contemporaneity in "Historicizing 'Contemporary Art': Some Discursive Practices in *Gendai Bijutsu* in Japan," *Positions: East Asia, Culture, Critique* 12, no. 3 (2004): 611–641; and in "'International Contemporaneity' in the 1960s: Discoursing on Art in Japan and Beyond," *Japan Review* 21 (2009): 123–147.

12. Translation by Reiko Tomii. In Kuroda, "Kyūshū-ha as a Movement," 20.

13. Taniguchi Harumichi, "Tanima no jidai no seishun no kyōsō—Watashi ni totte no Kyushu-ha," in *Kyūshū-ha-ten*, Fukuoka Art Museum (Fukuoka: Fukuoka-shi Bijutsukan Kyōkai, 1988), 11.

12. Kyushu-ha: Between Three Worlds

1. Hariu Ichirō, "Kyūshū-ha tenmatsuki," in *Kyūshū-ha-ten: Han-geijutsu purojekuto*, edited by Fukuoka Art Museum (Fukuoka: Fukuoka-shi Bijutsukan Kyōkai, 1988), 6–7.

2. This was a large sum in those days: approximately 80,000 yen in today's prices.

3. Hataraki Tadashi, "Shin'ai naru Kyūshū-ha no minasama e," *Kyushu-ha* 6 (March 1962): 2.

4. Kuroda Tatsuya, *Gendai Kyushu shishi (zōhoban)* (Fukuoka: Ashishobō, 1974), 83.

5. Boin was the name for the group of poets; it was also the title of the journal they produced.

6. Maruyama Yutaka, "Shishi *Boin* no shiori," in *Fukkokuban Boin: shiryōhen*, edited by Fukuoka-ken Shijin Kai (Fukuoka: Sōgensha, 1993), 17.

7. For a history of the journal *Boin*, see Tanaka Yūko, "Shishi *Boin* ni atsumatta gunzōtachi," *Ishin: shi to shiron* 66–70 (August 1987–May 1989). (This is a five-part series.) For the influence of Tanigawa Gan, see part four, *Ishin: shi to shiron* 69 (November 1988): 30–38. Also see Sawamiya Yū, *Hōrō to tsuchi to bungaku: Takaki Mamoru, Matsunaga Goichi, Tanigawa Gan* (Tokyo: Gendai Shokan, 2005), 24–85.

8. Although the original plan was to publish the journal quarterly, it was published with extreme irregularity.

9. [Matano Mamoru], "Kyushu-ha," *Kyushu-ha* 1 (September 1957): 1.

10. See Matei Calinescu, *Five Faces of Modernity: Modernism, Avant-Garde, Decadence, Kitsch, Postmodernism* (Durham, NC: Duke University Press, 1987).

11. Kuroda, *Gendai Kyushu shishi (zōhoban)*, 122–123.

12. Itabashi Kenkichi, "'Shika' no kotoba," *Shika* 1 (May 1954): 25.

13. Sakurai, Matano, and Tanigawa Gan were all employed by the journal *Kyushu shijin* (Kyushu Poets) in the late 1950s. Kyushu-ha organized a conference in 1959 at the Farmer's Assembly Hall in Fukuoka City that featured Tanigawa Gan, Sekine Hiroshi, and Hariu Ichirō. For more, see Yamaguchi Yōzō, "Kyushu-ha to Sākuru Mura: sono kankei o meguru nōto," in *Bunka shigen toshite no tankōten*, edited by Masaki Motoi and Ishizaki Takashi (Tokyo: Meguro Museum of Art, 2009), 154–158.

14. Tanigawa Gan, "Kōsakusha no ronri," in *Kōsakusha sengen* (Tokyo: Shio Shuppansha, 1977), 12. I use Reiko Tomii's translation, which appears in Kuroda, "Kyūshū-ha as a Movement," 13.

15. Tanigawa Gan, "Sōkan sengen—sara ni fukaku shūdan no imi o," *Sākuru mura* 1 (September 1958): 3.

16. Sakurai Takami, "Majimena hanashi," *Kyushu-ha* 4 (July 1961), 2–4.

17. Reiko Tomii, "Introduction: Collectivism in Twentieth-Century Japanese Art with a Focus on Operational Aspects of Dantai," *Positions: East Asia Critique* 21, no. 2 (2013): 225–267.

18. Reiko Tomii, "After the 'Descent to the Everyday': Japanese Collectivism from Hi Red Center to The Play, 1964–1973," in *Collectivism after Modernism: The Art of Social Imagination after 1945*, edited by Blake Stimson and Gregory Sholette (Minneapolis: University of Minnesota Press, 2007), 48.

19. Shibata Katsunori and Matsuura Hitoshi, eds., "Terada Ken'ichirō no ayumi," in *Terada Ken'ichirō-ten*, edited by Fukuoka Art Museum (Fukuoka: Fukuoka Art Museum, 1987), 86, 90.

20. Thomas Havens, *Artist and Patron in Postwar Japan* (Princeton, NJ: Princeton University Press, 1982), 105–143.

21. Tomii, "Introduction: Collectivism in Twentieth-Century Japanese Art," 243.

22. Akiyoshi Soseki, ed., *Bi o motomete 60-nen, Nika Seijinsha no kiroku* (Fukuoka: Akiyoshi Soseki, 1998).

23. Kikuhata Mokuma, *Hangeijutsu kidan*, in *Kikuhata Mokuma chosakushū*, vol. 2, 111–112.

24. Terada Ken'ichirō, *Ekaki no shōkyūshi* (Fukuoka: Nishi Nihon Shinbunsha, 1986), 79.

25. Yamaguchi ed., *Shiriizu Kyushu-ha zaihō 1*, 2.

26. Sakurai Takami, "Kyushu-ha no kigen Ochi Osamu ni tsuite," in *I Discover Jesus Curist* [*sic*] *Is a Woman*, edited by Sakurai Takami (Fukuoka: Tōka Shobō, 1987), 289–307.

27. Ibid., 290.

28. Many people have recognized Ochi as the most gifted artist in Kyushu-ha. In addition to Okamoto Tarō's praise of his early work, the critic Nakahara Yūsuke included his *Deguchi nashi* (No Exit) in his list of the best ten postwar works of art; see *Geijutsu shinchō* 44, no. 2 (February 1993): 53. Kuroda Raiji also recognizes him as one of the few Kyushu-ha members who were in the same class as Kudō Tetsumi and Shinohara Ushio; see Kuroda, "Kyūshū-ha as a Movement," 27. Unfortunately, of all Kyushu-ha members, he has left the fewest works behind.

29. Yamaguchi, *Shiriizu Kyushu-ha zaihō 1*, 2.

30. It would be wrong, however, to think of Kyushu-ha as a group of officially rejected artists. Most members were not actually rejects. Some, such as Tabe, refused invitations to submit at the art society exhibits, while others, such as Sakurai, Kuroki, and Terada, continued to exhibit at Nika through 1958.

31. Hariu Ichirō, quoted in Yamaguchi ed., *Shiriizu Kyushu-ha zaihō 1*, 6.

32. Ming Tiampo, "Gutai and Informel: Post-War Art in Japan and France, 1945–1965" (PhD diss., Northwestern University, 2003), 57.

33. An essential resource on Informel's arrival in Japan is Katō Mizuho, Warashina Hideya, and Yamamoto Atsuo, eds. *Sōgetsu to sono jidai 1945–1970* (Ashiya Municipal Museum and Chiba Municipal Museum, 1998), 83–195.

34. Osaki Shin'ichirō has also shown that the abstract expressionist and Informel artists were already being introduced and discussed in Japan before the cloudburst of the Art of the World Today exhibition. This early appreciation of Informel in Japan does not alter the fact, however, that it was the exhibition and artists' visits to Japan in 1957 that had the greatest impact. Osaki Shin'ichirō, "Anforumeru," in *Bijutsu hihyō to sengo bijutsu*, edited by Bijutsu Hyōronka Renmei (Tokyo: Brücke, 2007), 123–144.

35. Yamaguchi ed., *Shiriizu Kyushu-ha zaihō 1*, 4.

36. William Marotti, *Money, Trains, and Guillotines: Art and Revolution in 1960s Japan* (Durham, NC: Duke University Press, 2013), 127.

37. Ibid., 117–131.

38. From 1949 to 1954, the title was the Nihon Andepandan-ten (Japan Independent Exhibition); from 1955 to 1956, it was the Yomiuri Nihon Andepandan-ten (Yomiuri Japan Independent Exhibition); and from 1957 to 1963, it was the Yomiuri Andepandan-ten (Yomiuri Independent Exhibition). The Nihon Bijutsu Kai's Nihon Andepandan-ten never changed its name; it continues to this day. Segi Shin'ichi, *Sengo kūhakuki no bijutsu* (Tokyo: Shichōsha, 1996), 51.

39. Kuroda, "Kyūshū-ha as a Movement," 20.

40. As listed in Yamaguchi Yōzō's timelines in *Shiriizu "Kyushu-ha zaihō 1"* and *Shiriizu "Kyushu-ha zaihō 2"* (Fukuoka: Fukuoka Art Museum, 2007).

41. Kikuhata, *Hangeijutsu kidan*, 126–127.

42. In contrast, in 1958, the Prefectural Exhibition exhibited 460 works out of 1,471 submissions. In 1959, it exhibited 368 works out of 1,561 submissions. Fukuoka Prefectural Museum of Art, *Fukuoka Kentenshi 1940–1994* (Fukuoka: Fukuoka-ken Bijutsu Tenrankai Jikkōiinkai, 1999), 671.

43. It is important to note that, while Kyushu-ha challenged the authority of the judges who guarded access to the various juried exhibitions in Fukuoka, Kyushu-ha received solid support from the two major local newspapers, *Nishinippon shinbun* (a regional paper) and *Fukunichi shinbun* (the Fukuoka prefectural paper).

44. A copy of the letter is in the Kyushu-ha collection at the Fukuoka Museum of Art. The incident was also reported in both *Nishinippon* and *Fukunichi*. According to the coverage in *Nishinippon*, the spark that set off the protest was the news that two of the eight judges for the *yōga* section were staying on past their five-year term limits.

45. Masaki Motoi, "Chihō no zen'ei," in *Yasei no kindai: saikō—sengo Nihon bijutsushi, kirokushū*, edited by Shima Atsuhiko and Nakai Yasuyuki (Osaka: Kokuritsu Kokusai Bijutsukan, 2006), 155–157.

46. Kuroda, "Kyūshū-ha as a Movement," 19.

47. A good introduction to this period in Fukuoka's contemporary art is Kikan Henshū Iinkai, ed., *Tokushū: Shūdan Kumo to Moriyama Yasuhide, Kikan* 16 (1987).

48. Ibid.

49. Author's interview with Tabe Mitsuko, June 30, 2006.

50. Thomas Crow, *Modern Art in the Common Culture* (New Haven, CT: Yale University Press, 1996), 1–38, 35.

51. Clement Greenberg, "Avant-Garde and Kitsch," *Partisan Review* 6, no. 5 (1939): 34–49.

52. Kuroda, "Kyūshū-ha as a Movement," 20.

53. Both Tabe and Surusumi claim to have coined this alternate name. Yamaguchi, ed., *Shiriizu Kyushu-ha zaihō 1*, 4.

54. Hariu, "Kyushu-ha tenmatsuki," 6.

55. Kuroda, "Kyūshū-ha as a Movement," 20.

56. Ibid.

57. Crow, *Modern Art in the Common Culture*, 36–37.

58. John Roberts, *The Intangibilities of Form: Skill and Deskilling in Art after the Readymade* (New York: Verso, 2007), 168, italics in original.

59. Thomas Crow, *The Rise of the Sixties* (New York: Harry N. Abrams, 1996), 23.

60. Ibid., 69–103.

13. Kyushu-ha's Art

1. Kikuhata Mokuma, "Kyushu-ha," *Bijutsu techō* (October 1971), 54–55.

2. Tabe Mitsuko, *Nisennen no ringo: Watashi no datsugeijutsuron* (Fukuoka: Nishinippon Shinbunsha, 2001), 30–31.

3. The process of building this history arguably began around 1970 in a series of special issues of the journal *Bijutsu techō*. First is a series of essays by Yoshida Yoshie that was later collected in *Kaitaigeki no makuorite* (Tokyo: Zōkeisha, 1982). This was followed by "Shūdan no nami, undō no nami: 60-nendai bijutsu undō wa dō ugoitaka," *Bijutsu techō* (October 1971); and "Hyōgen/jōkyō: 60-nendai bijutsu wa dō ugoitaka," *Bijutsu techō* (December 1971). See also Akatsuka Yukio, Tone Yasunao, and Hikosaka Naoyoshi, eds., *Nenpyō: gendai bijustsu no 50-nen*, special double issue, *Bijutsu techō* (April–May 1972).

4. Testimony from other Kyushu-ha members attests to the force of Sakurai's personality. Kyushu-ha's strength as a group correlates with the level of his engagement.

5. Sakurai Takami, *Hige no kiseki: Sakurai Takami shobunshū* (Fukuoka: Tōka Shobō, 1979), 6–14.

6. Sakurai, "Kyushu-ha no kigen Ochi Osamu ni tsuite," 291.

7. The exhibition, which was held in November 1955, was organized by Sakurai and Matano themselves. It was held at the Hyutte Chabo (Hütte Tearoom), which later became an informal meeting place for Kyushu-ha. Yamaguchi, ed., *Shiriizu Kyushu-ha zaihō 1*, 4.

8. Andrew Gordon, "Contests for the Workplace," in *Postwar Japan as History*, edited by Andrew Gordon (Berkeley: University of California Press, 1993), 378–383.

9. Fukuoka City Hall, ed. *Fukuoka shishi*, vol. 8 (Fukuoka: Fukuoka City Hall, 1978), 586.

10. Sakurai, "Kyushu-ha no kigen Ochi Osamu ni tsuite," 290–291.

11. Tabe, *2000-nen no ringo*, 30–31.

12. Kuroda, "Kyūshū-ha as a Movement," 26.

13. Peter Boswell, "Beat and Beyond: The Rise of Assemblage Sculpture in California," in Wight Art Gallery, *Forty Years of California Assemblage* (Los Angeles: Wight Art Gallery, 1989), 65.

14. Ibid., 69.

15. Kuroda, "Kyūshū-ha as a Movement," 28. Kuroda's research has also shown that the city of Fukuoka was rapidly increasing the number of paved roads in the late 1950s, so tar was a common part of everyday life in the city. It was also used in waterproofing and printing.

16. See Kitazawa Noriaki, "Dentō ronsō: 60-nendai avangyarudo e no airo," in *Bijutsu hihyō to sengo bijutsu*, edited by Bijutsu Hyōronka Renmei (Tokyo: Brücke, 2007), 103–122.

17. Sakurai Takami, "Dentō o koeru mono," *Kyushu-ha* 1 (September 1957): 7.

18. Michael Davidson, *The San Francisco Renaissance: Poetics and Community at Mid-Century* (Cambridge: Cambridge University Press, 1989), 63.

19. Sakurai, "Dentō o koeru mono," 7.

20. Tanigawa Gan, "Genten ga sonzai suru," *Boin* 18 (May 1954), reprinted in *Genten ga sonzai suru* (Tokyo: Shio Shuppansha, 1978), 10.

21. Sakurai Takami, "Majimena hanashi," *Kyushu-ha* 4 (July 1961): 2–3.

22. This was the Kyushu-ha Exhibit in December 1963, held in Fukuoka.

23. Tabe Mitsuko, *Jutai geijutsu* (Fukuoka: Kashoin, 1997), 106.

24. Ibid., Ishibashi Yasuyuki was another person who stayed with Kyushu-ha from beginning to end.

25. Kokatsu Reiko has also written an excellent account of Tabe's individual development as an artist in "Tabe Mitsuko shiron: 'Zen'ei (Kyushu-ha)' o koete," *Bijutsu Undōshi Kenkyūkai nyūsu* 93 (May 2008): 1–12.

26. Tabe's maiden name is Ishibashi; no relation to Ishibashi Yasuyuki.

27. Author's interview with Tabe Mitsuko, June 30, 2006.

28. Ibid.

29. Kuroda, "Kyūshū-ha as a Movement," 18; and Fukuoka City Hall, ed., *Fukuoka-shishi*, 584–585.

30. Tabe Mitsuko, "Purakādo no tame ni," *Kyushu-ha* 5 (September 1961): 7.

31. Author's interview with Tabe Mitsuko, June 30, 2006.

32. Tabe Mitsuko, "Gyozoku," *Kyushu-ha* 2 (December 1957): 6.

33. Tabe Mitsuko, "Purakādo no tame ni," *Kyushu-ha* 5 (September 1961), 7.

34. Author's interview with Tabe Mitsuko, June 25, 2006.

35. Tabe, *Nisennen no ringo*, 20–21.

36. Midori Yoshimoto also points out the tension between the ominous assemblage and the optimism of Tabe's interpretation in *Into Performance: Japanese Women Artists in New York* (New Brunswick, NJ: Rutgers University Press, 2005), 26. Tabe's reading of the piece is that it is a celebratory fantasy of liberation. The bristles on the women's pelvises, for instance, are intended to create a warm and fuzzy impression. Author's interview with Tabe Mitsuko, June 30, 2006.

37. "Joseiki ni idomu geijutsuka-tachi," *Doyō manga*, October 20, 1961, 32–33.

38. Tabe, *Nisennen no ringo*, 131.

39. The 1970 World Expo in Osaka was controversial among artists and intellectuals because it glorified technological progress while ignoring examples of modernization's ambivalent effects such as global inequality, the threat of nuclear weapons, and the continuing violence of the Vietnam War. See "Expo '70 and Japanese Art: Dissonant Voices," edited by Yoshimoto Midori, special issue, *Josai University Review of Japanese Culture and Society* XXIII (2011). A copy of Tabe Mitsuko's letter is held in the archives of the Fukuoka Art Museum.

40. Kawanami Chizuru, "Hitori no taido o megutte," in *Tabe Mitsuko: Recent Works,* edited by T. M. T Studio (Fukuoka: Gallery Toile, 2002), 42.

41. Tabe Mitsuko, *Onna to otoko no jikū: Nihon joseishi saikō* (Tokyo: Fujiwara Shoten, 1995).

42. Tabe, *Nisennen no ringo*, 131.

43. Quoted in Jeffrey C. Wright, "Menus of the Soul: Assemblages Implode Loaded Symbols," in *Tabe Mitsuko: Recent Works*, edited by T. M. T Studio (Fukuoka: Gallery Toile, 2002), 27.

44. Ibid.

45. *Hangeijutsu kidan* first appeared as a serialization in 1981 in *Mainichi shinbun*. It was published as a book in 1986.

46. Fukuoka Art Museum held an authoritative retrospective of his work in 2011. Kurokawa Noriyuki, ed., *Kikuhata Mokuma sengo/kaiga* (Tokyo: grambooks, 2011).

47. *Bijutsu hihyō* (November 1956): 35.

48. Kikuhata Mokuma, "Yukkuri yonde kudasai. Majime ni kaita mono desu," *Kyushu-ha* 6 (March 1962): 7–8.

49. Yamane Yasuchika, "Kyokushiteki mikurokosumosu to tendōsetsu no aida de," in *Kikuhata Mokuma-ten*, edited by Yamane Yasuchika (Fukuoka: Kita Kyushu Municipal Museum of Art, 1988), 25.

50. Kikuhata Mokuma, "'Ankēto' Naze jintai o sakuhin no ichibu ni toriageru no ka: sakka no tō," *Bijutsu techō* (October 1965): 13. Quoted in Yamane, "Kyokushiteki mikurokosumosu to tendōsetsu no aida de," 27.

51. Kawanami Chizuru, ed., *Miyazaki Junnosuke-ten* (Fukuoka: Fukuoka Prefectural Museum of Art, 1998), 20–21.

14. A Cruel Story of Anti-Art

1. Miyakawa Atsushi, "Anforumeru igo," *Bijutsu techō* (May 1963): 86–96. Reiko Tomii's work has been important in interpreting the importance of Miyakawa's theorization. See Reiko Tomii, "Miyakawa Atsushi saidoku: 'Anforumeru igo' o chūshin ni," in *Bijutsushi no supekutorumu: sakuhin, gensetsu, seido*, edited by Wakayama Eiko and Kōdera Tsukasa (Kyoto: Kōrinsha, 1996), 143–152.

2. Tomii, "Historicizing 'Contemporary Art,'" 615.

3. Mitsuda Yuri, "Hihyō no eiyūjidai: *Bijutsu hihyō* (1952–1957) shi ni okeru gendai bijutsu hihyō no seiritsu," *Gekkan aida* 110–115 and 117 (February–July and September 2005). This is a seven-part series that was republished as Mitsuda Yuri, "*Bijutsu hihyō* (1952–1957) shi to sono jidai: 'gendai bijutsu' to 'gendai bijutsu hihyō' no seiritsu," *Pb: Fuji Xerox Art Bulletin* 2 (2006).

4. Mitsuda Yuri, "Hihyō no eiyūjidai," *Gekkan Aida* 111 (March 2005): 2–9.

5. Tomii, "Historicizing 'Contemporary Art,'" 614, 617.

6. Mitsuda Yuri, "Hihyō no eiyūjidai," *Gekkan aida* 110 (February 2005): 5.

7. The special issues were published in December 1956 and January 1957. The exhibition began in Tokyo in November 1956 and toured the country through early 1957.

8. Osaki, "Anforumeru," 135. See also Segi Shin'ichi, "Anforumeru o meguru sukyandaru," *Geijutsu shincho* (February 1958): 54–66.

9. For an analysis of the discourse surrounding Anti-Art, see Reiko Tomii, "Geijutsu on Their Minds: Memorable Words on Anti-Art," in *Art, Anti-Art, Non-Art: Experimentations in the Public Sphere in Postwar Japan, 1950–1970*, edited by Charles Merewether with Rika Iezumi Hiro (Los Angeles: Getty Research Institute, 2007), 35–62.

10. Here I use Nakahara Yūsuke's periodization, which divides the fifteen years of the Yomiuri into three periods. The final period, from 1958 to 1963, is what he classifies as the "late period of confused variety." Nakahara Yūsuke, "Yomiuri Independanten o kaerimite sakka no jishu unei," *Yomiuri shinbun* (evening edition), March 16, 1964. Quoted in Mitsuda, "Geijutsu/fuzai/nichijō," 145.

11. Doryun Chong, "When the Body Changes into New Forms: Tracing Tetsumi Kudo," in *Tetsumi Kudo: Garden of Metamorphosis*, edited by Doryun Chong (Minneapolis: Walker Art Center, 2008), 26.

12. Kudō Tetsumi was not a member of Kyushu-ha or Neo Dada.

13. Ann Sherif, "The Aesthetics of Speed and the Illogicality of Politics: Ishihara Shintarō's Literary Debut," *Japan Forum* 17, no. 2 (2005): 185–211.

14. Every year at the beginning of March, the Yomiuri newspaper featured reviews and pictures of its Independent Exhibition. Takiguchi Shūzō was contracted to write the main review each year.

15. Tōno Yoshiaki, "Amerika no bijutsukai," *Yomiuri shinbun* (evening edition), August 25, 1959, 3.

16. Quoted in Mitsuda, "Geijutsu/fuzai/nichijō," 155–156.

17. A point also made in Kuroda Raiji, "A Flash of Neo-Dada: Cheerful Destroyers in Tokyo," translated by Reiko Tomii with Justin Jesty, *Josai University Review of Japanese Culture and Society* 17 (December 2005): 57.

18. Ebara Jun, "Garō kara," *Mizue* 679 (November 1961): 76.

19. Kuroda Raiji, "A Flash of Neo-Dada: Cheerful Destroyers in Tokyo," 53, 63, 59.

20. Kawakita Michiaki, "Rokabirii-ha to yosokuteki chisei-ha," *Bijutsu techō* (May 1958): 26–27.

Epilogue

1. Tyrus Miller, *Singular Examples: Artistic Politics and the Neo-Avant-Garde* (Evanston: Northwestern University Press, 2009), 7–8.

2. Solnit, *Hope in the Dark*, 100.

3. Maurice Merleau-Ponty, *Sense and Non-Sense*, translated by Hubert L. and Patricia Allen Dreyfus (Evanston, IL: Northwestern University Press, 1964), 25.

4. For more detail on this series, see Thomas Schnellbacher, *Abe Kōbō, Literary Strategist: The Evolution of His Agenda and Rhetoric in the Context of Postwar Japanese Avant-garde and Communist Artists' Movements* (Munich: Iudicium, 2004), 190–207; and Toba Kōji, "Ruporutāju shiriizu: Nihon no shōgen ni tsuite." *Bungei to hihyō* 8, no. 10 (1999): 41–57.

5. Abe theorized that human language was originally indexical. Song came into being as people moved around the physical world with each other: songs designated places and pointed the way through the world as they passed from person to person. Abe Kōbō, "Abata no myūzu," (1952), in *Abe Kōbō zenshū*, vol. 3 (Tokyo: Shinchōsha, 1997–2001), 300–305.

6. Tanigawa Gan, "Sōkan sengen—sara ni fukaku shūdan no imi o," *Sākuru mura* 1 (September 1958): 3.

7. See Tetsuo Najita, "Civil Society in Japan's Modernity—An Interpretive Overview," in *Civil Society, Religion and the Nation: Modernization in Intercultural Context: Russia, Japan, Turkey*, edited by Gerrit Steunebrink and Evert Van Der Zweerde (Amsterdam: Rodopi, 2004), 101–115.

8. Susan Pharr, "Conclusion: Targeting by an Activist State: Japan as a Civil Society Model," in *The State of Civil Society in Japan*, edited by Frank Schwartz and Susan Pharr (New York: Cambridge University Press, 2003).

9. Simon Andrew Avenell, *Making Japanese Citizens: Civil Society and the Mythology of the* Shimin *in Postwar Japan* (Berkeley: University of California Press, 2010), 3.

10. Shisō no Kagaku Kenkyūkai, ed., *Kyōdō kenkyū: shūdan* (Tokyo: Heibonsha, 1976).

11. Avenell, *Making Japanese Citizens*, 44–61. Avenell also implies that the use of the term *minzoku* for "the people" in the 1950s is objectionable, but he never demonstrates any specific problematic ideas or organizational habits that derived from it. His translation of *minzoku* as "ethnic nation" is also highly questionable in light of Oguma Eiji's studies of how postwar discourses of the people and nationalism have changed over time.

12. The essay that launched the attack on modernization theory was John Dower's introduction to a collection of E. H. Norman's writings, "E. H. Norman, Japan, and the Uses of History," in *Origins of the Modern Japanese State*, edited by John W. Dower (New York: Pantheon Books, 1975), 3–101. For a retrospective overview of these developments, see Sheldon Garon, "Rethinking Modernization and Modernity in Japanese History: A Focus on State-Society Relations," *Journal of Asian Studies* 53, no. 2 (May 1994): 346–366.

13. Sheldon Garon, *Molding Japanese Minds: The State in Everyday Life* (Princeton, NJ: Princeton University Press, 1997), 152.

14. Ibid., 200–205, 190, 192, 160.

15. See, for instance, Robert Pekkanen, *Japan's Dual Civil Society: Members without Advocates* (Stanford, CA: Stanford University Press, 2006).

16. Kitagawa Kenzō, *Sengo no shuppatsu: bunka undō, seinendan, sensō mibōjin* (Tokyo: Aoki Shoten, 2000), 15–16. Kitawaga cites a 1950 survey conducted by the Fukushima Prefecture Social Education Section. He notes there may be some double counting in the number.

17. Ibid., 13–54.

18. Justin Jesty, "Hokkaidō tankō rōdōsha no kyōdō seisaku: 1950-nen no 'Jinmin saiban kirokuga' o megutte," in *Bunka shigen toshite no tankō-ten* [The coal mine as cultural resource exhibition], edited by Masaki Motoi and Ishizaki Takashi (Tokyo: Meguro Museum of Art, 2009), 128–139.

19. Solnit, *Hope in the Dark*, 4.

20. Particularly in the work of Alain Badiou. *Being and Event*, translated by Oliver Feltham (New York: Continuum, 2005).

Bibliography

Special Collections

Fukuoka Art Museum, Fukuoka
    Kyushu-ha Collection
Museum of Contemporary Art, Tokyo
National Research Institute for Cultural Properties, Tokyo
    Sasaki Shigeo Collection
Private collection of Shimazaki Kiyomi
Private collection of Takamori Shun

Journals

Bek 1 (May 1950). Newsletter published by Seiki (Century).

Bijutsu undō (Art movement), January 20, 1947–. Journal of the Nihon Bijutsu Kai (Japan Art Society).

Geijutsu nōto (Art notes) 1–6 (April 1961–December 1963). Journal of the Zen'ei Bijutsu Kai (Avant-Garde Art Society).

Genzai (Present). Journal of the Genzai no Kai (Present Society). Nos. 1–14 (June 1952–September 1955).

Hihyō undō (Critical movement). Nos. 12–18 (February 1956–October 1960).

Konnichi no bijutsu (Art of today) 2–6 (May 1953–October 1954). Journal of Seinen Bijutsu Rengō (Youth Art Alliance).

Kyushu-ha 1–8 (September 1957–May 1968).

Riarizumu (Realism). Nos. 1, 2, 4, 6–11 (May 1955–1956). Journal of the Seisakusha Kondankai (Producers' Talking Group).

Seikigun (Century collection) 1–7 + *Gashū* (Collection of illustrations) (September–December 1950). Booklets published by Seiki.

Seiki nyūsu (Seiki news). Newsletter published by Seiki. Nos. 1–3, 5 (March 1949–December 1950).

Sōbi panfuretto (Sōbi pamphlet) 1–8 (July 1952–January 1957). Booklets published by Sōzō Biiku Kyōkai.

Sōzō biiku (Creative aesthetic education), December 1957–. Newsletter of Sōzō Biiku Kyōkai.

Interviews

Hani Susumu, Hataraki Jun, Ikeda Tatsuo, Katsuragawa Hiroshi, Kikuhata Mokuma, Maruyama Teruo, Morinaga Jun, Nakamura Hiroshi, Obana Shigeharu, Ochi Osamu, Osaka Kōji, Sakurai Takami, Shimazaki Kiyomi, Tabe Mitsuko, Takamori Shun, Taniguchi Toshio, Yamauchi Jūtarō

Books and Articles

Abe Kōbō. "Abata no myūzu" (1952). In *Abe Kōbō zenshū*. Vol. 3. Tokyo: Shinchōsha, 1997–2001, 300–305.

——. "Atarashii realizumu no tame ni: ruporutāju no igi." *Riron* 18 (August 1952): 29–36.

——. "Ruporutāju no igi." In *Ruporutāju to wa nani ka?* Edited by Genzai no Kai. Tokyo: Hakurin Shobō, 1955.

——. "Shūruriarizumu hihan." *Mizue* 525 (August 1949). In *Abe Kōbō zenshū*. Vol. 2. Tokyo: Shinchosha, 1997–2001, 260–267.

Adachi Gen. *Zen'ei no idenshi: anakizumu kara sengo bijutsu e* [Memes of the Japanese avant-garde: From anarchism to postwar art]. Tokyo: Brücke, 2012.

Aitken, Ian. *European Film Theory and Cinema: A Critical Introduction*. Bloomington: Indiana University Press, 2001.

Akiyoshi Soseki, ed. *Bi o motomete 60-nen, Nika Seijinsha no kiroku*. Fukuoka: Akiyoshi Soseki, 1998.

Alschuler, Rose H., and La Berta Weiss Hattwick. *Painting and Personality: A Study of Young Children*. Chicago: University of Chicago Press, 1947.

Amano Masako. *'Tsukiai' no sengoshi: Sākuru, nettowāku no hiraku chihei*. Tokyo: Yoshikawa Kōbunkan, 2005.

Aoyanagi Tamotsu, and Ōno Motoaki, eds. *Sōzō shugi bijutsu kyōiku ni tai suru hantairon*. N.p., 1952.

Arai Tetsuo. "Kubo Sadajirō: bijutsu kyōiku kanren chosaku nenpu." *Gunma Daigaku Kyōiku Gakubu kiyo* 30 (1995): 67–109.

——. "Kubo Sadajirō no bijutsu kyōikuron (2): Sono sōzōsei no gainen o megutte." *Bijutsu kyōiku: Daigaku Bijutsu Kyōka Kyōiku Kenkyūkai hōkoku* 16 (1995): 13–25.

——. "Kubo Sadajirō no bijutsu kyōikuron (5): Kubo Sadajirō no jidōga hyōka." *Gunma Daigaku Kyōiku Gakubu kiyo* 39 (2004): 81–113.

——. "'Sōzō Biiku undō' to sono konnichitekina imi." *Biiku bunka* 55, no. 3 (2005): 22–27.

Ashiya Shiritsu Bijutsu Hakubutsukan, ed. *Biiku: Sōzō to keishō*. Ashiya: Ashiya Shiritsu Bijutsu Hakubutsukan, 2000.

Avant-Garde Art Society. "Avant-Garde Art Society Manifesto." In *Sengo Nihon no riarizumu* [Realism in postwar Japan, 1945–1960], 29. Edited by Nagoya City Art Museum. Nagoya: Nagoya City Art Museum and Sengo Nihon no Riarizumu Jikkō Iinkai, 1998.

Avenell, Simon. *Making Japanese Citizens: Civil Society and the Mythology of the* Shimin *in Postwar Japan*. Berkeley: University of California Press, 2010.

Ayers, Anne. "Directions in California Assemblage." In Wight Art Gallery, *Forty Years of California Assemblage*, 49–64. Los Angeles: Wight Art Gallery, 1989.

Ayers, William. *On the Side of the Child: Summerhill Revisited*. New York: Teachers College Press, 2003.

Badiou, Alain. *Being and Event*. Translated by Oliver Feltham. New York: Continuum, 2005.

Barbosa, Ana Mae. "The Escuales de Pintura al Aire Libre in Mexico: Freedom, Form, and Culture." *Studies in Art Education* 42, no. 4 (2001): 285–297.

Berger, John. *Selected Essays*. Edited by Geoff Dyer. New York: Vintage, 2001.

Boswell, Peter. "Beat and Beyond: The Rise of Assemblage Sculpture in California." In Wight Art Gallery, *Forty Years of California Assemblage*, 65–71. Los Angeles: Wight Art Gallery, 1989.

Calinescu, Matei. *Five Faces of Modernity: Modernism, Avant-Garde, Decadence, Kitsch, Postmodernism*. Durham, NC: Duke University Press, 1987.

Certeau, Michel de. *The Practice of Everyday Life*. Translated by Steven Rendall. Berkeley: University of California Press, 1984.

Chinzei Yoshimi, Fujii Aki, Yamada Satoshi, and Iwata Taka'aki, eds. *Nakamura Hiroshi: Zuga jiken 1953–2007* [Hiroshi Nakamura: Pictorial disturbances, 1953–2007]. Tokyo: Tokyo Metropolitan Museum of Modern Art, 2007.

Chong, Doryun, ed. *Tokyo: 1955–1970: A New Avant-Garde*. New York: Museum of Modern Art, 2012.

——. "When the Body Changes into New Forms: Tracing Tetsumi Kudo." In *Tetsumi Kudo: Garden of Metamorphosis*, 24–29. Edited by Doryun Chong. Minneapolis: Walker Art Center, 2008.

Croall, Jonathan. *Neill of Summerhill: The Permanent Rebel*. New York: Pantheon Books, 1983.

Crow, Thomas. *Modern Art in the Common Culture*. New Haven, CT: Yale University Press, 1996.

——. *The Rise of the Sixties*. New York: Harry N. Abrams, 1996.

Davidson, Michael. *The San Francisco Renaissance: Poetics and Community at Mid-Century*. Cambridge: Cambridge University Press, 1989.

Debord, Guy. *The Society of the Spectacle*. Translated by Donald Nicholson-Smith. New York: Zone Books, 1999.

Dower, John W. "E. H. Norman, Japan, and the Uses of History." In *Origins of the Modern Japanese State*, edited by John W. Dower, 3–101. New York: Pantheon Books, 1975.

——. *Embracing Defeat: Japan in the Wake of World War II*. New York: W. W. Norton & Company, 1999.

——. "Peace and Democracy in Two Systems: External Policy and Internal Conflict." In *Postwar Japan as History*, edited by Andrew Gordon, 3–33. Berkeley: University of California Press, 1993.

——. "War, Peace, and Beauty: The Art of Iri Maruki and Toshi Maruki." In *The Hiroshima Murals: The Art of Iri Maruki and Toshi Maruki*, edited by John Dower and John Junkerman, 9–26. Tokyo: Kodansha International, 1985.

Ebara Jun. "Garō kara." *Mizue* 679 (November 1961): 76.

Efland, Arthur D. *A History of Art Education: Intellectual and Social Currents in Teaching the Visual Arts*. New York: Teachers College Press, 1990.

Ei-Kyū. "Kibō wa jiyū naru soshiki ni." *Demokrāto* 1 (1953): 5–8.

Elliott, David, and Kazu Kaido, ed. *Reconstructions: Avant-Garde Art in Japan 1945–1965*. Oxford: Museum of Modern Art, 1985.

Filliou, Robert, and John Cage. *Lehren und Lernen als Auffuehrungskuenste*. New York: Koenig, 1970.

Fukkokuban Sākuru Mura. 4 vols. Tokyo: Fuji Shuppan, 2006.

Fukuoka Art Museum, ed. *Kyūshū-ha-ten: Han-geijutsu purojekuto* [Group Kyūshū-ha: Anti-art project]. Fukuoka: Fukuoka Art Museum, 1988.

Fukuoka City Hall, ed. *Fukuoka shishi*. Vol. 8. Fukuoka: Fukuoka City Hall, 1978.

Fukuoka Prefectural Museum of Art, ed. *Fukuoka kentenshi 1940–1994*. Fukuoka: Fukuoka-ken Bijutsu Tenrankai Jikkōiinkai, 1999.

Fukuoka Shijin Kai, ed. *Fukkokuban Boin*. 3 vols. Fukuoka: Sōgensha, 1993.

Fukushima Tatsuo. "Izon shinai hito ni kyōryoku dekiru hito ni, kimi ni soshite wareware ni." *Demokrato* 1 (1953): 1–4.

Furuhata, Yuriko. *Cinema of Actuality: Japanese Avant-Garde Filmmaking in the Season of Image Politics*. Durham, NC: Duke University Press, 2013.

Furukawa Sōichirō [Kurahara Korehito]. "Puroretaria geijutsu undō no soshiki mondai." *Nappu* (June 1931). In *Kurahara Korehito hyōronshū*, 109–136. Vol. 2. Tokyo: Shin Nihon Shuppansha, 1966–1979.

Garon, Sheldon. *Molding Japanese Minds: The State in Everyday Life*. Princeton, NJ: Princeton University Press, 1997.

——. "Rethinking Modernization and Modernity in Japanese History: A Focus on State-Society Relations." *Journal of Asian Studies* 53, no. 2 (1994): 346–366.

Gayle, Curtis Anderson. *Marxist History and Postwar Japanese Nationalism*. New York: RoutledgeCurzon, 2003.

Gerteis, Christopher. *Gender Struggles: Wage-Earning Women and Male-Dominated Unions in Postwar Japan*. Cambridge: Harvard University Press, 2009.

Gluck, Carol. "The Past in the Present." In *Postwar Japan as History*, 64–95. Edited by Andrew Gordon. Berkeley: University of California Press, 1993.

Gordon, Andrew. "Contests for the Workplace." In *Postwar Japan as History*. Edited by Andrew Gordon, 373–394. Berkeley: University of California Press, 1993.

——. *The Wages of Affluence: Labor and Management in Postwar Japan*. Cambridge: Harvard University Press, 1998.

Grilli, Elise. "Bijutsu kyōiku katei ni okeru sokkyō ni tsuite." *Sōbi panfuretto* 8 (1957): 34.

Hanada Kiyoteru. *Avangyarudo geijutsu*. In *Hanada Kiyoteru chosakushū*. Vol. 3. Tokyo: Miraisha, 1970.

——. *Fukkōki no seishin*. In *Za Kiyoteru*. Tokyo: Daisan Shokan, 1986.

——. "Riarizumu josetsu." In *Atarashii geijutsu no tankyū*, 143–178. Edited by Yoru no Kai. Tokyo: Getsuyō Shobō, 1949.

Hani Setsuko. "Sōzō no kyōiku." *Sōzō biiku* 2, nos. 11–12 (1958): 1.

Hani Susumu. *Engi shinai shuyakutachi*. Tokyo: Chuō Kōronsha, 1958.

——. *Jiyū Gakuen monogatari*. Tokyo: Kōdansha, 1984.

——. *Kamera to maiku*. Tokyo: Chuō Kōronsha, 1960.

——. *Ningenteki eizōron* [A theory of the human image]. Tokyo: Chukō Shinsho, 1972.

Hariu Ichirō. "Kirokusei." *Bijutsu hihyō* (January 1955): 51–59.

——. "Kyūshū-ha tenmatsuki." In *Kyūshū-ha-ten: Han-geijutsu purojekuto*, edited by Fukuoka Art Museum, 6–9. Fukuoka: Fukuoka Art Museum, 1988.

——. "Shakaiteki shudai to riarizumu." *Bijutsu hihyō* (January 1954): 6–14.
——. "Sengo bijutsu no saikentō no tame ni." *Bijutsu undo* 53 (April 1957): 4–5, 21.
——. "Shin gushō no hōkō." *Bijutsu hihyō* (December 1954): 5–11.
——. "Viruherumu teru no ringo." *Bijutsu hihyō* (April 1956): 22–34.
Hataraki Tadashi. "Shin'ai naru Kyūshū-ha no minasama e." *Kyūshū-ha* 6 (March 1962): 2.
Havens, Thomas. *Artist and Patron in Postwar Japan*. Princeton, NJ: Princeton University Press, 1982.
——. *Radicals and Realists in the Japanese Nonverbal Arts: The Avant-Garde Rejection of Modernism*. Honolulu: University of Hawai'i Press, 2006.
Hein, Laura. "The Art of Bourgeois Culture in Kamakura." In *Japan from 1945: From Postwar to Post-Bubble*, edited by Christopher Gerteis and Timothy George. London: Continuum Books, 2013.
——. "Reckoning with War in the Museum: Hijikata Teiichi and the Kamakura Museum of Modern Art." *Critical Asian Studies* 43, no. 1 (2011).
——. "Modern Art Patronage and Democratic Citizenship in Japan." *Journal of Asian Studies* 69, no. 3 (2010): 821–841.
Hein, Laura, and Rebecca Jennison, eds. *Imagination without Borders: Feminist Artist Tomiyama Taeko and Social Responsibility.* Ann Arbor: Center for Japanese Studies, The University of Michigan, 2010.
Higgins, Hannah. *Fluxus Experience*. Berkeley: University of California Press, 2002.
Hijikata Tei'ichi. "Rearizumu to moshasetsu." *Sōbi* 6–7 (August 1948): 14–18.
Hirasawa Gō. *Andāguraundo firumu ākaibuzu*. Tokyo: Kawade Shobō Shinsha, 2001.
Hoaglund, Linda, dir. *Art X War.* 2010.
Hōkokusho Sakusei Iinkai, ed. "Kamiyamada Togura seminâru hōkokusho." *Sōbi panfuretto* 8 (1957).
——, ed. "Yudanaka seminâru hōkokusho." *Sōbi panfuretto* 6 (1956).
Horio Teruhisa. *Educational Thought and Ideology in Modern Japan*. Translated and edited by Steven Platzer. Tokyo: University of Tokyo Press, 1988.
Hoshi Kiichi, ed. *Sunagawa tōsō 50-nen: Sorezore no omoi*. Tokyo: Keyaki Shuppan, 2005.
Hulme, T. E. *Speculations*. Edited by Herbert Read. London: Kegan Paul, Trench, Trubner, 1936.
Hyman, James. *The Battle for Realism: Figurative Art in Britain During the Cold War 1945–1960*. New Haven, CT: Yale University Press, 2001.
"Hyōgen/jōkyō: 60-nendai bijutsu wa dō ugoitaka." Special feature. *Bijutsu techō* (December 1971).
Ikeda Tatsuo, Fukuda Tsuneta, Sudō Shinichi, and Yamano Takuzō. "Tachikawa kichi." *Jinmin bungaku* (July 1953): 46–50.
Ikeda Tatsuo. *Geijutsu avangyarudo no senaka*. Tokyo: Chūsekisha, 2001.
——. "Kaiga ni okeru ruporutāju no mondai." *Konnichi no bijutsu* 2 (May–June 1953): 10–12.
——. *Mu/gen/ki: ichi gaka no jidai e no shōgen*. Tokyo: Gendai Kikakushitsu, 1990.
Imaizumi Yoshihiko. "Nakamura Hiroshi no koto." *Kikan* 15 (1990).
Inoue Masao. *Bunka to tōsō: Tōhō sōgi 1946–1948*. Tokyo: Shinyōsha, 2007.
Ishii Shigeo. "Kindai geijutsu e no ketsubetsu." *Bijutsu hihyō* (January 1957): 21–23.
Itabashi Kenkichi. "'Shika' no kotoba." *Shika* 1 (May 1954): 25.

Itō Toshio. "Sākuru zenshi no kokoromi." In *Kyōdō kenkyū: shūdan*, 45–67. Edited by Shisō no Kagaku Kenkyūkai. Tokyo: Heibonsha, 1976.

Ivy, Marilyn. "Formations of Mass Culture." In *Postwar Japan as History*, edited by Andrew Gordon, 239–258. Berkeley: University of California Press, 1993.

Iwasaki Minoru. "Sengo Nihon kakumei no zasetu." In *Sengo Nihon sutadiizu 1: 40, 50-nendai*, edited by Iwasaki Minoru, Ueno Chizuko, Kitada Akihiro, Komori Yōichi, and Narita Ryūichi, 117–134. Tokyo: Kinokuniya Shoten, 2009.

Jackson, Shannon. *Social Works: Performing Art, Supporting Publics*. New York: Routledge, 2011.

Jay, Martin. *Downcast Eyes: The Denigration of Vision in Twentieth-Century French Thought*. Berkeley: University of California Press, 1994.

Jeong Hyeon-a. "1950-nendai riarizumu saikō: ruporutāju kaiga o chūshin ni." *Kyoto bigaku bijutsushigaku* 8 (March 2009): 99–135.

Jesty, Justin. "The Realism Debate and the Politics of Modern Art in Early Postwar Japan." *Japan Forum* 26, no. 4 (2014): 508–529.

——. "Hanga to hanga undō." *Gendai shisō* 35, no. 17 (2007): 152–161.

——. "Hokkaidō tankō rōdōsha no kyōdō seisaku: 1950-nen no 'Jinmin saiban kirokuga' o megutte." In *Bunka shigen toshite no tankō-ten* [The coal mine as cultural resource exhibition], 128–139. Edited by Masaki Motoi and Ishizaki Takashi. Tokyo: Meguro Museum of Art, 2009.

——. "Casting Light: Community, Visibility and Historical Presence in Reportage Art of the 1950s." *Quadrante: Areas, Cultures and Positions* 10 (2008): 187–253.

Jesty, Justin, and Tokunaga Keita. "Senda Umeji-ron." In *Bunka shigen toshite no tankō-ten*, 10–27. Edited by Masaki Motoi and Ishizaki Takashi. Tokyo: Meguro Museum of Art, 2009.

Jiyū Gakuen Joshibu Sotsugyōseikai, ed. *Jiyū Gakuen no rekishi*. 2 vols. Tokyo: Fujin no Tomosha, 1991.

"Joseiki ni idomu geijutsuka-tachi." *Doyō manga*, October 20, 1961, 32–33.

Kahn, B. Winston. "Hani Motoko and the Education of Japanese Women." *The Historian* 59, no. 2 (1997): 391–401.

Kaikō Takeshi. "Hadaka no ōsama." *Bungakkai*, December 1957. In *Kaikō Takeshi zensakuhin: shōsetsu*, 111–162. Tokyo: Shinchōsha, 1973.

Kaneda Takuya. "The Concept of Freedom in Art Education in Japan." *The Journal of Aesthetic Education* 37, no. 4 (Winter 2003): 12–19.

Katō Mizuho, Warashina Hideya, and Yamamoto Atsuo, eds. *Sōgetsu to sono jidai 1945–1970*. Ashiya City Museum of Art & History and Chiba City Museum of Art, 1998.

Katsuragawa Hiroshi. *Haikyo no ze'nei: Kaisō no sengo bijutsu*. Tokyo: Ichiyōsha, 2004.

——. "Kōyō to botsuraku no sedai 1950–1955." *Keishō* 4 (July 1960): 11–23.

——. "Nihon bijutsu no dotai wa doko kara kawari hajimete iru no ka." *Bijutsu undo* (June 1954): 6–7.

——. "'Shūdan toshite no bijutsuka' wa nani o subekika?" *Konnichi no bijutsu* 1 (April 1953): 7–9.

Kawakita Michiaki. "Rokabirii-ha to yosokuteki chisei-ha." *Bijutsu techō* (May 1958): 26–27.

Kawanami Chizuru. "Hitori no taido o megutte." In *Tabe Mitsuko: Recent Works*, 41–44. Edited by T. M. T Studio. Fukuoka: Gallery Toile, 2002.

——, ed. *Miyazaki Junnosuke-ten* [Miyazaki Junnosuke exhibition]. Fukuoka: Fukuoka Prefectural Museum of Art, 1998.

Kester, Grant. *Conversation Pieces: Community and Communication in Modern Art*. Berkeley: University of California Press, 2004.

——. *The One and the Many: Contemporary Collaborative Art in a Global Context*. Durham, NC: Duke University Press, 2011.

Key, Margaret S. *Truth from a Lie: Documentary, Detection, and Reflexivity in Abe Kōbō's Realist Project*. Lanham: Lexington Books, 2011.

Kido Noboru. *Tokyo Nanbu sengo sākuru undōshi nenpyō: Haisen kara 60-nen Anpo tōsō made*. Tokyo: Me no Kai, 1992.

Kikan Henshū Iinkai, ed. *Tokushū: Shūdan Kumo to Moriyama Yasuhide*. *Kikan* 16 (1987).

Kikuhata Mokuma. *Kikuhata Mokuma chosakushū*. Vol. 2. Fukuoka: Kaichōsha, 1993.

——. *Tennō no bijutsu*. Kikuhata Mokuma chosakushū. Vol. 1. Fukuoka: Kaichōsha, 1993.

——. "Yukkuri yonde kudasai. Majime ni kaita mono desu." *Kyushu-ha* 6 (March 1962): 7–8.

Kitagawa Kenzō. *Sengo no shuppatsu: Bunka undō, seinendan, sensō mibōjin*. [The beginning of the postwar: Culture movements, youth groups, war widows] Tokyo: Aoki Shoten, 2000.

Kitagawa Tamiji. *Bijutsu kyōiku to yūtopia: Kitagawa Tamiji bijutsu kyōiku ronshū*. Edited by Kubo Sadajirō and Shimazaki Kiyomi. Tokyo: Sōgensha, 1969.

——. *E o kaku kodomotachi*. Tokyo: Iwanami Shoten, 1952.

——. *Kodomo no e to kyōiku*. Tokyo: Sōgensha, 1952.

Kitazawa Noriaki. "Dentō ronsō: 60-nendai avangyarudo e no airo." In *Bijutsu hihyō to sengo bijutsu*, edited by Bijutsu Hyōronka Renmei, 103–122. Tokyo: Brücke, 2007.

Ko Youngran. *'Sengo' to iu ideorogii: rekishi, kioku, bunka*. Tokyo: Fujiwara Shoten, 2010.

Kokatsu Reiko. "Tabe Mitsuko shiron: 'Zen'ei (Kyushu-ha)' o koete." *Bijutsu Undōshi Kenkyūkai nyūsu* 93 (May 2008): 1–12.

Konishi, Sho. *Anarchist Modernity: Cooperatism and Japanese-Russian Intellectual Relations in Modern Japan*. Cambridge: Harvard University East Asia Center, 2013.

Koschmann, J. Victor. *Revolution and Subjectivity in Postwar Japan*. Chicago: University of Chicago Press, 1996.

Kozawa Setsuko. *Genbaku no zu: Egakareta "kioku," katarareta "kaiga."* Tokyo: Iwanami Shoten, 2002.

Kubo Sadajirō. *Hanga shūshū no hiketsu*. Vol. 9, *Kubo Sadajirō: Bijutsu no sekai*. Tokyo: Kubo Sadajirō Kankōkai, 1987.

——. *Jidō no mikata*. Tokyo: Dainihon Tosho, 1954.

——. *Kubo Sadajirō bijutsu kyōiku ronshū*. 2 vols. Ed. Shimazaki Kiyomi and Takamori Shun. Tokyo: Sōfūsha, 2007.

——. *Watashi no deatta geijutsukatachi*. Tokyo: Keishōsha, 1978.

——, ed. *Jidōga wa dō shidō shitara yoi ka: Chiizekku jidō bijutsu kyōiku no mondō*. N.p., 1952.

Kubo Sadajirō o Kataru Henshū Iinkai, ed. *Kubo Sadajirō o kataru*. Tokyo: Bunka Shobō Hakubunsha, 1997.

Kuroda Raiji. "A Flash of Neo-Dada: Cheerful Destroyers in Tokyo." Translated by Reiko Tomii with Justin Jesty. *Josai University Review of Japanese Culture and Society* 17 (December 2005): 51–71.

——. "Kyūshū-ha as a Movement: Descending to the Undersides of Art." Translated and edited by Reiko Tomii. *Josai University Review of Japanese Culture and Society* 17 (December 2005): 12–50.

Kuroda Tatsuya. *Gendai Kyushu shishi (zōhoban)*. Fukuoka: Ashi Shobō, 1974.

Kusakabe Kyūshirō. *Eizō o tsukuru hito to kigyō: Iwanami Eiga no sanjūnen*. Tokyo: Mizuumi Shobō, 1980.

Laclau, Ernesto and Chantal Mouffe. *Hegemony and Socialist Strategy: Towards a Radical Democratic Politics*. New York: Verso, 2001.

Lane, Homer. *Talks to Parents and Teachers*. New York: Hermitage Press, 1949.

Marotti, William. *Money, Trains, and Guillotines: Art and Revolution in 1960s Japan*. Durham, NC: Duke University Press, 2013.

——. "Politics and Culture in Postwar Japan: Akasegawa Genpei and the Artistic Avant-Garde 1958–1970." PhD diss., University of Chicago, 2001.

Maruyama Yutaka. "Shishi *Boin* no shiori." In *Fukkokuban Boin: Shiryōhen*, edited by Fukuoka-ken Shijin Kai, 17. Fukuoka: Sōgensha, 1993.

Masaki Motoi. "Chihō no zen'ei." In *Yasei no kindai: saikō—sengo Nihon bijutsushi, kirokushū* [The savage mind in the modern age: Reconsidering postwar Japanese art history, report], edited by Shima Atsuhiko and Nakai Yasuyuki, 146–177. Osaka: Kokuritsu Kokusai Bijutsukan, 2006.

——. "Demokurāto bijutsuka kyōkai sōron: Bunken kirihari ni yoru shaken." In *Kaihō sareta sengo bijutsu: Demokurāto*, 15–20. Edited by Takano Akihiro, Yasugi Masahiro, Okubo Shizuo, Morimoto Shigeharu, and Teraguchi Yoshiaki. Miyazaki Prefectural Art Museum, The Museum of Modern Art, Wakayama, The Museum of Modern Art, Saitama, The Yomiuri Shimbun, The Japan Association of Art Museums, 1999.

Masuda Kingo. "A Historical Overview of Art Education in Japan." *Journal of Aesthetic Education* 37, no. 4 (Winter 2003): 3–11.

[Matano Mamoru]. "Kyushu-ha." *Kyushu-ha* 1 (September 1957): 1.

Matsukawa Bunshū Hensan Iinkai, ed. *Shinjitsu wa kabe o tōshite*. Tokyo: Getsuyō Shobō, 1951.

Matsukawa Tarō. "Kinpyō o kinpyō ni." *Sōzō biiku* 3, no. 7 (July 1959): 1.

Matsumoto Toshio. *Eizō no hakken: Avangyarudo to dokyumentari*. Tokyo: San'ichi Shobō, 1979.

Matute, Laura Gonzáles. "Kindaika e no michinori: nijūseiki Mekishiko bijutsu." Translated by Hōjō Yukari. In *Mekishiko nijūseiki kaigaten: camino a la modernidad, maestros de la pintura Mexicana*, 41–45. Edited by Katō Kaoru and Laura Gonzáles Matute. Exhibition organized by Setagaya Bijutsukan. Tokyo: NHK Promotions, 2009.

McDonough, Tom, ed. *Guy Debord and the Situationist International*. Cambridge: The MIT Press, 2002.

McLagan, Meg, and Yates McKee. *Sensible Politics: The Visual Culture of Nongovernmental Activism*. New York: Zone Books, 2012.

Mehl, Scott Richard. "The Concept of Expression in Modern Japanese Poetics: Thought, Consciousness, Language." PhD diss., University of Chicago, 2013.

Merleau-Ponty, Maurice. "Cezanne's Doubt." In *Sense and Non-Sense*, 9–25. Translated by Hubert L. and Patricia Allen Dreyfus. Evanston, IL: Northwestern University Press, 1964.

Michiba Chikanobu. *Senryō to heiwa: Sengo to iu keiken*. Tokyo: Seidosha, 2005.

——. *Shimomaruko Bunka Shūdan to sono jidai*. Tokyo: Misuzu Shobō, 2016.

——. "Shimomaruko Bunka Shūdan to sono jidai." Special issue. *Gendai shisō*, 35, no. 17 (December 2007): 38–101.

——. "Ueno Eishin *Oya to ko no yoru*, sono ni." *Mirai* 472 (January 2006): 14–21.

——. "Ueno Eishin *Oya to ko no yoru*, sono san." *Mirai* 474 (March 2006): 6–13.

Miller, Tyrus. *Singular Examples: Artistic Politics and the Neo-Avant-Garde*. Evanston: Northwestern University Press, 2009.

Mita Genjirō. "Atarashii E no Kai." In *Nihon bijutsu kyōiku sōkan sengo hen*, edited by Nihon Bijutsu Kyōiku Rengō, 324–329. Tokyo: Nihon Bunkyō Shuppan Kabushiki Gaisha, 1966.

Mitsuda Yuri. "*Bijutsu hihyō* (1952–1957) shi to sono jidai: 'Gendai bijutsu' to 'gendai bijutsu hihyō no seiritsu." *Pb: Fuji Xerox Art Bulletin* 2 (2006).

——. "Geijutsu / fuzai / nichijō: Hangeijutsu o meguru hihyō gensetsu." In *Bijutsu hihyō to sengo bijutsu*, edited by Bijutsu Hyōronka Renmei, 145–168. Tokyo: Brücke, 2007.

——. "Hihyō no eiyū jidai: *Bijutsu hihyō* (1952–1957) shi ni okeru gendai bijutsu hihyō no seiritsu." *Gekkan Aida* 110–115, 117 (February–July, September 2005).

Miyakawa Atsushi. "Anforumeru igo." *Bijutsu techō* (May 1963): 86–96.

Mizutamari Mayumi. *Sākuru Mura to Morisaki Kazue: kōryū to rentai no vijon*. Tokyo: Nakanishiya Shuppan, 2013.

——. "1950-nendai kōhan no sākuru undō to shōshūdan ron." *Kokugo kokubun kenkyū* 128 (August 2005): 1–16.

——. "Tankō ni okeru sākuru undō no tenkai: bungaku sākuru o chūshin ni." *Kokugo kokubungaku kenkyū* 133 (2007): 31–42; and 134 (2008): 44–54.

Moore, Joe. *Japanese Workers and the Struggle for Power, 1945–1947*. Madison: University of Wisconsin Press, 1983.

Munroe, Alexandra, ed. *Japanese Art After 1945: Scream against the Sky*. New York: Abrams, 1994.

Murata Masahiro and Takahashi Shūji, ed. *Kitagawa Tamiji-ten* [Kitagawa Tamiji retrospective]. Nagoya: Aichi Prefectural Museum of Art and Kitagawa Tamiji ten Jikkō Iinkai, 1996.

Nagai Kiyoshi. "Bijutsu o meguru hansei." Special issue "Bunka mondai to Nihon Kyōsantō." *Zen'ei* (March 1957): 88–94.

Nagoya City Art Museum, ed. *Sengo Nihon no riarizumu* [Realism in postwar Japan, 1945–1960]. Nagoya: Nagoya City Art Museum and Sengo Nihon no Riarizumu Jikkō Iinkai, 1998.

Najita, Tetsuo. *Ordinary Economies in Japan: A Historical Perspective, 1750–1950*. Berkeley: University of California Press, 2009.

——. "Civil Society in Japan's Modernity—An Interpretive Overview." In *Civil Society, Religion and the Nation: Modernization in Intercultural Context: Russia, Japan, Turkey*, 101–115. Edited by Gerrit Steunebrink and Evert Van Der Zweerde. Amsterdam: Rodopi, 2004.

Nakamura Hiroshi. "Fushin no 'jiko hihan.'" *Bijutsu undō* 53 (April 1957). In *Kaigasha 1957–2002*, 13–15. Tokyo: Bijutsu Shuppansha, 2003.

——. "Kaiga senden 1: Koritsu suru taburō." In *Kaigasha 1957–2002*. Tokyo: Bijutsu Shuppansha, 2003, 21–22.

——. "Seiji, taburō, jiko hihan." Interview by Kikuhata Mokuma. *Kikan* 15 (1990): 14–40.

——. "Tenkanki no geijutsu ideorogii" [Ideology of art at the turning point]. *Keishō* 4 (1960): 24–31.

——. *Nakamura Hiroshi: Zuga jiken* [Hiroshi Nakamura: Pictorial disturbances, 1953–2007]. Tokyo: Museum of Contemporary Art, 2007.

Nanjō Tetsu. "Bijutsu sensen ni okeru kokumin kōryō no gutaika no tame ni." *Zen'ei* (February 1954): 70–95.

Narita Ryūichi. "Dansō no jidai." *Shisō* 980 (December 2005): 95–112.

——. "'Heibon' to sono jidai." In *Sengo Nihon sutadiizu 1: 40, 50-nendai*, edited by Iwasaki Minoru, Ueno Chizuko, Kitada Akihiro, Komori Yōichi, and Narita Ryūichi, 219–243. Tokyo: Kinokuniya Shoten, 2009.

——. "'Sākuru undō' no jidai: 1950-nendai 'Nihon' no bunka no basho." In *Rōkaru hisutorii kara gurōbaru hisutorii e: Tabunka no rekishigaku to chiikishi*, edited by Kawanishi Hidemitsu, Namikawa Kenji, and M. William Steele, 245–260. Tokyo: Iwata Shoin, 2005.

Neill, A. S. *A Dominie's Log*. New York: Robert McBride and Company, 1915.

——. *Neill! Neill! Orange Peel*. New York: Hart Publishing, 1972.

——. *Summerhill: A Radical Approach to Child Rearing*. New York: Hart Publishing, 1960.

Nenkan Iinkai, ed. "Sōbi nenkan 1956." *Sōbi panfuretto* 7 (1956): 1–110.

Nihon Bijutsu Kyōiku Rengō, ed. *Nihon bijutsu kyōiku sōkan sengo hen*. Osaka: Nihon Bunkyō Shuppan, 1966.

Nihon Kyōshokuin Kumiai, ed. *Nihon no kyōiku*. Tokyo: Kokudosha, 1955.

Nishizawa Harumi. "Ikeda Tatsuo no datsuryōikiteki katsudō: 1950-nendai kara 60-nendai o chūshin ni," *Tsukuba Studies in Art and Design* 13 (2009): 87–97.

Nornes, Abé Mark. *Forest of Pressure: Ogawa Shinsuke and Postwar Japanese Documentary*. Minneapolis: University of Minnesota Press, 2007.

Oguma Eiji. *Minshu to aikoku: Sengo Nihon no nashonarizumu to kōkyōsei*. Tokyo: Shin'yōsha, 2002.

Okamoto Tarō, Nagai Kiyoshi, and Hanada Kiyoteru. "Avangyarudo no seishin." *Sōgō bunka* (April 1948): 2–13.

Okazaki Akio. "An Overview of the Influence of American Art Education on the Development of Japanese Art Education." *Journal of Multi-Cultural and Cross-Cultural Research in Art Education* 2, no. 1 (1984): 82–82.

Okumura Yukinori. *Genbaku no zu zenkoku junkai*. Tokyo: Shinjuku Shobō, 2015.

Ōno Saiji. "Hitotsu no hanron." *Konnichi no bijutsu* 2 (May–June 1953): 7–8.

Ōnuki Noboru and Takahashi Toshimaru, eds. "Sōzōshugi no bijutsu kyōiku undō nenpyō." In *Sōzōshugi bijutsu kyōiku bunken mokuroku*. N.p., 1952.

Osaki Shin'ichirō. "Anforumeru." In *Bijutsu hihyō to sengo bijutsu*, edited by Bijutsu Hyōronka Renmei, 123–144. Tokyo: Brücke, 2007.

——, ed. *Konseki: Sengo bijutsu ni okeru shintai to shikō* [Traces: Body and idea in contemporary art]. Tokyo: National Museums of Modern Art, 2004.

Ōsawa Shin'ichirō. "Sākuru no sengoshi." In *Kyōdō kenkyū: shūdan*, 68–92. Edited by Shisō no Kagaku Kenkyūkai. Tokyo: Heibonsha, 1976.

Ōtsuki Takeshi. *Sengo minkan kyōiku undōshi*. Tokyo: Ayumi Shuppan, 1982.

Ozaki Masato. "Akebonomura monogatari kara, soshite Akebonomura monogatari e." *Yamashita Kikuji-ten / Yamashita Kikuji*, 146–151. Edited by Harada Hikaru, Egawa Yoshihide, Arikawa Ikuo, and Ozaki Masato. Kanagawa Kenritsu Kindai Bijutsukan, Tokushima Kenritsu Kindai Bijutsukan, Miyagi-ken Bijutsukan, Itabashi Kuritsu Bijutsukan, 1996.

Ozaki Shōkyo. "Sōbi sentā." *Sōbi panfuretto* 8 (1957): 77.

Pekkanen, Robert. *Japan's Dual Civil Society: Members without Advocates*. Stanford, CA: Stanford University Press, 2006.

Pharr, Susan. "Conclusion: Targeting by an Activist State: Japan as a Civil Society Model." In *The State of Civil Society in Japan*. Edited by Frank Schwartz and Susan Pharr. New York: Cambridge University Press, 2003.

Pincus, Leslie. "A Salon for the Soul: Nakai Masakazu and the Hiroshima Culture Movement." *Positions: East Asia, Cultures, Critique* 10, no. 1 (2002): 173–194.

Placzek, Beverley R., ed. *Record of a Friendship: The Correspondence of Wilhelm Reich and A. S. Neill, 1936–1957*. New York: Farrar, Straus, Giroux, 1981.

Rancière, Jacques. *Dis-agreement: Politics and Philosophy*. Translated by Julie Rose. Minneapolis: Minnesota University Press, 1999.

——. *On the Shores of Politics*. Translated by Liz Heron. New York: Verso, 2007.

——. *The Ignorant Schoolmaster*. Translated by Kristin Ross. Stanford, CA: Stanford University Press, 1991.

——. *The Nights of Labor: The Workers' Dream in Nineteenth-Century France*. Translated by John Drury. Philedelphia: Temple University Press, 1989.

Read, Herbert. *Education for Peace*. New York: Charles Scribner's Sons, 1949.

——. *Education through Art*. New York: Pantheon Books, 1942.

Ridgely, Steven. *Japanese Counterculture: The Antiestablishment Art of Terayama Shūji*. Minneapolis: Minnesota University Press, 2010.

Roberts, John, *The Intangibilities of Form: Skill and Deskilling in Art after the Readymade*. New York: Verso, 2007.

Rodowick, D. N. *The Crisis of Political Modernism: Criticism and Ideology in Contemporary Film Criticism*. Berkeley: University of California Press, 1995.

Sakaguchi, Eiko. *Bonds of Civility: Aesthetic Networks and the Political Origins of Japanese Culture*. New York: Cambridge University Press, 2005.

Sakurai Takami. "Atarashii kamigami no tanjō." *Kyushu-ha* 2 (December 1957): 5

——. "Dentō o koeru mono." *Kyushu-ha* 1 (September 1957): 6–7.

——. "Eiyūtachi no daishūkai ripōto." *Kyushu-ha* 7 (October 1963): 2–32.

——. *Hige no kiseki: Sakurai Takami shobunshū*. Fukuoka: Tōka Shobō, 1979.

——. "Kyushu-ha no kigen Ochi Osamu ni tsuite." In *I Discover Jesus Curist* [*sic*] *Is a Woman*, edited by Sakurai Takami, 289–302. Fukuoka: Tōka Shobō, 1987.

——. "Majimena hanashi." *Kyushu-ha* 4 (July 1961): 2.

——. "Meirei suru geijutsu: Eiyū daishūkai Nyū Yōku ni tsuite." *Kyushu-ha* 7 (October 1963): 2–32.

——. *Paradaisu e no michi*. Fukuoka: Tōka Shobō, 1989.

——. "Shusseki sareru kata no tame ni." *Kyushu-ha* 6 (October 1962): 1.

Sandler, Mark, ed. *The Confusion Era: Art and Culture of Japan During the Allied Occupation, 1945–1952*. University of Washington Press, 1997.

Sasaki Ki'ichi. "Kiroku Geijutsu no Kai ni tsuite." *Gunzō* 12, no. 10 (1957): 262.

Sasaki-Uemura, Wesley Makoto. *Organizing the Spontaneous: Citizen Protest in Postwar Japan*. Honolulu: University of Hawai'i Press, 2001.

Satō Yō. "Kyoto Kiroku Eiga o Miru Kai ni tsuite, sono zenshi." *Engeki eizōgaku* (2013): 41–55.

Satō Yūko. "Zōkei kyōiku no genten o tashikametsutsu habahiroi shichō o kesshū suru." In "Minkan bijutsu kyōiku undō," *Āto edyukēshon* 2, no. 3 (1990): 10–13.

Sawamiya Yū. *Hōrō to tsuchi to bungaku: Takaki Mamoru, Matsunaga Goichi, Tanigawa Gan*. Tokyo: Gendai Shokan, 2005.

Scalapino, Robert A. *The Japanese Communist Movement, 1920–1966*. Berkeley: University of California Press, 1967.

Schilller, Friedrich. *On the Aesthetic Education of Man in a Series of Letters*. Edited and translated by Elizabeth M. Wilkinson and L. A. Willoughby. Oxford: Clarendon Press, 1967.

Schnellbacher, Thomas. *Abe Kōbō, Literary Strategist: The Evolution of His Agenda and Rhetoric in the Context of Postwar Japanese Avant-garde and Communist Artists' Movements*. Munich: Iudicium, 2004.

Segi Shin'ichi. "Anforumeru o meguru sukyandaru." *Geijutsu shincho* (Feburary 1958): 54–66.

——. *Kūhakuki no sengo bijutsu*. Tokyo: Shichōsha, 1996.

——. *Nihon no zen'ei 1945–1999*. Tokyo: Seikatsu no Tomosha, 2000.

——. *Sengo kūhakuki no bijutsu*. Tokyo: Shichōsha, 1996.

Sekine Hiroshi. "Banchi no nai machi." *Kaizō* (April 1954).

——. "Kakuritsu no kuni: Jittai naki niji no tanima." *Kaizō* (December 1954).

Senda Umeji. *Tankō shigoto uta bangakan*. Fukuoka: Urayama Shobō, 1990.

Seraphim, Franziska. *War Memory and Social Politics in Japan, 1945–2005*. Cambridge: Harvard University Asia Center, 2006.

Sherif, Ann. *Japan's Cold War: Media, Literature and the Law*. New York: Columbia University Press, 2009.

——. "The Aesthetics of Speed and the Illogicality of Politics: Ishihara Shintarō's Literary Debut." *Japan Forum* 17, no. 2 (2005): 185–211.

Shimazaki Kiyomi, Kubo Sadajirō, and Nonome Keizō. "Taidan: Eiga *E o kaku kodomotachi* to Sōzō Biiku Undō." *Biiku bunka* 41, no. 5 (1991): 20–27.

Shimizu Ikutarō, Miyahara Seiichi, and Ueda Shōzaburō. *Kichi no ko: Kono jijitsu o dō kangaetara yoika* [Children of the base: How can we think about this issue?] Tokyo: Kōbunsha, 1953.

Shimazaki Kiyomi and Takamori Shun, eds. *Kubo Sadajirō bijutsu kyōiku ronshū*. 2 vols. Tokyo: Sōfūsha, 2007.

Shinkai Akashi. "Sunagawa Tōsō no jōkyō to nōmin no kao o egaku to iu sōdaina chichi no mokuhyō." In *Sunagawa Tōsō 50-nen: sorezore no omoi*, edited by Kiichi Hoshi, 89–91. Tachikawa: Keyaki Shuppan, 2005.

Shinkai Kakuo. "Riarizumu bijutsu ni tsuite." *Akahata*, November 14, 1955.

Shishū Shimomaruko. Tokyo: Shimomaruko Shūdan, 1951. In *Tokyo Nanbu sākuru zasshi shūsei*. Tokyo: Fuji Shuppan, 2009.

Shōda Akira. "Domon Ken no yūki to gosan." Interview by Ueda Hiroshi. *Sākuru mura* (April 1960): 13–16.

"Shūdan no nami, undō no nami: 60-nendai bijutsu undō wa dō ugoitaka." *Bijutsu techō* (October 1971): 25–112.

Smith, Peter. *The History of American Art Education: Learning about Art in American Schools.* Westport, CT: Greenwood Press, 1996.

Solnit, Rebecca. *Hope in the Dark: Untold Histories, Wild Possibilities.* Chicago: Haymarket Books, 2016.

Sommer, Doris. *The Work of Art in the World: Civic Agency and Public Humanities.* Durham, NC: Duke University Press, 2014.

"Sōbi to dōtoku kyōiku." *Sōzō biiku* 2, no. 4 (April 1958): 8.

Sōzō Biiku Kyōkai Aichi Shibu, ed. *Yoi e yokunai e.* Nagoya: Reimeisha, 1956.

Sōzō Biiku Kyōkai, ed. *Sōbi nenkan.* Tokyo: Bunka Shobō Hakubunkasha, 1978.

Stahl, David C. *The Burdens of Survival: Ooka Shohei's Writings on the Pacific War.* Honolulu: University of Hawai'i Press, 2003.

Sugiura Minpei. "Chōchōsan fushinnin." *Kaizō* (February 1955).

——. "Chōkai giin ichinensei." *Akahata*, January–April 1957.

Suzuki Katsuo. "Shūdan no yume: 50-nendai o tsuranuku rekishiteki patosu." In *Jikkenba: 1950s*, 10–39. Edited by Suzuki Katsuo, Masuda Tomohiro, and Ōtani Shōgo. Tokyo: National Museum of Modern Art, 2012.

Suzuki Katsuo, Masuda Tomohiro, and Ōtani Shōgo, eds. *Jikkenba 1950s.* Tokyo: National Museum of Modern Art, 2012.

Tabe Mitsuko. "Gyozoku." *Kyushu-ha* 2 (December 1957): 6.

——. *Jutai geijutsu.* Fukuoka: Kashoin, 1997.

——. *Nisennen no ringo: Watashi no datsugeijutsuron.* Fukuoka: Nishinippon Shimbunsha, 2001.

——. "Purakādo no tame ni." *Kyushu-ha* 5 (September 1961): 7.

Takei Toshifumi. "Sunagawa tōsō to bijutsuka tachi." *Fuchū Bijutsukan kenkyū kiyo* 16 (2012): 9–21.

Takeuchi Kingo. "Taburō hitei no ron." *Konnichi no bijutsu* 1 (April 1953).

Takeyama Hiroko and Kokatsu Reiko, eds. *No ni sakebu hitobito: Kita Kantō no sengo hanga undō* [The print art movement in the northern Kanto region: 1946–1966]. Utsunomiya: Tochigi Prefectural Museum of Fine Arts, 2000.

Takimoto Masao. *Ningen kaihō no bijutsu kyōiku.* Nagoya: Reimei Shobō, 1976.

Tanaka, Kathryn M. "Through the Hospital Gates: Hansen's Disease and Modern Japanese Literature." PhD diss, University of Chicago, 2012.

Tanaka Yūko. "Shishi *Boin* ni atsumatta gunzōtachi." *Ishin: Shi to shiron* 66–70 (August 1987–May 1989).

Tang, Xiaobing. "Echoes of *Roar China!* On Vision and Voice in Modern Chinese Art." *Positions: East Asia, Cultures, Critique* 14, no. 2 (2006): 467–494.

Tanigawa Gan. "Genten ga sonzai suru." *Boin* 8 (May 1954).

——. "Kōsakusha no ronri." In *Kōsakusha sengen.* Tokyo: Shio Shuppansha, 1977, 5–21.

——. "Sōkan sengen: Sara ni fukaku shūdan no imi o." *Sākuru mura* 1 (September 1958): 2–7.

Tanigawa Gan, Yoshimoto Takaaki, Haniya Yutaka, Morimoto Kazuo, Umemoto Katsumi, and Kuroda Kanichi, eds. *Minshushugi no shinwa.* Tokyo: Gendai Shichōsha, 1960.

Tashiro Shun'ichirō. *Kakenuketa zen'ei.* Fukuoka: Kashoin, 1996.

Terada Ken'ichirō. *Ekaki no shōkyūshi.* Fukuoka: Nishinippon Shimbunsha, 1986.

Tiampo, Ming. "Gutai and Informel: Post-War Art in Japan and France, 1945–1965." PhD diss., Northwestern University, 2003.

Toba Kōji. *1950 nendai: "kiroku" no jidai*. Tokyo: Kawade Books, 2010.
——. "Chizu de miru sākuru bunka no bokkō." *Shūkan Nihon no rekishi*, May 25, 2014, 16–17.
——. "Ruporutāju shiriizu: Nihon no shōgen ni tsuite." *Bungei to hihyō* 8, no. 10 (1999): 41–57.
Tokyo Nanbu sākuru zasshi shūsei. Tokyo: Fuji Shuppan, 2009.
Tomii, Reiko. "Introduction: Collectivism in Twentieth-Century Japanese Art with a Focus on Operational Aspects of Dantai." *Positions: Asia Critique* 21, no. 2 (2013): 225–267.
——. "After the 'Descent to the Everyday': Japanese Collectivism from Hi Red Center to The Play, 1964–1973." In *Collectivism After Modernism: The Art of Social Imagination after 1945*, edited by Blake Stimson and Gregory Sholette, 44–76. Minneapolis: University of Minnesota Press, 2007.
——. "*Geijutsu* on Their Minds: Memorable Words on Anti-Art." In *Art, Anti-Art, Non-Art: Experimentations in the Public Sphere in Postwar Japan, 1950–1970*, edited by Charles Merewether with Rika Iezumi Hiro, 35–62. Los Angeles: Getty Research Institute, 2007.
——. "Historicizing 'Contemporary Art': Some Discursive Practices in *Gendai Bijutsu* in Japan." *Positions: East Asia, Culture, Critique* 12, no. 3 (2004): 611–641.
——. "'International Contemporeneity' in the 1960s: Discoursing on Art in Japan and Beyond." *Japan Review* 21 (2009): 123–147.
——. "Miyakawa Atsushi saidoku: 'Anforumeru igo' o chūshin ni." In *Bijutsushi no supekutorumu: sakuhin, gensetsu, seido*, edited by Wakayama Eiko and Kōdera Tsukasa, 143–152. Kyoto: Kōrinsha, 1996.
Tomotsune Tamotsu. "Minshū hanga undō no 50-nendai." In *Jikkenba 1950s*, edited by Suzuki Katsuo, Masuda Tomohiro, and Ōtani Shōgo, 86–99. Tokyo: National Museum of Modern Art, 2012.
Tone Yasunao and Hikosaka Naoyoshi with Akatsuka Yukio, eds. "Nenpyō: Gendai bijustsu no 50-nen." Special double issue, *Bijutsu techō* (April 1972): 1–251; and (May 1972): 25–186.
Tōno Yoshiaki. "Amerika no bijutsukai." *Yomiuri shinbun*, evening edition, August 25, 1959, 3.
Tsurumi Shunsuke. "Naze sākuru o kenkyū suru ka." In *Kyōdō kenkyū: shūdan*, 3–21. Edited by Shisō no Kagaku Kenkyūkai. Tokyo: Heibonsha, 1976.
Uchida Iwao. *Kaiga no rinri*. Tokyo: Shoshi Hitosugi, 1953.
Uchino, Tatsurō. *Japan's Postwar Economy*. Tokyo: Kodansha International, 1983.
Uda Hideshi. Entry in "Kumamoto Bunko shuyō bunken kaidai." *Biiku bunka* 55, no. 3 (2005): 40.
Ueda Seikichi and Gotō Shōjirō. *Ayamatta saiban*. Tokyo: Iwanami Shinsho, 1960.
Ueno Eishin. "Atogaki: Akai jūjika." (1958) In *Chitei no shuki: Kunigami Nobuo ikōshū*, 91–110. Edited by Nittan Takamatsu Bungaku Sākuru. Fukuoka: Nittan Takamatsu Bungaku Sākuru, 1958.
——. *Owareyuku kōfutachi*. Tokyo: Iwanami Shinsho, 1960.
——. *Oya to ko no yoru*. Illustrated by Senda Umeji. Tokyo: Miraisha, 1982.
Ueno Eishin and Chō Kunje, eds. *Shashin manyōroku: Chikuhō*. Fukuoka: Ashi Shobō, 1984.
Ueno Eishin and Tanigawa Gan. "Taishū keishiki to rōdōsha no kao: Ueno Eishin cho *Oya to ko no yoru* o megutte." *Sākuru mura* 2, no. 12 (1959): 8–12.

Viola, Wilhelm. *Child Art*. Kent: University of London Press, 1942.

Welfield, John. *An Empire in Eclipse: Japan in the Postwar American Alliance System*. London: Athlone Press, 1988.

Wight Art Gallery. *Forty Years of California Assemblage*. Los Angeles: Wight Art Gallery, University of California Los Angeles, 1989.

Williams, Raymond. "Culture Is Ordinary." (1958). In *The Raymond Williams Reader*, edited by John Higgins, 10–24. Oxford: Blackwell, 2001.

——. *The Long Revolution*. New York: Columbia University Press, 1961.

Winther-Tamaki, Bert. *Maximum Embodiment: Yōga, the Western Painting of Japan, 1912–1955*. Honolulu: University of Hawai'i Press, 2012.

Wright, Jeffrey C. "Menus of the Soul: Assemblages Implode Loaded Symbols." In *Tabe Mitsuko: Recent Works*, 27. Edited by T. M. T Studio. Fukuoka: Gallery Toile, 2002.

Yamada Mitsuharu. *Ei Kyū hyōden to sakuhin*. Tokyo: Seiryūdō, 1976.

Yamagata Hiroshi. *Nihon bijutsu kyōikushi*. Nagoya: Reimei Shobō, 1967.

Yamaguchi Isamu. *Sōzō Biiku o koete*. Tokyo: Reimei Shobō, 1956.

Yamaguchi Yōzō, ed. *Shiriizu "Kyushu-ha zaihō 1"* [Revisit Group Kyushu-ha 1]. Fukuoka: Fukuoka Art Museum, 2006.

——. *Shiriizu "Kyushu-ha zaihō 2"* [Revisit Group Kyushu-ha 2: Serial exhibition for the 50th anniversary of the founding of Group Kyushu-ha's organization]. Fukuoka: Fukuoka Art Museum, 2007.

——. "Kyushu-ha to Sākuru Mura: Sono kankei o meguru nōto." In *Bunka shigen toshite no tankō-ten*, edited by Masaki Motoi and Ishizaki Takashi, 154–158. Tokyo: Meguro Museum of Art, 2009.

Yamamoto Atsuo. "Oto no jikken." In *Sōgetsu to sono jidai*, 246–249. Edited by Katō Mizuho, Warashina Hideya, and Yamamoto Atsuo. Ashiya Municipal Museum and Chiba Municipal Museum, 1998.

Yamane Yasuchika. "Kyokushiteki mikurokosumosu to tendōsetsu no aida de." In *Kikuhata Mokuma-ten*, edited by Yamane Yasuchika, 24–33. Fukuoka: Kita Kyushu Municipal Museum of Art, 1988.

Yamashita Kikuji. *Kuzureru numa: Gaka Yamashita Kikuji no sekai*. Tokyo: Subaru Shobō, 1979.

Yoshida Yoshie. "Eiyū izukoni owasu: Nippon saijo no hantotachi." *Sansai* (July 1963): 60–63.

——. *Kaitaigeki no maku orite*. Tokyo: Zōkeisha, 1982.

——. "Sengo zen'ei yukari no aragoto jūhachiban: Kyushu-ha no eiyūtachi." *Bijutsu techō* (October 1971): 222–230.

Yoshimoto, Midori. *Into Performance: Japanese Women Artists in New York*. New Brunswick, NJ: Rutgers University Press, 2005.

Yoshimoto Takaaki. "Gisei no shūen." In *Minshushugi no shinwa*, edited by Tanigawa Gan, Yoshimoto Takaaki, et al., 43–76. Tokyo: Gendai Shinchosha, 1960.

——. "Zensedai no shijintachi" (1955). In *Yoshimoto Takaaki zenchosakushū*, vol. 5, 38–55. Tokyo: Kinsō Shobō.

Yoshimoto Takaaki and Takei Teruo. *Bungakusha no sensō sekinin*. Tokyo: Awaji Shobō, 1956.

INDEX